Forecasting Cyber Crimes in the Age of the Metaverse

Hossam Nabil Elshenraki
Dubai Police Academy, UAE

A volume in the Advances in Digital Crime, Forensics, and Cyber Terrorism (ADCFCT) Book Series

IGI Global
PUBLISHER of TIMELY KNOWLEDGE

Published in the United States of America by
IGI Global
Information Science Reference (an imprint of IGI Global)
701 E. Chocolate Avenue
Hershey PA, USA 17033
Tel: 717-533-8845
Fax: 717-533-8661
E-mail: cust@igi-global.com
Web site: http://www.igi-global.com

Library of Congress Cataloging-in-Publication Data

Names: Elshenraki, Hossam Nabil, 1971- editor.
Title: Forecasting cyber crimes in the age of the metaverse / edited by Hossam Elshenraky.
Description: Hershey, PA : Information Science Reference, [2024] | Includes bibliographical references and index. | Summary: "This book forecasts by scientific method the expected crimes in the meta verse and how it will affect the police capabilities in combating crimes"-- Provided by publisher.
Identifiers: LCCN 2023037442 (print) | LCCN 2023037443 (ebook) | ISBN 9798369302200 (hardcover) | ISBN 9798369302217 (paperback) | ISBN 9798369302224 (ebook)
Subjects: LCSH: Computer crimes. | Metaverse.
Classification: LCC HV6773 .F67 2024 (print) | LCC HV6773 (ebook) | DDC 364.16/8--dc23/eng/20231106
LC record available at https://lccn.loc.gov/2023037442
LC ebook record available at https://lccn.loc.gov/2023037443

This book is published in the IGI Global book series Advances in Digital Crime, Forensics, and Cyber Terrorism (ADCF-CT) (ISSN: 2327-0381; eISSN: 2327-0373)

British Cataloguing in Publication Data
A Cataloguing in Publication record for this book is available from the British Library.

Advances in Digital Crime, Forensics, and Cyber Terrorism (ADCFCT) Book Series

Bryan Christiansen
Southern New Hampshire University, USA
Agnieszka Piekarz
Independent Researcher, Poland

ISSN:2327-0381
EISSN:2327-0373

Mission

The digital revolution has allowed for greater global connectivity and has improved the way we share and present information. With this new ease of communication and access also come many new challenges and threats as cyber crime and digital perpetrators are constantly developing new ways to attack systems and gain access to private information.

The **Advances in Digital Crime, Forensics, and Cyber Terrorism (ADCFCT) Book Series** seeks to publish the latest research in diverse fields pertaining to crime, warfare, terrorism and forensics in the digital sphere. By advancing research available in these fields, the **ADCFCT** aims to present researchers, academicians, and students with the most current available knowledge and assist security and law enforcement professionals with a better understanding of the current tools, applications, and methodologies being implemented and discussed in the field.

Coverage

- Telecommunications Fraud
- Malicious Codes
- Vulnerability
- Criminology
- Mobile Device Forensics
- Cyber Warfare
- Database Forensics
- Data Protection
- Identity Theft
- Digital Crime

IGI Global is currently accepting manuscripts for publication within this series. To submit a proposal for a volume in this series, please contact our Acquisition Editors at Acquisitions@igi-global.com or visit: http://www.igi-global.com/publish/.

The Advances in Digital Crime, Forensics, and Cyber Terrorism (ADCFCT) Book Series (ISSN 2327-0381) is published by IGI Global, 701 E. Chocolate Avenue, Hershey, PA 17033-1240, USA, www.igi-global.com. This series is composed of titles available for purchase individually; each title is edited to be contextually exclusive from any other title within the series. For pricing and ordering information please visit http://www.igi-global.com/book-series/advances-digital-crime-forensics-cyber/73676. Postmaster: Send all address changes to above address.

Titles in this Series

For a list of additional titles in this series, please visit: www.igi-global.com/book-series

Cyber Security Policies and Strategies of the World's Leading States
Nika Chitadze (International Black Sea University, Georgia)
Information Science Reference • copyright 2023 • 295pp • H/C (ISBN: 9781668488461) • US $250.00 (our price)

Exploring Cyber Criminals and Data Privacy Measures
Nuno Mateus-Coelho (Lapi2s, Copelabs, Lusófona University, Portugal) and Manuela Cruz-Cunha (Polytechnic Institute of Cavado and Ave, Portugal)
Information Science Reference • copyright 2023 • 324pp • H/C (ISBN: 9781668484227) • US $275.00 (our price)

Modeling and Simulation of Functional Nanomaterials for Forensic Investigation
Allah Rakha (Department of Forensic Medicine/Medical Jurisprudence, University of Health Sciences, Pakistan) Anam Munawar (Department of Forensic Medicine/Medical Jurisprudence, University of Health Sciences, Pakistan) Virat Khanna (Department of Mechanical Engineering, Maharaja Agrasen University, India) and Suneev Anil Bansal (Department of Mechanical Engineering, Bharat Institute of Engineering and Technology, India)
Information Science Reference • copyright 2023 • 378pp • H/C (ISBN: 9781668483251) • US $250.00 (our price)

Handbook of Research on War Policies, Strategies, and Cyber Wars
Fahri Özsungur (Mersin University, Turkey)
Information Science Reference • copyright 2023 • 463pp • H/C (ISBN: 9781668467411) • US $315.00 (our price)

Global Perspectives on the Psychology of Terrorism
Nika Chitadze (International Black Sea University, Georgia)
Information Science Reference • copyright 2023 • 330pp • H/C (ISBN: 9781668453117) • US $215.00 (our price)

Aiding Forensic Investigation Through Deep Learning and Machine Learning Frameworks
Alex Noel Joseph Raj (Shantou University, China) Vijayalakshmi G. V. Mahesh (BMS Institute of Technology and Management, India) Ruban Nerssison (Vellore Institute of Technology, India) Ang Yu (Carolina University, USA) and Jennifer Gentry (Carolina University, USA)
Information Science Reference • copyright 2022 • 273pp • H/C (ISBN: 9781668445587) • US $250.00 (our price)

Dark Web Pattern Recognition and Crime Analysis Using Machine Intelligence
Romil Rawat (Shri Vaishnav Vidyapeeth Vishwavidyalaya, India) Shrikant Telang (Shri Vaishnav Vidyapeeth Vishwavidyalaya, India) P. William (Sanjivani College of Engineering, Savitribai Phule Pune University, India) Upinder Kaur (Akal University, Talwandi Sabo, India) and Om Kumar C.U. (School of Computer Science and Engineering (SCOPE),Vellore Institute of Technology, India)
Information Science Reference • copyright 2022 • 281pp • H/C (ISBN: 9781668439425) • US $250.00 (our price)

IGI Global
PUBLISHER of TIMELY KNOWLEDGE

701 East Chocolate Avenue, Hershey, PA 17033, USA
Tel: 717-533-8845 x100 • Fax: 717-533-8661
E-Mail: cust@igi-global.com • www.igi-global.com

Table of Contents

Detailed Table of Contents

One of the digital transformation features of the new generation of cyber world is the meta verse. It is expected to establish a self-sustainable virtual ecosystem of fully immersive environments, real-time experiences with numerous chances to interact with the world for users and industrial businesses. With the introduction of new networks and enabling technological tools, the meta verse will succeed in the long term. However, with increasing interaction using new meta verse and a lot of third-party services, there would be an arena for many possibilities of cybercrime threats. Hence, combating cybercrimes is critical for the meta verse, and they should be investigated since the commercial adoption of the meta verse is imminent. Therefore, this chapter discusses many cybercrime methods and techniques which are expected in the meta verse environment, (AI) related cyber-attacks are expected, and solutions to the meta verse is possible.

In an emerging era of virtual reality, cybercrimes become a significant challenge. The metaverse is a digital realm where people can socialize, work, play, invest, learn, entertain, and much more. The nature of the metaverse raises the concerns of cybercrimes. In this chapter, a deep understanding of potential threats is discussed. Several threats will be highlighted, such as virtual identity theft and impersonation, virtual real estate frauds, malware and ransomware, virtual espionage, advanced phishing, and social engineering. To forecast these threats, insights from cybercrimes are adapted and extrapolated to fit the unique environment of the metaverse. This will guide law enforcement, technical people, policymakers, regulators, and researchers.

The rise of the metaverse—a virtual world where individuals can interact with each other and digital objects in a fully immersive environment—has led to new challenges in the world of cybersecurity. As

implications, along with tech firms' oversight, can escalate cybercrime. Complex evolving cybercrime patterns hinder guilt proof. Criminalizing tech use in terrorism planning and financing is crucial. Social media users face risks like deepfakes, fostering doubt and inciting terrorism. Tech-security agency partnership is vital. Growing digital interconnectedness heightens cybersecurity issues. Metaverse's growth and internet use call for strengthened anti-terrorism and IT crime laws.

The future of cybercrimes and cyber warfare in the metaverse is a topic of concern. Understanding the emerging landscape is crucial. With technological advancements and the pervasive influence of the metaverse, new cyber threats have emerged. This chapter provides an overview of challenges and ramifications associated with cybercrimes and cyber warfare in the metaverse. It explores evolving cyber threats in the metaverse, considering AI, machine learning, and quantum computing. Cybercrimes include virtual asset theft, identity theft, phishing, harassment, and online extortion. Cyber warfare in the metaverse involves state-sponsored attacks, espionage, information warfare, and manipulation of virtual defense systems. Robust cybersecurity measures, collaboration among stakeholders, and cyber literacy are essential to mitigate risks.

The metaverse represents a transformative concept that has amassed substantial attention in recent years, with big corporations vying to gain hegemony over this domain. While revolutionizing the way we interact with and experience our environment, the metaverse unlocks a vast potential for cyber criminals and nation-states to take advantage of the present voids in its security. By analyzing existing literature and emerging trends, the authors delve into the uncharted territory of the metaverse, examining the ways in which users' digital avatars and assets are at risk- including poor security of NFTs, the scope for financial fraud, the dark verse, and social engineering, among other issues. This chapter provides insight into the real-world implications of cyber-attacks in the metaverse and examines the legal and ethical challenges of regulating cyber activity in virtual environments so that Law Enforcement Agencies, planners, and companies can navigate this field to create a safe virtual world for all.

Throughout history, terrorism has adeptly leveraged technological advancements to further its ominous objectives. As societies have evolved, so too have the methods employed by extremists. From the early

Preface

In the era of the metaverse, where virtual and augmented realities seamlessly merge with our physical world, the landscape of cyberspace is undergoing a transformative shift. *Forecasting Cyber Crimes in the Age of the Metaverse* offers a comprehensive exploration of the challenges and opportunities presented by this emerging digital frontier. This overview provides a glimpse into the key themes and considerations that shape the narrative of the book.

The metaverse represents a convergence of virtual and augmented realities, creating immersive digital spaces where users can interact, transact, and engage in activities mirroring the physical world. As this digital realm expands, so do the complexities and vulnerabilities that cybercriminals exploit to perpetrate a new breed of cybercrimes.

The book navigates through the intricate tapestry of immersive technologies that constitute the metaverse, including virtual reality (VR), augmented reality (AR), and extended reality (XR). Within these immersive environments, cyber threats transcend conventional boundaries, giving rise to novel forms of attacks such as virtual identity theft, digital asset fraud, and manipulation of augmented realities for malicious purposes.

The heart of this exploration lies in the proactive anticipation and understanding of cyber threats within the metaverse. Drawing on historical trends, current threat vectors, and expert insights, the book equips readers with the knowledge to forecast and address emerging cyber threats effectively. Case studies and real-world examples illuminate the dynamic nature of metaverse-related cybercrimes, providing a practical understanding of the challenges faced by cybersecurity professionals.

As users immerse themselves in the metaverse, the protection of digital identities becomes paramount. The book delves into the intricacies of securing virtual personas, safeguarding sensitive information, and implementing robust authentication mechanisms to counter the evolving tactics of cyber adversaries.

Navigating the metaverse requires a holistic approach that extends beyond technological solutions. The book explores the legal and regulatory frameworks necessary to combat cybercrimes in the metaverse, emphasizing the importance of collaboration between policymakers, law enforcement, and the private sector to create a secure and resilient digital environment.

Forecasting Cyber Crimes in the Age of the Metaverse is not only a theoretical exploration but a practical guide. The book provides actionable insights, best practices, and strategies that cybersecurity practitioners, organizations, and policymakers can implement to mitigate risks and respond effectively to metaverse-related cyber threats.

As we embark on this journey into the metaverse, this book serves as a beacon, illuminating the path toward a safer and more secure digital future. By forecasting cyber threats and proactively addressing the challenges of the metaverse, we can collectively shape a resilient cyberspace that empowers users, protects digital identities, and fosters innovation within this immersive digital frontier.

"In the Age of the Metaverse," the phrase itself evokes a sense of futuristic wonder and boundless possibilities. As the world hurtles towards an era where digital and physical realities intertwine seamlessly, so too do the challenges and threats in cyberspace. *Forecasting Cyber Crimes in the Age of the Metaverse* stands at the forefront of this paradigm shift, providing a timely and essential guide to understanding, predicting, and mitigating the evolving landscape of cyber threats.

In the contemporary world, technology is not just an integral part of daily life but a transformative force that shapes economies, societies, and individual experiences. The advent of the metaverse amplifies this influence, introducing immersive digital environments that redefine how we communicate, collaborate, and conduct business. However, with innovation comes risk, and the metaverse presents a new frontier for cybercriminals to exploit vulnerabilities and perpetrate sophisticated cybercrimes.

This book is a beacon of insight amid the complexities of the metaverse. It fits squarely into the contemporary discourse on cybersecurity, addressing the urgent need to comprehend and confront the unique challenges posed by this emerging digital realm. Here's where *Forecasting Cyber Crimes in the Age of the Metaverse* finds its place in the world today:

The metaverse is uncharted territory, and this book serves as a navigational guide for individuals, organizations, and policymakers. It provides a roadmap to understand the intricacies of immersive technologies, the potential risks they introduce, and how to fortify defenses against novel cyber threats.

In a world where cyber threats are ever-evolving, cybersecurity preparedness is paramount. This book equips readers with the foresight needed to proactively address emerging cyber threats within the metaverse. It is a valuable resource for cybersecurity professionals striving to stay ahead of the curve in an environment where the attack surface is constantly expanding.

With our lives increasingly intertwined with digital interactions, protecting our digital identities is crucial. This book sheds light on the unique challenges of safeguarding virtual personas within the metaverse, offering practical strategies for securing sensitive information and countering cyber threats that target the very fabric of our digital existence.

As the metaverse blurs the lines between physical and digital realms, policy and regulation must adapt to safeguard individuals and organizations. This book delves into the legal and regulatory frameworks necessary to combat metaverse-related cybercrimes, highlighting the importance of collaborative efforts to create a secure and regulated digital environment.

in a landscape where technological advancements outpace traditional cybersecurity measures, strategic insights are paramount. *Forecasting Cyber Crimes in the Age of the Metaverse* provides actionable strategies and best practices that bridge the gap between theory and practical implementation, ensuring that cybersecurity measures align with the dynamic challenges of the metaverse.

Forecasting Cyber Crimes in the Age of the Metaverse is meticulously crafted to cater to a diverse and dynamic audience, recognizing the multidimensional impact of cyber threats within immersive digital environments. The target audience encompasses professionals, experts, and stakeholders from various domains who seek to navigate the intricate landscape of cybersecurity in the evolving metaverse. This book is designed for:

Cybersecurity practitioners, including information security analysts, ethical hackers, incident responders, and cybersecurity managers, will find the book essential for staying abreast of emerging threats within the metaverse. It offers practical insights, forecasting methodologies, and strategic guidance to fortify defenses against novel cyber risks.

Technology professionals, IT specialists, system administrators, and software developers will benefit from a deep dive into the technological intricacies of the metaverse. The book provides insights into immersive technologies, potential vulnerabilities, and technical aspects of cyber threats, empowering experts to bolster their knowledge and refine their cybersecurity approaches.

Policymakers, legislators, and regulatory bodies will find the book invaluable for understanding the legal and regulatory challenges associated with the metaverse. It offers a nuanced exploration of the intersection between technology and law, providing insights to craft policies that ensure a secure and regulated digital space.

CEOs, CIOs, CISOs, and other business leaders will gain strategic insights for making informed decisions about investments in immersive technologies and cybersecurity measures. The book addresses the potential risks and rewards of the metaverse, offering guidance on organizational resilience in the face of evolving cyber threats.

Academics, researchers, and educators in the fields of cybersecurity, computer science, and technology studies will find the book to be a valuable reference. It contributes to the academic discourse on emerging cyber threats, providing case studies, forecasting methodologies, and insights that can inform research and educational curricula.

Attorneys, legal professionals, and compliance officers will gain a comprehensive understanding of the legal implications and compliance requirements associated with the metaverse. The book explores issues such as digital identity theft, data protection, and regulatory compliance within immersive digital spaces.

Entrepreneurs, startups, and innovators exploring opportunities within the metaverse will find this book to be a guide for navigating the cybersecurity landscape. It offers insights into building secure platforms, protecting digital assets, and fostering innovation while mitigating risks associated with cyber threats.

Students pursuing degrees in cybersecurity, computer science, information technology, and related fields will find the book to be a valuable educational resource. It provides foundational knowledge, real-world examples, and insights that can aid in their academic pursuits and future careers in the dynamic field of cybersecurity.

Forecasting Cyber Crimes in the Age of the Metaverse is designed to be accessible to both technical and non-technical readers, offering a holistic understanding of the metaverse's impact on cybersecurity. By catering to a diverse audience, the book aims to foster a collaborative and informed approach to addressing the challenges posed by cybercrimes in the evolving digital landscape.

Forecasting Cyber Crimes in the Age of the Metaverse stands as a pivotal contribution to the ever-evolving field of cybersecurity, offering profound insights and practical guidance that resonate with the contemporary challenges posed by the metaverse. As the digital landscape continues to metamorphose, this book plays a crucial role in shaping the discourse and responses to emerging cyber threats within immersive digital environments.

The book significantly impacts the field by providing actionable strategies and best practices that reshape cybersecurity practices in the age of the metaverse. It goes beyond theoretical discussions, offering tangible solutions to fortify defenses, anticipate threats, and proactively address the dynamic challenges presented by immersive technologies.

In the face of evolving cyber threats, preparedness is paramount. This book contributes by equipping cybersecurity professionals, organizations, and policymakers with the knowledge and foresight needed to enhance their preparedness and resilience. By forecasting potential cybercrimes, stakeholders can adopt preemptive measures to safeguard digital identities, secure virtual environments, and protect critical infrastructure.

The impact of the book extends to fostering interdisciplinary collaboration. By addressing the technological, legal, regulatory, and strategic aspects of the metaverse, it encourages collaboration among cybersecurity experts, legal professionals, policymakers, and technology innovators. This interdisciplinary approach is essential to comprehensively address the multifaceted challenges posed by metaverse-related cybercrimes.

The book contributes significantly to the formulation of legal and regulatory frameworks tailored to the metaverse. As policymakers and regulators grapple with the complexities of the digital age, this resource offers a roadmap for creating effective laws and regulations that balance innovation with security, protecting individuals and organizations from potential cyber threats.

Innovators and entrepreneurs exploring opportunities within the metaverse find empowerment in the insights provided by the book. By understanding the cybersecurity landscape, they can innovate responsibly, building secure platforms and digital experiences that thrive within the evolving digital ecosystem.

The impact of the book extends to educational realms, informing curricula in cybersecurity, computer science, and technology studies. By offering foundational knowledge, case studies, and practical insights, it becomes a valuable resource for educators and students, shaping the next generation of cybersecurity professionals.

As immersive technologies raise ethical considerations, the book navigates these complexities. It encourages ethical practices within the metaverse, addressing issues of privacy, digital identity, and responsible innovation. By fostering an ethical mindset, the book contributes to building a more trustworthy and secure digital environment.

Ultimately, the book significantly advances the dialogue on cybersecurity in the metaverse. It prompts ongoing discussions about the ever-evolving threat landscape, stimulates further research, and encourages a collective, global effort to tackle cybercrimes within this dynamic digital frontier.

In conclusion, *Forecasting Cyber Crimes in the Age of the Metaverse* is not merely a static observation of the metaverse's impact on cybersecurity; it is a dynamic catalyst for change. By offering actionable insights, fostering collaboration, and guiding stakeholders across various domains, the book leaves an enduring impact on the field, contributing to the ongoing mission of creating a secure and resilient digital future within the metaverse.

CHAPTER 1

Forecasting Cybercrimes in the Metaverse Era: Future Criminal Methods - Readiness Requirements

Professor / Hossam Nabil Elshenraki

One of the digital transformation features of the new generation of cyber world is the meta verse, it is expected to establish a self-sustainable virtual ecosystem of full immersive environment, real-time experiences with numerous chances to interact with the world for users and industrial businesses. With the introduction of new networks and enabling technological tools, the meta verse will succeed in the long term. However, with increasing interaction using new meta verse and a lot of third-party services, there would be an arena for many possibilities of cyber crimes threats. Hence, combating cyber crimes is critical for the meta verse, they should be investigated since the commercial adoption of the meta verse is imminent. Therefore, this paper discusses many cyber crime methods and techniques which are expected in the meta verse environment, (AI) related cyber-attacks are expected, and solutions to the meta verse is possible.

CHAPTER 2

Future Cybercrimes in the Metaverse: A Comprehensive Forecast

Dr. Ibtesam Alawadhi

In an era where virtual reality emerges in our life, cybercrimes become a challenge. With Metaverse, the potential dangerous maximized. In this chapter, deep understanding of potential threats is discussed. Several threats will be highlighted such as: virtual identify theft and impersonation, virtual real estate frauds, malware and ransomware, virtual espionage, advanced phishing, and social engineering. To forecast these threats, insights from cybercrimes are adapted and extrapolated to fit the unique environment of the metaverse. This will be a guide for law enforcement, tech firms, policymakers, regulators, and researchers.

CHAPTER 3

Navigating the Metaverse: Forecasting Cybercrime in the New Age of Virtual Reality

Akashdeep Bhardwaj

The rise of the metaverse - a virtual world where individuals can interact with each other and digital objects in a fully immersive environment - has led to new challenges in the world of cybersecurity. As more individuals and businesses move towards this new frontier, the potential for cybercrime is also increasing. In this chapter, we explore the diverse types of cybercrime that may emerge from virtual theft and fraud to privacy violations and hacking. We also discuss the unique challenges faced by law enforcement and security professionals in detecting and preventing these crimes in a fully virtual environment. To aid in forecasting these crimes, we examine current trends and technological developments that may impact the future of the metaverse, including the growth of decentralized technologies, the increasing prevalence of artificial intelligence, and the potential for quantum computing. By understanding the potential risks and challenges of the metaverse, we can better prepare ourselves for a future where virtual and physical crime intersect.

CHAPTER 4

Online Crime in the Metaverse: A Study on Classification, Prediction, and Mitigation Strategies

John Blake

With the burgeoning growth of the metaverse and online virtual environments, new security challenges have been introduced that require careful exploration and mitigation. An increasing proportion of human interactions and transactions now take place in these digital spaces, making it essential to protect users and ensure the safety and integrity of virtual worlds. This chapter explores three dimensions of this issue. First, through a study of the types of crimes that occur in these environments, we can gain a holistic understanding of the cybercrime technoscape. Second, we use a two-pronged approach to increase the safety of the metaverse by targeting both potential perpetrators and victims. This is achievable by identifying indicators that may be used to detect potential perpetrators or victims. Thirdly and finally, strategies and techniques to make these online communities safer are suggested.

CHAPTER 5

Predicting Future Cybercrime Trends in the Metaverse Era

Wasswa Shafik

The Metaverse is a virtual world where users can engage with each other and digital objects in real time, and its usage is growing significantly. However, the rise of virtual environments comes with the risk of cybercrime. This chapter presents the current cybercrime overview in the metaverse by examining recent incidents and standard methods cybercriminals employ. Moreover, it explores factors that could influence cybercrime trends in the Metaverse era, including technological advancements and evolving security measures. Furthermore, it evaluates current and potential cybersecurity measures to prevent or mitigate cybercrime in virtual environments and the importance of user education and responsible online behavior. Finally, we emphasize the need for industry, government, and users to collaborate to mitigate cybercrime in the Metaverse era due to possible negative impacts on social, economic, and environmental settings and its merits benefit people at different levels of endeavors.

CHAPTER 6

Societal Risks of Using Cyber Metaverse Technology

Amar El-Bably

AI's widespread use poses challenges, especially accountability and legal readiness for metaverse's unique traits. This study addresses AI's current hurdles, focusing on regulating AI-related crimes, including metaverse. It aims to define responsibilities and penalties. Metaverse's societal, reputational, and security implications, along with tech firms' oversight, can escalate cybercrime. Complex evolving cybercrime patterns hinder guilt proof. Criminalizing tech use in terrorism planning and financing is crucial. Social media users face risks like deepfakes, fostering doubt and inciting terrorism. Tech-security agency partnership is vital. Growing digital interconnectedness heightens cybersecurity issues. Metaverse's growth and internet use call for strengthened anti-terrorism and IT crime laws.

CHAPTER 7

The Future of Cyber-Crimes & Cyber War in the Metaverse

Sameer Saharan, Shailja Singh, Ajay Bhandari, Bhuvnesh Yadav

The future of cybercrimes and cyber warfare in the metaverse is a topic of concern. Understanding the emerging landscape is crucial. With technological advancements and the pervasive influence of the metaverse, new cyber threats have emerged. This chapter provides an overview of challenges and ramifications associated with cybercrimes and cyber warfare in the metaverse. It explores evolving cyber threats in the metaverse, considering AI, machine learning, and quantum computing. Cybercrimes include virtual asset theft, identity theft, phishing, harassment, and online extortion. Cyber warfare in the metaverse involves state-sponsored attacks, espionage, information warfare, and manipulation of virtual defense systems. Robust cybersecurity measures, collaboration among stakeholders, and cyber literacy are essential to mitigate risks.

CHAPTER 8

A Prelude to Cybersecurity Challenges in the Metaverse

Shashwath Bhaskar, Aiesha Kuna, Akshaya Jayakumar, Lakshmi D

The metaverse represents a transformative concept that has amassed substantial attention in recent years, with big corporations vying to gain hegemony over this domain. While revolutionizing the way we interact with and experience our environment, the metaverse unlocks a vast potential for cyber criminals and nation-states to take advantage of the present voids in its security. By analyzing existing literature and emerging trends, we delve into the uncharted territory of the metaverse, examining the ways in which users' digital avatars and assets are at risk- including poor security of NFTs, the scope for financial fraud, the dark verse and social engineering among other issues. This chapter provides insight into the real-world implications of cyber-attacks in the metaverse and examines the legal and ethical challenges of regulating cyber activity in virtual environments so that Law Enforcement Agencies, planners, and companies can navigate this field to create a safe virtual world for all.

CHAPTER 9

Potential Threats: Extremism and Terrorism in the Metaverse

Ehab Khalifa

Throughout history, terrorism has adeptly leveraged technological advancements to further its ominous objectives. As societies have evolved, so have the methods employed by extremists. From the early utilization of print media to spread propaganda, to the more recent harnessing of social media platforms for recruitment and radicalization, terrorist groups have consistently exploited the cutting edge of available technology. Now, with the dawn of the Metaverse, the terrorism is about to be at another pivotal intersection. This digital realm, characterized by immersive virtual environments and complex interactivity, offers a new frontier for these malevolent actors. The metaverse not only provides concealed platforms for communication and coordination but also introduces potential grounds for training, recruitment, and even virtual staging of attacks. we venture deeper into this digital epoch, it's imperative that we remain vigilant, recognizing that as technology advances, so too will the tactics of those intent on using it for harm.

CHAPTER 10

Metaverse Forensics: A Preliminary Analysis of Opportunities and Challenges

Faouzi Kamoun, Farkhund Iqbal, Siem Zeresenay, Richard Ikuesan, Sened Abraham, Zainab Khalid

The metaverse is poised to offer an immersive virtual environment for people to meet, socialize, collaborate, play, and conduct business transactions. Although the metaverse has not yet reached its full maturity, it has already been misused to launch illegal activities that can jeopardize the safety and well-being of individuals, and cause harm to organizations. Despite its increased importance, "metaverse forensics" remains an unexplored research topic. This chapter starts by reviewing the state-of-the-art research related to metaverse cybersecurity threats and underlying ethical, privacy, and legal issues. It then presents the results of a forensic investigation analysis performed on the VRChat and AltspaceVR metaverse platforms. We present new insights into metaverse forensics in terms of accessing digital containers and retrieving useful information for forensic investigators. Additionally, we highlight the primary obstacles encountered in metaverse digital forensic investigations and put forth recommendations for future research directions.

CHAPTER 11

Machine Learning Based Prediction Analysis of Unlawful Activities to Aid Law Enforcement

Vijayalakshmi Mahesh, Shilpa Hiremath, Chandra Prabha R

One of our society's most significant and pervasive issues is crime. Numerous crimes are perpetrated often each day. The development of policing strategies and the implementation of crime prevention and control depend greatly on crime prediction. The most popular prediction technique right now is machine learning. Few research, however, has rigorously contrasted various machine learning approaches for crime prediction. The dataset in this instance consists of the date and the annual crime rate for the corresponding years. The crime rate used in this project is only based on robberies. Utilising historical data, we employ linear and random forest regression algorithms to estimate future crime rates. The algorithm receives the date as input, and the result is the total number of crimes that year.

CHAPTER 12

Investigating Forensic Evidence in Metaverse: A Comparative Analytical Study

Ramy El-Kady

The study deals with the issue of Investigating Forensic Evidence in Metaverse. The importance of the study stems from its handling of the Metaverse technology, as one of the most prominent technological topics on the global scene at present, which is expected to shine in the coming times as the most prominent form of the development of the internet, which moves humanity to new technological dimensions. Spatial and temporal boundaries. The importance of this study is evident in light of the legislative vacuum that exists in the face of all forms of violations that occur in the Metaverse. The study aims to shed light on ways to collect digital evidence in the Metaverse. The study concluded with a set of recommendations, most notably: the need for concerted international efforts to amend international conventions on cybercrime, led by the Budapest Convention, or to aspire to develop a new international convention that regulates the responsibility of Metaverse service providers and obliges them to comply with cooperation in combating crimes.

In conclusion, *Forecasting Cyber Crime in the Age of Metaverse* stands as a significant contribution to the field, offering invaluable insights and foresight into the evolving landscape of cyber threats within the rapidly expanding metaverse. The book not only addresses current challenges but also anticipates future trends, providing a comprehensive guide for professionals, researchers, and policymakers.

One of the key strengths of the book lies in its proactive approach to cybercrime prevention and mitigation. By delving into the metaverse, it sheds light on novel attack vectors and vulnerabilities that are likely to emerge as technology advances. This foresight equips readers with the knowledge necessary to stay ahead of cybercriminals, fostering a proactive security mindset crucial for navigating the intricate metaverse ecosystem.

Furthermore, the book bridges the gap between theoretical discourse and practical application. Through case studies, real-world examples, and practical scenarios, it provides readers with tangible insights that can be directly applied to enhance cybersecurity measures. This practical orientation enhances the book's utility, making it an essential resource for professionals seeking actionable strategies to safeguard their digital assets in the metaverse.

The interdisciplinary nature of the book is another noteworthy aspect. It seamlessly weaves together insights from cybersecurity, technology, law, and ethics, offering a holistic understanding of the challenges posed by cybercrime in the metaverse. This interdisciplinary approach is crucial for comprehensively addressing the multifaceted nature of digital threats, ensuring that readers gain a well-rounded perspective on the subject matter.

As the metaverse continues to evolve, the relevance of this book will only intensify. Its forward-looking perspective positions it as a guide for navigating the ever-changing cybersecurity landscape. By fostering a deeper understanding of the unique challenges and opportunities presented by the metaverse, the book empowers its readers to develop adaptive and resilient strategies, ultimately contributing to the ongoing dialogue surrounding cybersecurity in this new era.

In summary, *Forecasting Cyber Crime in the Age of Metaverse* is a pioneering work that not only illuminates the intricacies of cybersecurity within the metaverse but also empowers its readers with the knowledge and tools needed to proactively address the dynamic challenges that lie ahead. Its impact on the field is profound, providing a foundation for future research, policy development, and practical implementation in the ongoing battle against cyber threats in the age of the metaverse.

Hossam Nabil Elshenraki
Dubai Police Academy, UAE

Chapter 1
Forecasting Cyber Crime in the Metaverse Era:
Future Criminal Methods – Readiness Requirements

Hossam Nabil Elshenraki
https://orcid.org/0000-0002-8131-5586
Dubai Police Academy, UAE

ABSTRACT

One of the digital transformation features of the new generation of cyber world is the meta verse. It is expected to establish a self-sustainable virtual ecosystem of fully immersive environments, real-time experiences with numerous chances to interact with the world for users and industrial businesses. With the introduction of new networks and enabling technological tools, the meta verse will succeed in the long term. However, with increasing interaction using new meta verse and a lot of third-party services, there would be an arena for many possibilities of cybercrime threats. Hence, combating cybercrimes is critical for the meta verse, and they should be investigated since the commercial adoption of the meta verse is imminent. Therefore, this chapter discusses many cybercrime methods and techniques which are expected in the meta verse environment, (AI) related cyber-attacks are expected, and solutions to the meta verse is possible.

INTRODUCTION: PROBLEM AND AIM OF THE BOOK EXPLAINED

Online users are exposed to many crimes such as online bullying, image-based abuse, such as sexual extortion, inciting children to sexual behaviour and exploitation, and given the high prevalence of interactive online games among children and youth.

Game environments can enable criminals to use avatars, disguising their real age and identity to target children. They can also provide a platform to post child pornography. In realistic scenarios generated by metaverse technology, children may not have yet developed critical thinking to help them identify risks.

DOI: 10.4018/979-8-3693-0220-0.ch001

There were already concerns about online user safety, as it was found that more than 50% of girls had experienced online abuse.

Added to these online personal safety challenges are the risks to the police of personal data. Websites record the circulation of large amounts of data, including biometrics, location, and personal information.

This can provide new opportunities for criminals to commit identity theft, online fraud, and deception. Along with the growth of virtual currencies, which can provide unlimited space for criminals to defraud and steal users. (elliptic metaverse report, 2022)

BACKGROUND

Forecasting cybercrimes in the metaverse age is important because it is reflecting the need to proactively address emerging threats and safeguard the security and well-being of individuals within virtual environments, Forecasting helps in identifying potential cyber threats and criminal activities that may emerge within the metaverse, giving Early detection enables law enforcement and cybersecurity professionals to implement preventive measures before significant harm occurs, Understanding potential cybercrime trends allows for the development and implementation of proactive security measures, law enforcement can work collaboratively with technology providers to integrate security features and safeguards into virtual platforms, Forecasting assists law enforcement agencies in allocating resources efficiently based on anticipated cybercrime trends, prioritizing resources in areas with higher forecasted risks ensures a more targeted and effective response, Agencies can develop strategic plans for cybercrime prevention and response by aligning resources with forecasted threats, planning ahead helps in building specialized units, acquiring necessary technologies, and training personnel, it allows policymakers to anticipate changes needed in legal and regulatory frameworks to address emerging cyber threats, Timely updates to laws can provide a more robust legal foundation for prosecuting cybercriminals in the metaverse, that is why it is essential for adopting a proactive and strategic approach to cybersecurity, by anticipating and preparing for emerging threats, law enforcement, policymakers, and technology providers can collaboratively create a safer virtual environment for users and uphold the principles of security, privacy, and justice in the digital realm.

LITERATURE REVIEW

1- lik-hang lee, tristan braud, pengyuan zhou, lin wang, dianlei xu, zijun lin, abhishek kumar, carlos bermejo, and pan hui, fellow, ieee, all one needs to know about metaverse: a complete survey on technological singularity, virtual ecosystem, and research agenda, journal of latex class files, vol. 14, no. 8, September 2021 (Lik-Hang et al., 2021), the research study published in the Latex Class Files magazine, which is one of the magazines classified within the global Scopus index.

The study discussed the concept of mixed reality, and how the digital world will be from the perspectives of the ecosystem, which is meta verse world, with its new and completely different personalities, with what we live and see today.

The study concluded that with the involvement of emerging and progressive technologies to develop and improve ecosystems, and virtual world or digital twins may appear in another shape in the next years, also the digitalization in the future will be better interactive, embodied, alive, and the multimedia due to presence of quantum computing devices and wearable devices,

There are still many challenges to overlap that should be done before meta verse integration into real world and daily life.

The study recommended the need to follow a comprehensive approach to building the meta virus, as we consider that the meta verse will be a large entity in parallel with our physical reality., While the research will anticipate future crimes considering the new world, legal challenges, and ways to confront them.

2- Nuno Cadilhe, Augmented Reality for the Mobile Police Force, A dissertation submitted in the partial fulfilment of master's degree in science, Specialization Area of Sistemas Gráficos e Multimedia, Supervisor: Filipe de Faria Pacheco, Porto, June 26, 2022.

This master's thesis entitled "Using Augmented Reality for Police Patrol Forces" and the thesis discussed the concept of meta verse as well as its use in training traffic policemen on the required behaviour and avoiding problems resulting from inappropriate behaviour as well as safe road applications and also presents the experience of the Dutch police in training on the use of meta verse in Police work and shows all the results and mechanisms of application, which is what the research group will benefit from in this study in some of its parts.

The study will also deal with criminal patterns under the meta verse will predict what the situation will be like regarding the crime and its methods of commission, as well as the legal position on this crime, and how the situation will be legalized in the meta virus.

3- Mitra Pooyandeh, Ki-Jin Han and Insoo Sohn, Cybersecurity in the AI-Based Metaverse: A Survey, 2022, Switzerland, an open access article distributed under the terms and conditions of the Creative Commons Attribution (CC BY) license (https://cre-ativecommons.org/licenses/by/4.0/).

The article discussed Metaverse as multi-user virtual environment combines real world and VR, and the study discussed also the three technologies uses to create Metaverse which are immersive tech, AI, blockchain, so Companies subsequently making investments in creating AI Metaverse, with consequence turn cybersecurity to be more crucial, which led to the increase of cybercrime, it is evident that a comprehensive study of Metaverse security based on AI is lacking, the growth of denial-of-service attacks and identity theft attacks made it essential to conduct comprehensive and inclusive research in this field in order to identify the Metaverse's vulnerabilities and weaknesses. the study summarizes a comprehensive vision of AI-based Metaverse cybersecurity and discussed security challenges, based on identification which has important role in presented works, for which biometric methods are important because of its uniqueness, susceptible to misuse, AI cyber-situation management system should analyse data volumes by algorithms, so to prepare researchers who will pursue this topic, this article provides a comprehensive summary of research on cybersecurity in Metaverse based on AI.

As AI-based Metaverse not considered in some aspects of security research, authors considered various aspects of Metaverse apps as possible and make results available to other researchers, in the field of cybersecurity, authentication is a great interest to researchers, biometric methods are important and widely used, and because of its uniquity; it's hard to be cheated, however, that there are concerns, such as error detection and possibility of biometric information misuse.

Considering AI effective solutions to solve cybersecurity problems in Metaverse, authors analysed the role of AI in security, and found that neural network algorithms can improve attack detection accuracy, conduct attack detection, authentication methods could use algorithms.

Alternatively, hackers can also make use of AI to attack the Metaverse. Various types of attacks have been described using AI algorithms in several papers, the results of this study suggest that researchers in this area face a very basic challenge regarding access to specific Metaverse data, while AI and machine learning can defend cyber-attacks, but hackers can defeat security algorithms by targeting data.

Hackers can use AI to compromise systems and develop malwares to deceive firewalls.

AI systems can produce faulty results, consequences of data manipulation could be catastrophic if institutions failed to detect it, also they can struggle to recover correct information that support AI systems, to develop AI- based Metaverse cybersecurity, collecting and classifying data is a great idea, as implicit algorithms require large data sets.

the paper basically focused on new methods of cybercrimes which may appear in the age of metaverse that predicted according to trends in studies of the impact of new technologies on cyber threats, so this paper focused on the effects of AI on criminal methods in metaverse.

4- A scoping study of crime facilitated by the metaverse, Juliana Gómez-Quintero, Shane D Johnson, Hervé Barrion, and Samantha Lundrigan, the study results Considered the top ten risks identified in a little more detail, five of these were sexual in nature. The types of sexual offenses identified are all contemporary problems, some of which – such as child sexual abuse material, child grooming, non-consensual sexual image offenses take place online, whereas rape and sexual assaults, as defined in law, currently only take place in real life.

In all cases, attributes of metaverse have potential to make these types of offenses worse than their online equivalents, Decentralisation may make it easier for offenders to escape detection or perceive that they will do so. There will likely be a tension between privacy and security, but attention should be given to balancing the two to make the metaverse a safe place. Relative to similar crimes committed in 2D environments, the level of immersion facilitated by metaverse technologies will also likely increase the rewards to offenders, and the harm experienced by victims.

Four of the offenses considered were other types of crimes against the person. Each of these already take place in the real world or online, but again, the immersion associated with the metaverse will mean that their effects are amplified for victims. The hyper-spatiality of the metaverse may make offenses such as stalking easier to commit and the use of avatars may help to conceal an offender's activity.

Virtual-physical hybridity may also mean that the effects of these offenses are not constrained to impacting upon victims in virtual worlds but may also affect them in real world contexts.

While many of the above crimes are expressive ones, the motivation for other forms of offending is clearly financial, and hence it is unsurprising that financial crimes were included in the top ten.

Investment scams are currently rife on the internet, with recent incarnations including cryptocurrency frauds, such as initial coin offerings for fake currencies.

Such scams will be possible in the metaverse, but as there will be other forms of ownership in the metaverse –which will be recorded on blockchains which lack a central controller to monitor activity – the opportunities for financial crime will increase substantially and, as the metaverse is expected to be a multi-user environment, this will facilitate offending at scale.

In terms of the likely scale of the crime harvests that might emerge, participants rated how frequent they anticipated each threat might be. However, what these actual frequencies are likely to be will depend on how ubiquitous the use of the metaverse is, who uses it, and for what purposes.

Because of its emerging nature, there is currently uncertainty about this. In their report, outline three scenarios regarding its trajectory: low orbit, double star, and big bang.

In the low orbit scenario, the Metaverse becomes a 'specialty market' that complements existing platforms/technologies but does not replace them and is not fully integrated to daily life.

In the double star scenario, the metaverse becomes a 'mainstream market' with many applications but one that lacks interoperability which leads to a few major players dominating the metaverse.

Lastly, the 'big bang' scenario considers a complete overhaul of how we experience the internet today, with this becoming an immersive world where most businesses and consumers are involved.

All three scenarios could facilitate crime harvests, but the scale of the problems generated will depend on which scenario plays out.

The big bang scenario would create the greatest crime opportunity and, because there would be the most actors involved, it would also be the most complicated to design security for, and to monitor place manager's compliance with any guidelines, standards or regulation that are proposed.

The situation is made more complex by the fact that the metaverse is a convergence of technologies, each of which will have their own vulnerabilities and their own standards and regulations.

THE EFFECTS OF THE METAVERSE IN DEVELOPING CRIMINAL METHODS

By the beginning of the year 2026, there are expectations that 25% of persons in the world will spend more than hour daily in the metaverse world - which opens possibilities to be victims of cybercrimes, the possibilities of committing cyber-crimes against children will rise, such as stealing digital assets, impersonation, sexual exploitation, ethnic harassment. metaverse means has a special nature which need organizational concern so it needs to adopt an approach of a multi-stakeholder, because of the fast development of the technology, **so I will address it through:**

The metaverse will include many types of technologies which will be as blocks in a building, each of them will come with different risks, cybercrimes which exist like fraud, impersonation, credential stealing, technology debt, espionage, and disinformation, will follow us into metaverse, crimes in Metaverse will be More Harmful As digital commerce in meta verse grows in scope and scale, Estimates reaching $1 trillion annually, and financial crimes will increase in frequency and aggressiveness, Security threats should be clear and the awareness of them should be enhanced and we can see the layers of the metaverse to conclude that. (Brenner, 2008)

The Social Engineering Techniques

Phishing scams committed by using social engineering techniques are the most dangerous primary attacks cybercriminals use to commit their crimes.

Because of the effectiveness of exploiting psychological weakness of users, social engineering will be a challenge in Metaverse and users who been scammed by phishing promoting fraudulent crypto-tokens, land sales illegally, shady Web 3.0 phishing scammer use impersonate popular Ethereum-based metaverse environment, deceiving users by entering their wallet's pass codes, allowing scammers to steal users' virtual money.

Phishing attacks in metaverse can be visualized using deep fake technology to impersonate famous organizations or avatars, standards that allow users to verify authenticity of organizations and avatars is needed to interact with, without violating user's privacy, Organizations should care about the verification of avatars' identities and protect them from identity theft.

Users should be trained to be able to discover the new methods of criminals in the metaverse which exploit social engineering techniques in cybercrimes and how to be safeguarding personal identities.

Figure 1. Social engineering techniques

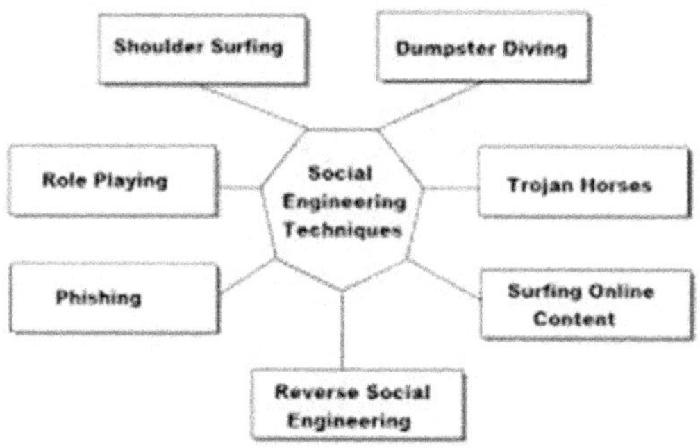

Malware which is used to attack crypto wallets and to hack people's cryptocurrency wallets, tokens, and non-fungible tokens, Online blackmailing and ransomware attacks are among the most famous and lucrative cybercrime, So, in the metaverse world it will take complicated forms, but they will still be very risky.

A high percentage of attacks against existing Web 3.0 platforms and Divi protocols are made possible by vulnerabilities in the underlying software, or the smart contracts used.

The most serios thefts usually result in code exploits. So, breaches are a serious threat to user's digital assets in the world of Metaverse.

VR and AR wearables devices are essentially computers but have special capabilities, it observed that it uses software and memory tools courage cybercriminals to target them.

Research conducted by a university results that VR and AR headsets can be hacked to access sensitive data sent by voice commands, such as credit card data and passwords.

Correcting bugs, backdoors and vulnerabilities in platforms, smart contracts, and AR& VR headsets to protect from cyber-attacks and malware attacks are important considerations in security. (Falchuk, Loeb, & Neff, 2018) (Figure1)

Interactive Content Risks in Metaverse Environment

Phishing, sexual, and ethnic harassment are current problems on all digital and virtual reality gaming platforms, This type of behavior has a long experience in virtual world- but the interactivity of VR means it can negatively affect user's psychological health, The risks of sexual exploitation on children are high, so they are likely not to explore metaverses before their parents, which could lead to be victims of sexual exploitation and force them to see sexual content without informing their parents.

VR world introduces several tools to combat cybercrimes, like personal spaces, muting, blocking, and reporting against bad behavior, providing awareness training on new cybercriminals techniques to users and vulnerable women and children, on how to use these tools is very important to enhance capabilities of users in that. (Chamara Sandeepa, 2023)

READINESS REQUIREMENTS TO CONFRONT CYBERCRIME IN THE META VERSE

To forecast the future of cybercrime in the metaverse age, organizations which in the Metaverse should collaborate with security and risk management teams in the very beginning to identify what could be at stake and to detect expected vulnerabilities and secure it, they must appropriately educate the developers to mitigate such risks and test the applications according to the rules before publishing it.

End users also their awareness must be raised that using any new technologies like metaverse put them in a threats of being a cybercriminals victim, users also need to learn about the threats of social engineering and phishing scams, as well as best practices on the safe use of the internet and specially the metaverse for the best use and protection of their assets on the metaverse, wallets, and identities, Policy makers must play do their best to put suitable plans to protect users from cyber criminals' attacks on their important information in the metaverse, they should set regulations to safeguarding women and children on the metaverse and other consumers without affecting creativity negatively.

So that is why the need to define how ethics, consumer protection, and governance are critical in the presence of these new technologies such metaverse, also identifying the right actions about contacting others in the metaverse world? Which jurisdiction should apply? What is a haven? These questions are complex and urgent.

To answer it a multi-stakeholder approach, forward-thinking, and innovative policy measures that put safety first should be adopted. Unique biometrics must be extracted from optical imaging sensors embedded in the wrist wearable devices to authenticate user. Experimental results show that systems have a high continuous validation accuracy. (Collard, 2022)

Identity Authentication Across Domains

Metaverse usually contains different security domains created by a lot of operators and by using many standards.

Identity authentication through security applications in the Metaverse virtual world is important to offer services in the metaverse virtual world that could be used easily by the users and their avatars.

Identity Authentication via Blockchain

By restricting the trust third parties, the blockchain is important to build zero trust avatars for the users of the metaverse in all domains because sub-Metaverses must use services on heterogeneous blockchain to be compatible with the requirements of excellent Services, and effective cross-chain so authenticating it is essential for smooth services by using a lot of sub-metrics (Figure 2)

Decentralized authentication design block chain-based protocol to solve identity retention, where the identity verifications preserved in the blockchain ledger to remove certification authority System management which use encrypt blockchains for supporting verify the public keys and to use hash codes which has been circulated to enable the public key lookup and centralizing the Exists tools by using blockchain which are primarily based on transferring digital assets, and identity authentication in Metaverse. (Loozen, Chedid, & Buchanan, 2022)

Figure 2. Identity authentication in blockchain

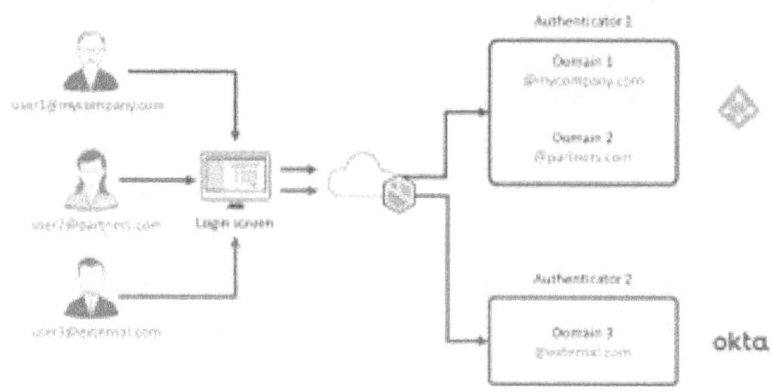

Managing Data

Metaverse is a virtual world built in virtual versions of real world, so the virtual entity called avatar, is a value created to represent users activities, digital twins which are virtual models created to be like physical things in shape and objectives, so as behavior of avatars will issue specific values in virtual world which called metaverse, where cyber security is important for developing the metaverse, and the elements of data privacy and security are In Metaverse, securing data in in the metaverse virtual world in terms of data reliability and quality, and data source are as follows:

Data Authenticity of Content Established by AI, Digital Twin, and Real Input

using AI in the Metaverse like generative Adversarial networks could be useful in generating a very high-quality dynamic scenarios and the context image in the Metaverse environment, on the other hand it can be considered a security threats like adversarial threats which consider cannot be detected in real world as suggested stress-based opposite training to counteract antagonistic samples in training the AI sample and improve learning methods by sampling antagonistically as a section of training, could be used to combat attacking threats in metaverse crime scene reconstruction.

To discuss the reliability of data in the metaverse file in terms of augmented reality device inputs and a digital twin, to Introduce a threat to the authenticate actual augmented reality hardware inputs in location-based on augmented reality games, introduce a reliable replication technique for synchronous digital twins, also to recognize 7 requirements in metaverse design, However, the reliability of the data

Figure 3. Digital twin element

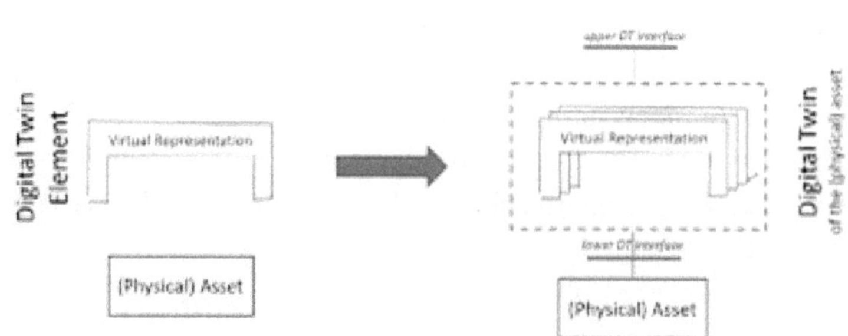

gathered from many data storage have not been studied in addressing that problem, Metaverse combines blockchain technology to build a reliable platform for information exchange and errors diagnosis to create digital twin by different data sources (Figure 3)

Quality of User Generated Content and Data Input

Data which is low-quality which received by sensors will lead to degrade quality of Metaverse Services which produced by Avatar for users, while high quality control tools is essential for providing high quality reverse services and to preserve sustainable innovative economy, So, keeping the psychology of human beings well, offer safety management methods to be sure that data generated by the wearable devices in the Metaverse is always available.

also, the multi-hop and node-potential transmissions, a step-by-step data redundancy scheme for IoT sensors proposed, which could assure achieving available data even in situation of high node failure scenarios, a vehicle service access model capable of evaluate access quality also proposed and designed, Access service routing strategies based on network conditions, and aware of data collection privacy method designed to enhance the quality of results for IoT services in the metaverse world, However, the proposed method overlooks the accuracy of data pooling results. (Leenes, 2010)

Data Source Quality

Data source can achieve timing traceability of a piece of the content which create by users, which is needed to assess the quality of data storage, track data source, reproduce processing on data generation, conducting auditing trails, and identify persons responsible for data very fast.

Source Information in Metaverse

such as the source of trading conditional data, intermediate processing stored in blockchain tokens, so it became hard to track and monitor in the accurate time. IoT data source can provide understanding of User generated content in the Metaverse.

Blockchain-Based Cloud Source Architecture

always includes three phases which are:

A- Source data collection, verification, and storage.
B- User privacy.
C- cloud storage reliability.

Those form the life cycle of the three worlds and a lot of substations, which could be more complex than similar in regular IoT. Besides, scalability, reliability, and efficiency as a delay replay remain a challenge in establishing huge three worlds in the large-scale metaverses. (Amaizu et al., 2022)

IMPROVE PRIVACY

Privacy in interactive games in Metaverse:

VR&AR games are popular in the Metaverse world among users, as game platform have three phases:

(1) Collecting sensory data from users and their surroundings.
(2) Identifying objects according to the context.
(3) Performing Senses for Engagement: Existing work demonstrated many concerns related to metaverse games using case studies, also qualitative studies which conducted using (AR headsets), so results shows that players can interact with AR experiences and treat virtual objects as real, Revealing security.

For the privacy and safety issues, a new attack identified while tracking user's location in games Location-based on AR by using player's network traffic, then experiments confirm that proposed attack model achieved the accurate geolocation of players with high accuracy.

To reduce potential privacy violations in Metaverse games, the principles of privacy by design were introduced into virtual games from a qualitative and quantitative perspective, that they included 19 privacies contain 3 levels to assess privacy, where distinction between individual and group privacy indicates preservation of privacy in interactive design of the game.

So Metaverses of behavioral traits, purchasing patterns, and communication, video, image, location, and users' data, while the user's data refers to privacy associated with users' gropes.

Strict Access Control and Usage Auditing for Content Creation

The content generated by Avatars is essential to maintain creativity and sustainability in the Metaverse virtual world, Since UGCs inevitably contain user information, effective control of access to UGC, and review of usage.

Access control systems are different from the traditional ones which require unique access system for each content and need to design a scalable access control system to give the levels of access privilege to share user-create media content in each cloud.

Detailed build based on scalable mechanism presented with official security manual.

However, systems will not be able to facilitate time-domain access control or addressing problems proposed a time-attribute-based access control mechanism by implemented security mechanism to share user-creation video contents in the cloud.

Allowed access time embedded in the ciphertext and keys, so just the authorized users within the predefined periods of time can decrypting, the Queries also built in earlier periods of time with accurate features updated, However, authorized entities working on illegal distribution created by users to be able to counter such threats, new encrypted and secure sharing systems by tracking cloud via re-encryption to secure sharing and tagging mechanism which prepared is focused on access control, in the same time usage control is ignored. (Hanke, 2022) (Figure 4)

Sharing And Processing User-Generated Content While Preserving Privacy

existing privacy-preserving systems for data sharing and processing focus primarily on four areas: differential privacy, federated learning, cryptographic approaches such as: secure multiparty computations, isomorphic encryption, zero-knowledge proof, and trusted computing.

It offers secure data collaboration in which wearable sensors periodically send model updates trained on their own sensory data to a server that synthesizes a global paradigm to detect health. (Siyaev & Jo, 2021)

To enhance the privacy protection of the blockchain-based Metaverse, use ZKP to enable the block chain of the current account model with privacy-preserving functions in terms of hiding sender-receiver association, account balances, and transaction amounts. Determining the privacy threat of a shared photo in the social metaverse that a shared photo may contain not only the individual privacy but also the privacy of others in the photos. Besides, the software managers designed a custom facial recognition method to distinguish shared photo owners without revealing their privacy in users' private photos. The privacy-preserving user-generated content handling of Metaverse has also attracted different attention. (Mukherjee, 2022)

Protect the Confidentiality of User

Generated Content and Physical Input within Metaverse To prevent leakage of private data and exposure of sensitive data Identity management, access control, and privacy computing technologies are conducive to maintaining the confidentiality of UGC in Metaverse.

Protecting Digital Fingerprints

The digital fingerprints inside avatars could be classified into 3 types:

a) Personal Data (avatar profiling)
b) The Default behaviors
c) Interactions and connections between avatars digital Footprints can be tracked by stalking and spying attacks virtually in the Metaverse world to reveal user's physical identity and all kinds of private Data (shopping behavior, location, bank information's).

A possible solution is to clone avatars, create multiple virtual copies of avatars that have the same appearance and objectives to deceive attackers.

Other privacy-preservations ways like invisibility, private enclave, also lockout, the Invisibility indicates that avatars have been temporarily become invisible.

RAISING THE AWARENESS

Raising the awareness of the situation is considered a powerful tool to monitor the security situation and achieve early warning of cybercrimes threats in complex, large-scale systems such as Metaverse world.

In the Metaverse, the situational awareness is essential to keep an effective monitor for each security domain also to raise and enhance the global awareness of any situation, it can give technical support in early warning of cyber-attacks targeting multiple subgroups:

Awareness of Local Conditions

awareness of the conditions of devices and systems based on mixed reality technology, increasing interest in Metaverse.

By Reviewing the display of information in AR headsets and discussing all possibilities of applying it to enhance users' awareness of situations in perceiving and getting comprehensive understanding on all surrounding environments.

VR technology can improve the awareness capabilities of any kind of situations in all types of applications.

Enhancing the Awareness of the Global Situation

Situational awareness could provide a comprehensive understanding of all security situations in defending all large-scale cyber-attacks in the Metaverse virtual world.

Each of them uses a data-driven approach of global awareness of situation in such large-scale power grids distributed.

TRUSTED USER GENERATED ASSET/RESOURCE TRADING

Blockchain Technologies For example, NFT's are irreplaceable and indivisible tokens in a blockchain and considered unique tradable virtual assets associated with metaverse objects. (Wang et al., 2022)

Economic Fairness to Prevent Manipulation

Economic Fairness in Metaverse when circumvention of market laws is committed by strategy, gratuitous utilization, and users' complicity. Pro-strategic incentive mechanisms, for example, honest auctions and honest contracts, can prevent the avatar from manipulating the market. However, honest participation also violates user privacy, for example, the fact that bidding in auctions may reveal the user's true valuation of items. Primarily privacy-preserving auctions rely on encryption mechanisms, which can lead to significant system overheads for power-limited wearables. Or the low utility of big data in practical metaverse applications.

Digital Asset Ownership Tracking

In the Metaverse world, Blockchains can provide a lot of solutions to handle challenges which affect the protection of assets and tracking ownerships in the different phases of managing virtual assets by preserving evidence of authenticating the metaverse content.

Because all recorded activities on blockchains ledgers are held by most entities in the Metaverse virtual world, it is a guarantee to keep being immutable, undeniable, transparent, and auditable.

CURRENT POTENTIAL SOLUTIONS FOR PHYSICAL SAFETY IN METAVERSE IN THE FOLLOWING RESPECTS

Solutions Depending on Insurance

Electronic insurance provides a financial tool to mitigate the risks of sensitive infrastructure in cyber threats.

To get such requirement of high premiums in traditional insurance offered by insurers, he proposed Federal Insurance in each Power System where alliance premium calculated by analyze losses distributions, all vulnerabilities, budgetary compliance in all insurance coalitions.

However, when applying to Metaverse, formation of dynamic and scalable insurance coalitions combined with a fair design diverted with cyber threats (eg, forensic countermeasures) requires further investigation. (Murray, 2022)

CPSS-Based Solutions

Provide training on defense against cyber threats to protect physical integrity in Metaverse. Providing physical cybersecurity indicators to measure the security of energy grid infrastructures.

Deploying Virtual probes on all host systems targeting profiling each system's activity, and each record has been created using structure data, and random Bayesian models which has been constructed using diffusion algorithms.

Designing dynamic water technology which uses indelible patterns to indicate misconduct like tampering with malicious sensor signals or actuators.

For solving problems in the task-based programming model, a service-oriented model must be prepared with a QoS-aware process and resource-aware deployment to achieve the best support in implementing and reconfiguring the incremental system with no interruption.

Metaverse is different from the CPSSs, in that it is an interactive, hyper-interactive spatiotemporal virtual space with a sustainable ecosystem, which adds much more challenges in the use of solutions. (Figure 5)

Figure 5. Cyber physical social systems

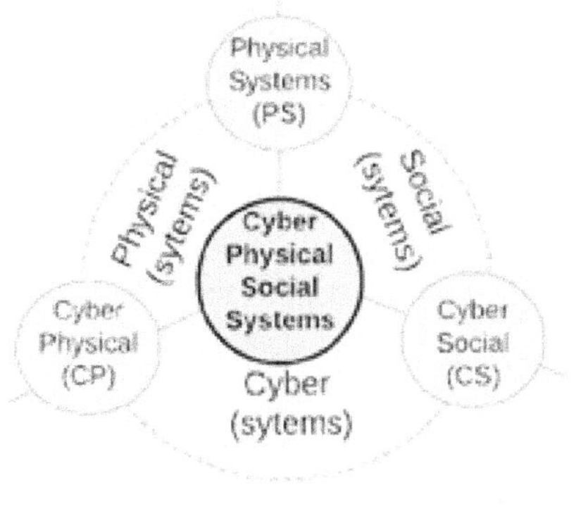

NEW DIMENSIONS OF CYBERCRIME BY METAVERSE

Cyberbullying

The risk of cyberbullying is likely to increase no more by participation in the metaverse world than by using the web.

Cyber Theft and Fraud

Many new methods of cybertheft and cybercrud will appear in virtual worlds specially in social networks such as Second Life, and where business virtual networks are, in those virtual worlds' cryptocurrencies will be used by converting it into real money in trades in a deceiving ways to fraud the victims and it will be punishable if someone intentionally sells a virtual item that does not in reality comply with agreed requirements upon or assumed upon purchase. (Laue, 2011)

The Internet is an important area for scam traders, as it is where they hide behind usernames or avatars.

In addition, the possibility of people logging in with a fake identity provides ample opportunities for them to commit their crimes.

The jurisdictions in the cybertheft of metaverse objects in that virtual environment will be very difficult because of the legal challenges and understanding the law principles in this world.

Where will also appear a new types of abuse, which can be imagined in a social virtual world, also Digital currencies in the virtual worlds will have a new quantitative dimension, and metaverses will

Figure 6. Cyber theft and fraud

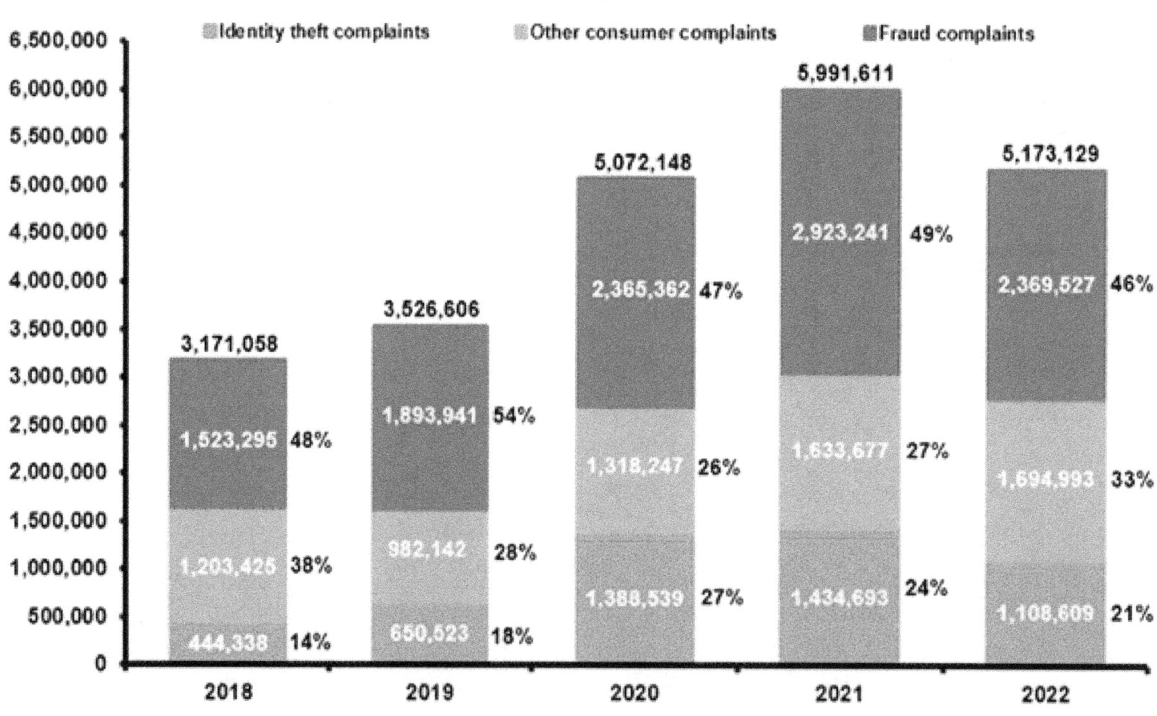

provide different economic activities with their crypto currencies that are able to exchange for local currencies which will facilitate money laundering and terrorism financing.

However, we will not be able to know if the ecosystem in the metaverse a core of contact for money laundry crimes will really be.

So, the web will be an ideal place for illegal money laundering. (Numaan Huq, Reyes, Lin, & Swimmer, n.d.).

A certain role because it provides all the components of money laundering. However, it is not enough to just be a tycoon in the metaverse to convert illegal money to legal one. (Figure 6)

Cyber Pornography

Metaverse introduces new ways of distributing pornographic images. In 2007, Second Life ran into problems because individual users designed avatars that looked like children and were presented in porn, no limitation of punishment due to the fact that these images were only fake, according to the public opinion, for the term child porn publications were shown virtual child porn images that Avatars as subjects were widely - especially in Germany - in the media and the site was under a lot of pressure.(Kusch 2000)

It was also easy to buy real child porn, i.e., non-fake porn images by e-mail from site users and pay for them with cryptocurrency.

The business opportunities provided by Linden Lab for the dissemination of child pornography, this can be seen as at least a quantitative extension of Internet capabilities Distributing pornographic fliers to minors, Second Life does not have any effective age controls, which means that minors can easily log in.

Thus, it is relatively easy for them to view the porn offered by website however, virtual worlds do not offer possibility on websites which also do not have effective age controls to sum up, social virtual worlds offer new avenues for pornography distribution, especially regarding the delusional supply of child pornography.

Sexuality and pornography are part of a pool of potential content in virtual worlds. However, there is the possibility of concealing the circulation of child pornography in the world of Second Life where users are accessible, and the investigative authorities have weak control, So, operators of virtual worlds must limit misuse. (Gee et al., 2010)

Cyber Violence

The Internet provides many advantages to its users, including the possibility of making social contacts, and considering the reduction of social contacts on the Internet. Aggression and social violence have developed across the network, and there are many examples of this, including the reality of 13-year-old Megan Mayer, who committed suicide in 2006 after being abandoned by her hypothetical lover called "Josh Evans", who raised by a former classmate of hers at school, her mother, and the neighbor of the victim's family in the chat room on the Internet.

Myspace", and successfully lured Megan into humiliating her, and then one day Josh ended their relationship with hateful insults and shaming her online. The girl could not stand it and hanged herself. In November 2008, the court sentenced her classmate's 49-year-old mother for computer fraud because she logged in under a false name. And the state has enacted legislation on cyberbullying. This case did not happen in Metaverse, but in the widespread "Myspace" showing that this type of bullying is not limited to virtual worlds but was already possible in the current Internet. (Tredinnick, Smith, & Ponto, 2019)

However, the social virtual world opens like “Second Life” has many possibilities. There are “components” such as bullying in “Myspace”, where the establishment of social contacts between virtual characters is the goal, but this encourages many target children to exploit this, as in the case of Megan Meyer, an adult criminal and a young victim, and there are two similar cases from Germany:

In 2009, a ruling On Christian J. He had met women online and then met them in the real world, which caused the death of two of those women. At first glance, it seems doubtful that these crimes were caused by the Internet. (Zubaska & Academy in Szczytno, 2018)

However, when you read that the accused had virtually no social contacts in real life and was only able to make contacts by establishing a second—virtual—existence, the opportunity to make social contacts over the Internet is probably not a sufficient condition of the crime, but it is a necessary one. This becomes even more apparent when you consider the famous case of the “cannibal of Rothenburg”, Armin Meiwes.

In February 2001, he killed and ate a man he met online who had agreed to kill and maim. In this case, it is difficult to imagine that the perpetrator and the victim who consented to him would have met outside the Internet. Here also, the Internet appears to have been a necessary condition for crime, and there is debate as to whether it makes sense to regard this case as a cybercrime.

What is remarkable here is that the perpetrators would not have been in contact with their subsequent victims without the aid of the Internet. In the case of the “cannibals”, the Internet provided an extremely low probability of meeting the consensual victim.

The range of social contacts has been greatly expanded. In his reality “Chat Room Killer”, the killer assumed a virtual identity, which made him attractive to victims. The fact is that metaverses provide an opportunity to build virtual identities, and this is its goal.

However, metaverses are not a new dimension for the Internet to commit crimes because these possibilities already exist on the Internet - as can be seen in the two cases above. However, social virtual worlds pose another challenge in two respects.

There is the relevant criminal behavior of users in the virtual world and there are potential ramifications between virtual world use and behavior in real world **(Figure7).**

Figure 7. Cyber violence
(Ciencias Sociales y Humanas 2021)

Dimensions of the scale (3 to 15 points)	Concept Scale			Cyber-victimization Scale		
	Global mean (SD)	Female mean (SD)	Male mean (SD)	Global mean (SD)	Female mean (SD)	Male mean (SD)
Deviating from female sexuality norms	11.92 (2.77)	11.96 (2.85)	11.91 (2.74)	4.41 (1.07)	4.44 (1.12)	4.38 (1.01)
Going against compulsory heterosexuality norms	12.81 (2.58)	12.85 (2.67)	12.80 (2.61)	4.28 (.99)	4.28 (1.04)	4.27 (.93)
Imposed heteronormative models of beauty	12.63 (2.65)	12.68 (2.73)	12.57 (2.71)	4.49 (1.08)	4.52 (1.14)	4.46 (1.02)
Sexual violence	13.45 (2.57)	13.45 (2.66)	13.41 (2.59)	4.26 (.94)	4.28 (1.00)	4.24 (.87)
Violence associated with myths of romantic love	11.88 (3.04)	11.93 (3.03)	11.91 (3.03)	4.68 (1.55)	4.70 (1.59)	4.66 (1.52)

THE FUTURE OF THE METAVERSE AND ITS REPERCUSSIONS ON POLICE WORK

Crime will inevitably move into the virtual world. Indeed, even at this early development stage, criminals are starting to exploit the metaverse. This new technology offers a new opportunity to commit age-old crimes such as theft, assault, and money laundering – and could open new risks as well.

When it comes to dealing with the threat posed by new technologies, police forces globally have often been slow to respond. As the Internet rose in prominence at the end of the last century, law enforcement officials could see the risk of digital and cybercrime coming but the development of preventative interventions and legal frameworks were very slow.

Crime had to reach a certain level before governments took note or allocated sufficient cybersecurity funds. In other words, policing's response was reactive, not proactive.

Given that we can clearly see the risks that are coming over the horizon, do we really want to make the same mistake again? Do we wait another 10 years before thinking about how best to regulate and police the metaverse – at which point the risks will have increased substantially? Or should we act now to ensure the metaverse grows in a safe, proportionately governed way?

While regulation does not have to be punitive or a barrier to the metaverse's growth, there evidently needs to be some form of governance structure. The role of the police is to identify the risks and combat them effectively. Many of these risks are like those the police deal with every day in the real world, albeit in a new environment.

New Platform, Old Crimes

The proliferation of non-fungible tokens and other digital assets, for example, raises the prospect of digital theft and property-based crime. Especially given that global brands are increasingly entering the metaverse market, an avatar's digital assets could be highly valuable and therefore a target for criminals, just like in the real world.

The metaverse will require some form of police presence and enforcement mechanisms to deter such crimes from taking place and prosecute those who do commit offences, as the metaverse develops, the use of haptic feedback is increasing. We've already seen the creation of Tesla suit – a full-body suit that enables users to navigate the metaverse in a more immersive way through sense of touch. As costs fall, these suits are likely to become much more mainstream, and more sophisticated.

Fully immersive haptic suits would mean that, if an avatar touches an object in the metaverse, the user feels as if they are touching it in real life. Such technology could ultimately mean that users are able to physically engage with others as they can in the real world, this opens the risk of bodily crime. Avatars could be assaulted by criminal actors. In such cases, the physical pain suffered may not be precisely the same as that which is inflicted in real-world crimes, however they clearly involve a physical intrusion with real consequences – not least distress.

The metaverse has not yet reached a stage where VR technologies are fully integrated or widely available. However, even without this, law enforcement bodies are already seeing crimes such as the theft of digital property, cyberstalking, and cyber-harassment in the virtual world, as well as the forgery of cryptocurrencies and NFTs. The question of how we deter crimes that take place in a virtual setting is therefore pressing.

CRIME PREVENTION

While the police will always have a role in the prevention of crime, software providers and tech companies also have a part to play in the regulation of the metaverse. How could they do this? One theory is 'Crime Prevention Through Environmental Design' (CPTED).

In the context of the metaverse, this approach would mean that so many safeguards are built into the metaverse that certain crimes become much harder to commit.

For example, the metaverse could be programmed to mean that an avatar is not able to touch another avatar unless explicit consent is given. CPTED would be unlikely to eradicate the risks completely but could go some way to making the metaverse a significantly safer place.

At this stage, it appears that many players in the space are reluctant to go down this route. Why? Because there is often an ideological commitment to decentralisation and a misplaced belief that regulation is either pointless or an obstacle to innovation. Many are also of the view that if crimes such as theft do take place, they are usually traceable on the blockchain and therefore easily resolvable.

While this is the case in theory, cryptocurrencies and decentralised financial instruments are already being used for criminal purposes. The United Nations claims that up to 20 per cent of terrorist attacks may be crypto-financed or linked to digital assets. Blockchain analysis firm, Chain analysis, has also determined that, in 2021, criminals laundered $8.6 billion through crypto.

This is where the principles underpinning the metaverse, such as decentralisation, can come into tension with the duties of law enforcement agencies – tasked with preventing these crimes and prosecuting those responsible for committing them.

Virtual police force should be possible to resolve tensions in a way that encourages innovation while ensuring metaverse does not become an environment where crimes go unpunished.

This means looking at formulating and implementing appropriate legislation: rules which are not overburdensome but protect users, given the way in which metaverse promises to tear down physical borders, this process may also involve establishing super-governmental regulatory bodies. And it will also require effective policing.

Platforms such as Second Life suggest there may be a role for volunteers. On this platform, there is an entire community of users who operate in the Second Life metaverse as police officers, taking it upon themselves to prevent criminal behaviour. There may also be a role for algorithms that can automatically spot criminal activity and trigger the necessary next steps, it is also likely that traditional law enforcement agencies will develop a virtual presence to police the metaverse. Ajman Police in the UAE has already taken initial steps towards doing this, last year becoming the world's first law enforcement agency to provide metaverse-based services.

Of course, this raises a whole range of questions. How does a police force obtain a virtual presence? From where would it obtain the authority to patrol the metaverse? What would a virtual police officer look like? To what extent would the use of virtual force be legitimate? How will we establish virtual courts and prosecutions? What penalties would be in place for those found guilty of committing crimes?

These are all deeply complex questions – but ones to which police forces will need to find answers as the metaverse continues to expand its reach.

The metaverse could bring a huge array of advantages to individuals and enterprises around the world. Indeed, police forces themselves are set to benefit from this innovation. For example, immersive technology means that trainee officers could be put into the middle of highly realistic situations, such as terrorist incidents and natural disasters, and learn how best to respond.

Being excited about the endless possibilities the metaverse offers does not mean, however, that we should not proceed with caution. The primary duty of any police force is to keep its citizens safe and strive to do so in the real world every day. It is imperative that authorities globally act now to ensure they can do so in the virtual world too. (Gareth lee Stubbs,2023)

POLICY ISSUES RELATED TO METAVERSE AND ITS EFFECTS ON THE CYBERCRIMES

The emergence and growth of the metaverse bring forth various policy issues related to cybersecurity and the potential increase in cybercrimes. Addressing these challenges requires a comprehensive approach involving policymakers, law enforcement agencies, technology developers, and the private sector.

The metaverse involves the collection and processing of vast amounts of user data, raising concerns about privacy and data protection, so Policymakers need to establish and enforce robust privacy regulations, ensuring that users have control over their personal information. Transparency in data practices and user consent mechanisms are crucial.

The immersive nature of the metaverse may create opportunities for identity theft and various forms of fraud, Policy Response should be Developing and enforcing regulations addressing identity verification, authentication mechanisms, and penalties for fraudulent activities within the metaverse. Establish clear guidelines for platforms to prevent and respond to identity-related cybercrimes.

The metaverse may witness an increase in online harassment, bullying, and other forms of harmful behaviour, the Policy Response is Implement and enforce policies that explicitly address harassment and bullying in virtual environments. Collaboration between platform providers and law enforcement is essential to identify and address instances of online abuse.

The metaverse involves the creation and trading of virtual assets, leading to concerns about theft and fraudulent transactions so the policy Response is to Establish legal frameworks for virtual property rights and enforce regulations to prevent theft or unauthorized transactions of virtual assets. Work with technology providers to implement secure transaction mechanisms.

The metaverse presents new opportunities for child exploitation, including grooming, harassment, and sharing of explicit content, so the policy Response: Strengthen laws and regulations related to child protection online. Implement age verification measures, enhance content moderation capabilities, and increase collaboration between law enforcement agencies and platform providers to identify and combat child exploitation.

virtual platforms may become targets for cyberattacks, compromising user data and platform integrity so the policy so develop and enforce cybersecurity standards for virtual platforms, ensuring that they implement robust security measures, encryption protocols, and regular security audits. Encourage collaboration between platforms to share threat intelligence.

The metaverse operates across borders, making it challenging to enforce laws and regulations consistently, so it needs to Promote international cooperation and agreements on cybersecurity and digital crimes, establish clear guidelines for cross-border jurisdiction and collaboration between law enforcement agencies globally.

Rapid technological advancements within the metaverse may outpace regulatory frameworks, so foster agile regulatory frameworks that can adapt to emerging technologies, encourage collaboration between policymakers, technologists, and other stakeholders to stay ahead of potential risks and challenges.

users will not understand the terms of service, risks, and potential harms associated with metaverse platforms, so Implementing consumer protection measures, including transparent terms of service, clear disclosures about potential risks, and mechanisms for dispute resolution is needed, empowering users to make informed decisions about their participation in the metaverse.

The use of AI and algorithms in the metaverse may raise ethical concerns, including bias and discriminatory practices, so developing guidelines for the ethical use of AI within virtual environments is needed, encourage transparency in algorithms, promote fairness, and establish mechanisms for auditing and addressing algorithmic biases, addressing these policies requires a multi-stakeholder approach, involving collaboration between governments, technology companies, civil society, and academia.

Policymakers should stay informed about technological developments, engage with relevant stakeholders, and continuously update regulations to ensure the responsible and secure development of the metaverse. (Europol (2022), Policing in the metaverse)

DISCUSSION

we can forecast the future of the cybercrimes in the metaverse age when we analyse the initiatives and strategies on that, the global police organization unveiled the first ever Metaverse specifically designed for law enforcement worldwide, interact with other officers via their avatars, and even take immersive training courses in forensic investigation and other policing capabilities, it is provided through the Secure Cloud, ensuring its neutrality.

Trend reports show crime has increasingly moved online as the pace of digitalization has increased, If the boundaries of our physical world move ever further into a digital – and seemingly borderless – realm, the panel discussion asked, 'how can law enforcement continue to protect communities and guarantee the rule of law.

The metaverse might enhance police capabilities and change our lifestyle, whether in terms of crime patterns or mechanisms to confront and combat crime, and the potential impact of the metaverse on police capabilities and its influence on lifestyle, crime patterns, and crime-fighting mechanisms is an evolving and complex topic. While there are opportunities for enhancement, challenges and ethical considerations also need careful consideration. Here are some potential ways the metaverse could influence policing: Enhanced Surveillance and Data Analysis, the metaverse may provide new avenues for surveillance, enabling law enforcement to monitor virtual spaces for potential criminal activities, Increased surveillance raises concerns about privacy and the ethical use of data. Striking a balance between security and individual rights will be crucial.

Law enforcement may adapt to prevent crimes that emerge within the metaverse, such as virtual theft, fraud, or harassment, Policing virtual spaces requires expertise in cybercrime and an understanding of the unique challenges presented by the metaverse. Legal frameworks for prosecuting virtual crimes may need refinement.

Police departments could use the metaverse for community engagement, education, and crime prevention initiatives, ensuring that community engagement is inclusive and effective in virtual spaces and addressing potential misinformation or misuse of virtual community spaces, the metaverse may offer realistic training simulations for law enforcement, allowing officers to practice responding to various scenarios, Ensuring the ethical use of simulations, and addressing potential biases in training scenarios.

Virtual reality technologies could be used to recreate crime scenes and aid investigators in solving cases, Ensuring the accuracy and integrity of virtual crime scene reconstructions, and addressing potential challenges in presenting virtual evidence in legal proceedings, the metaverse could facilitate international collaboration in combating cross-border cybercrimes and virtual offenses, developing consistent legal frameworks and cooperation mechanisms among countries to address jurisdictional challenges in virtual spaces.

Policing virtual communities may involve building trust, ensuring online safety, and preventing crimes within these spaces but it may could not maintain Balancing freedom of expression with the prevention of harmful activities, and addressing potential biases or discrimination in policing virtual communities.

Law enforcement agencies could use the metaverse to monitor and prevent virtual terrorism or extremist activities, but it may face Challenges related to Defining the boundaries between monitoring potential threats and infringing on individuals' rights and addressing the global nature of virtual extremism, there are good possibilities to adopt legal frameworks by policymakers to address the new challenges and opportunities in the metaverse but developing comprehensive and adaptable policies that safeguard individual rights, privacy, and security while addressing the dynamic nature of the metaverse consider as challenges, the metaverse could enhance public trust of law enforcement by demonstrating technological innovation in law enforcement, its challenges are building, maintaining public trust in ethical and responsible use of metaverse technologies, addressing concerns related to potential misuse or overreach.

Enhancing police awareness of threats and harnessing opportunities in the context of evolving technologies and digital landscapes requires a strategic and adaptive approach.

CONCLUSION

Metaverse users grows, and the technology further develops, the list of possible crimes will only expand to potentially include crimes against children, data theft, money laundering, financial fraud, counterfeiting, ransomware, phishing, and sexual assault and harassment.

For law enforcement, some of these threats are likely to present significant challenges, because not all acts that are criminalized in the physical world are considered crimes when committed in the virtual world, "By identifying these risks from the outset, we can work with stakeholders to shape the necessary governance frameworks and cut off future criminal markets before they are fully formed,"

"Only by having these conversations now can we build an effective response.", Metaverse holds many benefits for law enforcement, notably in terms of remote work, networking, collecting, and preserving evidence from crime scenes, and delivering training.

Capacity building in the Metaverse holds promise, offering students more opportunities to collaborate and network, ensuring a greater engagement through immersion and enabling hands-on activities, experts delivered a training course on travel document verification and passenger screening using capabilities in a Metaverse classroom. Students were then teleported to an airport where they were able to apply their newly acquired skills at a virtual border point, "The Metaverse has the potential to transform every aspect of our daily lives with enormous implications for law enforcement," "But in order for police to understand the Metaverse, we need to experience it."

Cybercrimes in the age of metaverse will be more complicated to handle and the law enforcement agencies will face a lot of challenges to investigate those crimes because of the multidimensions of the environment, also that crimes will be in many types such sexual harassment and trademarks steeling and forgery.

From the tech perspective the types of cybercrimes will be more deferent that the new tech in communication Metaverse is not a new dimension for the Internet to commit crimes because these possibilities already exist on the Internet - as can be seen in the two cases above. However, the metaverse poses another challenge in two respects.

There is the relevant criminal behaviour of users in the metaverse and there are potential ramifications between the behaviour in metaverse environment and the behaviour in real world, So to be ready for that expected methods of crimes law enforcement agencies should enhance the collaboration channels with the community in the metaverse, the law enforcement presence in the metaverse should be proactive, and all member states law enforcement agencies should present in the metaverse and enhance their police tools to chase criminal activities, while the metaverse holds potential for enhancing certain aspects of police capabilities and changing lifestyle dynamics, it also introduces new challenges that require careful consideration, striking a balance between security, privacy, and individual rights will be crucial in shaping the future of policing in virtual environments, policymakers, law enforcement agencies, and technology developers must work collaboratively to ensure that the integration of the metaverse into policing aligns with societal values and legal standards.

REFERENCES

Brenner, S. W. (2008). Fantasy Crime: The Role of Criminal Law in Virtual Worlds. *Vanderbilt Journal of Entertainment and Technology Law, 11*(1), 61–65. https://scholarship.law.vanderbilt.edu/cgi/viewcontent.cgi?article=1317&context=jetlaw

Chukwunonso, A. G., Njoku, J. N., Lee, J.-M., & Kim, D.-S. (2022). *Security in Metaverse: A Closer Look* (Conference Paper). Research Gate. https://www.researchgate.net/publication/358948229SecurityinMetaverseACloserLook?enrichId=rgreq-1532b32e0303a88ccfddf15ca27f8419XXX&enrichSource=Y292ZXJQYWdlOzM1ODk0ODIyOTtBUzoxMTI5MDAwNDU4MDI3MDA4QDE2NDYxODYwOTMxNTU%3D&el=1x2&esc=publicationCoverPdf

Collard, A. (2022, August 18). *Crime in the Metaverse is Very Real. But How Do We Police a World With No Borders or Bodies?* World Economic Forum. https://www.weforum.org/agenda/2022/08/crime-punishment-metaverse/

Europol. (2022). *Policing in the metaverse, what law enforcement needs to know, An Observatory Report from the Europol Innovation Lab*. Politiet. https://www.politiet.no/en/rad/trygg-nettbruk/police-online-patrol/

Falchuk, B., Loeb, S., & Neff, R. (2018). The Social Metaverse: Battle for Privacy. *IEEE Technology and Society Magazine, 37*(2), 52–61. https://www.semanticscholar.org/paper/The-Social-Metaverse%3A-Battle-for-Privacy-Falchuk Loeb/b4c1ade08edba966a44765e32117eb2c9cb114c2. doi:10.1109/MTS.2018.2826060

Gee, A. P., Escamilla-Ambrosio, P. J., Webb, M., Mayol-Cuevas, W., & Calway, A. (2010, October 29). *Augmented Crime Scenes: Virtual Annotation of Physical Environments for Forensic Investigation.* In MiFOR'10 Conference, Firenze, Italy. https://www.researchgate.net/publication/228418927_Augmented_crime_scenes_Virtual_annotation_of_physical_environments_for_forensic_investigation

Hanke, J. (2022). *Value Creation in the Metaverse: The Real Business of the Virtual World.* McKinsey & Company. https://www.mckinsey.com/~/media/mckinsey/business%20functions/marketing%20and%20sales/our%20insights/value%20creation%20in%20the%20metaverse/Value-creation-in-the-metaverse.pdf

Huq, N., Reyes, R., Lin, P., & Swimmer, M. (2023). Cybersecurity Threats Against the Internet of Experiences. *Trend Micro.* https://documents.trendmicro.com/assets/white_papers/wp-metaverse-or-metaworse-cybersecurity-threats-against-the-internet-of-experiences.pdf

Laue, C. (2011). Crime Potential of Metaverses. In K. Cornelius & D. Hermann (Eds.), *Virtual Worlds and Criminality* (pp. 19–25). Springer-Verlag Berlin Heidelberg. doi:10.1007/978-3-642-20823-2_2

Leenes, R. (2010). *Privacy in the Metaverse: Regulating a Complex Social Construct in a Virtual World.* Springer. https://link.springer.com/content/pdf/10.1007/978-0-387-79026-8_7.pdf

Lik-HangL.TristanB.PengyuanZ.LinW.DianleiX.ZijunL.PanH. (2021). All One Needs to Know about Metaverse: A Complete Survey on Technological Singularity. Virtual Ecosystem, and Research Agenda. *Latex Class Files, 14.* https://pengyuan-zhou.github.io/papers/metaversearxiv.pdf

Loozen, T., Chedid, F., & Buchanan, L. (2022). *Journey to the Centre of the Metaverse: A Perspective on the Metaverse and What It Means for Telcos.* Ernst & Young., https://assets.ey.com/content/dam/ey-sites/ey-com/en_gl/topics/telecommunications/ey-metaverse-for-telcos.pdf?download

Mukherjee, S. (2022). Fighting Cybercrime in the Metaverse: As More Money Enters the Metaverse, the More Hackers Will Try to Take Advantage of Everyday Crypto Users. *Analytics India.* https://analyticsindiamag.com/fighting-cybercrime-in-metaverse/

Murray, M. D. (April 2022). *Ready Lawyer One: Lawyering in the Metaverse* (pp. 2-5). Research Gate. https://www.researchgate.net/publication/359931632

Report, E. M. (2022). *The Future of Financial Crime in the Metaverse, Fighting Crypto crime in Web3.0* Elliptic. https://www.elliptic.co/hubfs/Crime%20in%20the%20Metaverse%202022%20final.pdf

Siyaev, A., & Jo, G. S. (2021). Towards Aircraft Maintenance Metaverse Using Speech Interactions with Virtual Objects in Mixed Reality. *Sensors (Basel), 21*(6), 1–21. doi:10.339021062066 PMID:33804253

Stubbs, G. (2023). *How should we police the metaverse?* DWTC. https://www.dwtc.com/en/industry-insights/how-should-we-police-the-metaverse/

Tredinnick, R., Smith, S., & Ponto, K. (2019, November). A Cost-Benefit Analysis of 3D Scanning Technology for Crime Scene Investigation. *Forensic Science International. Reports, 1*, 100025. https://www.sciencedirect.com/science/article/pii/S2665910719300258. doi:10.1016/j.fsir.2019.100025

Wang, Y., Su, Z., Li, J., Zhang, N., Zhang, K., Choo, K.-K. R., & Liu, Y. (2022). Blockchain-Based Secure and Cooperative Private Charging Pile Sharing Services for Vehicular Networks. *IEEE Transactions on Vehicular Technology, 71*(2), 1857–1874. doi:10.1109/TVT.2021.3131744

Zubaska, M., & Szczytno, P. (2018, January). Improvement of Crime Scene Examination and Reduction of Cognitive Deficit: The Need to Implement a New Imaging and Dimensioning Technique. *Issues in Forensic Science, 302,* 54-62.

Chapter 2
Future Cybercrimes in the Metaverse: A Comprehensive Forecast

Ibtesam Mohammed Alawadhi
Dubai Police Academy, UAE

ABSTRACT

In an emerging era of virtual reality, cybercrimes become a significant challenge. The metaverse is a digital realm where people can socialize, work, play, invest, learn, entertain, and much more. The nature of the metaverse raises the concerns of cybercrimes. In this chapter, a deep understanding of potential threats is discussed. Several threats will be highlighted, such as virtual identity theft and impersonation, virtual real estate frauds, malware and ransomware, virtual espionage, advanced phishing, and social engineering. To forecast these threats, insights from cybercrimes are adapted and extrapolated to fit the unique environment of the metaverse. This will guide law enforcement, technical people, policymakers, regulators, and researchers.

1. INTRODUCTION

The term "Metaverse" was introduced in 1992 by Neal Stephenson in his novel Snow Crash (Stephenson, 2003, page number). Neal's definition of the metaverse was a virtual world that humans can interact with for art and commerce. Metaverse is the new digital life where people can entertain, learn, socialize, work, play, and invest. Metaverse also could be identified as virtual worlds partly overlapping with the physical world as the virtual world allows users to be presented as avatars and interconnect with each other (Weinberger, 2022). As the metaverse presents great positive opportunities, it can also be used to perform suspicious activities. Threats in the metaverse differ significantly from traditional threats due to the unique characteristics and complexities of the metaverse. Cybersecurity measures have been developed to indicate known vulnerabilities (Rahman et al., 2022). However, the metaverse introduces new technologies that must be evaluated to eliminate security concerns. Potential threats could include security, privacy, and ethical implications. Generally, those suspicious activities committed in the digital

DOI: 10.4018/979-8-3693-0220-0.ch002

realm are called cybercrime, and they could be committed through unauthorized access, data modification, data interception, or theft of information (Saini et al., 2012). Metaverse applies the new technologies of artificial intelligence, blockchain, and innovation in a platform that offers a whole engagement experience. As people adopt this technology fast, the opportunity for people with malicious intentions arises. Hackers, scammers, and exploiters seek to use any new technology for their gain. It is essential to critically examine the potential threats from using the metaverse and prepare for the new era.

2. PURPOSE

This chapter will discuss cybersecurity challenges to navigate possible risks and put hands on potential threats and vulnerabilities. Furthermore, strategies and countermeasures that should be implemented will also be suggested. Nowadays, we need to collaborate to unify standards and introduce robust security measures to protect individuals and businesses.

3. TYPES OF THREAT ACTORS

Different motivations and capabilities lead to a diverse range of hackers. State-sponsored, cybercriminal organizations and hacktivist groups are different threat actors. State-sponsored hackers are individuals or groups that conduct cyber-attacks like advanced persistent threats for economic, political, military, or other potential purposes (Akoto, 2021). Cybercriminal organizations are identified as hackers who perform illegal activities such as data theft, ransomware, and identity theft to gain profit (Nicolae Sfetcu, 2023). Individual hackers are hackers who perform different types of attacks individually, like unauthorized access, data theft, and disruption of services, and they are also known as black hat hackers (Gerstenfeld, J. 2023). Hacktivist groups are usually motivated by political goals or social agendas and conduct illegal actions like website defacement, denial of service attacks, and data breaches to raise awareness about specific issues (Ulrich et al.; S., 2023).

4. POTENTIAL RISKS

4.1 Virtual Identity Theft and Impersonation

Virtual identity theft and impersonation are the malicious acts of stealing someone's personal information, such as identification numbers, credit card details, and login credentials. Etc. (Popa, Stoklossa and Mazumdar 2023). This act is performed to impersonate the victim later and gain unauthorized access to their accounts to perform suspicious activities, resulting in financial losses, reputation damage, emotional distress, legal repercussions, and trust issues. In the Metaverse, these activities can result in unauthorized access to virtual assets, impersonation of avatars, and misleading communications.

Key Aspects

1. Phishing: Sending misleading emails or messages and pretending to be legitimate to trick the victims into submitting their personal details or login credentials.
2. Data breaches: Attacking systems to steal sensitive data of large-scale user details.
3. Keylogging: Capturing login details when the user types it and records keystrokes.
4. Impersonation: deceiving others online by using stolen identity to commit a crime that could be in:
   A. Social impersonating: faking social media profiles using stolen information to impersonate victims.
   B. Financial Impersonation: Opening bank accounts or applying for loans or purchases using a stolen identity.
   C. Professional impersonation: Pretending to be doctors, lawyers, teachers…etc., to gain trust and then manipulate victims to steal their personal or financial details.
   D. Dating Scam impersonation: creating fake accounts and establishing a romantic relationship with the victims until that leads to personal or financial exploitation.

Implementation in the Metaverse

In the metaverse, such activities can occur as acquiring unauthorized personal details to perform an illegal activity, such as stealing virtual currency or valuable virtual assets, copying an avatar's appearance, or impersonating the victim's character to conduct fraudulent activity. In the metaverse, sending misleading messages in chat rooms, taking over sensitive details from business owners, or convincing users to download malicious programs are all valid.

4.2 Virtual Real Estate Frauds

Metaverse recently caught the public attention of obtaining digital assets NFTs (Non-Fungible Tokens). Those digital assets on blockchains represent the ownership of a unique item in the platform, allowing the metaverse users to have their cryptocurrencies (Kennedy, 2023). Buying and selling virtual assets in the metaverse emphasizes the need to identify comprehensive and interdisciplinary transaction law. Thus, the metaverse represents unique challenges in real estate transactions, which require creating laws, regulations, and policies to maintain stakeholders' interests (Kalyvaki, 2023). Due to the lack of well-defined regulations in the metaverse world, fraudulent activities are expected to occur, especially with the expansion in demand to obtain virtual assets. Online platforms are mainly used to buy and sell those virtual assets. Virtual real estate frauds affect this market, and there are financial and legal consequences for those acts.

Key Aspects

1. Phantom Listing: This is a type of fraud where scammers fake a list of virtual real estate platforms to convince buyers or renters by below-market prices or attractive features. After the customer (victim) shows interest, the scammer requests advance payment to hold as a security deposit ap-

plication fee or other fees. Once the scammer receives the payment, the scammer disappears, and the victim realizes the fraud.

2. Identity Theft and Title Fraud: Scammers may impersonate property owners to conduct fraudulent transactions. Scammers might also try to change property ownership records to change the ownership of the virtual assets.
3. Rental Frauds: Scammers post fake listings to grab the attention of interested tenants. Once they are convinced of the fake offer, the scammer asks for a deposit or advance payment. After victims pay, the scammers disappear and block any contact with the victim.
4. Misleading Property Descriptions: False details or descriptions about the condition, size, location, actual price, photos …etc. Let the victim make decisions that might not be accurate due to the misleading information.
5. Forged Documents: Forged documents of property title deeds, agreements, contracts…etc, might be created to convince the victim that the transaction is legitimate.

Implementation in the Metaverse

Real estate fraud in the metaverse could be a unique challenge because of the unique nature of those assets. Fake listing could be promoted over the metaverse. Pretending to be a legitimate owner or broker over Metaverse or offering a fake rental opportunity is also valid.

4.3 Malware

Malware is malicious software that disturbs a computer, server, client, or network to gain unauthorized access. It is also essential to understand that ransomware is malware that threatens to publish the victim's information or block their access unless they pay a ransom (Al-rimy, Maarof, The threat of both malware and ransomware has become a critical concern. Many articles emphasize the measures and techniques that should be mitigated to prevent malware and ransomware attacks (Lee & Choi, 2021). With all the technology and interconnected digital environment, the metaverse is a target of malicious attacks. Those malicious threats affect the individual experience and lead to significant consequences. As the challenges posed in the metaverse, strategies to mitigate are crucial.

Key Aspects

Malware can be one of the following:

1. Viruses: self-replicated programs that attach themselves to files and software and spread once the infected file is executed.
2. Worms: a self-replicated standalone program that can spread across the networks without needing a host file.
3. Trojans: Presented as legitimate software but includes hidden malicious code that can be executed to harm a system.
4. Ransomware: encrypt the victim's files and ask for a ransom to decrypt the files.
5. Spyware: gathering information from the victim's device and sending it to a third party without consent.

6. Adware: Displaying unwanted advertisements.
7. Rootkits: Malicious software hides in the operating system and is usually challenging to detect.
8. Botnets are network-compromised devices controlled by an attacker to launch distributed denial of service attacks.
9. Keyloggers: records strokes made by users to capture sensitive information such as passwords or band details.

Implementation in the Metaverse

Viruses might be able to infect objects, assets, or even avatars, and that could be replicated and spread within the metaverse. Women can also be represented in the metaverse and self-replicate via interconnected networks. Trojans could be represented in the metaverse as a legitimate asset that waits for the interaction of a user and one that a malicious code can harm the victim's asset. Ransomware in the metaverse can be done by locking users' virtual assets or virtual real estate, including digital collectibles, NFTs, or virtual currencies. Attackers request a ransom to give the access back to the owners. Avatars can also be affected by restricting the avatar's movement, and for the users to use it again, they need to pay a ransom. Spyware could also be valid in the metaverse as virtual surveillance collects information about the users and sends it to third parties without consent to perform illegal actions. Adware can be presented as intrusive virtual advertisement, potentially generating revenue for attackers. Rootkit can interfere with the platform's security or environment and be challenging to detect. Distributed Denial Attack could be represented in the metaverse if an attacker takes the lead of several assets and avatars over the platform, leading them to conduct illegal attacks. Keyloggers: Keyloggers could be presented in the metaverse where the attackers could record user keystrokes to capture sensitive data.

4.4 Cyber Espionage

Cyber espionage could be identified as stealing sensitive data from the opposing party using malware. It is also called cyber spying or digital espionage. Cyber espionage aims to gain unauthorized access to sensitive data, trade information, intellectual property, strategic plans, and marketing campaign details. As well as political, economic, military, or competitive advancement data. The impact of malware can cause physical damage to critical and industrial infrastructure (Weinberger, 2022). Using malware attacks in political espionage poses a persistent threat to national security (Segal, 2013). Thus, understanding the impact and mechanism of malware leading to cyber espionage is crucial to understanding the nature of cyber threats and developing effective countermeasures.

Key Aspects

1. Government-sponsored espionage: conducted by governments to collect information about military, economic, or political information.
2. Corporate espionage involves organizations using others' secrets in trade, designs, or strategic plans.
3. Industrial espionage: Like corporate espionage, but with the urge to steal intellectual property.
4. Economic Espionage: Gaining sensitive information about the stock market, financial data, currency exchange, or other financial benefits.

5. Cyber espionage: accessing sensitive information about military abilities, strategies, or plans.
6. Technological espionage: stealing technological development or research ideas or findings.
7. Academic espionage: targeting academia to steal research ideas, intentions, progress, or intellectual property.
8. Healthcare espionage: taking information on medical research progress, sensitive details about patients, storage of medication, and medical capabilities in certain countries.

Implementation in the Metaverse

Cyber espionage is one of the threats that could occur in the metaverse. Business owners can conduct several activities over the metaverse. Business activities like meetings, discussions, transactions, or critical decisions are vulnerable to certain surveillance activities. Thus, those details could be tracked, monitored, and shared with opposes. Business owners could also be tracked to steal their intellectual property, trade secrets, and market insights. It is fertile ground for conducting virtual espionage through exchanging sensitive information, exploiting activity, or interrupting any intention of business increase. Cyber spies might create an avatar that will attend virtual meetings, forums, social parties, etc., to gain information. Cyber spies might also manipulate users to reveal information about their work. Access to sensitive information about virtual assets could affect the economic trust in the metaverse. Cyber spies might be able to monitor virtual exchanges between users in the metaverse. Collecting valuable information in the metaverse is the primary concern. Political competitors might engage in virtual espionage for their campaign, revealing opposing plans and gaining geopolitical advantages through sensitive information they acquired from virtual espionage. Information such as financial data, trade secrets, proprietary technology, strategic plans, or information about individuals or organizations is sensitive and could be exchanged with undesirable parties.

4.5 Advanced Phishing and Social Engineering

Phishing and social engineering are attacks where the attacker deceives the victim by pretending to be legitimate or gaining trust to share their confidential information (Gupta, Singhal, Based on the literature conducted by Singhal and Kapoor, a combination of social engineering and technical methods is implemented on victims to persuade them to reveal their data. They also identified that typical phishing attacks involve email spoofing or instant messaging. Usually, it attacks users who do not pay attention to the details or the importance of their privacy of digital accounts, bank accounts, or any other financial accounts. Different phishing tactics will be listed in this section. Phishing and social engineering attacks mainly rely on human exploits rather than technical vulnerabilities.

Key Aspects

1. Phishing: Attackers send deceptive emails, messages, or links that appear legitimate to fool the users and take sensitive data.
2. Social Engineering: Social impersonation of friends, colleagues, or trusted cohorts could be used by attackers to gain trust.
3. Pretexting: Attackers create a fake scenario to convince victims to provide information they will not share in ordinary circumstances.

4. Baiting: Attackers try to convince the use of a driver or download an application pretending to do something legitimate or solve a problem while infecting and attacking the system with malware.
5. Immersive deception is one of the critical aspects that attackers can use to convince victims. Attackers can use Metaverse's rich visual experience to introduce themselves as legitimate and show innocent intentions.
6. The attackers could quickly consider personalized targeting. They can target the victims depending on their interests, behaviors, conversations…etc.
7. Emotional exploitation could also be an essential aspect used by attackers targeting victims due to their feelings of fear, excitement, or curiosity.

Implementation in the Metaverse

Advanced phishing and social engineering techniques could quickly occur in the metaverse. Attackers can create a phishing message and send it to different users in avatars in the metaverse. Deceiving individuals through malicious tactics to gain access to personal information, financial data, and virtual assets can be sophisticated and challenging to identify. Attackers might pretend to be well-known organizations in one of the metaverse platforms and then message individuals to gain sensitive details. Pretending to offer support or assistance for the users over the metaverse, they might convince them to share personal or bank details.

5. STRATEGIES AND COUNTERMEASURES

Metaverse platforms are responsible for working together to create a safe and secure environment for individuals to reduce the potential risks discussed in this chapter. A robust authentication method should be enabled to protect users' metaverse accounts. Identity verification confirmation should be assured. Protecting personal data should also be applied by the different metaverse platforms. Antivirus scanning tools should be available for the users to protect their virtual assets, real estate properties, avatars…etc. Content scanning tools will be beneficial in detecting any malicious links. Reporting mechanisms should be introduced and regularly enhanced to identify and deal with individual problems. Behavioral analysis of the users needs to be indicated for any abnormal activities. Legal frameworks that address possible attacks over the metaverse should be established and identified clearly. Policies need to be regulated and encouraged to obtain. Cross-platform security measures should be established. Awareness campaigns need to take place to suggest good practices for the users, such as regular backups. Periodic risk assessments to identify vulnerabilities should also be obtained by the platforms.

6. LEGAL AND REGULATORY ASPECTS

Metaverse is a global platform where users from the whole world interact with each other's. Appropriate legal jurisdiction is needed to act against any criminal activities appropriately. Virtual property rights need to be obtained and identified for the users. Intellectual property to address trademarks, patents, and copyrights of all virtual assets needs an ownership agreement. Protection of digital identity needs to be fundamental in the metaverse. Contracts and agreements need to be legally recognized. Consumer protection rights also need to be ensured. Cross-border virtual assets need international cooperation and mechanisms. Finally, ethical frameworks need to be obtained and identified for virtual violence, addiction, minors …etc.

7. RAISE THE AWARENESS

It is essential to start raising awareness among the community regarding the potential threats when using the metaverse, which could be implemented differently. For example, education initiatives must be implemented to counteract all the risks and potential threats that might occur while using the metaverse. It is also important to mention that human error led to breaches in many cybersecurity cases (Nobles, 2018). To give some general examples, employees fall victim to phishing attacks, or individuals fall into social engineering attacks. Thus, it is vital to raise awareness regularly among employees and individuals to prevent such incidents. Security training and workshops within the metaverse can support and help individuals overcome any possible challenges. Engage the community to share their experience in the metaverse and what challenges and threats they think they might face. Regular meetings and sessions could affect the users' knowledge of this new technology and how to deal with it. Ensure that the security tools are easy to obtain and implement. Spreading the fact of self-protection via ant various software implementations or using two-step authentication techniques is very crucial. Regularly encourage the community to ensure security updates. Ethical hacking competitions could encourage users to search for any vulnerabilities in the platform and raise awareness of the importance of all the security measures to be taken seriously to avoid any exploits of sensitive or personal details.

8. TARGET AUDIENCE

Law enforcement, technological companies, policymakers, regulators, and researchers.

In conclusion, the experience that the metaverse provides is unique. Cybersecurity challenges and potential threats must be considered when using this technology. Several vital aspects of forecasting cybercrime in the metaverse were discussed in this chapter. Some countermeasures were also addressed in the chapter.

REFERENCES

Al-rimy, B. A. S., Maarof, M. A., & Shaid, S. Z. M. (2018). Ransomware threat success factors, taxonomy, and countermeasures: A survey and research directions. *Computers & Security*, *74*, 144–166. doi:10.1016/j.cose.2018.01.001

Gerstenfeld, J. (2023). Understanding the Connection Between Hackers and Their Hacks: Analyzing USDOJ Reports for HackerProfiles. *International Journal of Cybersecurity Intelligence & Cybercrime*, *6*(1), 59–76.

Gupta, S. (2016). A literature survey on social engineering attacks: Phishing attack. 2016 international conference on computing, communication, and automation (ICCCA). IEEE.

Kalyvaki, M. (2023). Navigating the Metaverse Business and Legal Challenges: Intellectual Property, Privacy, and Jurisdiction. *Journal of Metaverse*, *3*(1), 87–92.

Kennedy, J. (2023). Metaverse Property: Advocating for the Regulation of Metaverse Land and Property through a Real Estate Legal Regime. *Ohio St. Bus. LJ*, *17*, 323.

Lee, H., & Choi, K.-S. (2021). Interrelationship between Bitcoin, ransomware, and terrorist activities: Criminal opportunity assessment via cyber-routine activities theoretical framework. *Victims & Offenders*, *16*(3), 363–384.

Nobles, C. (2019). Establishing human factors programs to mitigate blind spots in cybersecurity. *MWAIS 2019 Proceedings, 22*.

Popa, M., Stoklossa, S. M., & Mazumdar, S. (2023). ChainDiscipline-Towards A Blockchain-IoT-Based Self-Sovereign Identity Management Framework. *IEEE Transactions on Services Computing*, *16*(5), 3238–3251. doi:10.1109/TSC.2023.3279871

Rahman, F. (2022). The future of cybersecurity in the age of quantum computers. *Future Internet*, *14*(11), 335.

Saini, H., & .... (2012). Cyber-crimes and their impacts: A review. *International Journal of Engineering Research and Applications*, *2*(2), 202–209.

Segal, A. (2013). The code not taken: China, the United States, and the future of cyber espionage. *Bulletin of the Atomic Scientists*, *69*(5), 38–45.

Sfetcu, N. (2023). *Intelligence Info, Volumul 2, Numărul 1, Martie*. Nicolae Sfetcu.

Stephenson, N. (2003). *Snow crash: A novel*. Spectra.

Ulrich, F., Müller, S. D., & Flowers, S. (2023). The Professionalization of Hackers: A Content Analysis of 30 Years of Hacker Communication. *Communications of the Association for Information Systems*, *52*(1), 12.

Weinberger, M. (2022). What Is Metaverse? A Definition Based on Qualitative Meta-Synthesis. *Future Internet*, *14*(11), 310.

Chapter 3
Navigating the Metaverse:
Forecasting Cybercrime in the New Age of Virtual Reality

Akashdeep Bhardwaj
https://orcid.org/0000-0001-7361-0465
University of Petroleum and Energy Studies, India

ABSTRACT

The rise of the metaverse—a virtual world where individuals can interact with each other and digital objects in a fully immersive environment—has led to new challenges in the world of cybersecurity. As more individuals and businesses move towards this new frontier, the potential for cybercrime is also increasing. In this chapter, the authors explore the diverse types of cybercrime that may emerge from virtual theft and fraud to privacy violations and hacking. They also discuss the unique challenges faced by law enforcement and security professionals in detecting and preventing these crimes in a fully virtual environment. To aid in forecasting these crimes, the authors examine current trends and technological developments that may impact the future of the metaverse, including the growth of decentralized technologies, the increasing prevalence of artificial intelligence, and the potential for quantum computing. By understanding the potential risks and challenges of the metaverse, we can better prepare ourselves for a future where virtual and physical crime intersect.

1. INTRODUCTION

As technology continues to evolve and become more integrated into our daily lives, the threat of cybercrime (What is Cyber Crime? Types, Examples, and Prevention, 2023) is becoming increasingly prevalent. The rise of the metaverse, a virtual world that is being created by the convergence of the physical and digital worlds, is presenting new challenges and opportunities for those looking to commit cybercrimes. Forecasting cybercrimes in the age of the metaverse is becoming a critical issue for law enforcement agencies, governments, and businesses. Forecasting cybercrimes in the age of the metaverse is becoming increasingly important as the metaverse continues to grow and evolve. The metaverse is creating new

DOI: 10.4018/979-8-3693-0220-0.ch003

opportunities for cybercriminals to commit crimes and new challenges for law enforcement agencies and businesses to detect and prevent cybercrime. The metaverse (What Does Metaverse Mean and How Does This Virtual World Work?, 2023) is an emerging technology that has the potential to change the way we interact with each other and with the digital world. It is a virtual environment where users can create and explore digital spaces, socialize with other users, and participate in various activities. However, with the emergence of the metaverse comes new challenges and opportunities for cybercriminals.

Cybercrime is a type of criminal activity that is committed using the internet, computers, or other digital devices. Cybercriminals can use a variety of techniques to commit cybercrime, including hacking, phishing, malware, and social engineering. With the metaverse, cybercriminals have a new platform to commit cybercrime, and they are already taking advantage of this opportunity. One of the most significant risks of cybercrime in the metaverse is virtual currency theft. In the metaverse, users can earn virtual currency by participating in various activities, and this virtual currency can be exchanged for real-world goods and services. Cybercriminals (Cybercriminals – Definition, 2023) can steal virtual currency by hacking into user accounts or by using social engineering techniques to trick users into giving them access to their virtual wallets. Another significant risk of cybercrime in the metaverse is virtual identity theft. In the metaverse, users create virtual avatars that represent them in the virtual world. Cybercriminals can steal these avatars and use them to commit virtual crimes or to access the user's personal information. Virtual identity theft can be especially dangerous because it can lead to real-world identity theft and financial fraud. Cybercrime in the metaverse can also take the form of virtual harassment and cyberstalking. In the virtual world, users can communicate with each other using text, voice, or video chat. Cybercriminals can use these communication channels to harass or stalk other users. This type of cybercrime can be particularly challenging to detect and prevent because it takes place in a virtual environment.

To address these and other cybercrime risks in the metaverse, businesses, governments, and law enforcement agencies are taking steps to increase awareness, prevention, and response. They are developing innovative technologies and strategies to detect and prevent cybercrime, such as using artificial intelligence to detect unusual patterns of activity or developing blockchain technology to create a more secure virtual environment. Other companies are creating virtual crime units to investigate and prosecute cybercriminals in the metaverse. Despite these efforts, the risks of cybercrime in the metaverse are likely to persist and evolve. As the metaverse continues to grow and become more integrated into our daily lives, it will become increasingly important to develop effective strategies to prevent and address cybercrime. This will require collaboration between governments, businesses, and individuals to ensure that the benefits of the metaverse are realized without compromising our safety and security.

2. EVOLUTION OF METAVERSE AND CYBERCRIME

The concept of the metaverse has captured the imagination of tech enthusiasts, science fiction writers, and futurists for decades. It envisions a virtual reality space that goes beyond the boundaries of the physical world, offering immersive, interconnected experiences for users. While the idea of the metaverse dates to the early 1990s, its evolution has been a complex journey marked by technological advancements, societal shifts, and economic developments. In this exploration of the metaverse's evolution, we will trace its roots, examine key milestones, and consider future possibilities. The origins of the metaverse can be traced back to science fiction, notably Neal Stephenson's 1992 novel 'Snow Crash' and Vernor Vinge's 1981 novella 'True Names'. Both works depicted immersive virtual worlds where individuals assumed avatars and interacted with one another. These early visions set the stage for the concept of a shared, digital realm where people could escape into new realities, engage with one another, and transcend physical limitations.

The first practical steps towards the metaverse came in the form of online communities and virtual worlds. In the late 1990s and early 2000s, platforms like Second Life, The Sims Online, and Active Worlds allowed users to create avatars, build virtual spaces, and interact with other participants. While these environments were far from the fully immersive metaverse we envision today, they laid the groundwork for the concept by introducing the idea of shared, digital spaces.

Gaming played a pivotal role in advancing the metaverse. Massively multiplayer online games (MMOs) such as World of Warcraft and EVE Online enabled thousands of players to inhabit persistent digital worlds. These virtual realms provided not only entertainment but also social interaction, economies, and complex ecosystems. Gamers formed communities, collaborated, and competed, mirroring aspects of the metaverse's social and economic potential. The mid-2000s saw the rise of Web 2.0, a shift towards more dynamic, user-generated content on the internet. Platforms like MySpace, Facebook, and later Twitter connected people globally and introduced the concept of virtual identities. While not immersive in the way we think of the metaverse, these social networks were an important step in forging digital connections and creating spaces for self-expression and interaction.

The 2010s brought significant advancements in virtual reality (VR) technology. The Oculus Rift, released in 2016, was a pivotal moment, making VR more accessible and immersive. VR headsets allow users to step into virtual environments, bringing them closer to the metaverse's immersive vision. This technology opened new possibilities for gaming, education, and social interaction. The introduction of blockchain technology, primarily through cryptocurrencies like Bitcoin, marked another turning point in the metaverse's evolution. Blockchain offered secure and transparent record-keeping, which was essential for digital asset ownership and trading. Non-fungible tokens (NFTs) emerged, enabling unique digital assets to be bought, sold, and owned on the blockchain. This innovation laid the groundwork for digital property rights and asset ownership within the metaverse. The development of decentralized virtual worlds built on blockchain technology is a notable milestone. Projects like Decentraland and The Sandbox allowed users to create, buy, and sell virtual land and assets. These platforms incorporated blockchain technology to ensure ownership, scarcity, and provenance of digital items, setting the stage for an economy within the metaverse.

Tech giants like Facebook (now Meta), Google, and Microsoft have recognized the potential of the metaverse and entered the arena. Meta's announcement of its metaverse vision in 2021 and rebranding marked a significant shift. These companies are investing heavily in VR and augmented reality (AR) technologies, creating platforms and ecosystems that aim to connect users in immersive digital spaces. This corporate interest has injected substantial resources and attention into the metaverse's development. The metaverse's evolution is also characterized by efforts to create cross-platform compatibility. Users should have the freedom to move seamlessly between different metaverse spaces and experiences. The development of open standards, interoperability, and cross-platform avatars are key components of this vision, allowing for a more interconnected and versatile metaverse. The metaverse has the potential to reshape various aspects of society and the economy. From a social perspective, it offers opportunities for diverse communities and experiences, fostering connections in virtual environments. Education, healthcare, entertainment, and work could all be transformed by the metaverse, providing new possibilities and addressing limitations of the physical world.

Economically, the metaverse introduces a new frontier for commerce. Digital real estate, virtual goods, and services are already generating substantial revenue. Job opportunities related to content creation, virtual architecture, and metaverse development are on the rise. This economic dimension is expected to expand further as the metaverse evolves. The metaverse's journey is not without challenges and concerns. Privacy and security issues are at the forefront, as users generate vast amounts of personal data within digital spaces. Ensuring the protection of user data and digital identities is a critical concern. Additionally, questions about governance, moderation, and content regulation within the metaverse have arisen. Balancing freedom of expression with the need to prevent harm and ensure a safe environment is a complex challenge. Economic disparities within the metaverse are also a concern. As virtual real estate and digital assets appreciate, there is a risk of wealth concentration and exclusion. Efforts to address these disparities will be crucial for a more equitable metaverse.

The metaverse's evolution is far from complete, and its future holds many possibilities. Advancements in VR and AR technology will continue to improve the immersive quality of virtual experiences. As metaverse platforms become more open, interoperable, and user-friendly, adoption is likely to increase. One significant trend is the integration of AI and virtual assistants within the metaverse. These intelligent systems can enhance user experiences, provide information, and facilitate interactions, making the metaverse more engaging and functional. The metaverse's role in education is expected to expand, offering new methods of learning and skill development. Virtual classrooms, immersive simulations, and collaborative environments could revolutionize education, making it more accessible and engaging. Healthcare could also benefit from the metaverse. Telemedicine, rehabilitation, and mental health services are areas where the metaverse can provide innovative solutions, reaching patients in more convenient and effective ways. The metaverse's economic impact will continue to grow. Digital real estate, virtual goods, and services will be traded on a larger scale, creating new business opportunities and challenges. The metaverse could even give rise to entirely new economic systems and business models.

The metaverse is a virtual world that is created by the convergence of the physical and digital worlds. It is a collective virtual shared space that is created by the convergence of virtual reality, augmented reality, and the internet. The metaverse is a place where people can interact with each other in a digital environment that is as real as the physical world. In the metaverse, people can create their avatars, explore virtual environments, and engage in social activities with others. The metaverse is being driven by advances in technology such as virtual reality, artificial intelligence, and blockchain. These technologies are enabling the creation of a more immersive and interactive virtual world that is becoming increasingly popular. The metaverse is already being used for gaming, socializing, and even commerce. As the metaverse continues to grow, it is becoming a critical part of our digital lives. Metaverse is a virtual reality environment that allows users to interact with each other and the environment in a highly immersive way. To create this environment, Metaverse developers use a variety of tools and technologies. The underlying technology that drives the Metaverse is called the Metaverse Protocol, which is a set of rules that govern the interactions between users and the virtual environment. The protocol specifies how information is exchanged between users, how actions are executed, and how objects are represented.

Metaverse is a complex virtual environment that requires a variety of advanced technologies to create and operate. These technologies include the Metaverse Protocol, 3D engines, 3D modeling tools, scripting languages, networking infrastructure, security protocols, and input and output devices. Using these technologies, developers can create highly immersive virtual environments that allow users to interact with each other and the environment in entirely new ways. One of the key components of the Metaverse is the 3D engine, which is responsible for rendering the virtual environment in real time. This engine uses advanced graphics technologies to create a highly realistic and immersive environment, including advanced lighting and shading techniques, physics simulations, and artificial intelligence algorithms. To create the virtual objects that populate the Metaverse, developers use a combination of 3D modeling tools and scripting languages. 3D modeling tools allow developers to create and manipulate 3D objects while scripting languages allow developers to create interactive objects that can respond to user input and interact with other objects in the environment.

Another important aspect of the Metaverse is its networking infrastructure. Metaverse must be able to support many users interacting with each other in real time. To achieve this, Metaverse uses a variety of networking technologies, including peer-to-peer networking, client-server architecture, and cloud computing. To ensure security and privacy within the Metaverse, developers use a variety of encryption technologies and security protocols. This includes encryption of data in transit and at rest, secure login processes, and the use of digital signatures to authenticate users and transactions. Finally, the Metaverse relies on a variety of input and output devices to provide users with a highly immersive experience. These devices include virtual reality headsets, motion controllers, and haptic feedback devices, which provide users with a sense of touch and physical presence within the virtual environment.

The metaverse, with its immersive digital environments and interconnected user experiences, has not only been a source of fascination but also a terrain for potential cybercrime. As the metaverse has evolved, so has the nature of cyber threats and illicit activities within these virtual realms. In this exploration of the historical context of the metaverse's interrelation with cybercrime, we will delve into the evolving landscape of virtual crime, the risks it poses, and the efforts to mitigate these threats. The concept of the metaverse took its initial steps in the form of virtual communities and online worlds in the 1990s. Platforms like Second Life and The Sims Online allowed users to create avatars and interact within digital spaces. While these environments were relatively innocent, they were not immune to early instances of cybercrime.

One of the earliest forms of virtual crime in these spaces was avatar harassment and theft. Users could create malicious avatars and engage in activities like griefing, harassment, or even stealing virtual property from others. These actions, while relatively benign compared to today's cybercrimes, revealed the potential for malicious behavior within the metaverse. Virtual economies also became breeding grounds for fraud and exploitation. In games like EverQuest, virtual currencies and items had real-world value, leading to activities like item theft and account hacking. These early cases hinted at the emerging economic aspect of the metaverse and the vulnerabilities it could introduce. The metaverse's evolution continued with the rise of massively multiplayer online games (MMOs). Games like World of Warcraft, EVE Online, and RuneScape attracted millions of players into vast digital worlds. As the user base expanded, so did the opportunities for cybercrime. One significant form of virtual crime in MMOs was account hacking. Players invested considerable time and money in building characters and accumulating virtual assets. Hackers, therefore, sought to gain unauthorized access to accounts, stealing items, currency, and in some cases, real-world financial information. This led to the emergence of a lucrative underground market for stolen virtual goods and accounts.

Phishing scams, often through in-game chat or fake websites became another common threat. Players would receive messages that appeared to be from the game developers or official sources, asking for login credentials or payment information. These scams aimed to compromise accounts and steal valuable assets. The use of Bot programs to farm in-game currency or items also became widespread. These automated scripts allowed players to accumulate virtual wealth without actively participating in the game. This practice not only disrupted the in-game economy but also violated the terms of service.

The proliferation of virtual worlds and the concept of the metaverse introduced new forms of digital commerce. Virtual real estate, in-game items, and virtual currencies started to hold real-world value, and this transformation attracted the attention of cybercriminals. Virtual real estate scams became prevalent as platforms like Decentraland and The Sandbox gained popularity. Criminals would create fraudulent listings or misrepresent virtual property, duping buyers into purchasing non-existent or illegitimate assets. These fraudulent transactions extended into the realm of non-fungible tokens (NFTs) as well, with counterfeit NFTs and art sales deceiving collectors. Virtual currency, often used for in-game purchases, also became a target for cybercriminals. Phishing attacks, ransomware, and fraudulent exchanges sought to compromise players' digital wallets or steal their virtual currency. The convergence of virtual and real-world economies made these forms of cybercrime more lucrative and enticing.

As the metaverse grew, the lines between virtual and real-world consequences blurred. This transformation was exemplified by acts of swatting and doxxing. Swatting involved malicious individuals reporting fake emergencies at the physical addresses of their victims, often during livestreams or in response to disputes within the metaverse. These hoaxes not only posed a serious risk to the victims but also consumed valuable law enforcement resources. Doxxing, on the other hand, was the practice of revealing a person's private or sensitive information, such as their real name, address, or contact details. This tactic was used to intimidate, harass, or seek revenge against individuals within the metaverse. The consequences were not confined to the virtual world, as victims often faced real-world harassment and threats.

With the metaverse becoming a more complex ecosystem, the risks to user privacy and data security increased. Virtual worlds began to collect extensive user data, from communication logs to behavioral patterns. The potential for data breaches and privacy violations escalated. Incidents of data breaches within virtual worlds raised concerns about the safety of user information. Attackers could gain access to personal data, potentially leading to identity theft, financial fraud, or further cybercrimes. Users had to grapple with the trade-off between the convenience of a more immersive metaverse and the security of their personal information. Ransomware attacks in the metaverse have been a particularly concerning development. In virtual worlds and gaming, attackers have targeted users by encrypting their in-game assets or holding their virtual property hostage. Victims were then presented with ransom demands in exchange for the release of their virtual assets or accounts. The success of these attacks often depended on the perceived value of the virtual assets to the victim. In some cases, the emotional attachment players had to their in-game achievements or digital possessions made them more likely to pay the ransom, creating a financial incentive for cybercriminals.

The metaverse's growing economic significance has made it a target for various forms of fraud and exploitation. Virtual currencies, in-game assets, and NFTs have seen substantial price appreciation, drawing the attention of cybercriminals seeking financial gain. Pump-and-dump schemes, fraudulent auctions, and scams involving virtual assets have proliferated. Economic disparities within the metaverse have also given rise to concerns about wealth concentration and exclusion. As some users amass virtual wealth, others are left at a disadvantage, which can lead to tensions and potential conflicts within the virtual community. Efforts to mitigate cybercrime in the metaverse have evolved alongside the threats themselves. Virtual world operators and game developers have implemented security measures to protect user data, detect fraud, and prevent in-game cheating.

Law enforcement agencies have also adapted to address metaverse-related cybercrime. Cybercrime units investigate incidents of virtual theft, fraud, and harassment, seeking to identify and apprehend offenders. International collaboration is crucial, as metaverse-related crimes often transcend borders.

Additionally, user education and awareness campaigns have played a vital role in preventing cybercrime. Players are encouraged to use strong, unique passwords, avoid sharing personal information, and be cautious of phishing attempts and suspicious links within virtual spaces. The metaverse's economic impact will likely lead to an escalation in financial cybercrimes. Virtual asset theft, fraudulent NFT sales, and investment scams

The emergence of the metaverse, a virtual universe where users can interact with each other and digital objects in a fully immersive environment, has brought about new opportunities for entertainment, socialization, and commerce. However, it has also created new risks and challenges in terms of cybercrime. In this essay, we will explore how cybercrime and the metaverse are linked together and the implications of this relationship. As with any technology, the Metaverse is not immune to cybersecurity vulnerabilities. Some of the potential vulnerabilities that could be exploited by cybercriminals include:

- Data breaches (Data Breach – Definition, 2021): Since the Metaverse collects and stores user data, it could be vulnerable to data breaches that could result in the theft of sensitive user information, such as login credentials, payment information, and personal data.
- Malware and viruses (12 Types of Malware + Examples That You Should Know, 2023): Users could inadvertently download malware or viruses while interacting with the Metaverse. This could lead to the theft of personal information, financial loss, or other types of cyber-attacks.
- Social engineering (What is Social Engineering? | Definition, 2023): Cybercriminals could use social engineering tactics to trick users into revealing their login credentials or other sensitive information. This could include phishing emails, fake login pages, or other types of social engineering attacks.
- Insecure APIs (The Threat of Insecure Interfaces and APIs, 2023): The Metaverse relies on APIs (Application Programming Interfaces) to communicate with other software systems. If these APIs are not properly secured, they could be vulnerable to attacks such as SQL injection or cross-site scripting.
- Virtual asset theft (Skin Trade: Preventing and Punishing Digital Asset Theft – Gamma, 2023): The Metaverse allows users to purchase and trade virtual assets, which could be vulnerable to theft or fraud. Cybercriminals could use phishing attacks or other tactics to steal virtual currency or assets from users.
- Distributed Denial of Service (DDoS) attacks (What is a DDoS Attack? DDoS Meaning, Definition & Types | Fortinet, 2023): The Metaverse could be vulnerable to DDoS attacks, in which many requests are sent to the system, overwhelming its servers and causing the system to crash or become unavailable.
- Virtual identity theft (What is Digital Identity Theft? - Bitdefender Cyberpedia, 2023): Users could have their virtual identities stolen, which could be used to gain access to their accounts or other sensitive information. This could include the theft of virtual avatars or other virtual identities.

To mitigate these risks, Metaverse developers should take steps to ensure the security of their systems, such as implementing strong encryption, conducting regular security audits, and providing users with security awareness training. Additionally, users should take steps to protect their data, such as using strong passwords, enabling authentication, and avoiding clicking on suspicious links or downloading unknown files. One of the primary ways in which cybercrime and the metaverse are linked is through the theft of virtual goods and currencies. In virtual worlds like Second Life, and World of Warcraft, users can acquire and trade virtual goods and currencies that have real-world value. These goods and currencies can be stolen or scammed through a variety of techniques, including hacking, phishing, and social engineering. As mentioned above the virtual game Eve Online was hit by a massive virtual currency theft that resulted in the loss of over $60,000 worth of virtual currency. The attacker used a technique called social engineering to gain access to an employee's computer and steal login credentials, allowing them to access the game's database and transfer the virtual currency to their account. Similarly, in 2019, a user in the virtual world of Second Life had their virtual store hacked and over $1,700 worth of virtual goods stolen. Virtual currency and goods theft are not just limited to gaming environments. In the metaverse, where virtual experiences and services are becoming increasingly common, there are also opportunities for fraud and theft. For example, scammers could create fake virtual storefronts or services, offering products or experiences that they have no intention of delivering.

Another area where cybercrime and the metaverse are linked is through the use of virtual identity theft. In the metaverse, users create virtual identities that they use to interact with other users and digital objects. Hackers may use a variety of methods to gain access to user accounts, including phishing scams, malware, and social engineering tactics. Once they gain access, they may use the victim's virtual identity to commit fraud or other types of online crimes. For example, the virtual world of Roblox had its virtual avatar stolen and used to scam other users out of virtual currency. The attacker would message other users, posing as the victim, and ask for virtual currency or items. They would promise to trade back but never follow through on the deal. This scam was repeated multiple times, resulting in the loss of virtual currency for several Roblox users. Virtual identity theft can have serious consequences for users, including the loss of virtual goods and currency, damage to their reputation, and even real-world financial losses if their virtual identity is linked to their real identity. In the exploration of cybercrimes within the metaverse, it is crucial to acknowledge the human element and the real-world implications beyond the technical aspects. While discussing incidents like the theft on 'Roblox' and other virtual crimes, it is essential to delve deeper into the emotional and psychological toll on victims. Beyond the loss of virtual assets, victims of cybercrimes within the metaverse often grapple with profound emotional distress, such as anxiety, fear, and a sense of violation. The human element in these cases includes the sense of helplessness, humiliation, and even real-world consequences that victims may face. Addressing these aspects not only grounds the theoretical discussions in real-world experiences but also highlights the urgent need for support mechanisms and preventative measures to protect the well-being of metaverse users.

Another area where cybercrime and the metaverse are linked is through the use of virtual espionage and sabotage. In the metaverse, virtual objects and environments can be used for espionage and sabotage, just as in the real world. Hackers may attempt to steal virtual secrets or use virtual objects to disrupt or damage virtual environments. For example, in the virtual world of Second Life, there have been instances of virtual espionage, where users have created virtual objects that can secretly gather information from other users or disrupt virtual environments. In some cases, these virtual objects have been used for real-world espionage purposes. Virtual sabotage can also have real-world consequences. For example, if a virtual environment is used for training or simulation purposes, a hacker could disrupt or sabotage the environment, leading to real-world consequences like reduced training effectiveness or even physical harm.

3. REAL-WORLD EXAMPLES OF CYBERCRIMES IN THE METAVERSE

Cybercrime refers to any illegal activity that is committed using a computer or a networked device. This includes a wide range of activities such as hacking, identity theft, fraud, and cyberstalking. Cybercrime is becoming increasingly prevalent as more people use the internet and digital devices for their daily lives. Cybercriminals are becoming more sophisticated and are using advanced technologies to carry out their illegal activities. The emergence of the metaverse, a virtual universe where users can interact with each other and digital objects in a fully immersive environment, has brought about new opportunities for entertainment, socialization, and commerce. However, it has also created new risks and challenges in terms of cybercrime. In this essay, we will explore how cybercrime and the metaverse are linked together and the implications of this relationship.

One of the primary ways in which cybercrime and the metaverse are linked is through the theft of virtual goods and currencies. In virtual worlds, users can acquire and trade virtual goods and currencies that have real-world value. These goods and currencies can be stolen or scammed through a variety of techniques, including hacking, phishing, and social engineering.

Another area where cybercrime and the metaverse are linked is through the use of virtual identity theft. In the metaverse, users create virtual identities that they use to interact with other users and digital objects. Hackers may use a variety of methods to gain access to user accounts, including phishing scams, malware, and social engineering tactics. Once they gain access, they may use the victim's virtual identity to commit fraud or other types of online crimes. Virtual identity theft can have serious consequences for users, including the loss of virtual goods and currency, damage to their reputation, and even real-world financial losses if their virtual identity is linked to their real identity.

Another area where cybercrime and the metaverse are linked is through the use of virtual espionage and sabotage. In the metaverse, virtual objects and environments can be used for espionage and sabotage, just as in the real world. Hackers may attempt to steal virtual secrets or use virtual objects to disrupt or damage virtual environments. For example, in the virtual world of Second Life, there have been instances of virtual espionage, where users have created virtual objects that can secretly gather information from other users or disrupt virtual environments. In some cases, these virtual objects have been used for real-world espionage purposes. Virtual sabotage can also have real-world consequences. For example, if a virtual environment is used for training or simulation purposes, a hacker could disrupt or sabotage the environment, leading to real-world consequences like reduced training effectiveness or even physical harm.

In addition to these specific examples, there are also broader implications of the link between cybercrime and the metaverse. The metaverse is a rapidly evolving space, with new technologies, platforms, and experiences emerging all the time. This section presents real-world examples of cybercrime performed in the metaverse in the past few years and reviews the impact of such cybercrimes on our lives. The chapter on cybercrime in the metaverse certainly provides a comprehensive overview of current challenges and mitigation strategies. However, to enhance its relevance and preparedness for the rapidly evolving metaverse, a more explicit exploration of emerging trends in cybercrime is essential. As the metaverse continues to evolve alongside technological advancements and a growing user base, the nature of cybercrimes within these digital realms is likely to change as well. By offering insights into these potential future trends, such as metaverse-specific ransomware, deepfake identity theft, and augmented reality-related threats, the chapter can better equip readers and stakeholders to anticipate and address the evolving challenges of cybercrime in the metaverse effectively. Understanding the potential trajectory of cybercrimes within this dynamic landscape is crucial for staying ahead of the curve in terms of security and prevention.

3.1 Virtual Currency Theft

One of the most common cybercrimes in the metaverse is virtual currency theft. In the metaverse, users can earn virtual currency by completing tasks, selling virtual goods, or participating in virtual events. This virtual currency can then be used to purchase real-world goods or services. Cybercriminals can steal virtual currency by hacking into user accounts or by tricking users into giving them access to their virtual wallets. In 2016, the popular virtual game "Eve Online" was hit by a massive virtual currency theft (Gamer steals from the virtual world to pay real debts | Reuters, 2023) that resulted in the loss of over $60,000 worth of virtual currency. The virtual currency theft that occurred in "Eve Online" in 2016 was a significant event in the gaming industry. The game is a massively multiplayer online game where players can engage in various activities, such as mining, trading, and combat, in a virtual universe. The virtual currency in "Eve Online" is called Interstellar Kredits (ISK), which players can earn by participating in various in-game activities.

The virtual game Eve Online was hit by a massive virtual currency theft that resulted in the loss of over $60,000 worth of virtual currency. The attacker used a technique called social engineering to gain access to an employee's computer and steal login credentials, allowing them to access the game's database and transfer the virtual currency to their account. Similarly, in 2019, a user in the virtual world of Second Life had their virtual store hacked and over $1,700 worth of virtual goods stolen. Virtual currency and goods theft are not just limited to gaming environments. In the metaverse, where virtual experiences and services are becoming increasingly common, there are also opportunities for fraud and theft. For example, scammers could create fake virtual storefronts or services, offering products or experiences that they have no intention of delivering.

The virtual currency theft in "Eve Online" involved a group of cybercriminals who had been planning the attack for several months. The attack was conducted using a complex combination of social engineering and hacking techniques. The cybercriminals began by infiltrating a corporation within the game that had a significant amount of virtual currency stored in its corporate wallet. They used social engineering techniques to gain the trust of the corporation's members and eventually convinced them to give the cybercriminals access to their virtual wallets. Once the cybercriminals had access to the wallets, they began transferring the virtual currency to other accounts that they controlled. They used various techniques to cover their tracks, such as using proxy servers and creating fake accounts to move the stolen virtual currency. The theft was discovered when players in the game noticed that large amounts of virtual currency were being transferred out of the corporation's wallet. The game's developers were alerted to the situation and were able to track down the cybercriminals responsible for the theft.

The cybercriminals were eventually caught and prosecuted, and the stolen virtual currency was returned to its rightful owners. However, the incident highlighted the risks of virtual currency theft in online games and the importance of security measures to prevent such incidents from occurring. One of the main vulnerabilities in the "Eve Online" virtual currency system was the use of passwords to protect user accounts. The cybercriminals were able to obtain the passwords through social engineering techniques and then use them to gain access to the virtual wallets. The virtual currency theft in "Eve Online" in 2016 had a significant impact on the game's economy and community. The loss of over $60,000 worth of virtual currency was a major blow to the affected players and the game's developer, CCP Games. The theft of such a large amount of ISK had a ripple effect on the game's economy, as it created an imbalance in the supply and demand of virtual goods. In addition to the economic impact, the theft also had social and psychological effects on the affected players. For many players, the virtual world of "Eve Online" is a significant part of their social life, and losing a large amount of virtual currency can have emotional consequences. The theft also highlighted the vulnerability of virtual currencies and virtual economies to cybercrime. It served as a wake-up call for game developers and players alike to take cybersecurity seriously and implement stronger measures to protect their virtual assets.

After the theft, CCP Games took steps to investigate and address the incident, including reversing some of the fraudulent transactions and permanently banning the accounts of the cybercriminals responsible for the theft. The company also implemented additional security measures to prevent similar incidents from occurring in the future. Overall, the virtual currency theft in "Eve Online" in 2016 had a significant impact on the game's economy and community, as well as highlighting the importance of cybersecurity in virtual worlds. In conclusion, the virtual currency theft in "Eve Online" in 2016 was a significant event that highlighted the risks of cybercrime in online games. The incident was carried out using a combination of social engineering and hacking techniques and resulted in the loss of a significant amount of virtual currency. The incident underscores the importance of implementing robust security measures to protect virtual assets in online games and virtual worlds.

3.2 Virtual Property Theft

In the metaverse, users can also own virtual property such as virtual real estate, virtual vehicles, or virtual businesses. Cybercriminals can steal virtual property by hacking into user accounts or by exploiting vulnerabilities in the virtual environment. In 2019, a user in the virtual world of "Second Life" had their virtual store hacked (Linden Lab, 2023) and over $1,700 worth of virtual goods stolen. The virtual world of "Second Life" is a popular online platform where users can create and customize avatars, interact with others, and participate in a wide range of activities. One of the most crucial features of "Second Life" is the ability for users to create and sell virtual goods, such as clothing, furniture, and other items. In 2019, a user in "Second Life" had their virtual store hacked, resulting in the loss of over $1,700 worth of virtual goods. The user's store was in a virtual shopping district called "The Marketplace," which is a popular location for virtual commerce in the game.

The hack was carried out by exploiting a vulnerability in the user's virtual store software. The cybercriminals responsible for the attack were able to gain access to the user's account and take control of their virtual store. Once in control, the hackers began transferring virtual goods from the user's store to their accounts. The user discovered the theft when they noticed a significant decrease in the number of virtual goods in their store. They contacted the game's support team, who investigated the incident and confirmed that the user's store had been hacked. The developers of "Second Life" have implemented various security measures to protect users' virtual assets, such as encryption, firewalls, and other security features. However, cybercriminals can still find vulnerabilities in users' software and exploit them to gain access to virtual assets. In this case, the vulnerability that was exploited in the user's virtual store software was likely a weakness in the login system. The cybercriminals may have used brute-force attacks or other methods to obtain the user's login credentials and gain access to their store.

The virtual store hack in "Second Life" in 2019 had a significant impact on the affected user and their virtual business. The loss of over $1,700 worth of virtual goods was a major blow to the user's profits and ability to operate their store. In "Second Life", users can create and sell virtual goods and services for virtual currency, known as Linden Dollars (L$). The theft of virtual goods can have a significant impact on a user's business and revenue stream. In addition to the economic impact, the theft also had social and psychological effects on the affected user. As with "Eve Online", virtual worlds like "Second Life" are often a significant part of their users' social lives, and losing virtual assets can have emotional consequences. The theft also highlighted the vulnerability of virtual businesses to cybercrime. Just like real-world businesses, virtual businesses can be targeted by cybercriminals seeking to exploit vulnerabilities in their security systems. After the theft, the user likely took steps to investigate and address the incident, such as reporting the theft to the platform's administrators and implementing additional security measures to prevent future hacks. Depending on the specific circumstances of the hack, the user may also have taken legal action to recover their losses.

Overall, the virtual store hack in "Second Life" in 2019 had a significant impact on the affected user's virtual business and highlighted the importance of cybersecurity in virtual worlds. To prevent similar incidents from occurring, users in "Second Life" are encouraged to use strong passwords and multi-factor authentication to protect their accounts. They should also keep their software up-to-date with the latest security patches and be vigilant for any suspicious activity in their accounts. In conclusion, the theft of virtual goods in "Second Life" in 2019 highlights the risks of cybercrime in virtual worlds and the importance of implementing robust security measures to protect users' virtual assets. The hack was likely carried out by exploiting a vulnerability in the user's virtual store software, and the cybercriminals were able to transfer virtual goods worth over $1,700 to their accounts. Users in virtual worlds should take steps to protect their accounts and virtual assets to prevent similar incidents from occurring.

3.3 Virtual Harassment and Cyberstalking

The metaverse can also be used as a platform for cyber harassment and cyberstalking. In the virtual world, users can communicate with each other using text, voice, or video chat. Cybercriminals can use these communication channels to harass or stalk other users. In 2015, a user in the virtual world of "Second Life" was charged with cyberstalking after he harassed and threatened another user for months. The case highlights the potential dangers of online harassment and the importance of online safety. According to reports, the accused user created multiple accounts and used them to harass and threaten the victim in "Second Life". The accused user allegedly sent threatening messages, made unwanted advances, and even created a virtual representation of the victim and harassed it in the virtual world.

The victim reported the harassment to "Second Life" administrators, who investigated the matter and provided evidence to law enforcement. The accused user was eventually arrested and charged with cyberstalking, which is a serious crime in many jurisdictions. Cyberstalking is a form of online harassment that involves repeatedly targeting a victim with unwanted and threatening communication. Cyberstalkers may use social media, email, instant messaging, or other digital platforms to harass their victims. Cyberstalking can cause emotional distress, anxiety, and even physical harm to the victim. In the case of the "Second Life" user, the accused was found guilty of cyberstalking and sentenced to prison. The case highlights the potential dangers of online harassment and the need for users to be vigilant about their online safety. In response to the case, "Second Life" and other virtual world platforms have implemented stronger measures to prevent and report online harassment. For example, "Second Life" now has reporting tools for users to report incidents of harassment or abuse, and administrators can take action against users who violate the platform's terms of service.

The final impact of the cyberstalking incident in "Second Life" was significant for both the victim and the accused user. The victim experienced emotional distress and anxiety because of the harassment and threats, while the accused user faced legal consequences for their actions. After the victim reported the incident to "Second Life" administrators and law enforcement, the accused user was arrested and charged with cyberstalking. The criminal charges and potential legal consequences likely had a significant impact on the accused user's life, including their reputation, employment prospects, and personal relationships. In addition to the legal consequences, the incident highlighted the potential dangers of online harassment and cyberstalking. It raised awareness about the need for online platforms to implement stronger measures to prevent and address incidents of online harassment and ensure the safety of their users. The case also demonstrated the importance of reporting incidents of online harassment and abuse. By reporting the incident to "Second Life" administrators and law enforcement, the victim was able to receive support and protection, and the accused user was held accountable for their actions.

Overall, the cyberstalking incident in "Second Life" in 2015 had a significant impact on both the victim and the accused user. It underscored the need for online safety and the importance of acting against online harassment and abuse. In conclusion, the case of cyberstalking in "Second Life" in 2015 underscores the importance of online safety and the need for users to be aware of the potential dangers of online harassment. Virtual worlds and other online platforms must continue to implement stronger measures to prevent and address incidents of online harassment and ensure the safety of their users.

3.4 Virtual Identity Theft

Virtual identity theft is a growing concern in online gaming and virtual worlds. Hackers may use a variety of methods to gain access to user accounts, including phishing scams, malware, and social engineering tactics. Once they gain access, they may use the victim's virtual identity to commit fraud or other types of online crimes. Cybercriminals can also use the metaverse to steal user identities. In the metaverse, users create virtual avatars that represent them in the virtual world. Cybercriminals can steal these avatars and use them to commit virtual crimes or to access the user's personal information. The attacker would message other users, posing as the victim, and ask for virtual currency or items. They would promise to trade back but never follow through on the deal. This scam was repeated multiple times, resulting in the loss of virtual currency for users. The victim eventually became aware of the situation and reported it to administrators. The administrators investigated the matter and were able to identify the attackers and act against them. The victim's account was also recovered, and their virtual avatar was returned to them. To protect against virtual identity theft, users should take steps to secure their accounts and be wary of suspicious messages or requests. Online platforms and virtual worlds should also implement strong security measures and educate their users on how to protect their accounts and personal information.

In the case of virtual identity theft, the victim and other affected users likely experienced a loss of virtual currency and items, which can have real-world value. However, the incident also served as a reminder of the importance of online security and the need for users to be vigilant about their virtual identities. To address these and other cybercrimes in the metaverse, law enforcement agencies, governments, and businesses are using a variety of approaches. These approaches include using artificial intelligence to detect and prevent cybercrime, developing blockchain technology to create a more secure virtual environment, and creating virtual crime units to investigate and prosecute cybercriminals in the metaverse. As the metaverse continues to grow and evolve, forecasting cybercrimes will become even more critical to ensure the safety and security of virtual communities.

4. EMOTIONAL AND PSYCHOLOGICAL TOLL OF METAVERSE CYBERCRIMES

The growing prevalence of cybercrimes within virtual environments, often referred to as the metaverse, has brought to the forefront the significant emotional and psychological toll that victims can experience. Research and surveys have shed light on the profound impact of these digital offenses on individuals who have fallen prey to such activities. Understanding the mental health repercussions is essential to appreciate the gravity of these crimes and to develop effective strategies for prevention and support. Victims of virtual crimes, such as online harassment, doxxing, or in-game theft, often experience a range of negative emotions, including fear, anxiety, and distress. Research has shown that the anonymity and detachment offered by virtual spaces can embolden offenders, leading to more extreme and frequent forms of harassment. This can leave victims feeling helpless and exposed, with their mental well-being significantly affected.

A study conducted by the Pew Research Center found that 41% of Americans had personally experienced some form of online harassment, and 73% had witnessed it happening to others. Such experiences can lead to heightened levels of stress and anxiety, affecting not only the immediate mental state but also long-term emotional health. Victims may develop symptoms of post-traumatic stress disorder (PTSD), including intrusive thoughts, nightmares, and hypervigilance. Virtual environments can be especially conducive to cyberbullying, where individuals face persistent harassment or humiliation. A survey conducted by the Cyberbullying Research Center found that victims of cyberbullying often reported feelings of sadness, depression, and anxiety, with some experiencing suicidal ideation. These severe emotional consequences underscore the need for addressing the mental health impact of metaverse cybercrimes.

In cases of doxxing, where personal information is exposed, victims can suffer from extreme anxiety and paranoia. A study published in the Journal of Interpersonal Violence found that the victims of doxxing often lived in fear of physical harm and had a reduced sense of personal safety. The emotional distress arising from the invasion of one's privacy can be long-lasting and challenging to overcome. The emotional toll of virtual crimes extends beyond the immediate victims to the broader metaverse community. Witnessing or hearing about such incidents can create a culture of fear and mistrust, negatively impacting the mental well-being of individuals within these digital spaces. Users may become apprehensive about participating, sharing information, or forming relationships, all of which can lead to a sense of isolation and anxiety. Furthermore, in the realm of virtual economies, financial cybercrimes like in-game theft or fraudulent NFT sales can result in significant monetary losses. The financial burden and the realization that one has been manipulated or cheated can lead to feelings of humiliation and shame, compounding the emotional distress. A survey by Norton LifeLock found that 73% of respondents who had experienced cybercrime reported feeling anger, and 38% reported feeling violated.

Research also suggests that the emotional and psychological impact of metaverse cybercrimes can extend into the offline world. Victims may become more cautious, anxious, and mistrusting of others, affecting their overall quality of life. The emotional scars can lead to long-lasting mental health issues, affecting relationships, work, and daily functioning. The mental health repercussions of metaverse cybercrimes highlight the urgent need for support and intervention strategies. Virtual communities, platform operators, and law enforcement agencies must take proactive steps to prevent and address these issues. Educational campaigns on online safety, reporting mechanisms, and mental health resources are vital to assist victims and mitigate the emotional trauma associated with cybercrimes within the metaverse. Additionally, raising awareness about the emotional and psychological toll of these crimes is crucial for fostering empathy and understanding within the digital community and society.

4.1 Interaction Between Metaverse Virtual Economies and Real-World Economies

The metaverse, with its virtual economies, has become an increasingly influential player in the broader context of real-world economies. This interaction is driven by the recognition that virtual assets and transactions often carry real-world value, impacting individuals, businesses, and even national economies. The interplay between metaverse virtual economies and their real-world counterparts is a complex and dynamic relationship, with several key aspects.

- Virtual Asset Valuation: The metaverse has seen the emergence of virtual assets with tangible real-world value. These assets, such as virtual real estate, in-game items, and non-fungible tokens (NFTs), can be bought, sold, and traded in digital marketplaces. Their value is determined by supply, demand, and perceived scarcity, much like physical assets. Some virtual items have fetched astonishing prices in real-world auctions, further blurring the line between the metaverse and reality.
- Economic Activity and Earnings: Virtual economies have provided opportunities for individuals to earn real income. Gamers, content creators, and virtual entrepreneurs can generate revenue through activities within the metaverse. For instance, professional gamers can earn significant incomes from competitive gaming, while artists and designers can monetize their creations through NFT sales. These earnings contribute to real-world economic activity, impacting personal finances and spending.
- Job Creation and Entrepreneurship: The growth of the metaverse has led to the creation of new jobs and entrepreneurial opportunities. Virtual architects, digital artists, virtual event planners, and metaverse developers are just a few examples of professions that have emerged. The metaverse's economic dimension has also fostered startups and businesses dedicated to metaverse-related services and products.
- Cross-Platform Transactions: The real-world impact of virtual economies is further emphasized by the ability to convert virtual assets into real-world currency. Virtual currencies can be exchanged for fiat currency on digital platforms, and NFTs can be sold for substantial sums in cryptocurrency. These transactions bridge the virtual and real-world economies, enabling users to transform their virtual assets into tangible assets or income.
- Investment and Speculation: The metaverse's economic potential has attracted investors and speculators. Cryptocurrencies, which often play a central role in virtual economies, have experienced substantial price appreciation, with investors eyeing metaverse-related assets and technologies. This speculative interest can lead to fluctuations in real-world financial markets, influenced by metaverse trends and developments.
- Cross-Industry Impact: Metaverse-related technologies and applications are not confined to a single sector. They have the potential to influence various industries, from entertainment and gaming to education, healthcare, and real estate. The growth of virtual economies can create ripple effects in these industries, altering business models, customer engagement strategies, and economic dynamics.
- Economic Disparities and Regulatory Challenges: The metaverse's economic impact is not without its challenges. It can exacerbate economic disparities, as individuals with access to metaverse opportunities can accumulate virtual wealth while others may be left at a disadvantage.

Additionally, regulatory challenges arise as governments seek to navigate the taxation and oversight of virtual assets and transactions.

- Technological Advancements: The evolution of the metaverse and its technologies, including virtual reality and blockchain, has led to advancements that extend beyond the virtual realm. These technologies have broader applications in real-world industries, such as healthcare, training, and collaborative work environments, transforming the way we engage with and interact within the physical world.

The interaction between metaverse virtual economies and real-world economies is multifaceted and continues to evolve. The recognition of virtual assets as having real-world value, the generation of income within the metaverse, and the increasing investment interest have led to a complex relationship. As the metaverse's influence grows, it presents both opportunities and challenges, requiring careful consideration by individuals, businesses, and policymakers to ensure that the real world and virtual economies can coexist harmoniously and responsibly.

4.2 Understanding and Mitigating the Risks Faced by Young Users in the Metaverse

The metaverse, with its immersive digital environments and interconnected experiences, has garnered a substantial user base, including many young individuals. While the metaverse offers exciting opportunities for entertainment, education, and social interaction, young users may also be more susceptible to certain types of cybercrimes due to their potentially limited understanding of the risks involved. This section explores the specific risks faced by young users in the metaverse and outlines preventative measures to safeguard their online experiences.

- Cyberbullying and Online Harassment: Young users in the metaverse are particularly vulnerable to cyberbullying and online harassment. These forms of digital abuse can include hurtful messages, hate speech, or the spreading of false information, leading to emotional distress and harm to the victim's self-esteem. Young individuals may be more emotionally affected by such incidents, and the consequences can extend into their offline lives. Preventative Measures include:
    - Open Communication: Encourage open communication with children or young users about their online experiences. Teach them how to recognize and respond to cyberbullying and emphasize the importance of reporting such incidents to responsible adults.
    - Awareness Programs: Schools and parents can conduct awareness programs on cyberbullying and online harassment, educating young users about the negative effects and how to protect themselves.
- Inappropriate Content Exposure: The metaverse contains a wide range of content, not all of which is suitable for young audiences. Exposure to inappropriate or explicit content can have adverse effects on a child's emotional and psychological well-being. Young users inadvertently come across such content while exploring virtual spaces or interacting with other users. Preventative Measures include:
    - Parental Controls: Utilize parental control software and settings to restrict access to age-inappropriate content. These tools can help filter out explicit material and ensure a safer virtual environment.

   - Education: Teach young users how to recognize and report inappropriate content. Make them aware of the potential risks and the need to exercise caution while navigating the metaverse.
- Privacy and Data Security: Young users might not fully grasp the importance of safeguarding their personal information in the metaverse. Sharing sensitive details can make them targets for identity theft, harassment, or other forms of cybercrime. Their limited understanding of privacy issues can put them at risk. Preventative Measures include:
   - Education on Privacy: Educate young users about the significance of personal privacy and the potential consequences of sharing personal information online. Emphasize the importance of keeping sensitive data confidential.
   - Privacy Settings: Assist young users in configuring the privacy settings of their metaverse accounts to limit the sharing of personal information. Teach them to use strong and unique passwords.
- Grooming and Predatory Behavior: Young users become targets for online predators and grooming, where individuals with harmful intentions seek to manipulate and exploit their trust. Groomers often pretend to be of a similar age to establish a connection with their victims, making it challenging for young users to identify the risks. Preventative Measures include:
   - Open Conversations: Encourage young users to openly communicate about their online interactions. Teach them about the potential dangers of sharing personal information or meeting strangers on the internet.
   - Supervision: Depending on the age and maturity of the child, supervision of their online activities may be necessary to ensure their safety.
- Virtual Theft and Scams: Young users may lack the experience to recognize virtual theft and scams in the metaverse. Scammers may promise virtual goods or currency in exchange for real-world money, ultimately resulting in financial loss and disillusionment. Preventative Measures include:
   - Educate about Scams: Teach young users to be cautious about any offers that seem too good to be true. Make them aware of common virtual scams and the importance of verifying the legitimacy of transactions.
   - Monitor Transactions: Supervise and monitor their virtual transactions and financial activities, especially when real money is involved.
- Exposure to Addictive Behavior: The metaverse can be engaging, and some activities, such as gaming, can become addictive for young users. Overindulgence in virtual activities can lead to negative consequences on their physical and mental health, affecting their academic and social lives. Preventative Measures include:
   - Set Time Limits: Establish time limits for metaverse activities to strike a balance between the virtual and real worlds. Encourage healthy offline activities and hobbies.
   - Monitor Behavior: Be attentive to changes in behavior, such as withdrawal from social interactions or declining academic performance, which might signal excessive use of the metaverse.
- Encourage Critical Thinking and Digital Literacy: Young users should be encouraged to develop critical thinking and digital literacy skills. This includes the ability to evaluate information critically, distinguish between credible and false sources, and understand the consequences of their online actions. Preventative Measures include:

- Digital Literacy Education: Schools and parents should incorporate digital literacy into the curriculum to teach young users how to evaluate information, identify misinformation, and think critically about the content they encounter.
- Promote Media Literacy: Encourage discussions on media and digital content, emphasizing the importance of verifying information before accepting it as fact.

Metaverse presents a unique set of risks for young users due to their limited understanding of the potential dangers. Preventative measures should focus on education, supervision, and open communication with parents, teachers, and guardians. Empowering young users with digital literacy skills and awareness of the risks can help them navigate the metaverse safely and responsibly. By addressing these challenges, we can ensure that young users can fully enjoy the benefits of the metaverse while staying protected from its potential pitfalls.

5. LITERATURE SURVEY

The author reviewed several research papers from journals, the most relevant ones are mentioned below.

Currently, the metaverse concept has captured significant attention across various sectors, thanks to the rapid advancements in blockchain and Web3 technologies. The decentralized metaverse ecosystem is experiencing a surge in users and investments. However, this growth has also led to a rise in financial crimes like scams, code exploitation, wash trading, money laundering, and illegal services due to the absence of industry standards and regulations. This underscores the need to categorize and address financial security threats within the Web3-driven metaverse for its sustainable development. In a recent study by Wu et al. (2023), the authors delved into the background and applications of the Web3 metaverse and provided a comprehensive classification of security risks and financial crimes that have emerged in this decentralized environment. They discussed existing definitions, relevant cases, and academic research related to each type of financial crime. Additionally, the paper examined current anti-crime measures and technologies, drawing from academic research and government policies. It concluded by exploring opportunities and challenges in behavioral mining and potential regulation of financial activities in the metaverse. This overview aims to enhance readers' understanding of security threats in this emerging ecosystem and serve as a valuable resource for combating financial crimes.

Analyzing crime patterns in large cities presents a complex spatiotemporal challenge. This difficulty is primarily rooted in two key factors: the infrequent occurrence of criminal activities and their distribution across vast geographical areas. The rarity of crimes hinders the effectiveness of most time series analysis methods, while the sheer size of urban areas makes the computational costs of such methods impractical. Additionally, visualizing the various patterns hidden within crime time series data is a daunting task due to the multitude of potential patterns that can emerge from such analyses. In a recent study by García-Zanabria et al. (2022), a novel methodology was introduced to address these challenges, allowing for the analysis of spatiotemporal crime patterns at a street-level of granularity. This approach consists of two primary components tailored to address the issues of spatial sparsity and the dispersion of crimes across citywide areas. The first component leverages a stochastic mechanism to visually identify potential intensive crime hotspots, revealing crucial patterns that standard intensity-based hotspot visualizations might miss. The second component utilizes deep learning techniques to embed crime time series data into Cartesian space, enabling the identification of spatial locations where these time series exhibit similar behavior. These two components have been integrated into an online analytical tool known as CriPAV (Crime Pattern Analysis and Visualization), facilitating both a global and street-level examination of crime patterns. Developed in collaboration with domain experts, CriPAV's effectiveness has been demonstrated through a series of case studies involving real crime data in São Paulo, Brazil. These experiments and case studies showcase CriPAV's ability to identify patterns, such as locations with low crime intensity but a high probability of criminal activity and locations that are geographically distant but exhibit similar crime patterns.

In recent years, there has been a growing interest among researchers in using machine learning and deep learning techniques to predict and understand patterns and trends in criminal activities. A review paper authored by Mandalapu et al. (2023) explored a substantial body of research, comprising over 150 articles, to investigate the application of machine learning and deep learning algorithms in crime prediction. The paper not only delves into the datasets employed by researchers for crime prediction but also thoroughly analyzes the various methods and algorithms used in these technologies, shedding light on the different aspects and factors associated with criminal behavior. Furthermore, the review identifies potential gaps in the existing research and suggests future directions that could enhance the accuracy of crime prediction models. The comprehensive insights presented in this paper offer a valuable reference for researchers working in this domain. By gaining a more profound understanding of crime prediction techniques, law enforcement agencies can develop more effective strategies to prevent and respond to criminal activities, ultimately contributing to improved public safety. The study primarily focused on the cities of San Francisco and Chicago in the USA for experimental analysis. In these cities, the proposed model demonstrated impressive performance metrics, with a Mean Absolute Error of 0.008 and 0.02, a Coefficient of Determination of 0.95 and 0.94, and a Symmetric Mean Absolute Percentage Error of 1.03% and 0.6%, respectively. The model outperformed several other well-known models, showcasing its effectiveness in crime prediction.

Predicting crime is a complex task due to the multifaceted nature of criminal activities, and the sheer volume of daily crime incidents in various locations makes this prediction even more challenging. Despite the availability of established machine learning and deep learning techniques, law enforcement agencies still face difficulties in preventing crimes proactively. To address this issue, a highly effective approach is essential to reduce crime rates. Tasnim et al. (2022) proposed a robust multi-module method for crime prediction using deep learning techniques. The method consists of two key modules: Feature Level Fusion and Decision Level Fusion. In the first module, the approach utilizes temporal-based Attention LSTM, Spatio-Temporal Stacked Bidirectional LSTM, and a Fusion model. The Fusion model leverages data from the previous two models. The temporal-based model serves as the source model for transfer learning on datasets from different cities, reducing the model's training time. In the second module, the spatio-temporal-based Attention, Stacked Bidirectional LSTM, and the outcomes of the feature-level fusion module work together to make the final prediction. This architecture forecasts future crime occurrences, specifically for the next hour, based on data from the preceding twenty-four hours. It provides estimates of the number of crimes in various categories for specific locations, allowing law enforcement to gain insights into future crimes based on factors like category, time, and location.

Crime prevention heavily relies on the practice of crime prediction, which is essential for law enforcement agencies to formulate effective patrol strategies. Numerous methods and solutions have been employed for forecasting criminal activities. However, the landscape and data sources for crime prediction are continually evolving. The rise of social media platforms for information sharing and idea exchange, particularly Twitter, has provided a valuable resource for capturing public sentiments, emotions, perspectives, and feedback. In this context, techniques have been developed to analyze the sentiment expressed in tweets on Twitter, helping determine whether the textual content conveys a positive or negative perspective on crime incidents. Data fusion is a vital approach to combining information from both crime data and tweets. Tam et al. (2023) harnessed semantic knowledge from text and historical crime data, incorporating them into a model designed for crime prediction. They employed a data fusion technique in conjunction with a ConvBiLSTM model to extract distinct vectors from both tweet and crime data modalities and amalgamate them into a single representation, effectively capturing information from all sources. The study involved conducting experiments using two datasets. The first dataset encompassed crime incident data sourced from the Chicago police department, specifically covering the period from September 1 to September 30, 2019. The second dataset consisted of tweets containing crime-related terms specific to Chicago. To assess the model's performance, it was benchmarked against the latest crime prediction models, including SVM, Logistic Regression, NAHC, DNN with feature-level data fusion, CrimeTelescope, ANN+BERT, and BERT-based crime prediction models. The experimental results demonstrated that the ConvBiLSTM model with multimodal data fusion outperformed other traditional deep-learning and BERT models, achieving an accuracy rate of 97.75%. This underscores the efficacy of their approach in crime prediction.

Crime prediction aims to forecast the number of crime incidents in various regions of a city by analyzing historical crime data. This field has garnered significant attention from both academic and industrial sectors due to its crucial role in enhancing urban safety and reducing financial losses. However, most existing methods assume that historical crime data are complete, which may not be the case in many real-world situations. Additionally, crime incidents are influenced by multiple factors and exhibit complex spatial, temporal, and categorical correlations, which are not fully harnessed by current approaches. Liang et al. (2023) proposed a novel framework called TD-Crime was introduced, based on tensor decomposition. TD-Crime directly addresses the issue of incomplete crime data. The authors structured the crime data as a tensor and applied nonnegative CP decomposition, which not only provides a natural solution to missing data but also implicitly captures spatial, temporal, and categorical correlations. Furthermore, the research aimed to explicitly leverage spatial and temporal correlations by learning directly from the crime data to enhance forecasting performance. The authors formulated a joint optimization problem and presented an efficient alternating optimization scheme to find a satisfactory solution. Extensive experiments conducted on real-world crime datasets demonstrated that TD-Crime effectively handles crime prediction tasks under various missing data scenarios, highlighting its practical utility.

6. FORECASTING CYBER CRIMES IN THE AGE OF THE METAVERSE

Forecasting cybercrimes in the age of the metaverse is becoming a critical issue for law enforcement agencies, governments, and businesses. The metaverse is creating new opportunities for cybercriminals to commit crimes such as theft, fraud, and cyberstalking. The metaverse is also creating new challenges for law enforcement agencies and businesses to detect and prevent cybercrime. Forecasting cybercrime in the Metaverse can be challenging due to the constantly evolving nature of technology and the increasing sophistication of cybercriminals. However, several options can be used to try and predict and prevent cybercrime in the Metaverse:

- **Threat intelligence**

Gathering threat intelligence from various sources can help identify potential cyber threats and vulnerabilities in the Metaverse. This could include monitoring social media, forums, and other online sources for discussions related to cyber-attacks or vulnerabilities. Threat intelligence can be a powerful tool for forecasting cybercrime in the metaverse. Threat intelligence involves gathering information about potential cyber threats and analyzing that information to identify patterns and trends that could indicate an impending cyber-attack. Here are some ways that threat intelligence can be used for forecasting cybercrime in the metaverse:

- Monitor Dark Web forums: Cybercriminals often use the dark web to communicate and plan their attacks. By monitoring dark web forums, threat intelligence analysts can identify potential threats and alert Metaverse platform owners to take appropriate action.
- Analyze Malware: Malware is a common tool used by cybercriminals to carry out attacks in the metaverse. Threat intelligence analysts can analyze malware to identify the tactics and techniques used by cybercriminals and predict future attacks.
- Monitor Social Media: Social media platforms are increasingly being used by cybercriminals to coordinate and plan attacks. By monitoring social media platforms, threat intelligence analysts can identify potential threats and alert Metaverse platform owners.
- Monitor Vulnerabilities: Threat intelligence analysts can monitor vulnerability databases to identify new vulnerabilities in Metaverse platforms. By identifying these vulnerabilities early, Metaverse platform owners can take action to patch them before they can be exploited by cybercriminals.
- Analyze Attack Patterns: Threat intelligence analysts can analyze attack patterns to identify trends and patterns that could indicate an impending cyber-attack. This can include identifying patterns of activity on Metaverse platforms, such as an increase in phishing attacks or a rise in virtual currency theft.
- Share Threat Intelligence: Sharing threat intelligence between Metaverse platforms and with law enforcement agencies can help to identify potential threats and prevent cybercrime in the Metaverse.

By using threat intelligence to forecast cybercrime in the metaverse, Metaverse platform owners can take proactive measures to prevent attacks and protect their users. It is important to note, however, that threat intelligence is just one tool in the fight against cybercrime, and it must be used in conjunction with other security measures to be effective.

- **Data Analytics**

Analyzing data related to user behavior, system logs, and other relevant data can help identify patterns and anomalies that could indicate a potential cyber-attack. This could include using machine learning and artificial intelligence to identify and predict potential cyber threats. Data analytics can be used to identify patterns and trends in data related to cybercrime in the metaverse, which can help to forecast potential threats and prevent attacks. Here are some ways that data analytics can be used for forecasting cybercrime in the metaverse:

- User Behavior Analysis: Data analytics can be used to analyze user behavior on Metaverse platforms to identify patterns and anomalies that could indicate potential cyber threats. For example, unusual login activity, excessive virtual currency transactions, or sudden changes in user behavior could all be indicators of cybercrime.

- Sentiment Analysis: Sentiment analysis involves analyzing data from social media and other sources to identify the sentiment and mood of users. This can help to identify potential threats, such as cybercriminals using social media to coordinate attacks.
- Network Analysis: Data analytics can be used to analyze network traffic on Metaverse platforms to identify patterns and anomalies that could indicate potential cyber threats. For example, an unusually high volume of traffic from a particular IP address could be a sign of a DDoS attack.
- Machine Learning: Machine learning algorithms can be trained on data related to past cybercrime incidents to identify patterns and trends that could indicate future attacks. For example, machine learning could be used to identify patterns in virtual currency theft incidents that could be used to predict future incidents.
- Predictive Analytics: Predictive analytics involves using statistical algorithms and machine learning to predict future outcomes based on past data. This can be used to forecast potential cyber threats in the metaverse.

By using data analytics to forecast cybercrime in the metaverse, Metaverse platform owners can take proactive measures to prevent attacks and protect their users. It is important to note however, that data analytics is just one tool in the fight against cybercrime, and it must be used in conjunction with other security measures to be effective. Additionally, privacy concerns must be taken into account when collecting and analyzing data from users.

- **Red teaming**

Conducting red team exercises, in which a team of experts simulates a cyber-attack against the Metaverse system, can help identify potential vulnerabilities and weaknesses in the system. This can help Metaverse developers and security professionals identify and address potential security flaws before they are exploited by cybercriminals. Red teaming is a security testing approach that involves creating simulated cyber-attacks to identify weaknesses in security controls and improve overall cybersecurity posture. In the context of forecasting cybercrime in the metaverse, red teaming can be used to identify potential vulnerabilities and threats to Metaverse platforms and test the effectiveness of existing security measures. Here are some ways that red teaming can be used for forecasting cybercrime in the metaverse:

- Penetration Testing: Penetration testing involves simulating cyber-attacks to identify weaknesses in security controls and exploit vulnerabilities. Penetration testing can be used to identify vulnerabilities in Metaverse platforms and test the effectiveness of security measures such as access controls, encryption, and firewalls.
- Social Engineering: Social engineering involves manipulating users into revealing sensitive information or performing actions that could compromise security. Red teams can use social engineering tactics to identify vulnerabilities in Metaverse platforms and test the effectiveness of security measures such as user awareness training.
- Red Teaming Exercises: Red teaming exercises involve simulating real-world cyber-attacks to identify weaknesses in security controls and test the effectiveness of incident response plans. Red

teaming exercises can be used to test the response of Metaverse platforms to cyber-attacks and identify areas for improvement.

By using red teaming to identify potential vulnerabilities and threats to Metaverse platforms, platform owners can take proactive measures to prevent attacks and improve their overall cybersecurity posture. Red teaming can help Metaverse platform owners identify gaps in their security controls, train employees on how to recognize and respond to cyber-attacks, and improve their incident response plans. However, it is important to note that red teaming should be used in conjunction with other security measures, such as threat intelligence and data analytics, to be effective in forecasting cybercrime in the metaverse.

- **Bug bounty programs**

Offering bug bounty programs, in which security researchers are rewarded for identifying and reporting vulnerabilities in the Metaverse system, can help identify and address potential security flaws before they are exploited by cybercriminals. Bug bounty programs are initiatives offered by organizations that invite ethical hackers to identify and report vulnerabilities in their software or platforms. In exchange for finding and reporting these vulnerabilities, the organization offers a reward or compensation to the ethical hacker. These programs have become an effective way for organizations to find and fix vulnerabilities before they can be exploited by malicious actors. In the context of forecasting cybercrime in the metaverse, bug bounty programs can be a valuable tool to identify potential vulnerabilities and improve the overall security posture of Metaverse platforms. Here are some ways that bug bounty programs can be used for forecasting cybercrime in the metaverse:

- Identifying Vulnerabilities: By offering rewards for the identification of vulnerabilities in Metaverse platforms, organizations can identify potential weaknesses in their security controls and take proactive measures to fix them before they can be exploited by cybercriminals.
- Encouraging Responsible Disclosure: Bug bounty programs can encourage ethical hackers to responsibly disclose vulnerabilities they have discovered, rather than selling them to the highest bidder on the black market. This can help Metaverse platforms to fix vulnerabilities before they are exploited by malicious actors.
- Improving Security Culture: Bug bounty programs can help improve the security culture of Metaverse platforms by promoting the idea that security is everyone's responsibility. By engaging with ethical hackers, organizations can gain a better understanding of potential threats and work to build a more robust security program.

However, it is important to note that bug bounty programs should not be seen as a replacement for other security measures, such as penetration testing and vulnerability assessments. Bug bounty programs should be used in conjunction with other security measures to be effective in forecasting cybercrime in the metaverse. Additionally, it is important to ensure that bug bounty programs are implemented properly and that rewards are offered responsibly to ensure that ethical hackers are incentivized to disclose vulnerabilities without putting the platform at risk.

- **Collaboration and information sharing**

Collaboration and information sharing among Metaverse developers, security professionals, and law enforcement agencies can help identify potential cyber threats and vulnerabilities in the Metaverse. This could include sharing threat intelligence, best practices, and other relevant information. Collaboration and information sharing are crucial in forecasting cybercrime in the metaverse. As the metaverse is a complex system involving multiple platforms, users, and stakeholders, it is essential to have a collaborative approach to cybersecurity. Here are some ways collaboration and information sharing can be used for forecasting cybercrime in the metaverse:

- Public-Private Partnerships: Collaboration between public and private sectors can help to gather intelligence on cyber threats in the metaverse. Public agencies can share information on cybercrime trends, while private entities can provide insights into the latest vulnerabilities and attack methods.
- Sharing of Best Practices: Sharing of best practices among stakeholders can help to raise awareness about potential cyber threats in the metaverse. For example, virtual world platforms can share guidelines on how to secure user accounts and detect suspicious activity.
- Information Exchange Platforms: Creating information exchange platforms where stakeholders can share information on cyber threats and vulnerabilities can help to improve situational awareness in the metaverse. These platforms can include forums, social media groups, and chat rooms.
- Collaboration among Security Researchers: Collaboration among security researchers can help to identify new vulnerabilities and threats in the metaverse. Researchers can share their findings with the broader community to help improve the overall cybersecurity posture of the metaverse.
- Cybersecurity Drills and Exercises: Conducting cybersecurity drills and exercises can help to prepare stakeholders for cyber threats in the metaverse. These drills can simulate cyberattacks and help stakeholders identify weaknesses in their cybersecurity defenses.

In conclusion, collaboration and information sharing are essential for forecasting cybercrime in the metaverse. By working together, stakeholders can improve their situational awareness, share best practices, and identify new vulnerabilities and threats. By utilizing these options, Metaverse developers and security professionals can work together to try and predict and prevent cybercrime in the Metaverse. However, it is important to note that predicting and preventing all cyber-attacks is not always possible, and therefore it is important to have a comprehensive incident response plan in place to quickly respond to and mitigate cyber-attacks when they occur. One of the challenges of forecasting cybercrimes in the metaverse is the evolving nature of technology. The metaverse is constantly evolving, and innovative technologies are being developed to create a more immersive and interactive virtual world. Cybercriminals are also constantly adapting and evolving their tactics to take advantage of these new technologies. As a result, it can be difficult to anticipate the new types of cybercrimes that may emerge in the metaverse. Another challenge in forecasting cybercrimes in the metaverse is the global nature of the virtual world. The metaverse is not limited by physical boundaries and is accessible to anyone with an internet connection. This makes it difficult for law enforcement agencies and governments to regulate and enforce laws in the metaverse. Cybercriminals can operate from anywhere in the world and can easily hide their identities in the metaverse.

6.1 The Balance Between Surveillance and Individual Privacy Rights

The metaverse, with its immersive digital environments and interconnected user experiences, has given rise to a complex debate regarding the balance between surveillance for security and individual privacy rights. On one hand, the potential for cybercrimes within the metaverse has made surveillance an essential tool for detecting and preventing illicit activities. On the other hand, the ever-present surveillance raises concerns about the erosion of individual privacy rights. Striking the right balance between these two interests is crucial to ensure both the security and well-being of users and the preservation of their fundamental rights. Surveillance within the metaverse is driven by the imperative to ensure user safety and maintain the integrity of the virtual environment. As virtual worlds and digital spaces become increasingly complex, they also become more susceptible to various forms of cybercrimes, including harassment, fraud, hacking, and other illicit activities. Surveillance tools, such as monitoring systems, data analysis, and behavior tracking, are essential for identifying and mitigating these threats.

One of the key advantages of surveillance in the metaverse is the ability to respond quickly to emerging threats. Whether it's tracking down cybercriminals, detecting in-game cheating, or identifying potential security breaches, surveillance can help prevent and mitigate harm in real time. It allows operators to take immediate action to protect users and safeguard the virtual environment. Moreover, surveillance can serve as a deterrent to potential wrongdoers. The knowledge that virtual actions are being monitored can dissuade individuals from engaging in harmful behavior, contributing to a safer and more secure metaverse. For example, the fear of being caught can discourage in-game harassment, cheating, and financial fraud. While surveillance in the metaverse has its merits, it also raises concerns about the erosion of individual privacy rights. Virtual spaces, like the physical world, should respect the right to privacy, autonomy, and personal freedom. Users should be able to engage in digital environments without feeling constantly monitored or exposed.

Intrusive surveillance can infringe on the right to privacy and can have a chilling effect on individuals, stifling free expression and discouraging participation in the metaverse. It can lead to self-censorship, as users may fear the consequences of their virtual actions being scrutinized. This inhibition can hinder creativity, collaboration, and the free exchange of ideas within the metaverse. Moreover, the collection and storage of user data in virtual environments raise concerns about data security and the potential for breaches. As users share personal information and engage in financial transactions within the metaverse, safeguarding this data becomes essential. Unauthorized access to user data can lead to identity theft, financial fraud, and various forms of abuse, further highlighting the importance of preserving individual privacy rights.

Balancing surveillance for security and individual privacy rights in the metaverse is a multifaceted challenge. It requires a nuanced approach that takes into account the unique characteristics of digital spaces. Here are several considerations to strike the right balance:

- Clear Policies and Transparency: Virtual world operators must establish clear policies on surveillance and data collection, providing users with full transparency regarding what is monitored and why. Users should have the opportunity to consent to the terms and conditions, knowing the extent of surveillance.
- Data Minimization: Collecting only the data necessary for security purposes and limiting the retention period of user information can help reduce the risk of privacy infringement. Data should be used solely for security and not for other purposes, such as targeted advertising.

- Consent and Opt-Out Options: Users should have the ability to opt out of certain types of surveillance, where possible, without compromising their safety. Offering opt-out mechanisms empowers users to make choices about their level of exposure to surveillance.
- Independent Oversight: Independent bodies or watchdog organizations can help ensure that surveillance practices within the metaverse adhere to ethical and legal standards. Regular audits and evaluations of surveillance systems can maintain transparency and accountability.
- Robust Security Measures: To protect the privacy of user data, virtual environments should implement robust security measures, including encryption and access controls, to prevent data breaches.
- Education and Awareness: Users should be educated about the risks and benefits of surveillance in the metaverse. Awareness campaigns can empower individuals to make informed choices about their virtual activities and privacy settings.

Ultimately, finding the right balance between surveillance for security and individual privacy rights is a dynamic and ongoing process. As the metaverse continues to evolve, it will be essential to adapt and refine these measures to ensure the safety and well-being of users while upholding their fundamental rights to privacy and autonomy.

6.2 Emerging Trends in Cybercrime

The metaverse, a burgeoning digital realm, has begun to transform the way we interact, conduct business, and experience the digital world. As technology continues to advance and the metaverse becomes more sophisticated, it presents a host of exciting opportunities but also novel challenges in the realm of cybercrime. This section explores the speculative future trends of cybercrime as we delve deeper into the metaverse's evolving landscape.

- Metaverse-Targeted Ransomware Attacks: Ransomware attacks have been a persistent threat in the digital realm, and they are likely to evolve and adapt to the metaverse. In the future, we can anticipate ransomware attacks that specifically target virtual assets and digital property within the metaverse. Cybercriminals may encrypt virtual items, in-game currencies, or even entire virtual real estate properties, demanding a ransom in exchange for their release. Such attacks could lead to real-world financial losses, affecting individuals and businesses that invest in the metaverse.
- Virtual Identity Theft and Deepfakes: As the metaverse's virtual environments become increasingly realistic, so too will the opportunities for virtual identity theft and deepfake creation. Cybercriminals may exploit advanced technologies to impersonate individuals within the metaverse, perpetrating various forms of fraud and deception. Users could find themselves facing not only financial losses but also damage to their reputation and trust within virtual communities.
- Spatial Computing-Related Threats: The integration of spatial computing technologies in the metaverse, such as augmented reality (AR) and virtual reality (VR), could introduce new types of cyber threats. Cybercriminals might exploit vulnerabilities in AR/VR systems to launch attacks that compromise users' sensory experiences. This could include visual or auditory manipulations, potentially leading to disorientation, misinformation, and even psychological harm.
- NFT Scams and Counterfeits: As non-fungible tokens (NFTs) gain more prominence within the metaverse, we can expect a surge in NFT-related cybercrimes. Scammers may create counterfeit NFTs, deceiving collectors and art enthusiasts. Additionally, fraudulent NFT sales and investment

schemes could prey on users' desire to own valuable virtual assets, potentially causing significant financial losses and disillusionment.

- Metaverse-Generated Malware: Cybercriminals are likely to develop metaverse-specific malware designed to exploit the virtual environments' unique features. These malware strains could target metaverse users, their assets, and the platforms themselves. They might include malicious scripts that manipulate in-game economies, steal virtual currencies, or facilitate unauthorized access to user accounts.]
- Enhanced Doxxing and Swatting: The metaverse's immersive nature, combined with the potential for real-world connections, may facilitate more insidious forms of harassment, including enhanced doxxing and swatting. Perpetrators could exploit the metaverse to gather extensive personal information about their victims and launch more sophisticated and potentially dangerous attacks, further blurring the line between the virtual and physical worlds.
- Metaverse-Enabled Espionage and Data Breaches: The interconnectedness of the metaverse could offer a fertile ground for cyber espionage. Nation-states and threat actors could exploit the metaverse for data breaches, surveillance, and intelligence gathering. This could have far-reaching implications, affecting national security, intellectual property, and individuals' privacy.
- Metaverse-Related Phishing and Social Engineering: Cybercriminals are likely to employ metaverse-specific phishing tactics and social engineering schemes to manipulate users. They might create virtual personas that gain trust within the metaverse community and use that trust to deceive users into sharing personal information or conducting fraudulent transactions. This could pose a significant risk to the metaverse's social fabric.
- Metaverse-Specific Regulations and Legal Challenges: As the metaverse evolves, legal frameworks and regulations may struggle to keep pace with the novel cyber threats it presents. The need for new, metaverse-specific laws and policies will emerge, as will debates on jurisdiction, accountability, and enforcement. Policymakers will need to collaborate across borders to address these complex challenges effectively.
- Ethical Dilemmas and Security Trade-offs: As metaverse technology advances, there will be ethical dilemmas and trade-offs between security and individual freedoms. Striking the right balance between surveillance for security and preserving privacy rights will remain an ongoing challenge, with significant implications for how users interact within the metaverse.
- Emerging Countermeasures and Solutions: In response to these evolving cyber threats in the metaverse, we can anticipate the development of advanced cybersecurity solutions, including metaverse-specific anti-malware software, enhanced encryption techniques, and blockchain-based security measures. Cross-platform collaboration and information-sharing will become increasingly vital to combat metaverse cyber crimes effectively.

Metaverse's rapid evolution and adoption create both opportunities and challenges. While the potential for enriching experiences and innovative business models is vast, the metaverse is not immune to cybercriminal activities. As technology advances and the metaverse becomes more sophisticated, individuals, businesses, regulators, and cybersecurity experts must stay vigilant and proactive in addressing the emerging trends in cybercrime. Developing robust security measures, fostering digital literacy, and promoting ethical and responsible behavior within the metaverse will be critical to navigating these future challenges successfully.

In the emergent metaverse, the ethical quandaries regarding surveillance and governance take center stage, presenting intricate challenges in the battle against cybercrime. As virtual worlds expand, so do the opportunities for surveillance, raising concerns about individual privacy and digital liberties. The ability of metaverse operators to monitor user activities and interactions for security purposes must strike a delicate balance between safeguarding against cyber threats and respecting user privacy. Stricter surveillance measures may help detect and prevent cybercriminal activities, but they can also infringe upon the fundamental principles of anonymity and personal freedom that many users cherish in virtual spaces. Moreover, governance within the metaverse is a complex issue, as it necessitates clear rules and regulations to address cybercrime while not stifling creativity and innovation. Striking the right balance between security and individual freedoms is a critical challenge that metaverse developers, policymakers, and users must grapple with in the quest to ensure a secure and ethical virtual realm.

7. ADDRESSING METAVERSE CYBERCRIMES

Addressing cybercrime in the Metaverse requires a multifaceted approach that involves a combination of technical, legal, and educational measures. One of the potential ways to address the challenge of forecasting cybercrimes in the metaverse is using artificial intelligence (AI). AI can be used to detect and prevent cybercrime in the metaverse by analyzing patterns and anomalies in user behavior. AI can also be used to create predictive models that can anticipate new types of cybercrimes in the metaverse. Another way to address the challenge of forecasting cybercrimes in the metaverse is through the development of blockchain technology. Blockchain technology can be used to create a more secure and transparent virtual environment in the metaverse. Blockchain technology can also be used to create a decentralized system of governance in the metaverse that is resistant to corruption and manipulation. Here are some ways in which cybercrime in the Metaverse can be addressed:

- **Strengthening Security Measures**

Metaverse developers and platform owners must implement robust security measures to prevent cyber-attacks. They should also conduct regular vulnerability assessments and penetration testing to identify potential vulnerabilities in the system. Strengthening security measures is one of the most effective ways to control cybercrime in the Metaverse. Here are some ways in which this can be achieved:

- Two-Factor Authentication: Metaverse platforms should implement two-factor authentication (2FA) to make it harder for cybercriminals to gain unauthorized access to user accounts. 2FA adds an extra layer of security by requiring users to provide a second form of authentication, such as a code generated by an app, in addition to their password.
- Encryption: Metaverse platforms should use encryption to protect user data and prevent cyber criminals from intercepting sensitive information. This includes encrypting user login credentials, virtual assets, and personal data.
- Intrusion Detection and Prevention: Metaverse platforms should use intrusion detection and prevention systems (IDPS) to detect and prevent cyber-attacks. IDPS can detect unusual behavior patterns that may indicate a cyber-attack and automatically block any suspicious activity.

- Vulnerability Assessments and Penetration Testing: Regular vulnerability assessments and penetration testing can help identify potential vulnerabilities in the Metaverse platform. This can help platform owners and developers patch security holes before cybercriminals can exploit them.
- Secure Development Practices: Metaverse platforms should follow secure development practices to prevent the introduction of security vulnerabilities during the software development lifecycle. This includes using secure coding practices, conducting code reviews, and implementing secure software development policies.
- Third-Party Audits: Third-party audits can be used to assess the security posture of Metaverse platforms. Independent auditors can identify security weaknesses and recommend best practices to improve security.

By implementing these security measures, Metaverse platforms can reduce the risk of cybercrime and protect users from malicious attacks. However, it is important to note that security is an ongoing process, and Metaverse platforms must continuously monitor and update their security measures to stay ahead of cybercriminals.

- **Raising User Awareness**

Users of the Metaverse should be educated on the risks associated with cybercrime, such as phishing, identity theft, and virtual asset theft. Platforms should provide user education and awareness training to help users protect themselves from cyber threats. Raising user awareness is an important aspect of forecasting cybercrime in the metaverse. As virtual worlds become more prevalent and accessible to a wider range of users, individuals must be educated about the risks associated with using these platforms and the steps they can take to protect themselves. One way to raise user awareness is through educational campaigns that highlight the potential risks and provide guidance on how to stay safe while using virtual worlds. This can include providing information on best practices for securing personal information, avoiding phishing scams, and recognizing fraudulent activity. Another approach is to provide users with tools and resources that can help them identify and report suspicious behavior. For example, virtual world platforms can implement reporting systems that allow users to flag inappropriate behavior or suspected cybercrime. This can help to quickly identify and respond to potential threats.

Furthermore, virtual world platforms can also implement features that help users protect their personal information and assets. Ultimately, raising user awareness is an important component of forecasting cybercrime in the metaverse, as it can help to prevent individuals from falling victim to cybercriminals and increase the overall level of security in virtual worlds. By providing users with the knowledge and tools they need to protect themselves, we can create a safer and more secure virtual environment for everyone.

- **Collaboration and Information Sharing**

Collaboration and information sharing among Metaverse developers, security professionals, and law enforcement agencies can help identify potential cyber threats and vulnerabilities in the Metaverse. This could include sharing threat intelligence, best practices, and other relevant information. Collaboration and information sharing can be crucial in forecasting and preventing cybercrime in the metaverse. The metaverse is a vast and interconnected virtual world, and it is not just one organization or individual's responsibility to ensure its security. It requires the collective effort of all stakeholders, including technology providers, virtual world platform owners, law enforcement agencies, security researchers, and the users themselves.

One way to promote collaboration and information sharing is to establish a public-private partnership. This partnership can bring together different organizations and individuals to work towards a common goal of ensuring the security and safety of the metaverse. Through this partnership, stakeholders can share information about potential threats and vulnerabilities, collaborate on security research, and develop best practices and guidelines for security measures. Another way to promote collaboration and information sharing is to establish a platform for reporting cybercrime incidents in the metaverse. This platform can serve as a central repository of information about cybercrime incidents, enabling stakeholders to track trends and identify patterns of criminal activity. Law enforcement agencies can use this information to investigate and prosecute cybercriminals, while technology providers and platform owners can use it to develop better security solutions and protect their users.

Moreover, technology providers and virtual world platform owners can encourage information sharing among their users. They can provide training and educational resources to help users identify potential threats and protect themselves from cybercrime. They can also create forums and discussion boards where users can share information about potential threats and vulnerabilities. In conclusion, collaboration and information sharing can be valuable tools in forecasting and preventing cybercrime in the metaverse. Establishing public-private partnerships, creating a platform for reporting cybercrime incidents, and promoting user awareness and education can all contribute to a safer and more secure metaverse for all stakeholders. It is essential to recognize that preventing cybercrime in the metaverse requires a collective effort and a shared responsibility among all stakeholders.

- **Legal Frameworks:**

Governments can play a significant role in addressing cybercrime in the Metaverse by implementing legal frameworks and regulations to prevent and punish cybercriminal activities. This includes creating laws and regulations to protect virtual assets, personal data, and intellectual property. The use of a legal framework is a critical component in forecasting and preventing cybercrime in the metaverse. A legal framework can provide a set of rules and regulations for the virtual world, just as it does for the physical world. These rules and regulations can help establish boundaries for acceptable behavior and can define the consequences for those who engage in cybercriminal activities.

One approach to creating a legal framework for the metaverse is to apply existing laws that govern the physical world to the virtual world. This approach can help ensure that criminal activities in the metaverse are treated the same way as they would be in the physical world. It can also make it easier for law enforcement agencies to investigate and prosecute virtual crimes. Another approach is to create new laws specifically for the metaverse. These laws can be tailored to address the unique challenges and characteristics of virtual environments. For example, laws could be created to address virtual currency theft or the use of virtual avatars for cyberstalking. Additionally, international cooperation is crucial for the success of a legal framework in the metaverse. As the metaverse is a global environment, cybercriminals can operate from anywhere in the world. Therefore, a coordinated effort among international law enforcement agencies is necessary to prevent and address cybercrime in the metaverse.

Furthermore, the use of a legal framework can also provide a sense of accountability and responsibility among virtual citizens. It can encourage individuals to take responsibility for their actions in the metaverse and discourage them from engaging in illegal activities. In conclusion, the use of a legal framework is a critical component in forecasting and preventing cybercrime in the metaverse. A legal framework can help establish boundaries for acceptable behavior, define the consequences for those who engage in cybercriminal activities, and provide a sense of accountability among virtual citizens. A coordinated international effort is essential for the success of a legal framework in the metaverse.

- **Cybercrime Investigation and Prosecution**

Law enforcement agencies must be trained to investigate cybercrime in the Metaverse and prosecute cybercriminals. This includes working with Metaverse platform owners and security professionals to identify and apprehend cybercriminals. Cybercrime investigation and prosecution play a crucial role in forecasting cybercrime in the metaverse. It is essential to have effective investigation and prosecution methods to deter cybercriminals from committing crimes in the virtual world. Law enforcement agencies need to work together with virtual platform providers to ensure that cybercriminals are brought to justice.

One of the primary challenges in investigating cybercrime in the metaverse is the lack of physical evidence. Therefore, digital forensics becomes critical in investigating and prosecuting cybercrime. Law enforcement agencies need to have access to the latest tools and techniques for digital forensics to gather evidence and build a strong case against cyber criminals. Another challenge in investigating cybercrime in the metaverse is the jurisdictional issues. Virtual platforms can be accessed from anywhere in the world, making it difficult to determine which law enforcement agency has jurisdiction over the case. Therefore, international cooperation and collaboration are essential to investigate and prosecute cybercrime in the metaverse. In addition to traditional investigation and prosecution methods, new techniques such as blockchain forensics and AI-based threat intelligence can also be used to investigate cybercrime in the metaverse. Blockchain forensics can be used to trace the flow of virtual currencies and identify the individuals behind the transactions. AI-based threat intelligence can be used to analyze large volumes of data to identify patterns and anomalies that could indicate cybercriminal activity.

In conclusion, cybercrime investigation and prosecution are essential components of forecasting cybercrime in the metaverse. Law enforcement agencies need to work together with virtual platform providers, have access to the latest digital forensics tools and techniques, and collaborate internationally to investigate and prosecute cybercrime in the metaverse. The use of new techniques such as blockchain forensics and AI-based threat intelligence can also help in investigating cybercrime in the metaverse.

8. CONCLUSION

The emergence of the metaverse presents both opportunities and challenges for individuals and organizations alike. The vast amounts of data generated by virtual worlds offer immense potential for innovation and growth but also create new avenues for cybercrime. As virtual worlds become more prevalent and sophisticated, we must develop effective strategies for forecasting and mitigating cybercrime in the metaverse. To effectively navigate the metaverse, a multi-pronged approach is required that includes strengthening security measures, leveraging threat intelligence, using data analytics, implementing red teaming, and utilizing bug bounty programs. Collaboration and information sharing between organizations and government agencies are also essential to ensure timely identification and mitigation of cyber threats.

It is important to recognize that as the metaverse continues to evolve, so too will the tactics and methods used by cybercriminals. Therefore, ongoing research and development in the field of cybersecurity will be critical to staying ahead of the curve and protecting against emerging threats. In short, forecasting cybercrime in the metaverse is a complex and dynamic challenge that requires a concerted effort from all stakeholders. By adopting a proactive and collaborative approach, we can maximize the potential of virtual worlds while minimizing the risks associated with cybercrime. Addressing cybercrime in the Metaverse requires a comprehensive approach that involves strengthening security measures, raising user awareness, collaboration and information sharing, legal frameworks, and cybercrime investigation and prosecution. By taking a proactive approach, the Metaverse can be a safe and secure space for users to enjoy immersive experiences without the risk of cybercrime.

REFERENCES

BizJournal. (2010). Linden Lab. *BizJournals.* https://www.bizjournals.com/boston/blog/mass-high-tech/2010/07/linden-labs-second-life-in-a-catch-22-over.html

Crowdstrike. (2023). *12 Types of Malware + Examples That You Should Know*. Crowdstrike. https://www.crowdstrike.com/cybersecurity-101/malware/types-of-malware/.

Cyberpedia. (2023). What is Digital Identity Theft? *Bitdefender Cyberpedia.* https://www.bitdefender.com/cyberpedia/what-is-digital-identity-theft/

CyberTalents. (2023). What is Cyber Crime? Types, Examples, and Prevention. *Cybertalents.* https://cybertalents.com/blog/what-is-cyber-crime-types-examples-and-prevention

Folger, J. (2022). What Does Metaverse Mean and How Does This Virtual World Work? *Investopedia.* https://www.investopedia.com/metaverse-definition-5206578

Fortinet. (2023). What is a DDoS Attack? DDoS Meaning, Definition & Types. *Fortinet.* https://www.fortinet.com/resources/cyberglossary/ddos-attack (accessed: Apr. 17, 2023).

García-Zanabria, G., Raimundo, M. M., Poco, J., Nery, M. B., Silva, C. T., Adorno, S., & Nonato, L. G. (2022, December 1). CriPAV: Street-Level Crime Patterns Analysis and Visualization. *IEEE Transactions on Visualization and Computer Graphics*, *28*(12), 4000–4015. doi:10.1109/TVCG.2021.3111146 PMID:34516376

Hoppe, D. (2021). *Skin Trade: Preventing and Punishing Digital Asset Theft*. Gamma. https://gammalaw.com/skin-trade-preventing-and-punishing-digital-asset-theft/

ISC2. (2021). *The Threat of Insecure Interfaces and APIs*. ISC2. https://www.isc2.org/Articles/the-threat-of-insecure-interfaces-and-apis.

Kaper Sky. (2023). *What is Social Engineering? Definition*. Kaspersky.

King, J. (2009). *Gamer steals from the virtual world to pay real debts.* Reuters. https://www.reuters.com/article/us-gaming-theft-idUSTRE56141L20090702.

Liang, W., Cao, J., Chen, L., Wang, Y., Wu, J., Beheshti, A., & Tang, J. (2023, October). Crime Prediction With Missing Data Via Spatiotemporal Regularized Tensor Decomposition. *IEEE Transactions on Big Data*, *9*(5), 1392–1407. doi:10.1109/TBDATA.2023.3283098

Mandalapu, V., Elluri, L., Vyas, P., & Roy, N. (2023). Crime Prediction Using Machine Learning and Deep Learning: A Systematic Review and Future Directions. *IEEE Access : Practical Innovations, Open Solutions*, *11*, 60153–60170. doi:10.1109/ACCESS.2023.3286344

Tam, S., & Tanriöver, Ö. Ö. (2023). Multimodal Deep Learning Crime Prediction Using Tweets. *IEEE Access : Practical Innovations, Open Solutions*, *11*, 93204–93214. doi:10.1109/ACCESS.2023.3308967

Tasnim, N., Imam, I. T., & Hashem, M. M. A. (2022). A Novel Multi-Module Approach to Predict Crime Based on Multivariate Spatio-Temporal Data Using Attention and Sequential Fusion Model. *IEEE Access : Practical Innovations, Open Solutions*, *10*, 48009–48030. doi:10.1109/ACCESS.2022.3171843

Trendmicro. (2023). Cybercriminals - Definition. *Trendmicro*. https://www.trendmicro.com/vinfo/us/security/definition/cybercriminals

Trendmicro. (2023). Data Breach - Definition. *Trendmicro*. https://www.trendmicro.com/vinfo/us/security/definition/data-breach (accessed: Apr. 17, 2023).

Wu, J., Lin, K., Lin, D., Zheng, Z., Huang, H., & Zheng, Z. (2023). Financial Crimes in Web3-Empowered Metaverse: Taxonomy, Countermeasures, and Opportunities. *IEEE Open Journal of the Computer Society*, *4*, 37–49. doi:10.1109/OJCS.2023.3245801

Chapter 4
Online Crime in the Metaverse:
A Study on Classification, Prediction, and Mitigation Strategies

John Blake
https://orcid.org/0000-0002-3150-4995
University of Aizu, Japan

ABSTRACT

With the burgeoning growth of the metaverse and online virtual environments, new security challenges have been introduced that require careful exploration and mitigation. An increasing proportion of human interactions and transactions now take place in these digital spaces, making it essential to protect users and ensure the safety and integrity of virtual worlds. This chapter explores three dimensions of this issue. First, through a study of the types of crimes that occur in these environments, to gain a holistic understanding of the cybercrime technoscape. Second, the authors use a two-pronged approach to increase the safety of the metaverse by targeting both potential perpetrators and victims. This is achievable by identifying indicators that may be used to detect potential perpetrators or victims. Thirdly and finally, strategies and techniques to make these online communities safer are suggested.

1. INTRODUCTION

Online virtual environments, such as the Metaverse, are interconnected, immersive spaces that transcend traditional digital boundaries, linking together multiple three-dimensional virtual worlds. This dynamic technoscape is able to amalgamate augmented reality and virtual reality. The metaverse has experienced exponential growth (Lee, 2022), becoming a nexus for social interaction, entertainment, education, and economic activity (Khalid, 2023). The combination of technological advancements, increased accessibility, and a shift towards remote engagement has fueled this expansion, transforming the metaverse into a complex transactional space where digital assets, services, and experiences are exchanged. In an era marked by digital convergence and globalization, the emergence of the Metaverse underscores a paradigmatic shift in how individuals interact, transact, and perceive both virtuality and reality. As

DOI: 10.4018/979-8-3693-0220-0.ch004

with real-world transactions of assets, services and experiences, such spaces also attract perpetrators of opportunistic or premeditated crimes. In the physical world a teenager who notices a mobile phone left on a seat, but pockets the device on the spur of the moment. Likewise, a player in a massive online multiplayer game may come across a naïve player who may be convinced to share details of passwords and usernames, that may ultimately result in the loss of the associated digital assets (DaCosta & Seok, 2020).

In the physical world, police forces serve a variety of essential functions aimed at maintaining public order, enforcing laws, and ensuring the safety and well-being of citizens. Through patrolling, community policing, and various crime prevention programs, police work to deter criminal activities before they occur, and maintain a safe and orderly environment for all members of the community. However, the concept of policing in the metaverse raises complex and evolving questions. Traditional policing within virtual environments is a developing and largely uncharted territory (Rosenberg, 2022).

While the ramifications of cybercrimes are well-understood (Aiken et al., 2019), there exists a significant research gap in the development of a comprehensive framework that can not only classify the diverse and evolving nature of these crimes but also predict potential perpetrators and victims, and proactively mitigate occurrences. Existing methods often suffer from fragmentation, relying on disparate tools and techniques that lack cohesion and adaptability to the fast-changing cyber landscape. The absence of a unified approach hampers the ability to understand, analyze, and effectively respond to cybercrimes, leaving communities and individuals at heightened risk. This article seeks to address this research gap by exploring avenues that can be adopted to address the unique challenges of cybercrime.

The following section provides an indicative taxonomy of crimes which may be committed in the Metaverse, some of these cybercrimes can be classed as fully online while others are hybrid, and include both digital-initiated and physical-initiated hybrid crimes. Chanda and Snowe (2022) proposed a multilevel theoretical taxonomy of cybercrimes with a focus on the target of the crime, namely the technological ecosystem or specific victims, e.g. indivdiuals or organisations. Different categories of crimes are next introduced beginning with the crimes most commonly associated with cybercrime, such as cyberstalking and identity theft (Awadallah et al., 2023). However, the multitude of crimes that can be committed or initiated online is much broader. Having established the range of crimes, the focus turns to prediction, specifically the prediction of potential perpetrators and victims. Sociodemographic factors related to perpetrators are first considered. The traits and behaviours of potential victims are next discussed. Statistical models that could be used for risk assessment are described and explained. The final focus is on ways to make online platforms safer though the use of various mitigation strategies, such as moderation, education, detection and regulation.

2. CRIME SPACES

Cybercrimes operate across distinct domains that can be categorized into three specific spaces: virtual, hybrid, and physical. In the virtual space, crimes are committed entirely online; the hybrid realm encompasses crimes transitioning between online and offline worlds; and the physical space refers to tangible geographic locations tied to criminal activities in the Metaverse. Each crime space presents its own challenges and intricacies. The term crime space denotes the environment in which these offenses take place, while geographic regions refer to the tangible locations connected to the crime, which may or may not coincide with the locations of the perpetrators or victims. The complex interplay between these creates a web of jurisdictional challenges, conflicting laws, data privacy concerns, and legal enforcement rights (Buck, 2022). These complexities magnify the difficulties in both apprehending offenders and protecting victims, particularly when they span different geographic regions. A detailed exploration of the three crime spaces and the geographic locations of crimes are subject of the subsequent sections.

2.1 Fully Online Crimes

Fully online cybercrimes are committed in the digital space. This means that the entire criminal activity, from inception to execution, takes place within the boundaries of the internet or a digital network. These types of crimes often exploit the anonymity provided by the Metaverse and can have global impacts due to the borderless nature of digital networks. One illustrative example is the propagation of ransomware, where malicious code is both crafted and transmitted online to encrypt victims' files, with ransom demands typically facilitated through cryptocurrencies (Bele, 2021). Another example is online identity theft, where personal information is illicitly obtained, traded, and exploited entirely within the confines of the digital network. These crimes may also encompass elaborate phishing schemes that deceive individuals into divulging sensitive information, akin to a complex web spun by a spider to ensnare unwitting prey. The inception, planning, and execution of these cybercrimes all occur in a virtual space, making them both challenging to trace and uniquely adaptable to the rapidly evolving technological landscape. The insular nature of these crimes necessitates specialized law enforcement techniques, tools, and collaboration across jurisdictions, mirroring the complex international efforts needed to combat infectious diseases that are confined to specific regions yet have far-reaching impacts.

2.2 Hybrid Crimes

Some crimes are neither purely digital nor physical but instead straddle both worlds, encompassing elements of online and offline interaction. These hybrid or cross-over crimes reflect the interconnectedness of our digital and physical lives. For instance, criminals may utilize virtual platforms like the Metaverse to find and contact potential victims, subsequently engaging in illegal activities in the physical world, such as theft, assault, or other forms of offline harm. An illustrative example is an online predator using a social networking site (SNS) to carefully cultivate a relationship with a potential victim, gradually building trust and intimacy, before arranging a physical meeting where they commit an assault or abduction. Another instance is an online scam where victims are skillfully manipulated to send money or provide personal information online, which the perpetrator then leverages offline to commit theft or fraud. These crimes are analogous to a bridge connecting two separate lands, where the digital initiation leads to tangible, real-world consequences. These types of crimes underscore the intricate web of connectivity between online activities and offline ramifications, reinforcing the need for comprehensive and detailed legal and protective measures.

Conversely, physical-initiated hybrid crimes begin in the offline world and culminate or extend into the digital domain. A case in point is a traditional burglary where stolen physical documents, such as credit cards or personal identification, are subsequently used online to make unauthorized purchases or create fraudulent digital identities. Another example is corporate espionage, where confidential information obtained through physical infiltration is then disseminated or sold online, transforming a localized crime into a global breach. This category of crimes can be likened to a river flowing from its source into a vast ocean, where the physical act is merely the beginning of a broader online exploitation. The dual nature of these crimes requires a multifaceted approach to prevention, investigation, and prosecution, embracing both the tangible origins and the virtual extensions of the criminal act. Together, digital- and physical-initiated hybrid crimes demonstrate the complexity and breadth of the challenges facing law enforcement and society in an increasingly interconnected world, calling for innovative and coordinated responses that transcend traditional boundaries.

2.3 Physical World Crimes

Physical assault and murder, as direct physical acts of violence, cannot be committed online. These crimes necessitate a tangible, real-world interaction between the offender and the victim. However, the line between the physical and virtual worlds is becoming increasingly blurred, and crimes such as these may find their origins in the Metaverse (Laue, 2011). Within this vast virtual environment, perpetrators can engage in victim selection, planning, and even conspiring with others. The use of the Metaverse for these preliminary activities has added a new dimension to traditional criminal patterns, intertwining the physical with the virtual. The connection between these worlds further complicates the nature of criminal investigations, as law enforcement must navigate both the digital trails left by criminals and the tangible evidence found in the physical world.

In addition to the challenges posed by the intertwining of the digital and physical worlds, the international nature of the crime space further complicates criminal investigations. Crimes may span across several geographic regions, weaving a complex web that transcends traditional borders. For example, a perpetrator located in the United Kingdom might target a victim in China, all within the virtual confines of the Metaverse, hosted on servers in the United States. This scenario is not merely theoretical but increasingly common in the age of global connectivity. Such international crimes raise intricate issues regarding jurisdiction, involving multiple legal systems, conflicting laws, and even language barriers. Law enforcement agencies must navigate multiple barriers, coordinating across different countries and cultures, to trace the intricate pathways of crime that flow between the physical locations of the offender, victim, and the virtual platforms that connect them. To better understand the crimescape (Dao & Thrill, 2022), it is necessary to gain a holistic overview of the categories of crimes that populate one or more of the crime spaces.

3. TYPES OF CRIMINAL OFFENSES

Crimes can be categorized by various factors, including the intent of the perpetrator and the nature of the act. For instance, heinous acts like murder or rape, which are considered inherently evil, fall under the category of *malum in se*. Conversely, crimes deemed *malum prohibitum* are not inherently evil but are prohibited by law. This classification is further nuanced by the jurisdiction in which a crime is committed, ranging from national and federal to provincial and municipal levels (Bovenzi, 2023). Different legal systems, such as Sharia law, common law, civil or continental law, tribal law, religious law, customary law, socialist law, and international law, offer unique interpretations and enforcements of criminal activities. Among these legal systems, distinctions emerge, such as the absence of legal precedents in civil law, in contrast to their importance in common law. Despite these variations, there are underlying commonalities in the types of acts considered criminal offenses across diverse legal systems. The following subsections introduce stereotypical digital and conventional crimes, but show how the borders between the types are becoming blurred.

3.1 Digital Crimes

Crimes occurring within the virtual environment of the Metaverse include a range of activities such as cyberstalking, online harassment, identity theft, cyber fraud, and cyberterrorism. These crimes often exploit the interconnected nature of the Metaverse and the anonymity it can provide. For example, cyberstalking and online harassment (Kaur et al., 2020), which involve persistent threats, intimidation, or abuse, are becoming increasingly prevalent within the virtual worlds of the Metaverse. Individuals may be targeted through virtual avatars or defamatory accusations, leading to emotional trauma or even real-world legal consequences. Identity theft, another pervasive crime within the Metaverse, often manifests through phishing scams (Qin & Hui, 2022). Perpetrators may use deceptive virtual storefronts or in-game communications to lure victims into divulging sensitive information, enabling fraudulent financial activities (Katterbauer 2023, Wu et al, 2022). The expansive and immersive nature of the Metaverse can make it difficult for users to differentiate between legitimate interactions and malicious intent. Similarly, cyber fraud encompasses a broad spectrum of scams executed through the various platforms and channels of the Metaverse. From bogus virtual real estate deals to fraudulent e-commerce transactions, these scams leverage the trust and ignorance of users to extract money or valuable digital assets. Lastly, cyberterrorism and hacktivism have found a new battleground within the Metaverse. Whether by sabotaging virtual infrastructure or using the platform to coordinate real-world attacks, these acts present unique challenges to national security and societal stability. An example might be the hacking of a prominent virtual city's security system within the Metaverse to make a political statement or demand change. These crimes highlight the complex landscape of criminal behavior within the Metaverse.

3.2 Conventional Crimes

Conventional crimes, rooted in the physical world, have long been recognized and categorized by legal systems worldwide. These crimes range from theft, assault, and robbery to more serious offenses like murder and arson. Traditional law enforcement has developed methodologies and practices to address these acts of criminality that manifest in tangible, physical spaces. However, with the advent of digital technology and the growth of online platforms, including the Metaverse, a shift has occurred, blurring the lines between conventional and digital crimes. This new frontier has given birth to hybrid crimes, where conventional criminal activities are initiated or executive online. Inchoate crimes, such as conspiracy to commit a physical crime, are now often planned and coordinated within the virtual space of the Metaverse. Criminal minds can convene in virtual meeting rooms to plot robberies or coordinate the smuggling of illegal goods (Lusthaus & Varese, 2017). Statutory crimes have also found a home online. Selling controlled substances or distributing child pornography, once confined to shadowy corners of the physical world, now operate through anonymous online marketplaces. A drug dealer in one country can connect with a buyer in another, all within the virtual walls of the Metaverse, leading to real-world transactions, facilitated by technological advancements of virtual reality and cryptocurrencies. Moreover, crimes such as human trafficking have begun to utilize online platforms for recruitment and coercion. The Metaverse may host virtual venues where traffickers lure unsuspecting victims, leading to real-life abductions and exploitation. This shift from conventional to hybrid crimes has introduced new challenges for law enforcement.

4. PREDICTING POTENTIAL PERPETRATORS AND VICTIMS OF CYBERCRIMES

Various factors can contribute to an individual's likelihood of becoming a perpetrator or victim of online crimes. These factors range from personal attributes such as age, gender, and occupation to behavioral tendencies and digital literacy. With the emergence of new technologies and methodologies, including predictive models and forensic linguistics, it is now possible to analyze the underlying patterns related to criminal activities. The following sections will explore how potential perpetrators and victims may be identified.

4.1 Potential Perpetrators

Potential perpetrators of online crimes can be analyzed through various dimensions, including the perception of anonymity, sociodemographic factors, personality traits, and previous criminal history. This section explores these aspects, helping to understand and predict who might engage in such activities.

The sense of anonymity online, created through the use of pseudonyms, VPNs, and other techniques to obscure true identity, can lower inhibitions and foster a detachment from reality. People who might never contemplate engaging in conventional crimes may be drawn to online criminal behavior, due to the perception that such actions are untraceable or exist behind a digital persona, reducing accountability. The effects of cybercrimes might be more abstract or distant compared to the immediate and visible impacts of physical crimes, creating a disconnect between actions and their real-world consequences.

Predicting the likelihood of an individual engaging in cybercrime is complex. Various sociodemographic factors, such as age, gender, education, and occupation, can provide insights. Teenagers with advanced technological skills, for example, may be more likely to participate in cybercrimes, and male perpetrators outnumber females, which is the case across all crime spaces. Individuals in IT-related fields are armed with the necessary skills to carry out cybercrimes.

Personality traits also play a role in predicting cybercriminal behavior. Traits such as high levels of curiosity, a preference for anonymity, a desire for thrill or challenge, and lower levels of empathy or moral engagement may be indicative. Narcissism and antisocial traits may also be common among cybercriminals.

Additionally, a previous criminal history, especially related to technology-based offenses, may indicate a higher propensity for future cybercriminal activities. Past behavior can often predict future behavior, particularly if it involves repetitive and compulsive criminal activities. However, the cybercrime context may also include first-time offenders who are technologically proficient without a previous criminal record.

While creating assessments and profiles to predict potential cybercriminal behavior might seem a laudable goal, the vast array of factors involved creates significant challenges. A comprehensive understanding that combines sociodemographic information, personality analysis, and exploration of past behaviors may offer valuable insights. Still, the dynamic and evolving landscape of online criminality requires ongoing research, vigilance, and adaptation. Understanding and addressing the unique characteristics of potential online criminals is crucial in the ongoing fight against cybercrime.

4.2 Potential Victims

Understanding the potential victims of online crimes involves examining factors such as the availability of personal information online, digital habits, and digital literacy, all of which can determine an individual's susceptibility to cybercrimes. The ease with which personal information can be accessed plays a vital role in making individuals potential targets. For example, those who actively participate and overshare in the metaverse may inadvertently expose themselves to cybercriminals. This information, such as personal details and preferences, can be exploited in highly personalized attacks like spear phishing or even lead to identity theft.

Individual digital habits also contribute to the likelihood of becoming a victim. Behaviors that may seem inconsequential, such as the use of weak or easily guessable passwords or downloading files from unverified sources, can significantly elevate the risk. The absence of robust security measures, like multi-factor authentication, leaves individuals more vulnerable to attacks.

Digital literacy, the competence to interact with technology safely and effectively, is a crucial determinant of vulnerability. Individuals who lack awareness of cybersecurity best practices or the risks associated with various online activities are more likely to fall prey to cybercrimes. The correlation between time spent in the metaverse and the likelihood of victimization underscores the importance of digital literacy in safeguarding against potential threats.

Furthermore, specific demographic groups may also be at higher risk. For example, younger or older individuals may lack the awareness or experience to recognize and ward off cyber threats, while those in high-profile or sensitive occupations may be specifically targeted for valuable information or access.

The profile of potential victims of cybercrimes is shaped by a combination of personal choices, behaviors, and levels of digital sophistication. Addressing these vulnerabilities requires not just technological solutions but also education and awareness. A multifaceted approach that encompasses robust security measures, awareness of potential risks, and responsible digital conduct can mitigate the risk and protect potential victims from the increasingly complex and targeted nature of online criminal activities. By understanding these dynamics, strategies can be developed to safeguard individuals and communities in both the physical world and the metaverse.

4.3 Predictive Models

The challenge of identifying potential perpetrators and victims of online crimes has led to the development of sophisticated techniques, leveraging both predictive models and forensic linguistics. These methods provide insights and offer innovative ways to predict and respond to online criminal activities, though they come with their own set of challenges and ethical considerations.

Predictive models, such as deep learning algorithms and Large Language Models (LLMs), have been employed to analyze various factors associated with both perpetrators and victims. By examining sociodemographic factors, digital behaviors, and other relevant indicators, these models can predict potential threats and vulnerabilities. For example, machine learning algorithms can analyze patterns in online behavior to detect individuals who might be more prone to engage in or fall victim to cybercrimes. However, the accuracy of predictive models can vary widely, influenced by the complexity and rapidly evolving nature of cybercrimes. Inconsistent data, shifting tactics of criminals, and the multidimensional aspects of online behavior can contribute to inaccuracies in prediction. Furthermore, privacy concerns arise from the extensive data collection required for these models, raising ethical questions about consent and the potential misuse of sensitive information.

Alongside predictive models, forensic linguistics presents a complementary approach. Forensic linguistics focuses on analyzing the language used in digital communication, uncovering hidden patterns, and identifying unique linguistic fingerprints. This can include the examination of word choices, syntax, and rhetorical strategies used by individuals online. For instance, forensic linguistics can reveal clues about the identity or intentions of potential perpetrators, such as recognizing specific speech patterns associated with antisocial behavior. Conversely, the language used by potential victims, such as expressions of naivete or lack of technical understanding, might signal vulnerability.

While both predictive models and forensic linguistics offer valuable tools in the fight against online crimes, they are not without limitations. The dynamic nature of language, the risk of false positives, and the ethical implications of surveillance and profiling must be carefully considered. The combination of predictive modeling and forensic linguistics provides a multifaceted approach to identifying potential perpetrators and victims of online crimes. The integration of these techniques, balanced with ethical considerations and a deep understanding of the complex nature of cybercrimes, can enhance the ability to detect and prevent criminal activities in both physical and digital realms. By continually refining these methods and considering their broader societal implications, it is possible to create more effective strategies to protect individuals and communities in an increasingly interconnected world.

When identities may be concealed or manipulated, the potential for malicious activities is a grave concern. Authorship profiling, a technique that constructs a profile of an unknown author based on their linguistic features, becomes an essential tool in tracking such individuals. By closely examining words, syntax, and style used in virtual interactions, platforms can discern patterns of abusive or fraudulent behavior. Once these patterns are detected, actions can be taken to warn, restrict, or ban the individuals responsible, helping to maintain a sense of trust and integrity within the virtual world. Ensuring the authenticity of interactions is another critical aspect of security. The Metaverse is likely to host many transactions and communications that require verification. Authorship attribution, with its capacity to match an unknown text to a known author, can assist in confirming the legitimacy of these communications or contracts. This technique can significantly reduce the risk of phishing or impersonation scams, safeguarding users from potential fraud. In cases where legal intervention is required, forensic linguistics can provide essential support. Using sophisticated machine learning algorithms and a detailed analysis of linguistic features, law enforcement can trace the source of these illegal activities. The application of forensic linguistics offers a toolkit for addressing safety and security challenges. By identifying malicious actors, ensuring authenticity, combating cyberbullying, and supporting law enforcement, forensic linguistics can make a valuable contribution to online safety.

5. MITIGATION STRATEGIES TO INCREASE SAFETY IN CYBERSPACE

The safety of online communities can be improved through various strategies, including effective moderation, education and awareness programs, the use of AI and machine learning for security, and stronger cyber laws. Effective moderation is essential in identifying and dealing with potentially harmful behavior. This involves monitoring online discussions or content to identify and respond to inappropriate behavior or content, which can include bullying, harassment, and misinformation. Education and awareness programs play a key role in reducing cybercrime. By teaching users how to recognize scams, use strong passwords, and adopt safe digital habits, we can greatly reduce their risk of becoming victims. AI may help enhance online security by automatically detecting and responding to threats. Stronger cyber laws and regulations could help deter potential cybercriminals and protect users. In order to enforce such laws, international cooperation is needed to effectively address cybercrime, given its global nature.

5.1 Moderation

Moderation is a standard method of both ensuring the suitability of content and increasing the safety of online forums. Online crime monitoring provides researchers with opportunities to improve both the prediction and detection of crimes (Décary-Hétu, 2017). Previously, such forums were primarily text-based, and moderators would be responsible for flagging and/or removing potentially harmful content, such as hate speech, misinformation, or content that violates community standards. With the move to multimodal virtual spaces that can display texts and images, and enable the sharing of audio and video files or streams, the role and complexity of moderation have evolved substantially. In these multimodal platforms, moderation must adapt to monitor not only written text but also visual and auditory content. For example, video-sharing platforms like YouTube employ both human moderators and sophisticated algorithms to review and manage a vast array of content ranging from user-generated videos to live streams. Similarly, social media platforms like Facebook and Instagram implement layered moderation processes, encompassing automated filters to detect explicit content, human oversight to handle nuanced context, and community-driven reporting systems. Virtual reality spaces, like those found in online gaming or the Metaverse, further push the boundaries of moderation by introducing real-time interactions that require immediate response to ensure safety and compliance with community guidelines. The task of moderation in these complex environments can be likened to the role of a traffic controller in a bustling city, coordinating the flow and behavior of various modes of transportation. Just as the controller must adapt to different vehicles and routes, online moderation must be dynamic and versatile, ready to respond to the myriad forms of content and interaction that digital technology enables. Moderation involves continuous collaboration between platform developers, content creators, users, and regulatory bodies to foster a safe and respectful virtual community.

5.2 Education

Education is presented as a solution to many societal problems. By integrating comprehensive educational programs that focus on the legal, ethical, and practical aspects of online conduct, we can cultivate a more responsible and aware digital citizenry. Such programs can be implemented at various educational levels, with a particular emphasis on the impressionable youth, to demonstrate that crimes committed online are tantamount to those committed in the physical world. Understanding the consequences of cybercrime not only enhances individual responsibility but also fosters a collective consciousness that prioritizes the safety and integrity of online platforms. This approach goes beyond mere punitive measures, addressing the root of the problem by instilling values that discourage engaging in unlawful online activities. The provision of education and awareness-raising programs acts as a preventative measure, thereby laying the foundation for a more secure and trustworthy digital environment. By investing in such initiatives, society can take a proactive stance against cybercrime, aligning education with the broader goal of technological advancement without sacrificing security and ethical conduct.

5.3 Automatic Threat Detection and Response

Automatic threat detection and response systems represent a sophisticated evolution in cyber-security measures, akin to predictive policing in the real world. Utilizing advanced algorithms and machine learning models, these systems can analyze patterns of behavior and historical data to identify potential hotspots where cybercrime is more likely to occur. Just as law enforcement might target dark streets in dangerous areas, these algorithms identify vulnerable nodes, suspicious users, and at-risk individuals within digital networks. By predicting potential threats, automatic response mechanisms can then be deployed to preemptively secure vulnerable areas, neutralize suspicious activities, or even warn potential targets before the crime occurs. Such proactive measures represent a significant shift from reactive security protocols, facilitating a more agile and adaptive defense against ever-evolving cyber threats. However, this approach also raises important ethical considerations, such as the risk of false positives or the potential infringement on individual privacy. The balance between enhanced security and the preservation of fundamental rights is a delicate one, necessitating rigorous oversight and transparent governance of these technological tools. Ultimately, the integration of automatic threat detection and response can be a valuable component in a multi-faceted strategy to create safer online platforms, provided it is implemented with a keen understanding of its potential benefits and challenges.

5.4 Increased Regulation and Cyber Laws

The safety of online platforms transcends the purview of individual responsibility, demanding a concerted effort between businesses, organizations, and governments through the formulation and enforcement of robust cyber laws and regulations, particularly the role of criminal law (Lee, 2022). This trilateral collaboration can be likened to the harmonious functioning of an ecosystem where each entity plays a vital role. Businesses, acting as the primary stakeholders in online platforms, must adhere to standardized security protocols, akin to following construction codes in physical infrastructure. Organizations, including NGOs and international bodies, serve as the mediators and policy advocates, paralleling watchdog groups that ensure environmental compliance. Governments, on the other hand, enact and enforce legislation, mirroring their role in regulating public health and safety. An illustrative example might be the General Data Protection Regulation (GDPR) in the European Union, where cross-sector collaboration has led to a comprehensive legal framework that protects user privacy and ensures corporate accountability. The interdependency between these entities creates a fabric of checks and balances, collectively advancing the shared goal of online safety. The synergy realized through this cooperative approach fosters a more resilient digital landscape, one in which the rules of engagement are clearly defined and uniformly applied, in the same way that traffic regulations that maintain orderly conduct on roadways. This unified strategy represents a sophisticated response to the complex challenge of cybercrime, aligning the interests and efforts of diverse stakeholders in the pursuit of a safer online world.

6.CONCLUSION

The advent and rise of the metaverse and online virtual environments present unique challenges that demand innovative solutions to ensure the safety and security of all users. This digital evolution has, unfortunately, given rise to new forms of crime that defy conventional regulations and law enforcement strategies, thus necessitating a thorough understanding of this changing landscape. In-depth exploration of the types of cybercrimes occurring in these new environments is crucial. This includes not only traditional forms of cybercrime like phishing, hacking, and identity theft, but also emerging crimes unique to virtual environments like virtual asset theft, abuse of avatars, and manipulation of virtual economies.

Identifying potential perpetrators is a complex but vital task. Understanding the sociodemographic factors, personality traits, and previous criminal history that could indicate potential cybercriminals helps law enforcement agencies in prediction, prevention, and timely intervention. It is important to note, however, that the anonymity and expansive nature of the metaverse can often obscure the identities of perpetrators. Sophisticated and technologically advanced identification techniques may be able to create models to identify potential crime spaces, and perpetrators. Equally important is the identification of potential victims. By recognizing the risk factors such as personal information availability, digital habits, and level of digital literacy, preventive measures can be effectively put into place. Education plays a key role here, by equipping users with the knowledge to navigate these virtual environments safely and wisely. Implementing effective safety strategies is the final and perhaps most critical step. This encompasses the development and enforcement of strong cyber laws, the use of AI and machine learning for improved security, the provision of robust moderation, and the establishment of comprehensive education and awareness programs.

The metaverse's potential is boundless, but with it comes a responsibility to ensure its spaces are safe and secure for all users. By committing to an ongoing understanding of cybercrimes, potential perpetrators and victims, and adopting innovative safety strategies, we can build a metaverse that is not only immersive and engaging but also a secure environment for users worldwide.

REFERENCES

Aiken, M., Mc Mahon, C., Haughton, C., O'Neill, L., & O'Carroll, E. (2019). A consideration of the social impact of cybercrime: examples from hacking, piracy, and child abuse material online. In *Crime and Society* (pp. 91–109). Routledge. doi:10.4324/9781351207430-7

Awadallah, A. M., Damiani, E., Zemerly, J., & Yeun, C. Y. (2023, March). Identity Threats in the Metaverse and Future Research Opportunities. In *2023 International Conference on Business Analytics for Technology and Security (ICBATS)* (pp. 1-6). IEEE. https://doi.org/10.1109/ICBATS57792.2023.10111122

Bele, J. L. (2021). Cryptocurrencies as facilitators of cybercrime. In *The 3rd Eastern European Conference of Management and Economics (EECME 2021) – Sustainable Development in Modern Knowledge Society*. (*Vol. 111*, p. 01005). SHS Web of Conferences. EDP Sciences. 10.1051hsconf/202111101005

Bovenzi, G. M. (2023, April). MetaCrimes: Criminal accountability for conducts in the Metaverse. In *Companion Proceedings of the ACM Web Conference 2023 (pp. 565-567).* ACM Digital Library. 10.1145/3543873.3587535

Buck, L., & McDonnell, R. (2022). Security and privacy in the metaverse: The threat of the digital human. *Proceedings of the 1st Workshop on Novel Challenges of Safety, Security and Privacy in Extended Reality.* ACM.

Chandra, A., & Snowe, M. J. (2020). A taxonomy of cybercrime: Theory and design. *International Journal of Accounting Information Systems, 38*, 100467. doi:10.1016/j.accinf.2020.100467

DaCosta, B., & Seok, S. (2020). Cybercrime in Online Gaming. In M. Khosrow-Pour D.B.A. (Ed.), Encyclopedia of Criminal Activities and the Deep Web (pp. 881-892). IGI Global. doi:10.4018/978-1-5225-9715-5.ch059

Dao, T. H. D., & Thill, J. C. (2022). CrimeScape: Analysis of socio-spatial associations of urban residential motor vehicle theft. *Social Science Research*, *101*, 102618. doi:10.1016/j.ssresearch.2021.102618 PMID:34823669

Décary-Hétu, D. (2017). *Online crime monitoring. The Routledge International Handbook of Forensic Intelligence and Criminology*. Routledge. doi:10.4324/9781315541945-20

Katterbauer, K., Hassan, S. Y. E. D., & Cleenewerck, L. (2022). Financial cybercrime in the Islamic finance metaverse. *Journal of Metaverse*, *2*(2), 56–61. doi:10.57019/jmv.1108783

Kaur, P., Dhir, A., Tandon, A., Alzeiby, E. A., & Abohassan, A. A. (2021). A systematic literature review on cyberstalking. An analysis of past achievements and future promises. *Technological Forecasting and Social Change*, *163*, 120426. doi:10.1016/j.techfore.2020.120426

Khalid, F. (2023). Metaverse is the Next Normal and Digital Future: A Systematic Review. In *2023 IEEE International Conference on Emerging Trends in Engineering, Sciences and Technology (ICES&T)* (pp. 1-7). IEEE. https://doi.org/10.1109/ICEST56843.2023.10138832

Laue, C. (2011). Crime potential of metaverses. In *Virtual worlds and criminality* (pp. 19–29). Springer Berlin Heidelberg. doi:10.1007/978-3-642-20823-2_2

Lee, L. H. (2022, October). The Digital Big Bang in the Metaverse Era. In *2022 IEEE International Symposium on Mixed and Augmented Reality Adjunct (ISMAR-Adjunct) (pp. 55-55)*. IEEE. 10.1109/ISMAR-Adjunct57072.2022.00020

Lee, W. S. (2022). A Study on the Role of criminal law in Metaverse. *Institute for Legal Studies Chonnam National University, 177-202*. doi:10.38133/cnulawreview.2022.42.3.177

Lusthaus, J., & Varese, F. (2021). Offline and local: The hidden face of cybercrime. *Policing*. *Policing (Oxford, England)*, *15*(1), 4–14. doi:10.1093/police/pax042

Qin, H. X., Wang, Y., & Hui, P. (2022). Identity, crimes, and law enforcement in the metaverse. arXiv preprint arXiv:2210.06134. https://doi.org//arXiv.2210.06134 doi:10.48550

Rosenberg, L. (2022, March). Regulation of the Metaverse: A Roadmap: The risks and regulatory solutions for largescale consumer platforms. In *Proceedings of the 6th international conference on virtual and augmented reality simulations* (pp. 21-26). ACM. 10.1145/3546607.3546611

Wu, J., Lin, K., Lin, D., Zheng, Z., Huang, H., & Zheng, Z. (2023). Financial Crimes in Web3-empowered Metaverse: Taxonomy, Countermeasures, and Opportunities. *IEEE Open Journal of the Computer Society*, *4*, 37–49. doi:10.1109/OJCS.2023.3245801

Chapter 5
Predicting Future Cybercrime Trends in the Metaverse Era

Wasswa Shafik
https://orcid.org/0000-0002-9320-3186
School of Digital Science, Universiti Brunei Darussalam, Brunei & Dig Connectivity Research Laboratory (DCRLab), Uganda

ABSTRACT

The Metaverse is a virtual world where users can engage with each other and digital objects in real time, and its usage is growing significantly. However, the rise of virtual environments comes with the risk of cybercrime. This chapter presents the current cybercrime overview in the metaverse by examining recent incidents and standard methods cybercriminals employ. Moreover, it explores factors that could influence cybercrime trends in the Metaverse era, including technological advancements and evolving security measures. Furthermore, it evaluates current and potential cybersecurity measures to prevent or mitigate cybercrime in virtual environments and the importance of user education and responsible online behavior. Finally, we emphasize the need for industry, government, and users to collaborate to mitigate cybercrime in the Metaverse era due to possible negative impacts on social, economic, and environmental settings and its merits benefit people at different levels of endeavors.

INTRODUCTION

The metaverse refers to the theoretical concept of a fully immersive virtual world where users can instantly interact with each other and digital objects (Jaipong et al., 2023). It is a virtual universe that can be retrieved through augmented reality (AR) and virtual reality (VR) devices, enabling users to experience a sense of presence and agency within the virtual environment. The metaverse concept was popularized in science fiction and video games, but it is now becoming a reality due to technological advancements in areas like VR/AR, blockchain, and artificial intelligence (Qamar et al., 2023).

The metaverse is gaining significant popularity due to its potential to revolutionize various industries, including entertainment, education, and e-commerce. For example, the metaverse could transform how people consume and create content in the entertainment industry, enabling more immersive and interac-

DOI: 10.4018/979-8-3693-0220-0.ch005

tive experiences (Seo et al., 2023; Shafik, 2023). For example, concerts, sports events, and theme parks could be recreated within the metaverse, providing users with a unique experience. Furthermore, the metaverse could enhance the learning experience in the education sector by enabling students to interact with virtual objects and simulations, providing a more engaging and practical approach to education. Therefore, in the e-commerce industry, the metaverse could provide new opportunities for businesses to reach customers and offer personalized and immersive shopping experiences (Wu et al., 2023).

However, the increasing popularity of the metaverse also raises concerns about privacy, security, and cybercrime. As more people engage in virtual environments, there is a risk of unauthorized access, data breaches, and other malicious activities (Amalia, 2023). In addition, the immersive nature of the metaverse also makes it an attractive target for cybercriminals looking to exploit vulnerabilities and steal sensitive information. This includes implementing secure authentication methods, such as two-factor authentication and biometric identification, to prevent unauthorized access. It also involves monitoring user behavior and promptly detecting and responding to security incidents (Ariesta & Tuti, 2023). In addition, users must be educated on responsible online behavior, such as avoiding suspicious links and phishing attempts and safeguarding personal information; examples of Tencent's Metaverse are presented in Figure 1.

Figure 1. Tencent's Metaverse, including virtual world and spatial software going mainstream, "premium" social media (more authentic, exclusive, fandom-focused), adoption of decentralized distributed and remote productivity technology, and democratization of e-commerce
(drwealth.com)

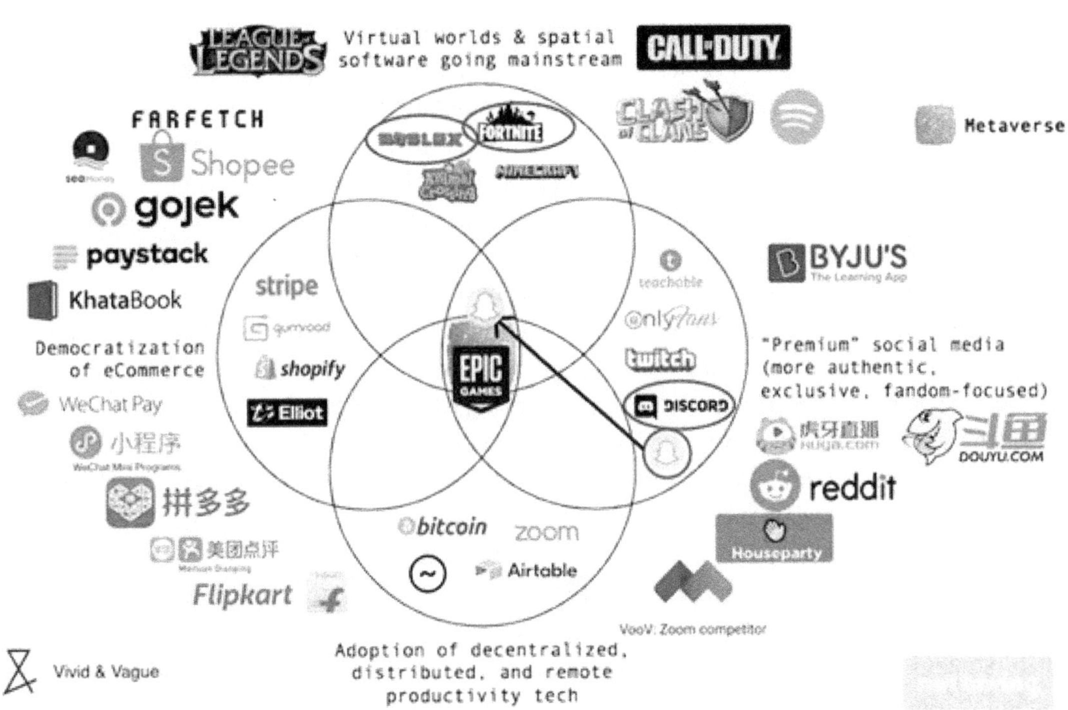

Moreover, the metaverse is a complex system that involves multiple stakeholders, including developers, service providers, and users (Grover et al., 2023). This includes establishing industry standards and guidelines for security and privacy and promoting accountability and transparency in using personal data within the metaverse. As the metaverse continues to gain popularity and evolve, it is essential to address these challenges and ensure virtual environments' safe and secure use. While the potential benefits of the metaverse are vast, it is crucial to prioritize privacy and security to avoid any potential negative consequences (Haber, 2023). By implementing robust security measures, educating users, and promoting collaboration between stakeholders, we can maximize the potential of the metaverse while minimizing its associated risks.

The future of the metaverse is exciting, but it is also unpredictable. Technological advancements will continue to shape the evolution of virtual environments, presenting both opportunities and challenges for users and stakeholders. As we move forward, we must stay vigilant and adapt to changing trends in cybercrime and security (Ariesta & Tuti, 2023; Qamar et al., 2023). The metaverse is a virtual universe gaining significant popularity due to its potential to transform various industries. Though, it also presents significant challenges related to privacy and security, which must be addressed through robust security measures, user education, and stakeholder collaboration (Q.-L. Han, 2023).

Importance of Discussing Cybercrime in the Metaverse Era

As virtual environments become increasingly popular and immersive, the potential for cybercrime is also rising. Cybercrime refers to criminal activities that are carried out using digital technology, such as hacking, identity theft, and data breaches (Olubuse, 2023; Seo et al., 2023). The metaverse presents new opportunities for cybercriminals to exploit vulnerabilities and steal sensitive information, making it essential to discuss and address cybercrime in this era. The importance of discussing cybercrime in the Metaverse era lies in the potential consequences of these crimes. For example, a successful cyberattack in the metaverse could lead to significant financial losses, reputation damage, and compromised sensitive information (Macpherson & Puplampu, 2023). In addition, cybercrime in the metaverse could have real-world consequences, such as the loss of physical property or harm to individuals.

Another reason why discussing cybercrime in the Metaverse era is essential is the potential impact on user trust and confidence. For example, suppose users do not feel secure in virtual environments. In that case, they may be hesitant to engage in activities that involve personal or financial information, hindering the growth and potential of the metaverse. Therefore, discussing and addressing cybercrime in the Metaverse era can promote a safe and secure virtual environment that inspires user trust and confidence (Ansari, 2023; Zhao et al., 2022). This involves implementing robust security measures, educating users on responsible online behavior, and promoting stakeholder collaboration to ensure a safe and enjoyable virtual experience. By prioritizing these issues, we can maximize the potential of the metaverse while minimizing its associated risks (Caglar, 2023; Grover et al., 2023).

Furthermore, discussing cybercrime in the Metaverse era is crucial for developing effective cybersecurity strategies. As the metaverse evolves, so do the tactics and methods used by cybercriminals to carry out their attacks. By staying informed about emerging trends and threats, we can develop and implement cybersecurity strategies that effectively mitigate these risks (Caglar, 2023). Additionally, discussing cybercrime in the Metaverse era is essential for promoting ethical and responsible behavior among users and stakeholders. This includes promoting transparency and accountability in using personal data

Figure 2. The seven layers of the metaverse include decentralization, creator economy, human interface, spatial computing, discovery, and experience, and infrastructure with their corresponding enablers and examples
(holonex.com)

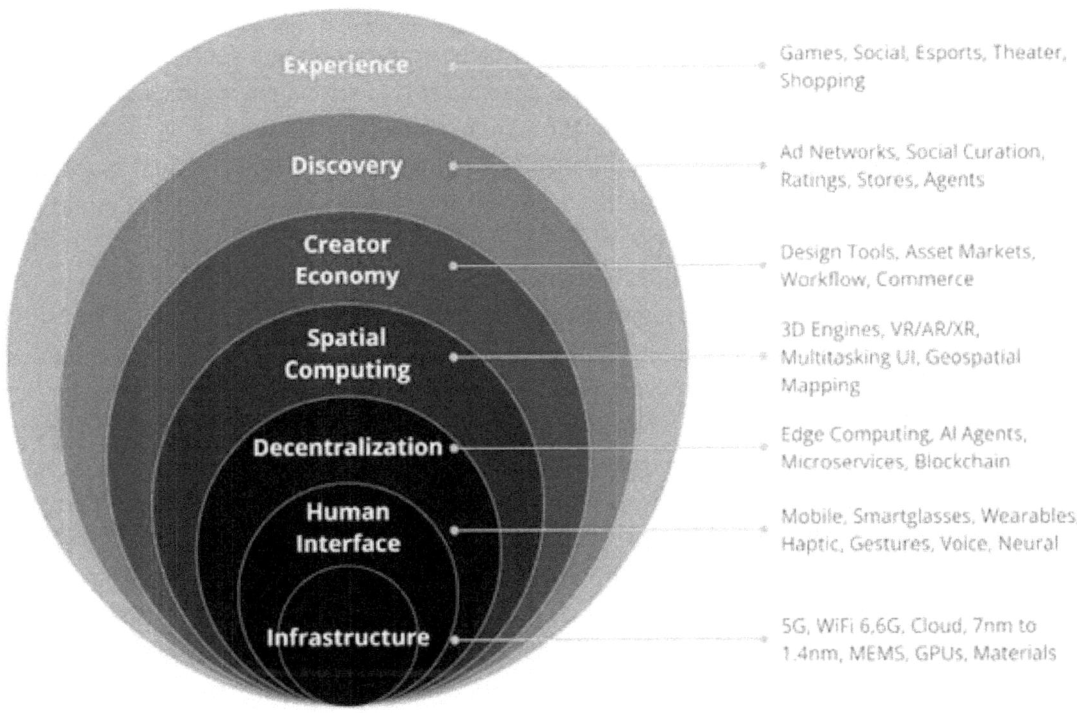

within virtual environments and adhering to industry standards and guidelines for security and privacy (Ansari, 2023; Filipova, 2023).

It is also worth noting that discussing cybercrime in the Metaverse era is crucial for promoting inclusivity and accessibility. As virtual environments become more prevalent in various industries, ensuring that all users, including those more vulnerable to cybercrime, feel safe and secure is essential (Macpherson & Puplampu, 2023; Wang et al., 2023). This involves implementing security measures that are inclusive and accessible, as well as educating users on how to protect themselves from potential cyber threats. Another aspect to consider when discussing cybercrime in the Metaverse era is the potential legal and regulatory implications; Figure 2 illustrates the seven layers that shape the Metaverse era.

As virtual environments become more complex, it is essential to establish clear legal frameworks that address the various challenges related to cybercrime (Gupta et al., 2023). This includes addressing data privacy, intellectual property, and online harassment. Furthermore, discussing cybercrime in the Metaverse era is critical for ensuring a safe and secure virtual environment that promotes innovation, growth, inclusivity, and accessibility (Kalyvaki, 2023). By prioritizing cybersecurity, promoting ethical behavior, staying informed about emerging trends and threats, and establishing clear legal frameworks, we can unlock the full potential of the metaverse while minimizing its associated risks.

Current State of Cybercrime in the Metaverse

As the metaverse continues to gain popularity and users, the potential for cybercrime also increases. Cybercrime in the Metaverse can take various forms, including hacking, identity theft, data breaches, and scams. One of the most common forms of cybercrime in the metaverse is phishing. Phishing refers to sending fraudulent messages or emails that appear to be from legitimate sources, aiming to steal personal information or login credentials (Koohang et al., 2023). In virtual environments, phishing can occur through messages sent to users' avatars or through fake links or websites.

Another common form of cybercrime in the metaverse is virtual asset theft. Virtual assets refer to digital items or currencies with value within the virtual environment, such as virtual real estate, digital art, or cryptocurrencies. Hackers can steal these virtual assets through various methods, such as hacking into user accounts or exploiting vulnerabilities in virtual marketplaces (Tugtekin, 2023). Moreover, virtual environments can also provide a platform for various types of online harassment, including cyberbullying, hate speech, and sexual harassment (Jaipong et al., 2023; Wang et al., 2023). This can have significant emotional and psychological impacts on users and negatively affect their virtual environment experience.

Implementing robust security measures, such as two-factor authentication, encryption, and firewalls, is essential to address these and other cybercrime threats in the metaverse. Educating users on responsible online behavior and promoting transparency and accountability in using personal data within virtual environments is also essential (Sia, 2023; Tugtekin, 2023). Additionally, a collaboration between stakeholders, including virtual environment providers, law enforcement, and cybersecurity experts, is critical in addressing the challenges posed by cybercrime in the metaverse. The metaverse is growing in popularity due to its potential to offer unique and immersive experiences in various industries (Hutson et al., 2023). As a result, it is expected to become a significant part of our daily lives.

The rest of this chapter is organized into five sections. Section 2 demonstrated the sources of Cybercrime in the Metaverse entailing, followed by the digital forensic techniques, entailing evidence collection and preservation, incident response in the metaverse, and end forensic techniques in Section 3. Section 4 demonstrates recent cybercrime incidents in a virtual environment, including some analysis of standard cybercrime methods used in the metaverse. Section 5 presents some forecasts for cybercrime future trends in two categories, that is to say, future cybercrime forecasting (these include increased use of virtual environments for data breaches, growing use of virtual environments for money laundering and other financial crimes, emergence of new types of phishing attacks in virtual reality (VR) and augmented reality (AR), use of deep learning and AI in cybercrime, use of virtual environments for social engineering attacks, increased supply chain attacks, routine of virtual environments for identity theft, growing use of virtual environments for ransomware attacks, increased use of botnets in virtual environments, and emergence of new types of cybercrime related to emerging technologies) and the top factors that could influence cybercrime in the metaverse era; this include security and privacy measures implemented by virtual environment developers, adoption rate of virtual environments, increasing complexity of virtual environments and emerging technologies, availability of tools and resources for cybercriminals, collaboration and information sharing between virtual environment developers and law enforcement, cross-border jurisdictional challenges, integration of real-world financial systems in virtual environments, accessibility and affordability of technology required to access virtual environments, cultural and societal attitudes towards virtual environments and cybercrime and also regulatory frameworks governing virtual environments and cybercrime. Section 6 illustrates ways to mitigate cybercrime in the metaverse, including implementing strong security measures, promoting user education, increasing collaboration, implementing secure and appreciative regulations, and developing new technologies. Lastly, section 7 presents the conclusion of the chapter and future research direction.

SOURCES OF CYBERCRIME IN THE METAVERSE

Addressing these concerns among the existing sources of cybercrimes necessitates the implementation of comprehensive security protocols, dissemination of user awareness programs, and potentially employment regulatory measures to ensure the safety of online environments. The digital landscape is an untamed and expansive domain, as detailed.

Phishing and Social Engineering Attacks

Within the Metaverse, phishing, and social engineering instances can materialize through intricately crafted virtual settings that closely resemble legitimate platforms. For example, a cybercriminal may fabricate a duplicate of a widely recognized virtual environment, disseminating invitations to those unaware of the copy's fraudulent nature (Amalia, 2023). Upon gaining access, individuals may inadvertently disclose their login credentials, enabling the assailants to breach their accounts. Social engineering involves manipulating interpersonal dynamics within virtual gaming environments (Seo et al., 2023). An illustrative instance involves a deceptive individual assuming the identity of a reliable acquaintance, persuading a participant to disclose personal data, or granting entry to virtual possessions.

Virtual Asset Theft and Fraud

The act of stealing virtual assets can be likened to the commission of digital grand larceny. Within a vast multiplayer online game, cybercriminals can employ hacking tools to illicitly acquire in-game currency or pilfer valuable items from the inventory of other players (Wu et al., 2023). Furthermore, it is essential to note that fraudulent schemes can potentially encompass activities such as selling counterfeit virtual assets or manipulating transactions within the virtual economy (Ariesta & Tuti, 2023). These deceptive practices can upset the equilibrium of the virtual ecosystem and result in financial detriment to the individuals involved in the virtual realm.

Data Breaches and Unauthorized Access

Data breaches can occur in virtual settings. Let us contemplate a hypothetical situation when the security of a Metaverse platform is hacked, resulting in the unauthorized disclosure of confidential user data. This may encompass personal data, financial information, and conversational records (Haber, 2023). The potential consequences of the fallout could transcend the confines of the virtual domain, exerting an impact on the personal privacy and security of users in the physical world.

Ransomware Attacks and Virtual Asset Extortion

The ransomware phenomenon exhibits a sinister transformation within the context of the Metaverse. Imagine a hypothetical scenario in which a malevolent actor infiltrates an individual's digital belongings through harmful software, subsequently encrypting valuable virtual resources. The targeted individual is subjected to a request for monetary compensation in return for providing a decryption key, thus employing their virtual possessions as leverage until a ransom is remitted (Ariesta & Tuti, 2023). The situation might be a cyber extortion event with tangible repercussions for the individual involved.

Identity Theft and Fraudulent Activities

Identity theft within the Metaverse encompasses a broader scope beyond the mere act of pilfering login credentials. Consider a hypothetical scenario when a malevolent individual generates a replicated digital representation, commonly referred to as an avatar, which closely mimics the characteristics and behaviors of an unwitting user. The impostor can partake in deceptive actions, compromising the actual user's credibility and potentially resulting in financial detriment (Qamar et al., 2023). The involvement of avatars in fraudulent activities, unlawful transactions, or virtual criminal acts can have tangible repercussions for those who fall victim to such conduct.

DIGITAL FORENSIC TECHNIQUES

Depending on the reality of digital forensic approaches, we briefly present some evidence collection and preservation, incident response in the metaverse, and end forensic techniques.

Evidence Collection and Preservation

Through the integration of these methodologies below, digital investigators are able to effectively navigate the intricate and ever-changing landscape of the Metaverse, thereby guaranteeing the precise acquisition and safeguarding of digital evidence (Q.-L. Han, 2023). Engaging in a digital archaeologist's role entails preserving virtual relics, allowing for meticulous examination and study.

Imaging Virtual Spaces

Within the Metaverse, the crime scene is not confined to a tangible physical setting but manifests as a multifaceted digital environment. Implementing best practices entails the creation of forensic photographs that surpass the mere acquisition of superficial data. This entails duplicating the observable components and comprehending the fundamental frameworks, information, and interconnections among virtual things (Macpherson & Puplampu, 2023). Comprehensive imaging techniques enable investigators to obtain a complete and all-encompassing perspective of the digital landscape, which is paramount in conducting a meticulous study.

Real-Time Monitoring

Real-time monitoring is an essential technique in virtual environments due to its dynamic nature. The functionality of investigative tools should facilitate the ongoing monitoring and documentation of actions within the Metaverse. This includes the surveillance of in-game communications, financial activities, and user engagements (Zhao et al., 2022). Through the real-time documentation of occurrences, investigators can collect temporally sensitive evidence, facilitating a comprehensive comprehension of the evolving digital storyline.

Blockchain Analysis

Several Metaverse platforms leverage the capabilities of blockchain technology to record transactions and establish ownership of virtual assets. It is essential to adhere to established conventions while comprehensively analyzing these decentralized ledgers (Grover et al., 2023). Utilizing blockchain technology provides a mechanism for establishing an immutable and readily observable ledger of activities, enhancing the capacity to monitor virtual transactions and adjustments inside the digital domain.

Memory Capture

Acknowledging the importance of immediate encounters, digital investigators must utilize memory capture techniques. This entails the preservation of volatile data that is stored in the random-access memory (RAM) of a computer. Researchers can acquire a momentary representation of the virtual environment by collecting active processes, open connections, and other transient data (Caglar, 2023). This enables them to gain valuable insights that may not be accessible through conventional disk imaging methods.

Metadata Documentation

Metadata plays a crucial role as an unobtrusive observer in digital investigations. The metadata documentation about virtual assets, files, and interactions is vital inside the Metaverse. The provided information encompasses details regarding file creation, modification, and access times (Ansari, 2023; Filipova, 2023). Thorough documentation plays a crucial role in establishing timelines, comprehending contextual links, and providing a comprehensive framework for the gathered data.

Collaboration With Platform Providers

Metaverse platforms function as the guardians of the digital domain. Establishing collaborative ties with these providers is a key component of best practices. This collaborative effort enhances the ability to access essential logs, gain insights into platform-specific functionalities, and develop a deeper comprehension of the virtual environment (Wang et al., 2023). Collaboration with platform providers significantly augments the investigator's capacity to navigate and comprehend the intricate aspects of the Metaverse.

Hashing and Digital Signatures

In order to uphold the veracity and genuineness of gathered evidence, digital investigators must utilize cryptographic methodologies, including hashing and digital signatures. The utilization of hashing enables the validation of data integrity, guaranteeing the preservation of the acquired evidence in its original state without any alterations (Kalyvaki, 2023). In contrast, digital signatures verify the evidence's origin, so establishing a reliable and secure possession sequence holds significant importance in legal contexts.

Documentation of Virtual Interactions

Recording Metaverse interactions, which frequently involve avatars and virtual entities, requires careful attention to detail due to their distinctive characteristics. Visual and contextual representations of events can be obtained through screenshots, chat logs, and records of in-game behaviors (Koohang et al., 2023). The provided documentation facilitates the reconstruction of virtual crime scenes and acts as tangible evidence in judicial procedures, providing a coherent narrative of the activities conducted within the virtual environment.

Incident Response in the Metaverse

A discussion on the phases of incident response, including preparation, identification, containment, eradication, and recovery, and how these apply to cybercrime in virtual environments and highlighting the role of virtual environment providers and organizations in establishing incident response teams and protocols are detailed (Jaipong et al., 2023). The incident response process in the Metaverse exhibits similarities to the conventional phases while presenting distinct obstacles and intricacies.

Preparation

The establishment of a comprehensive incident response strategy is contingent upon adequate preparation. Within the Metaverse, the task at hand encompasses establishing security measures for the virtual infrastructure and comprehending the distinct hazards presented by cyber threats within digital environments (Hutson et al., 2023). Virtual environment providers and organizations must collaborate to ensure effective incident response within the Metaverse. These endeavors should focus on establishing dedicated teams with comprehensive cybersecurity knowledge and the complexities inherent to the Metaverse (Jovanovic et al., 2023). This encompasses routine training, simulated exercises, and remaining updated on emerging virtual dangers.

Identification

Detecting an occurrence in the Metaverse necessitates a discerning observation of atypical patterns within the virtual realm. Potential indicators of atypical user conduct, unanticipated financial transactions, or indications of unlawful entry. Implementing effective monitoring systems by virtual environment providers is of paramount importance in this context, as it enables the detection of anomalies and initiating warnings (Jaipong et al., 2023). The prompt necessitates that incident response teams expeditiously evaluate these notifications to ascertain if they indicate a security incident.

Containment

After identifying an incident, the subsequent course of action involves containment measures to mitigate and averter any more harm or negative consequences. Within the Metaverse, potential actions to address security breaches could include isolating compromised virtual assets, suspending impacted accounts, or temporarily shutting specific virtual areas (Qamar et al., 2023). Virtual environment providers must establish procedures that enable prompt and efficient implementation of containment measures to respond to emergent situations successfully.

Eradication

The eradication process is centered on completely eliminating the underlying cause of the incident. The tasks mentioned above within the Metaverse encompass eliminating malevolent code within virtual environments, rectifying vulnerabilities, and enhancing security configurations (Wu et al., 2023). Virtual environment providers must collaborate closely with incident response teams in order to swiftly execute the essential remediation measures required to eliminate the danger.

Recovery

The process of recovery within the Metaverse encompasses more than mere system restoration since it also entails the restoration of the virtual economy and reestablishing user trust. Virtual environment providers must communicate transparently with users, clearly articulating the measures implemented to resolve the problem and offering assistance in safeguarding their virtual assets (Amalia, 2023). Incident response teams must engage in collaborative efforts during the post-event analysis phase in order to enhance and refine their future response plans. Notably, the virtual environment providers and organizations significantly impact incident response.

Establishing Incident Response Teams

It is recommended that virtual environment providers build specialized incident response teams that possess the necessary expertise and resources to effectively handle cyber occurrences within the Metaverse (Ariesta & Tuti, 2023). Organizations employing these virtual platforms must also cultivate their internal incident response capabilities, guaranteeing a synchronized and efficient response in the event of an issue.

Developing Protocols

Virtual environment providers and organizations must establish unambiguous and all-encompassing incident response processes. The protocols should delineate the various roles and corresponding responsibilities, provide effective communication channels, and delineate the sequential actions to be undertaken during each stage of incident response (Grover et al., 2023). It is imperative to conduct regular testing and refining of these protocols to ascertain their efficacy.

Collaboration

The effective management of incidents in the Metaverse necessitates a high degree of cooperation among virtual environment providers, organizations, and potentially law enforcement agencies. Establishing communication channels and collaborative mechanisms is of utmost importance to foster a cohesive and coordinated approach towards addressing cyber threats (Haber, 2023).

User Education

Both virtual environment providers and enterprises must place a high priority on the dissemination of knowledge on cybersecurity best practices within the Metaverse. The provided advise encompasses strategies for safeguarding virtual assets, identifying instances of phishing, and reporting any suspicious activity. Users with a high level of knowledge and understanding play a crucial role in enhancing the resilience of the virtual ecosystem. In conclusion, managing incidents inside the Metaverse necessitates the adoption of a proactive and collaborative methodology (Q.-L. Han, 2023). Collaboration between virtual environment providers and businesses is crucial to effectively address and mitigate cyber events in virtual environments' ever-changing and dynamic realm.

End Forensic Techniques

This subsection overviews the distinct forensic procedures employed for evidence collection within the metaverse. Potential focus areas encompass data recovery, memory analysis, network traffic analysis, and artifact extraction from virtual environments.

Data Recovery

The method of data recovery in the Metaverse is complex due to the inherent virtual nature of storage systems. Digital forensic experts employ specialized technologies built for virtual environments to retrieve files that have been deleted or destroyed. These software applications facilitate the exploration of virtual hard drives, cloud storage, and virtual machines to uncover crucial evidence (Caglar, 2023). Consider a hypothetical situation wherein a malevolent actor endeavors to obfuscate their digital footprints by eradicating potentially compromising data within a simulated environment. By employing rigorous methods of data retrieval, investigators can uncover these misplaced digital traces, thereby illuminating user behaviors, alterations, or records of communication (Wang et al., 2023).

Memory Analysis

Memory analysis within the Metaverse might be likened to immersing oneself in a virtual crime scene that is unfolding in real-time. The virtual environment's volatile memory (RAM) is captured and carefully examined by investigators, providing a dynamic representation of current actions (Kalyvaki, 2023). This may encompass details about active processes, established network connections, and transient data not permanently saved on a disk. Imagine a cyber incident in which an offender engages in real-time manipulation of virtual assets. Memory analysis serves as a digital tool that enables a closer inspection of the suspect's activities in the virtual realm, thereby offering valuable information for forensic investigation (Koohang et al., 2023).

Network Traffic Analysis

The examination of network traffic is a crucial task for forensic specialists while conducting an inquiry into the digital highways of the Metaverse. This methodology entails the analysis of the data transmission occurring among virtual entities, servers, and users. This analysis enables investigators to learn about communication patterns, potential points of unauthorized access, and indications of cyber risks (Hutson et al., 2023). Consider it as the process of understanding the digital traces that are left behind within the Metaverse. Network traffic analysis has a dual purpose in the realm of incident response. Firstly, it facilitates comprehension of the extent of an incident. Secondly, it plays a crucial role in reconstructing the chronological order of events that culminated in the security breach (J. Han et al., 2023).

Artifact Extraction From Virtual Environments

Virtual settings, such as archeological sites, generate digital artifacts, which are the traces of human interactions and system activities. The objects are meticulously extracted by forensic professionals in order to recreate events and establish chronological sequences. This entails doing an in-depth analysis of logs, scrutinizing the metadata linked to virtual assets, and reconstructing the remnants of files that have been deleted or altered (Anidjar et al., 2023; Chen, 2023). The Metaverse can be viewed as a digital crime scene, where the process of artifact extraction plays a crucial role in meticulously documenting virtual activities. This method aims to uncover traces that could potentially provide valuable insights into a cyber incident (Fusco, 2023).

Blockchain Analysis

Incorporating blockchain technology within the Metaverse presents a novel dimension of intricacy to forensic inquiries. Forensic professionals examine blockchain data to investigate the movement of digital currency, alterations in ownership, and potentially illicit behaviors documented within the decentralized ledger (Zaki & Santo, n.d.). This strategy is particularly relevant for addressing virtual asset theft or fraudulent transactions. Blockchain analysis offers investigators a transparent and immutable ledger of virtual transactions, providing a definitive path to pursue fraudsters operating within the digital domain (Sethuraman et al., 2023).

Steganography Analysis

Within the Metaverse, it is plausible for thieves to utilize the technique of steganography as a means to conceal information within digital files. Forensic professionals employ steganography analysis techniques to identify and extract hidden information from virtual assets that may appear harmless at first glance (Mittal & Bansal, 2023). This may involve revealing concealed messages inside various forms of digital content, such as photographs, audio files, or other digital components. Consider a hypothetical scenario whereby a digital artwork is employed to conceal a covert cryptographic message (Zainurin et al., 2023). The examination of steganography serves as a valuable tool in uncovering hidden information, shedding light on the intentions and techniques employed by cybercriminals.

File Carving

The issue of fragmentation or file destruction within virtual environments presents a unique challenge for forensic investigators. Using file carving techniques, experts can reconstruct fragmented or lost files by using remnants found on storage media. For example, engage in a theoretical examination of a scenario in which crucial evidence is intentionally erased inside the framework of the Metaverse (Olubuse, 2023). File carving is a digital reconstruction method used by investigators to recover and piece together fragmented or corrupted data. This approach aids in improving investigators' comprehension of the chronological order of events that occurred before a cybercrime (Fernandes & Werner, 2023).

Metadata Analysis

In the Metaverse, metadata assumes the role of an unobtrusive observer, retaining significant data on virtual assets, files, and user behaviors. Forensic professionals examine metadata analysis to construct chronological sequences, monitor alterations, and gain an understanding of the contextual elements of digital interactions (Hutson et al., 2023). Metadata can be conceptualized as the digital equivalent of DNA, providing valuable information regarding the identity, nature, and temporal aspects of virtual activities (Mitchell et al., 2023). The comprehensive examination assists researchers in reconstructing occurrences within the digital realm, providing a more profound comprehension of the sequence of events and the underlying motivations driving them.

EXAMPLES OF RECENT CYBERCRIME INCIDENTS IN VIRTUAL ENVIRONMENTS

There have been several notable cybercrime incidents in virtual environments in recent years. One high-profile example is the 2020 hack of the video game giant Ubisoft. Hackers accessed the company's servers and stole valuable intellectual property, including game source code and other sensitive data (Jovanovic et al., 2023). The hack is believed to have been motivated by the potential monetary gains from selling stolen intellectual property on the black market.

In 2021, a virtual real estate company called Decentraland was targeted by hackers who stole approximately $100,000 worth of the company's cryptocurrency. The hackers exploited a vulnerability in the company's smart contract, allowing them to drain funds from users' accounts (Jovanovic et al., 2023; Mittal & Bansal, 2023). Another recent incident involved a cyberattack on a virtual real estate marketplace called Nifty Gateway. Again, the attackers accessed users' accounts and made unauthorized purchases of digital artwork, resulting in financial losses for some users.

These incidents illustrate the potential financial impacts of cybercrime in virtual environments and the importance of implementing robust security measures and staying vigilant against emerging threats (Mitchell et al., 2023; Jun et al., 2021). Other examples of cybercrime in virtual environments include phishing attacks targeting virtual currency holders, online harassment within virtual communities, and using virtual environments to distribute malware and conduct botnet attacks. In response to these and other cybercrime incidents, virtual environment providers and cybersecurity experts are working to develop new technologies and strategies to improve security and mitigate risks (J. Han et al., 2023).

In addition to the incidents mentioned above, several high-profile cases of virtual asset theft have occurred in virtual environments. For example, in 2014, the famous online game World of Warcraft was targeted by hackers who stole virtual gold and other valuable in-game items worth an estimated $10 million (J. Han et al., 2023). In 2020, a player in the game EVE Online lost over $9,000 worth of in-game assets to a hacker who gained access to the player's account. The hacker could steal the player's virtual ships and other assets, which the player had accumulated over several years (Hutson et al., 2023; Mittal & Bansal, 2023).

These incidents highlight virtual assets' value in virtual environments and the potential financial impact of virtual asset theft. As virtual assets continue to gain popularity and value, it is crucial for virtual environment providers to implement strong security measures and for users to take steps to protect their accounts and assets (J. Han et al., 2023). Moreover, virtual environments are not immune to the risks associated with traditional cybercrime, such as data breaches and identity theft. For example, in 2020, the virtual event platform Hopin suffered a data breach that exposed the personal information of thousands of users, including names, email addresses, and other sensitive data (Hutson et al., 2023).

As virtual environments grow in popularity and complexity, cybercriminals will likely continue to target them. As a result, virtual environment providers, cybersecurity experts, and law enforcement must work together to develop effective strategies for preventing and responding to cybercrime in virtual environments (Buhalis et al., 2023). Organizations must implement robust cybersecurity measures, including access controls, encryption, intrusion detection, and incident response plans to address these cybersecurity concerns. Regular risk assessments, employee training, and compliance with data protection regulations are also essential (Sá & Serpa, 2023; Tlili et al., 2023). Technology integration into healthcare has revolutionized the industry, but it has also introduced new cybersecurity risks. Table 1 shows the actual cybercrime or breaching medical data with their reported details.

Table 1(a). Cybercrime in healthcare data (https://www.upguard.com/blog/biggest-data-breaches-in-health care)

Date	Data Breach	Impact (patients)	compromised	solution
September 2011	Tricare	5 million	prescription information, lab tests, clinical notes, personal health data, phone numbers, addresses, names, social security numbers	Data encryption policies
April-June, 2014	Community Health Systems	4.5 million	addresses, phone numbers, numbers, social security, birth dates, names	Teach employees to diagnose the threatening traits of malware injection attempts.
July 2015	UCLA Health	4.5 million	Some medical data: identification number, health plan number, Medicaid number, social security numbers, dates of birth, names	exhaustive investigation
August 2013	Advocate Health Care	4.03 million	Health insurance information, clinical information, Demographic information, dates of birth, addresses, names	physical security controls
July 2015	Medical Informatics Engineering	3.9 million	birth statistics, names of children, medical conditions, doctor names, disability codes, diagnosis, lab results, social security numbers, dates of information, and security questions	monitor for sensitive data

Table 1(b). Cybercrime in healthcare data (https://www.upguard.com/blog/biggest-data-breaches-in-health care)

July 2016	Newkirk Products	3.8 million	Invoice information, dates of birth, names of dependents, patient names, Medicaid ID number, and primary care provider information	Unceasingly scan servers for potential exploits.
August 2016	Banner Health	3.62 million	Information about the patient's health insurance, doctor appointments, social security number, birth date, address, and name.	regular security rating risk and assessment monitoring
May 2020	Trinity Health	3.3 million	Certain financial information, claim information, medications, lab results, medical record numbers, vaccination types, Dates of birth; addresses; email addresses; healthcare provider; date and types of health care; full names	the consciousness of the ransomware attack sequence
March 2022	Shields Healthcare Group	2 million	Diagnosis Information, Patient IDs, medical record numbers, and full names Insurance numbers, birth dates, Billing Information, Home Addresses, Provider Information, Social Security numbers	A zero-trust approach
January 2022	Broward Health	1.3 million	Medical data, insurance information, driver's license numbers, birth dates, addresses, and names	Protect all privileged access Supervision.
February 2022	Morley	521,046	Information about health insurance, treatment, medical diagnosis, client ID number, date of birth, social security number, addresses, and name.	Data breach security controls

Analysis of Standard Cybercrime Methods Used in the Metaverse

Cybercriminals in the Metaverse use various techniques to carry out their attacks. One standard method is phishing, where attackers create fake websites or emails that appear legitimate to trick users into revealing their personal information, such as login credentials and payment card details (Tlili et al., 2023). Another technique used in the metaverse is malware, which is malicious software designed to gain unauthorized access to a user's device or steal their personal information. Malware can be distributed through malicious links, downloads, or email attachments. Metaverse asset theft is also a prevalent form of cybercrime in the metaverse (Rawat & El Alami, 2023). Attackers can use various methods to access a user's virtual assets, such as stealing login credentials or exploiting the platform's security vulnerabilities.

Furthermore, social engineering is a common tactic used in the metaverse. For example, attackers may attempt to manipulate users into revealing their personal information or giving access to their accounts by pretending to be someone else or creating a false sense of urgency (Fusco, 2023). In addition, distributed denial-of-service (DDoS) attacks can disrupt virtual environments, causing downtime and preventing users from accessing their accounts (Demetis, 2023). Finally, hackers can use botnets or other techniques to flood a platform's servers with traffic, overwhelming the system and causing it to crash.

As virtual environments continue to evolve, cybercriminals will likely continue to develop new and innovative methods to carry out their attacks. Therefore, virtual environment providers must remain vigilant and implement robust security measures to protect their users' personal information and assets (Cork et al., 2023; Demetis, 2023). One emerging threat in the metaverse is the use of "deep fake" technology. Deepfakes are realistic and often convincing videos or images created using artificial intelligence and machine learning. Cybercriminals can use deep fakes to impersonate individuals, such as celebrities or high-profile individuals, in virtual environments to gain access to sensitive information or steal virtual assets (Huang et al., 2023).

Moreover, using blockchain technology and cryptocurrency in virtual environments has introduced new security challenges. For example, cryptocurrency transactions are irreversible, and if attackers gain access to a user's cryptocurrency wallet, they can quickly transfer the funds out of the wallet, making it difficult to trace the stolen assets (Aburayya et al., 2023). To mitigate these threats, virtual environment providers can implement multi-factor authentication, encryption, and other security measures to protect users' accounts and assets. Virtual environment users should protect their personal information and assets by using strong and unique passwords, avoiding clicking on suspicious links or downloading unknown files, and enabling two-factor authentication on their accounts (Yang et al., 2023).

Another significant challenge in addressing cybercrime in the metaverse is the international nature of virtual environments. Virtual environments may have users and servers located in different countries, making enforcing laws and regulations around cybercrime difficult (Radanliev, 2023). Moreover, the anonymity provided by virtual environments can make it challenging to identify and prosecute cybercriminals. For example, virtual environments may use pseudonyms or avatars, making it difficult to link virtual activities to real-life identities (Radanliev, 2023). This anonymity can also create a false sense of security for cybercriminals, who may believe they can carry out attacks without being caught.

To address these challenges, law enforcement agencies and cybersecurity experts must work together to develop international cooperation frameworks and establish best practices for identifying and prosecuting cybercrime in virtual environments (Radanliev, 2023; Zainurin et al., 2023). Moreover, virtual environment providers must proactively implement security measures to protect their users and platforms. It is also worth noting that the increasing popularity of virtual environments and the metaverse has led to the rise of virtual economies. Virtual assets, such as virtual currencies, virtual real estate, and in-game items, can have real-world value, creating virtual marketplaces and economies (Masera, 2023).

However, the growth of virtual economies has also led to increased cybercrime targeting virtual assets. Virtual asset theft, virtual money laundering, and virtual currency fraud are just a few examples of cybercrime in virtual economies. To address these challenges, virtual environment providers can work to implement policies and regulations around virtual economies to help prevent and mitigate cybercrime. This can include measures such as monitoring transactions and enforcing anti-money laundering policies. Moreover, virtual environment providers can work with law enforcement agencies and cybersecurity experts to develop best practices for identifying and prosecuting cybercriminals in virtual economies.

FORECASTING FUTURE CYBERCRIME TRENDS

Predicting the exact nature and scope of future cybercrime trends in the metaverse is challenging, given the rapid pace of technological development and the constantly evolving tactics of cybercriminals. However, it is possible to identify several areas of potential risk and emerging threats. One area of concern is the potential for cybercriminals to use virtual environments to conduct large-scale data breaches (Seo et al., 2023; Ariesta & Tuti, 2023). As more businesses and organizations move to virtual environments, they may become targets for cybercriminals looking to steal sensitive data. Cybercriminals could exploit vulnerabilities in virtual environment platforms to gain unauthorized access to servers and databases, leading to significant data breaches.

Another potential risk is using virtual environments for money laundering and other financial crimes. Cryptocurrency and other virtual assets are becoming increasingly common in virtual environments, making them attractive targets for cybercriminals seeking to launder money or engage in other financial crimes (Haber, 2023; Olubuse, 2023). Moreover, as virtual environments become more immersive and realistic, the potential for cybercriminals to use them for social engineering attacks increases. For example, cybercriminals could use deep fake technology to impersonate individuals, such as high-profile executives, to access sensitive information or steal virtual assets.

To address these potential threats, virtual environment providers and cybersecurity experts must work together to develop robust security measures and risk mitigation strategies. This could include using artificial intelligence and machine learning to detect and prevent cyberattacks and implementing multi-factor authentication and encryption to protect user accounts and data (Filipova, 2023; Q.-L. Han, 2023). The growth of virtual environments and the metaverse presents exciting opportunities for innovation and social connection. However, it also presents significant challenges and risks, particularly around cybercrime. By staying vigilant and proactive, virtual environment providers, cybersecurity experts, and law enforcement agencies can help mitigate these risks and ensure that virtual environments remain safe and secure for all users (Q.-L. Han, 2023; Sia, 2023). Emerging technologies, such as augmented reality (AR) and virtual reality (VR), may lead to new types of cybercrime in the metaverse. For example, as AR and VR become more widely adopted, cybercriminals may use these technologies to conduct phishing attacks that exploit users' trust in virtual environments. In addition, cybercriminals could create realistic virtual environments that mimic legitimate ones, leading users to disclose sensitive information unknowingly.

Another potential threat is using deep learning and artificial intelligence (AI) in cybercrime. Cybercriminals could use these technologies to automate attacks and bypass traditional security measures. For example, AI-powered malware could evade detection by traditional antivirus software, making it more difficult to detect and remove (Amalia, 2023; Filipova, 2023). In addition, cybercriminals could exploit vulnerabilities in third-party applications and services to gain unauthorized access to virtual environments and steal sensitive data or virtual assets. To address these emerging threats, virtual environment providers and cybersecurity experts must continue investing in research and developing new security technologies and strategies. This includes the development of AI and machine learning-based security solutions, as well as the adoption of security best practices for the supply chain management.

Future Cybercrime Forecasting

Therefore, the future of cybercrime in the metaverse is complex and ever-evolving. Virtual environment providers, cybersecurity experts, and law enforcement agencies must remain vigilant and proactive in identifying and mitigating emerging threats to ensure that virtual environments remain safe and secure for all users (Fernandes & Werner, 2023; Naqvi, n.d.). Based on the analysis of the current state of cybercrime in the metaverse and the potential risks and emerging threats, here are ten possible future cybercrime trends to consider, followed by the factors that could influence the metaverse era:

Increased Use of Virtual Environments for Data Breaches

The increased use of virtual environments for data storage and processing could lead to more cybercrime incidents involving data breaches. Cybercriminals could exploit vulnerabilities in virtual environment platforms to gain unauthorized access to servers and databases, potentially leading to the theft of sensitive information such as personal data, financial information, and intellectual property (Amalia, 2023; Sia, 2023). With the growing reliance on virtual environments for business operations, it is crucial to prioritize implementing robust security measures to safeguard against cyberattacks. Virtual environment providers and organizations must work together to identify and mitigate system vulnerabilities to prevent unauthorized access and protect sensitive data (Haber, 2023). Cybercriminals could exploit vulnerabilities in virtual environment platforms to gain unauthorized access to servers and databases, leading to significant data breaches.

The Growing Use of Virtual Environments for Money Laundering and Other Financial Crimes

Cryptocurrency and other virtual assets are becoming increasingly common in virtual environments, making them attractive targets for cybercriminals seeking to launder money or engage in other financial crimes (Koohang et al., 2023; Wang et al., 2023). The growing use of virtual environments for financial transactions and the rise of virtual assets such as cryptocurrencies may increase cybercrime incidents involving money laundering and other financial crimes. Cybercriminals could use virtual environments to launder money or engage in fraudulent activities, taking advantage of virtual assets' anonymity and decentralized nature. The potential for illicit activities in virtual environments poses a significant threat to the financial sector. Regulators and law enforcement agencies must monitor these transactions to detect and prevent such crimes (Kalyvaki, 2023). Virtual environment providers must also prioritize implementing strong security measures to prevent unauthorized access to virtual assets and sensitive financial information.

The Emergence of New Types of Phishing Attacks in AR and VR

The emergence of new phishing attacks in augmented reality (AR) and virtual reality (VR) environments is a potential future trend in cybercrime. With the increasing adoption of AR and VR technologies, cybercriminals could exploit these environments' immersive and interactive nature to create sophisticated phishing attacks (J. Han et al., 2023; Zainurin et al., 2023). For example, cybercriminals could use AR or VR to create realistic simulations of login screens or other authentication mechanisms to trick users into divulging their login credentials. As AR and VR continue to gain popularity, developing effective security measures to protect users against such attacks is crucial. AR and VR developers and security experts must collaborate to identify potential vulnerabilities and develop solutions to mitigate them. Additionally, user education and awareness programs may help users identify and avoid these new phishing attacks (Tlili et al., 2023). As AR and VR become more widely adopted, cybercriminals may use these technologies to conduct phishing attacks that exploit users' trust in virtual environments.

Use of Deep Learning and AI in Cybercrime

The use of deep learning and artificial intelligence (AI) in cybercrime is a potential future trend that could make cyber-attacks more sophisticated and challenging to detect. Cybercriminals could use AI algorithms to analyze and exploit vulnerabilities in networks and systems, creating customized and targeted attacks that evade traditional security measures (Fernandes & Werner, 2023; Szymanski, 2023). Additionally, AI could be used to automate attacks, making them faster and more efficient. As cybercriminals continue to use advanced technologies to carry out attacks, it is crucial to develop new security measures that can identify and mitigate these threats. Cybersecurity experts and researchers must work to develop AI and machine learning tools that can detect and respond to emerging cyber threats effectively (Scharfman, 2023). This requires a deep understanding of AI and its potential applications in cybercrime and ongoing research and development efforts to stay ahead of emerging threats.

Use of Virtual Environments for Social Engineering Attacks

As virtual environments become more immersive and realistic, the potential for cybercriminals to use them for social engineering attacks increases. Using virtual environments for social engineering attacks is a potential future trend in cybercrime (Hidayat et al., 2023). Cybercriminals could use virtual environments to create sophisticated and realistic simulations of social situations, allowing them to manipulate users into divulging sensitive information or performing actions that could compromise their security. For example, cybercriminals could create simulations of work environments or social events and use them to gain access to sensitive information or credentials. Therefore, as virtual environments become more prevalent, developing effective security measures to protect against social engineering attacks is crucial (Göknur et al., n.d.; Schmitt, 2023). This includes ongoing user education and awareness programs to help users identify and avoid falling victim to these attacks and implement strong authentication and access control mechanisms in virtual environments to prevent unauthorized access to sensitive information.

Increased Supply Chain Attacks

Cybercriminals could exploit vulnerabilities in third-party applications and services to gain unauthorized access to virtual environments and steal sensitive data or virtual assets. The increased use of technology in supply chain management has resulted in a rise in cybercrime, a potential future trend in supply chain attacks (Duranton et al., 2023). Cybercriminals can exploit vulnerabilities in supply chain systems to gain access to sensitive information, disrupt operations, or compromise products. With the growing complexity of supply chain systems, detecting and preventing these types of attacks is becoming increasingly challenging. To mitigate the risks associated with supply chain attacks, organizations must prioritize security throughout their supply chains (Zaki & Santo, n.d.). This includes implementing strong security measures and access controls, conducting regular security assessments and audits, and working with partners to ensure security standards are met throughout the supply chain (Poore, 2023). Additionally, security teams must stay abreast of emerging threats and adapt their security measures accordingly.

Use of Virtual Environments for Identity Theft

Using virtual environments for identity theft is a potential future trend in cybercrime. Cybercriminals could create realistic virtual identities, complete with social media profiles, credit histories, and other personal information, which they can use to commit fraud or other illegal activities (Narang, 2023). As virtual environments become more prevalent, cybercriminals may increasingly use these platforms for identity theft. To combat this, individuals and organizations must protect their personal information and identities by using strong passwords, enabling two-factor authentication, and avoiding sharing personal information online (BHATTACHARYA et al., n.d.; Chen, 2023). Organizations must also implement strong security measures to protect against unauthorized access to sensitive information, including identity data. Additionally, it is crucial to develop effective detection and response mechanisms to identify and mitigate identity theft incidents quickly (Betül, 2023). Cybercriminals could use deep fake technology to impersonate individuals, such as high-profile executives, to access sensitive information or steal virtual assets.

The Growing Use of Virtual Environments for Ransomware Attacks

Using virtual environments for ransomware attacks is an emerging trend in cybercrime that poses a significant threat to organizations. Ransomware attacks in virtual environments can be highly sophisticated, targeting critical data and systems and disrupting operations. For example, cybercriminals could use virtual environments to infiltrate a network, encrypt sensitive data, and demand payment in exchange for the decryption key (Figueiredo, 2023). As virtual environments become more prevalent, organizations must proactively protect against ransomware attacks by implementing robust security measures such as regular backups, network segmentation, and threat detection mechanisms. Organizations must also have effective incident response plans to respond quickly to ransomware attacks and minimize the impact of any data loss or disruption. It is crucial to continuously review and update security measures to avoid emerging threats as ransomware attacks become more advanced and sophisticated (Schmitt, n.d.). Cybercriminals could use virtual environments to deploy ransomware and other types of malware, potentially causing significant financial damage.

Increased Use of Botnets in Virtual Environments

The increased use of botnets in virtual environments is a potential future trend in cybercrime. Botnets are networks of compromised computers controlled by cybercriminals to carry out various malicious activities, such as Distributed Denial of Service (DDoS) attacks and spam campaigns (Zytko & Chan, 2023). As virtual environments become more prevalent, cybercriminals could use botnets to launch attacks on virtual platforms and networks, causing significant disruption and damage. To combat this, organizations must implement robust security measures such as network segmentation, regular vulnerability assessments, and threat detection mechanisms to detect and mitigate botnet attacks. Additionally, individuals and organizations must take proactive steps to prevent their computers from being recruited into botnets, such as using up-to-date antivirus software, avoiding suspicious email attachments, and regularly updating software and operating systems (Schmitt, n.d.). As botnets evolve and become more sophisticated, it is crucial to remain vigilant and proactive in protecting against these threats. For example, cybercriminals could use botnets to launch distributed denial-of-service (DDoS) attacks against virtual environment platforms, causing downtime and disruption.

The Emergence of New Types of Cybercrime Related to Emerging Technologies

As new technologies, such as quantum computing and 5G, continue to emerge, cybercriminals may find new ways to exploit them for criminal purposes. The emergence of new types of cybercrime related to emerging technologies is a significant concern in the future of cybersecurity. With the rapid pace of technological advancement, cybercriminals continually find new ways to exploit emerging technologies for malicious purposes (BHATTACHARYA et al., n.d.; Szymanski, 2023). For example, the proliferation of the Internet of Things (IoT) devices has created new opportunities for hackers to infiltrate networks and launch attacks. Similarly, the increasing use of artificial intelligence (AI) has opened up new possibilities for creating sophisticated phishing scams, while blockchain technology has created new avenues for financial crime. As these technologies continue to evolve, staying informed about emerging cybercrime trends and taking proactive steps to mitigate risks is essential (Hidayat et al., 2023; Schmitt, n.d.). Organizations must ensure that they have robust security measures to protect against emerging threats and continuously review and update their security strategies to stay ahead of the ever-evolving cybercrime landscape. While it is impossible to predict the nature and scope of future cybercrime trends in the metaverse, virtual environment providers, cybersecurity experts, and law enforcement agencies must remain vigilant and proactive in identifying and mitigating emerging threats (Zytko & Chan, 2023).

TOP FACTORS THAT COULD INFLUENCE CYBERCRIME IN THE METAVERSE ERA

Several factors could influence cybercrime in the Metaverse era. One significant factor is the security and privacy measures virtual environment developers implement. Inadequate security measures could make it easier for cybercriminals to exploit vulnerabilities and carry out attacks (J. Han et al., 2023). Additionally, the adoption rate of virtual environments could impact the frequency and severity of cybercrime incidents. As virtual environments become more widespread and widely used, they may become a more attractive target for cybercriminals. Moreover, the increasing complexity of virtual environments and emerging technologies such as AI and machine learning could create new opportunities for cybercriminals to carry out attacks (Radanliev, 2023). Effective collaboration between these agencies and virtual environment developers could be vital in identifying and mitigating cybercrime risks in virtual environments; below are some factors that could influence cybercrime in the Metaverse era (Gupta et al., 2023).

Security and Privacy Measures Implemented by Virtual Environment Developers

The security and privacy measures implemented by virtual environment developers will be crucial in predicting future cybercrime trends in the Metaverse era. Weak privacy policies and inadequate security measures could make virtual environments more vulnerable to cyberattacks and data breaches (Buhalis et al., 2023; Tlili et al., 2023). Therefore, virtual environment developers must prioritize security and privacy measures in their platform's development and maintenance. Cybercriminals may seek to exploit vulnerabilities in virtual environments, and developers must implement robust security protocols. Transparent privacy policies and explicit user consent for data collection or sharing are also essential (Li et al., 2023). The effectiveness of security and privacy measures will significantly influence the future of cybercrime in the Metaverse era.

The Adoption Rate of Virtual Environments

The adoption rate of virtual environments is a significant factor that could influence future cybercrime trends in the Metaverse era. As the use of virtual environments increases, so does the potential for cybercriminals to exploit these platforms for their criminal activities (Sethuraman et al., 2023). In addition, an increase in the adoption rate may increase the number of users, making virtual environments more attractive to cybercriminals. This could also result in a higher likelihood of cyberattacks as more potential targets exist. On the other hand, virtual environment developers may implement better security measures as the adoption rate grows, making these platforms less vulnerable to cyberattacks (Bhattacharya et al., n.d.). Therefore, understanding the adoption rate of virtual environments is crucial in forecasting future cybercrime trends in the Metaverse era.

The Increasing Complexity of Virtual Environments and Emerging Technologies

The increasing complexity of virtual environments and emerging technologies is another crucial factor that could influence future cybercrime trends in the Metaverse era. As virtual environments become more advanced and sophisticated, they may become more challenging to secure against cyberattacks (Fusco, 2023; Mittal & Bansal, 2023). Moreover, emerging technologies such as artificial intelligence, blockchain, and augmented reality could provide new opportunities for cybercriminals to carry out their malicious activities. Nevertheless, on the other hand, these same technologies could also be used to improve security measures and prevent cybercrime in virtual environments (Tlili et al., 2023). Therefore, the increasing complexity of virtual environments and emerging technologies must be carefully monitored and managed to forecast future cybercrime trends effectively.

Availability of Tools And Resources for Cybercriminals

The availability of tools and resources for cybercriminals is another significant factor that could influence future cybercrime trends in the Metaverse era. With the proliferation of online marketplaces and underground forums, cybercriminals have access to a wide range of sophisticated hacking tools, exploit kits, and malware (Li et al., 2023; Alabdulatif et al., 2023). Furthermore, the widespread availability of cryptocurrencies has made it easier for cybercriminals to profit from their illegal activities anonymously. As virtual environments continue to grow in popularity and complexity, the availability of such tools and resources will likely increase, providing more opportunities for cybercriminals to carry out their attacks (Demetis, 2023). Therefore, it is essential to monitor and regulate the availability of these tools to prevent and forecast future cybercrime trends.

Collaboration and Information Sharing Between Virtual Environment Developers and Law Enforcement

Collaboration and information sharing between virtual environment developers and law enforcement can be crucial in predicting and preventing cybercrimes in the Metaverse era. Developers can share information about vulnerabilities in their virtual environments with law enforcement, who can then use this information to develop effective strategies for mitigating cyberattacks (Sia, 2023). Similarly, law enforcement can share intelligence about cybercrime trends and emerging threats with virtual environment developers, who can use this information to strengthen the security of their platforms (Wang et al., 2023). This collaboration can create a more secure and resilient virtual environment that is less vulnerable to cybercrime.

Cross-Border Jurisdictional Challenges

Cross-border jurisdictional challenges refer to the difficulties law enforcement agencies face in investigating and prosecuting cybercriminals who operate across international borders. As virtual environments are accessible globally, cybercriminals can quickly launch attacks from one country while residing in another (Mittal & Bansal, 2023; Zainurin et al., 2023). In addition, the need for standardized laws and regulations across different countries further complicates the process. As a result, cybercriminals can only exploit these legal loopholes with practical international cooperation and coordination and evade justice (Zainurin et al., 2023). As a result, cross-border jurisdictional challenges are a significant factor that could influence cybercrime in the Metaverse era.

Integration of Real-World Financial Systems in Virtual Environments

Integrating real-world financial systems in virtual environments, such as blockchain-based currencies, can create new opportunities for cybercriminals. This could increase financial fraud, money laundering, and other financial crimes in the metaverse (Buhalis et al., 2023). Additionally, the cross-border nature of virtual currencies could pose challenges for law enforcement agencies in tracking and prosecuting cybercriminals operating in different jurisdictions (Tlili et al., 2023; Rawat & El Alami, 2023). Therefore, virtual environment developers and law enforcement must collaborate and implement adequate security measures to mitigate these risks.

Accessibility and Affordability of Technology Required to Access Virtual Environments

The accessibility and affordability of technology required to access virtual environments can influence cybercrime in the Metaverse era. As technology becomes more accessible and affordable, more individuals will likely be able to access virtual environments and potentially engage in cybercriminal activities (Schmitt, n.d.; Zainurin et al., 2023). This could lead to an increase in the number of cybercrime incidents in the metaverse. Additionally, the availability of technology and resources could make it easier for cybercriminals to develop and execute sophisticated cyber-attacks, making it more difficult for law enforcement to combat them. Therefore, it is crucial to consider the potential impact of technology accessibility and affordability when forecasting future cybercrime trends in the Metaverse era (Hidayat et al., 2023; Tlili et al., 2023).

Cultural and Societal Attitudes Towards Virtual Environments and Cybercrime

Cultural and societal attitudes toward virtual environments and cybercrime can also influence future trends. As virtual environments become more ubiquitous, cultural and societal attitudes toward them will shape their adoption and use (Ansari, 2023; Tlili et al., 2023). For example, if virtual environments are seen as more trustworthy and secure, people may be more likely to engage with them and use them for financial transactions. On the other hand, if virtual environments are seen as inherently risky or untrustworthy, this may lead to a decrease in adoption and use. Additionally, cultural attitudes towards cybercrime, such as tolerance for illegal activities, can impact the prevalence and severity of cybercrime in virtual environments (Koohang et al., 2023; Seo et al., 2023).

Regulatory Frameworks Governing Virtual Environments And Cybercrime

The regulatory frameworks that govern virtual environments and cybercrime are other factors that could influence the future of cybercrime in the Metaverse era. As virtual environments grow in popularity and become more integrated into daily life, governments worldwide are likely to develop regulations and laws to govern their use (Gupta et al., 2023; Koohang et al., 2023). These regulations could include requirements for virtual environment developers to implement more robust security and privacy measures and penalties for cybercriminal activity in these environments (Kalyvaki, 2023; Rawat & El Alami, 2023). The development and enforcement of these regulations will play a crucial role in shaping the future of cybercrime in the Metaverse era.

CHALLENGES IN METAVERSE FORENSICS

This section examines the distinct obstacles that arise when performing digital forensics in virtual environments, specifically focusing on the dynamic characteristics of virtual assets and the ability for user activities to be conducted anonymously.

Dynamic Nature of Virtual Assets

Within the Metaverse, virtual assets undergo continuous fluctuations, undergoing evolution and swiftly transitioning between different owners. The field of digital forensics encounters the formidable task of monitoring and safeguarding the authenticity and reliability of these ever-changing resources (Zainurin et al., 2023). In contrast to tangible proof, virtual assets such as in-game money, goods, or virtual real estate possess a higher susceptibility to manipulation, duplication, or transfer inside the virtual environment. The ever-changing nature of the virtual world necessitates that forensic professionals modify their methodology to capture a precise representation of the digital landscape at a particular point in time, guaranteeing the gathered evidence's precision and pertinence (Ansari, 2023).

Anonymity and Pseudonymity

The Metaverse offers a means of concealing one's identity and using pseudonyms, hence introducing challenges in determining the true source of acts performed by persons. Avatars and virtual identities can be quickly generated and discarded, making it challenging to relate digital activities to real-world organizations (Buhalis et al., 2023). Cybercriminals leverage the anonymity provided by the internet to perpetrate fraudulent transactions, participate in identity theft, and carry out various unlawful activities. The field of digital forensics in the Metaverse necessitates the utilization of sophisticated methodologies to track and assign acts to tangible individuals, taking into account the ever-changing and temporary nature of virtual identities (Wang et al., 2023).

Cross-Border Jurisdictional Issues

The Metaverse surpasses geographical boundaries, potentially enabling virtual crimes to involve individuals residing in disparate nations. A scenario presents intricate jurisdictional obstacles in digital forensics (Koohang et al., 2023). The investigation and prosecution of virtual crimes may need the establishment of cooperation mechanisms among law enforcement organizations operating in diverse jurisdictions. Disparities in legal frameworks, variations in data protection regulations, and the absence of standardized protocols for virtual criminal investigation can challenge the efficient implementation of forensic operations (Gupta et al., 2023).

Encryption and Security Measures

Virtual environments frequently utilize strong encryption and comprehensive security protocols to safeguard user data and facilitate secure transactions. Implementing these security mechanisms in the Metaverse presents certain obstacles for the field of digital forensics (Grover et al., 2023). The ability to decipher encrypted virtual communications, gain unauthorized access to protected virtual environments, and circumvent sophisticated security protocols necessitates a distinct set of specialized skills and knowledge (Ariesta & Tuti, 2023). Forensic professionals must be abreast of the ever-changing encryption technology to analyze and interpret encrypted data within virtual settings.

Virtual Ecosystem Diversity

The Metaverse encompasses a multitude of platforms that exhibit a wide range of characteristics and give distinct opportunities for engagement. The field of digital forensics necessitates accommodating a wide range of virtual environments, considering variations in data types, communication protocols, and asset management systems (Amalia, 2023). Examining a virtual offense may necessitate a comprehensive comprehension of a particular digital environment, hence demanding that forensic specialists possess adaptability and expertise across several virtual ecosystems (Seo et al., 2023).

Rapid Technological Advancements

The Metaverse is currently positioned at the vanguard of technical innovation, with platforms undergoing rapid evolution. The field of digital forensics encounters the formidable task of maintaining stride with the swift progressions in technology (Kalinaki et al., 2023). The Metaverse undergoes constant transformation due to the introduction novel features, advancements in virtual reality technologies, and evolving interaction methods (Seo et al., 2023). Consequently, forensic professionals must engage in ongoing learning and adaptation to proficiently conduct investigations and evaluate digital evidence within the most up-to-date virtual settings.

Decentralized and Blockchain Technologies

Numerous Metaverse platforms utilize decentralized technology and blockchain to facilitate transactions and manage assets. While utilizing these technologies augment the level of transparency, it concurrently introduces intricate challenges within digital forensics (Ansari, 2023). The process of blockchain analysis necessitates acquiring a particular skill set to precisely trace virtual transactions and changes in ownership (Filipova, 2023). The presence of decentralized structures poses a barrier to conventional investigative methodologies, requiring forensic professionals to be proficient in navigating and comprehending decentralized systems within the Metaverse.

Data Privacy and Consent

Virtual environments frequently accumulate enormous quantities of user data for personalization and analytics. The field of digital forensics necessitates the careful navigation of the intricate equilibrium between conducting investigations into virtual criminal activities and upholding the principles of user privacy (Wang et al., 2023). The acquisition of consent for forensic analysis, particularly in virtual platforms extending beyond international borders, presents ethical and legal implications. Reconciling forensic procedures with data protection standards while simultaneously upholding the efficacy of investigations presents a multifaceted and intricate dilemma (Macpherson & Puplampu, 2023). The field of digital forensics faces distinct obstacles when operating within the Metaverse due to the dynamic and diverse characteristics of virtual settings. To surmount these problems, it is imperative to employ a blend of specialized knowledge, flexibility, and cooperation among virtual environment providers, law enforcement agencies, and digital forensic professionals.

COLLABORATION BETWEEN FORENSICS AND CYBERSECURITY

Within this section, we highlight the significance of collaboration between professionals in digital forensics and cybersecurity, which is crucial when effectively addressing and mitigating cybercrime situations within virtual environments.

Incident Response Efficiency

In the event of a cyber incident within the Metaverse, the prompt resolution of the issue becomes crucial. Cybersecurity specialists play a crucial role in actively safeguarding against persistent threats (Gupta et al., 2023). The involvement of digital forensics professionals in collaboration facilitates a smooth progression from the initial identification and containment of an incident to the subsequent forensic investigation phase (Kalyvaki, 2023). Collaboration between different components enhances the incident response procedure's efficiency, reducing the adverse effects of the cyber attack on virtual resources and user data.

Forensic Readiness

The integration of these disciplines facilitates the development of cybersecurity protocols that prioritize the incorporation of forensic preparedness. Cybersecurity specialists can employ many technologies and methodologies to effectively gather and safeguard digital evidence (Koohang et al., 2023). Implementing this proactive strategy enhances the efficiency of the forensic investigation procedure in the event of an incident, facilitating prompt analysis and interpretation of the evidence by digital forensics specialists within the virtual realm.

Threat Intelligence Integration

Cybersecurity experts engage in the collection of real-time threat intelligence in order to enhance their defensive measures against constantly evolving cyber threats. By disseminating this information to professionals in the field of digital forensics, more extensive analysis may be conducted on patterns of attack, novel forms of malware, and developing strategies (Tugtekin, 2023). The dissemination of this collective knowledge enhances the efficacy of the preventive strategies employed by cybersecurity teams and bolsters the investigation proficiencies of digital forensics specialists, thus cultivating a more robust defense against cyber offenses.

Adaptive Security Measures

Virtual environments exhibit dynamic characteristics, while the nature of cyber threats is characterized by constant evolution. The collaboration between the fields of forensics and cybersecurity establishes a reciprocal relationship wherein insights gained from forensic investigations contribute to improving cybersecurity protocols (Sia, 2023). Utilizing this adaptive methodology enables firms to proactively modify security measures by leveraging knowledge acquired from previous occurrences, establishing a more resilient defense against recurring and emerging cyber threats in the Metaverse.

User Education and Awareness

The collaboration between cybersecurity and digital forensics encompasses the realm of user education within the Metaverse. Cybersecurity professionals can establish awareness programs to instruct users on optimal strategies for ensuring secure virtual interactions. Digital forensics professionals have the expertise to offer valuable insights into the ramifications of cyber risks, underscoring the significance of swiftly reporting any suspicious activities (Jaipong et al., 2023). This collective endeavor enables individuals to take the initiative in safeguarding themselves and their digital resources.

Legal and Compliance Alignment

The utilization of digital forensics frequently assumes a pivotal position in judicial processes after a cyber incident. Engaging in collaboration with cybersecurity professionals facilitates the alignment of both domains with legal and compliance obligations. This collaborative effort includes establishing protocols pertaining to the acquisition of evidence, preserving the chain of custody, and adhering to legislation concerning data privacy (Ariesta & Tuti, 2023). Establishing alignment is paramount in ensuring the efficacy of investigations and judicial proceedings about cybercriminal activities within the virtual domain.

Continuous Training and Skill Development

Professionals in the disciplines of cyber threats and virtual environments must maintain up-to-date knowledge of the newest technology and methodologies due to these domains' growing nature. Collaborative training programs and knowledge-sharing efforts play a crucial role in equipping cybersecurity and digital forensics experts with the necessary skills to effectively navigate the intricate dynamics of the Metaverse (Grover et al., 2023). The continuous collaboration fosters a collective of adaptable specialists with the skills necessary to address the ever-evolving complexities of virtual criminal activities.

RESEARCH AND ADVANCEMENTS

This section sheds light on current developments in the domain of metaverse digital forensics, encompassing research, tools, and technology improvements. This essay will examine how these advances assist investigators in maintaining a competitive advantage over cybercriminals.

Blockchain Analysis Tools

Utilizing blockchain technology is a fundamental component of numerous Metaverse platforms, as it serves the purpose of documenting virtual transactions and establishing ownership (Grover et al., 2023). Sophisticated tools for blockchain analysis have been developed to track and examine transactions, thereby offering forensic investigators enhanced and comprehensive insights (Haber, 2023). The primary objective of these tools is to augment the traceability of virtual assets, hence facilitating the examination of fraudulent activities, theft, and other cybercrimes occurring within the Metaverse.

Artificial Intelligence and Machine Learning for Anomaly Detection

The integration of artificial intelligence (AI) and ML is becoming more prevalent in digital forensics tools, namely for anomaly detection (Seo et al., 2023). Within the Metaverse, a virtual environment characterized by a wide range of user behaviors and interactions, the utilization of AI-driven technologies holds the potential to acquire knowledge of typical patterns and subsequently detect deviations that might signify suspicious activity (Olubuse, 2023). Implementing this proactive method enables investigators to identify and address potential dangers promptly.

Memory Forensics Advancements

The significance of analyzing volatile memory, specifically Random Access Memory (RAM), within the context of the Metaverse, highlights the noteworthy progress made in developing memory forensics tools. Scholars have been engaged in endeavors to enhance the efficacy of obtaining and evaluating memory snapshots derived from virtual environments (Macpherson & Puplampu, 2023). This includes software tools specifically developed to manage the intricacies of virtual memory architectures and retrieve pertinent data for investigative purposes.

Decentralized Forensics Techniques

Researchers are investigating decentralized forensics approaches in the Metaverse, given the widespread adoption of decentralized technologies like blockchain and peer-to-peer networks. These methodologies aim to address the difficulties inherent in examining occurrences within decentralized systems, enabling forensic investigators to effectively explore and analyze data within the framework of a decentralized Metaverse (Zhao et al., 2022).

Advanced Artifact Analysis

The utilization of advanced artifact analysis methods has facilitated the extraction of more significant data from virtual settings, enhancing the investigators' capabilities. This encompasses enhancements in the parsing of metadata linked to virtual assets, the analysis of chat logs, and the reconstruction of user activity (Grover et al., 2023). These technological improvements provide a more detailed comprehension of virtual crime scenes, hence assisting investigators in constructing full timelines.

Visualization and Simulation Tools

The development of visualization technologies is underway to create virtual reconstructions and simulations of crime scenes. These tools facilitate the visualization and manipulation of digital evidence within a simulated environment for investigative purposes (Seo et al., 2023). Utilizing this immersion methodology facilitates comprehension of the chronological order of occurrences, identification of possible avenues for attack, and augmentation of the entire investigation process.

Collaborative Platforms for Information Sharing

The significance of collaborative platforms that promote information sharing among professionals in the fields of digital forensics and cybersecurity has increased (Amalia, 2023). These platforms facilitate the immediate exchange of threat intelligence, knowledge, and optimal strategies about cyber dangers in the Metaverse. By facilitating collaboration, these platforms enable researchers to remain informed about emerging trends and collaboratively address developing strategies employed by cybercriminals (Ariesta & Tuti, 2023). Using advanced tools and methodologies, investigators can effectively navigate the intricate aspects of virtual environments, hence maintaining a competitive edge over cybercriminals and bolstering the overall resilience of cybersecurity measures within the Metaverse.

MITIGATING CYBERCRIME IN THE METAVERSE

As virtual environments continue to grow in popularity, developing effective strategies to mitigate cybercrime in the metaverse is crucial. One of the primary measures is to prioritize security and privacy during the design and development stages of virtual environments (Mitchell et al., 2023). This includes implementing robust encryption protocols, multi-factor authentication, and access controls. User education and awareness can also help prevent cybercrime by teaching users about common threats and best practices for protecting their information. Collaboration between virtual environment developers and law enforcement can also aid in identifying and addressing cybercrime incidents (Hutson et al., 2023; Aslam et al., 2023). Regulatory frameworks and international cooperation can be critical in establishing a unified approach to addressing cybercrime in the metaverse.

Implement Robust Security Measures

The implementation of concrete security measures can significantly mitigate cybercrime in the metaverse. This includes encryption, firewalls, and intrusion detection and prevention systems. Developers of virtual environments must prioritize security and take a proactive approach to identify and address vulnerabilities before cybercriminals can exploit them (J. Han et al., 2023; Seo et al., 2023). Additionally, using multi-factor authentication, regularly updated passwords, and user education can help prevent unauthorized access and phishing attacks. Regular security audits and testing can also help identify and address any weaknesses in the system (Fernandes & Werner, 2023; Olubuse, 2023). By implementing these measures, virtual environments can create a safer and more secure online space for users, reducing the risk of cybercrime.

Promote User Education

Users should be educated on the risks of cybercrime in virtual environments and how to protect themselves. This can include teaching them to identify phishing scams, avoid downloading suspicious files, and secure their personal information. Promoting user education can help mitigate cybercrime in the metaverse by raising awareness among users about the risks and threats associated with using virtual environments (Mittal & Bansal, 2023; Zainurin et al., 2023). User education programs can teach users how to recognize and avoid common cyber threats like phishing, malware, and identity theft. By educating users on the importance of using strong passwords, regularly updating software, and avoiding suspicious links or downloads, they can better protect their personal information and reduce the risk of falling victim to cybercrime (Filipova, 2023; Schmitt, n.d.). Educating users on the proper use of virtual environments can help prevent unintentional security breaches and reduce the overall risk of cyber-attacks.

Increase Collaboration

Increasing collaboration between virtual environment developers, law enforcement agencies, and cybersecurity experts can help mitigate cybercrime in the metaverse. Virtual environment developers can work with experts to identify potential security risks and develop more robust security measures (Sethuraman et al., 2023). Law enforcement agencies can provide support in investigating and prosecuting cybercrime cases in the virtual environment. Cybersecurity experts can offer guidance and best practices for securing virtual environments and preventing cyberattacks. Collaboration can also lead to sharing threat intelligence, which can help identify emerging threats and respond to them proactively (J. Han et al., 2023; Huang et al., 2023). Ultimately, a coordinated effort to combat cybercrime in the metaverse can make it more difficult for cybercriminals to operate and increase the overall security of virtual environments.

Implement Regulations

Governments should implement regulations that hold virtual environment developers accountable for security breaches and other cybercrime-related incidents. Implementing regulations can also help mitigate cybercrime in the metaverse (Zaki & Santo, n.d.). For example, governments and regulatory bodies can create and enforce laws and guidelines that require virtual environment developers and service providers to implement specific security and privacy measures. This can include the mandatory use of multi-factor authentication, encryption, and regular security audits. Regulations can also mandate reporting requirements for cyber incidents and data breaches, which can help law enforcement and security professionals promptly identify and respond to cyber threats (Fusco, 2023). Regulations can establish penalties for cybercrime, which can act as a deterrent and encourage virtual environment developers and users to prioritize security and take measures to prevent cybercrime.

Develop New Technologies

Developing new technologies can also play a significant role in mitigating cybercrime in the metaverse. For example, AI-based threat detection systems and blockchain-based security solutions can help prevent and detect cyberattacks (Fernandes & Werner, 2023; Schmitt, 2023). Biometric and multi-factor authentication can make it more difficult for cybercriminals to gain unauthorized access to virtual environments. Advancements in cryptography can also enhance security by ensuring secure data transmission and storage (Anidjar et al., 2023; Chen, 2023). Moreover, developing tools to track and monitor suspicious activities in virtual environments can aid in the early detection and prevention of cybercrime. Continued investment in research and development of innovative technologies can help keep up with the evolving threats in the metaverse (J. Han et al., 2023).

CONCLUSION

Cybercrime in the metaverse era is still in its early stages, and further research is needed to understand and predict future trends. Future research directions include investigating the impact of emerging technologies such as AI, blockchain, and quantum computing on cybercrime in virtual environments. The role of virtual environment developers in mitigating cybercrime, including examining the security and privacy measures implemented and tools available, as well as collaboration with law enforcement agencies, are also important research areas. Understanding cultural and societal attitudes towards virtual environments and cybercrime is critical as virtual environments become more integrated into daily life. Developing regulatory frameworks to protect users from cybercrime and ensure data privacy and security in the metaverse is another crucial area for future research. Ultimately, predicting future cybercrime trends in the metaverse era is a complex and rapidly evolving area of research. Continued investigation is necessary to understand better the factors influencing cybercrime in virtual environments and develop effective strategies to mitigate these risks. This research can inform the development of policies, regulations, and technological solutions to ensure the security and privacy of users in the metaverse era.

REFERENCES

Aburayya, A., Salloum, S., Alderbashi, K., Shwedeh, F., Shaalan, Y., Alfaisal, R., Malaka, S., & Shaalan, K. (2023). SEM-machine learning-based model for perusing the adoption of metaverse in higher education in UAE. *International Journal of Data and Network Science*, *7*(2), 667–676. doi:10.5267/j.ijdns.2023.3.005

Alabdulatif, A., Thilakarathne, N. N., Lawal, Z. K., Fahim, K. E., & Zakari, R. Y. (2023). Internet of nano-things (iont): A comprehensive review from architecture to security and privacy challenges. *Sensors (Basel)*, *23*(5), 2807. doi:10.339023052807 PMID:36905010

Amalia, R. F. (2023). Legal Protection for Virtual Land Trading Investment Transactions in the Metaverse. *3rd International Conference on Business Law and Local Wisdom in Tourism (ICBLT 2022)*, 488–496. 10.2991/978-2-494069-93-0_58

AnidjarL. Y.PackinN. G.PaneziA. (2023). The Matrix Of Privacy: Data Infrastructure In The Ai-Powered Metaverse. *Available at* SSRN. doi:10.2139/ssrn.4363208

Ansari, A. P. (2023). A Critique on Cybercrimes Concerning Online Games and Content: Need for Comprehensive Legal Framework in India. *Res Militaris*, *13*(3), 82–95.

Ariesta, W., & Tuti, T. (2023). Penerapan Doktrin Vicarious Liability Untuk Pertanggungjawaban Pelaku Tindak Pidana Dunia Maya. *Jurnal Penelitian IPTEKS*, *8*(1), 39–45.

Aslam, M. M., Tufail, A., Kim, K. H., Apong, R. A. A. H. M., & Raza, M. T. (2023). A Comprehensive Study on Cyber Attacks in Communication Networks in Water Purification and Distribution Plants: Challenges, Vulnerabilities, and Future Prospects. *Sensors (Basel)*, *23*(18), 7999. doi:10.339023187999 PMID:37766053

Betül, C. A. N. (2023). Metaverse Sosyal Alanına Meta Ekonomik Sermaye Açısından İslam Ülkeleri Ne Kadar Hazır? Ürün Uzayı Bağlamında Kesitsel Bir Değerlendirme. *Eskişehir Osmangazi Üniversitesi İlahiyat Fakültesi Dergisi*, *10*(1), 10–41. doi:10.51702/esoguifd.1213159

Bhattacharya, S., Hegde, P., & Maddikunta, P. K. R. (n.d.). *Metaverse for Healthcare: A Survey on Potential Applications*. Challenges and Future Directions.

Buhalis, D., Leung, D., & Lin, M. (2023). Metaverse as a disruptive technology revolutionising tourism management and marketing. *Tourism Management*, *97*, 104724. doi:10.1016/j.tourman.2023.104724

Caglar, E. (2023). Analysis of Metaverse Technology: Is It Real or Virtual? In Strategies and Opportunities for Technology in the Metaverse World (pp. 1–12). IGI Global.

Chen, Z. (2023). Metaverse office: Exploring future teleworking model. *Kybernetes*. Advance online publication. doi:10.1108/K-10-2022-1432

CorkD. A. D.FianiC.KhamisM.McGillM.MurdochS.RashidA.SaegheP. (2023). *REPHRAIN*.

Demetis, D. (2023). Organised crime-the cyber dimension. *A Research Agenda for Organised Crime*, 177–194.

Duranton, M., De Bosschere, K., Coppens, B., Gamrat, C., Gray, M., Hoberg, T., Munk, H., Robinson, C., Vardanega, T., & Zendra, O. (2023). *HiPEAC Vision 2023.*

Fernandes, F. A., & Werner, C. M. (2023). A Scoping Review of the Metaverse for Software Engineering Education: Overview, Challenges and Opportunities. *PRESENCE: Virtual and Augmented Reality*, 1–56.

Figueiredo, S. C. (2023). Rhetoric in the metaverse. *Convergence (London)*, *29*(1), 81–96. doi:10.1177/13548565221138399

Filipova, I. A. (2023). Creating the Metaverse: Consequences for Economy, Society, and Law. *Journal of Digital Technologies and Law*, *1*(1), 7–32. doi:10.21202/jdtl.2023.1

Fusco, M. (2023). *Moving towards virtual identity: Enabling accessible motion capture for Metaverse users and their avatars* [Master's Thesis]. University of Twente.

Göknur, E. G. E., YOUSSOUF, M. M., & DARNADJI, D. (n.d.). DIGITAL DIVIDE AND AFRICA IN THE UPCOMING METAVERSE ERA: A STUDY ON THE EXAMPLES OF CHAD AND DJIBOUTI. *Prof. Dursun KOSE, Ph. D.*, 388.

Grover, A., Arora, N., & Sharma, P. (2023). Social Commerce and Metaverse in a New Virtual World: Exploring Women's Adoption Intentions. In *Cultural Marketing and Metaverse for Consumer Engagement* (pp. 262–286). IGI Global. doi:10.4018/978-1-6684-8312-1.ch019

Gupta, A., Khan, H. U., Nazir, S., Shafiq, M., & Shabaz, M. (2023). Metaverse Security: Issues, Challenges and a Viable ZTA Model. *Electronics (Basel)*, *12*(2), 391. doi:10.3390/electronics12020391

Haber, E. (2023). (Forthcoming). The Criminal Metaverse. *Indiana Law Journal (Indianapolis, Ind.)*.

Han, J., Liu, G., & Gao, Y. (2023). Learners in the Metaverse: A Systematic Review on the Use of Roblox in Learning. *Education Sciences*, *13*(3), 296. doi:10.3390/educsci13030296

Han, Q.-L. (2023). The Era of Quality and Metaverse. *IEEE/CAA Journal of Automatica Sinica, 10*(1), 1–2.

Hidayat, W., Ramli, H., Ikhram, P. M. B., Ridhawi, A. R., Mukhtar, N. A., & Junedy, R. (2023). Analisa Clustering Phising Untuk Meningkatkan Kesadaran Mahasiswa Terhadap Keamanan Data Pribadi Mahasiswa Universitas Negeri Makassar. *Vokatek: Jurnal Pengabdian Masyarakat*, *1*(1), 28–33. doi:10.61255/vokatekjpm.v1i1.29

Huang, Y., Li, Y. J., & Cai, Z. (2023). Security and Privacy in Metaverse: A Comprehensive Survey. *Big Data Mining and Analytics*, *6*(2), 234–247. doi:10.26599/BDMA.2022.9020047

Hutson, J., Banerjee, G., Kshetri, N., Odenwald, K., & Ratican, J. (2023). Architecting the Metaverse: Blockchain and the Financial and Legal Regulatory Challenges of Virtual Real Estate. *Journal of Intelligent Learning Systems and Applications, 15.*

Jaipong, P., Siripipattanakul, S., Sriboonruang, P., Sitthipon, T., Jaipong, P., Siripipattanakul, S., Sriboonruang, P., & Sitthipon, T. (2023). A Review of Metaverse and Cybersecurity in the Digital Era. *International Journal of Computing Sciences Research*, *7*, 1125–1132. doi:10.25147/ijcsr.2017.001.1.122

Jovanovic, V., Kuzlu, M., Cali, U., Utku, D. H., Catak, F. O., Sarp, S., & Zohrabi, N. (2023). Digital Twin in Industry 4.0 and Beyond Applications. In Digital Twin Driven Intelligent Systems and Emerging Metaverse (pp. 155–174). Springer.

Jun, Y., Craig, A., Shafik, W., & Sharif, L. (2021). Artificial intelligence application in cybersecurity and cyberdefense. *Wireless Communications and Mobile Computing*, *1*, 1–10. doi:10.1155/2021/3329581

Kalinaki, K., Thilakarathne, N. N., Mubarak, H. R., Malik, O. A., & Abdullatif, M. (2023). *Cybersafe capabilities and utilities for smart cities. Cybersecurity for Smart Cities.* Springer., doi:10.1007/978-3-031-24946-4_6

Kalyvaki, M. (2023). Navigating the Metaverse Business and Legal Challenges: Intellectual Property, Privacy, and Jurisdiction. *Journal of Metaverse*, *3*(1), 87–92. doi:10.57019/jmv.1238344

Koohang, A., Nord, J. H., Ooi, K.-B., Tan, G. W.-H., Al-Emran, M., Aw, E. C.-X., Baabdullah, A. M., Buhalis, D., Cham, T.-H., Dennis, C., Dutot, V., Dwivedi, Y. K., Hughes, L., Mogaji, E., Pandey, N., Phau, I., Raman, R., Sharma, A., Sigala, M., ... Wong, L.-W. (2023). Shaping the metaverse into reality: A holistic multidisciplinary understanding of opportunities, challenges, and avenues for future investigation. *Journal of Computer Information Systems*, *63*(3), 1–31. doi:10.1080/08874417.2023.2165197

Li, T., Yang, C., Yang, Q., Zhou, S., Huang, H., & Zheng, Z. (2023). MetaOpera: A Cross-Metaverse Interoperability Protocol. *ArXiv Preprint ArXiv:2302.01600.*

Macpherson, I., & Puplampu, A. (2023). *15 Better than the Real You? VR, Identity, Privacy, and the Metaverse*. Virtual Identities and Digital Culture.

Masera, R. (2023). Web 1.0, 2.0, 3.0; InfoSphere; Metaverse: An Overview. Monetary, Financial, Societal and Geopolitical Transformation Cusps. *Monetary, Financial, Societal and Geopolitical Transformation Cusps (January 14, 2023).*

Mitchell, A. R., Ahlert, D., Brown, C., Birge, M., & Gibbs, A. (2023). Electrocardiogram-based biometrics for user identification–Using your heartbeat as a digital key. *Journal of Electrocardiology*, *80*, 1–6. doi:10.1016/j.jelectrocard.2023.04.001 PMID:37058746

Mittal, G., & Bansal, R. (2023). *Driving Force Behind Consumer Brand Engagement.*

Naqvi, A. A. (n.d.). *A COMPREHENSIVE ANALYSIS OF METAVERSE TECHNOLOGIES TO ATTEMPT A TREND ANALYSIS OF THE EMERGING CONCEPTUAL AND APPLIED ASPECTS OF METAVERSE.*

Narang, N. K. (2023). Mentor's Musings on Role of Standards, Regulations & Policies in Navigating Through Metaverse and its Future Avatars. *IEEE Internet of Things Magazine*, *6*(1), 4–11. doi:10.1109/MIOT.2023.10070410

OlubuseO. (2023). The Role of the Nigerian Lawyer in the Metaverse. *Available at* SSRN 4326585. doi:10.2139/ssrn.4326585

Poore, C. A. (2023). *Leadership in the Metaverse: Creating the Future of WebWe Through Strategy and Community Building*. Greenleaf Book Group.

Qamar, S., Anwar, Z., & Afzal, M. (2023). A systematic threat analysis and defense strategies for the metaverse and extended reality systems. *Computers & Security*, *128*, 103127. doi:10.1016/j.cose.2023.103127

Radanliev, P. (2023). *The Metaverse: Economic and Social Values and Risks of New Cryptocurrencies and Blockchain Technologies.*

Rawat, D. B., & El Alami, H. (2023). Metaverse: Requirements, Architecture, Standards, Status, Challenges, and Perspectives. *IEEE Internet of Things Magazine*, *6*(1), 14–18. doi:10.1109/IOTM.001.2200258

Sá, M. J., & Serpa, S. (2023). Metaverse as a Learning Environment: Some Considerations. *Sustainability (Basel)*, *15*(3), 2186. doi:10.3390u15032186

Scharfman, J. (2023). Additional Case Studies in Cryptocurrency Fraud. In *The Cryptocurrency and Digital Asset Fraud Casebook* (pp. 161–172). Springer. doi:10.1007/978-3-031-23679-2_11

SchmittM. (2023). Big Data Analytics in the Metaverse: Business Value Creation with Artificial Intelligence and Data-Driven Decision Making. *Available at* SSRN 4385347. doi:10.2139/ssrn.4385347

SchmittM. (n.d.). Securing the Digital World: Protecting Smart Infrastructures and Digital Industries with Artificial Intelligence (Ai)-Enabled Malware and Intrusion Detection. *Available at* SSRN 4397870. doi:10.1016/j.jii.2023.100520

Seo, S., Seok, B., & Lee, C. (2023). Digital forensic investigation framework for the metaverse. *The Journal of Supercomputing*, *79*(9), 1–19. doi:10.100711227-023-05045-1

Sethuraman, S. C., Mitra, A., Ghosh, A., Galada, G., & Subramanian, A. (2023). MetaSecure: A Passwordless Authentication for the Metaverse. *ArXiv Preprint ArXiv:2301.01770.*

Shafik, W. (2023). Cyber Security Perspectives in Public Spaces: Drone Case Study. In *Handbook of Research on Cybersecurity Risk in Contemporary Business Systems, 79–97.* IGI Global. doi:10.4018/978-1-6684-7207-1.ch004

Sia, C. C. (2023). The Role of Legal Governance Framework in the Metaverse World. In *Strategies and Opportunities for Technology in the Metaverse World* (pp. 321–330). IGI Global. doi:10.4018/978-1-6684-5732-0.ch017

Szymanski, T. (2023). *A Software-Defined Deterministic Internet of Things (IoT) with Artificial Intelligence (AI) for Quantum-Safe Cyber-Security.*

Tlili, A., Huang, R., & Kinshuk. (2023). Metaverse for climbing the ladder toward 'Industry 5.0'and' Society 5.0′? *Service Industries Journal*, *43*(3–4), 260–287. doi:10.1080/02642069.2023.2178644

Tugtekin, U. (2023). The Dark Side of Metaverse Learning Environments: Potential Threats and Risk Factors. In Shaping the Future of Online Learning: Education in the Metaverse (pp. 57–67). IGI Global.

Wang, J., Makowski, S., Cieślik, A., Lv, H., & Lv, Z. (2023). Fake News in Virtual Community, Virtual Society, and Metaverse: A Survey. *IEEE Transactions on Computational Social Systems*, 1–15. doi:10.1109/TCSS.2022.3220420

Wu, J., Lin, K., Lin, D., Zheng, Z., Huang, H., & Zheng, Z. (2023). Financial Crimes in Web3-empowered Metaverse: Taxonomy, Countermeasures, and Opportunities. *IEEE Open Journal of the Computer Society*, *4*, 37–49. doi:10.1109/OJCS.2023.3245801

Yang, R., Li, L., Gan, W., Chen, Z., & Qi, Z. (2023). The Human-Centric Metaverse: A Survey. *ArXiv Preprint ArXiv:2303.11123*. doi:10.1145/3543873.3587593

Zainurin, M. Z. L., Haji Masri, M., Besar, M. H. A., & Anshari, M. (2023). Towards an understanding of metaverse banking: A conceptual paper. *Journal of Financial Reporting and Accounting*, *21*(1), 178–190. doi:10.1108/JFRA-12-2021-0487

Zaki, M. R. S., & Santo, P. A. F. D. (n.d.). *International Labour Law Perspectives on the Metaverse*.

Zhao, L., Zhu, D., Shafik, W., Matinkhah, S. M., Ahmad, Z., Sharif, L., & Craig, A. (2022). Artificial intelligence analysis in cyber domain: A review. *International Journal of Distributed Sensor Networks*, *18*(4), 15501329221084882. doi:10.1177/15501329221084882

Zytko, D., & Chan, J. (2023). The Dating Metaverse: Why We Need to Design for Consent in Social VR. *IEEE Transactions on Visualization and Computer Graphics*, *29*(5), 2489–2498. doi:10.1109/TVCG.2023.3247065 PMID:37027706

Chapter 6
Societal Risks of Using Cyber Metaverse Technology

Amar Yasser El-Bably
Police Academy, Egypt

ABSTRACT

AI's widespread use poses challenges, especially accountability and legal readiness for metaverse's unique traits. This study addresses AI's current hurdles, focusing on regulating AI-related crimes, including metaverse. It aims to define responsibilities and penalties. Metaverse's societal, reputational, and security implications, along with tech firms' oversight, can escalate cybercrime. Complex evolving cybercrime patterns hinder guilt proof. Criminalizing tech use in terrorism planning and financing is crucial. Social media users face risks like deepfakes, fostering doubt and inciting terrorism. Tech-security agency partnership is vital. Growing digital interconnectedness heightens cybersecurity issues. Metaverse's growth and internet use call for strengthened anti-terrorism and IT crime laws.

INTRODUCTION

Today we are faced with the phenomenon of social media and Internet applications, which are phenomena that science fiction books have always dealt with in the past. Now, we see these technologies becoming an integral part of our lives, with three billion people interacting on the Facebook platform and two billion using Instagram every day. Estimates predict that the size of the Internet market will reach $1.6 trillion by 2030, and the value of electronic commerce is currently $50 billion (Fahd, 2022).

And with the advent of the concept of metaverse, we find that it will open the doors to new jobs such as virtual architects. Already, Mark Zuckerberg announced his future for Metaverse and pointed to the potential for jobs and investments in the European Union worth hundreds of billions.

The importance of technology management in this context cannot be denied. As we can witness how the Twitter platform has evolved from simply publishing short messages to a basic source for displaying our daily news. Social media has played a major role in promoting new media, and this is evident in how people rely on it to follow up on events and news, a development that may be an alternative to traditional news agencies and technology based on continuous management.

DOI: 10.4018/979-8-3693-0220-0.ch006

And with this technological advance, new challenges and potential risks emerge. Including the use of websites by terrorist groups for their purposes, It requires the development of coping mechanisms and the need for a proactive step by both legislators and those in charge of law enforcement to confront this danger by enacting legislation and making amendments to national laws and the need to adhere to the use of electronic signature to tighten control over commercial transactions that take place through Metaverse, and activate international agreements that combat Cybercrimes, setting legal requirements and rules for companies operating in the metaverse field to obtain licenses to carry out their work with criminal liability in case of violating these conditions and rules, and developing plans to protect metaverse users and activating the Information Technology Crime Law No. 175 of 2018.

This research deals The crime of propaganda and promotion of terrorism where Penalties are directed at those who use metaverse technology to spread and promote terrorist content or to recruit volunteers to participate in terrorist acts Those who use metaverse technology to plan or carry out terrorist attacks are punished, whether by directing actual attacks or providing training and mentoring to militants. And Criminalize the financing of terrorism using technology: Those who use metaverse technology in terrorist financing operations or exchange money to support terrorist activities will be held accountable.

THE STUDY PROBLEM

Importance the Study

I became The terrorism industry in light of the rapid technical progress is a very important topic In light of preserving societies from extremism and terrorism, Andin order to put lines of defense to confront the causes of terrorism through the cyber environment Preserving the cyber violations and penetrations of terrorist militias must be criminalized Use Information technologies such as metaverse in communication, tango, training, and setting scenarios for hostile and terrorist acts in light of the rise in Internet users and social communication, And must Inaugurating a strong partnership between technology companies and security and intelligence agencies To combat hostilities committed via advanced technologies and The crime of propaganda and promotion of terrorism: Penalties are imposed on those who use metaverse technology to spread and promote terrorist content or to recruit volunteers to participate in terrorist acts.

Objectives of the Study

- Identify the most important properties of Metaverse technology and its security and societal risks considering the digital development.
- Recognition The dangers of deep falsification technology through social networking sites and platforms and the risks of artificial intelligence related to deepfakes, Internet bots, spreading rumors, and how dangerous it is the dangers of the dark web Dark Web) in spreading rumors.
- Identify dangers of “metaverse” augmented reality associated with social networking sites and platforms in training and education on weapons and the danger of chatting in planning terrorist operations.
- Finding out about the latest UAE and Egyptian legislation regarding combating information technology crimes related to financing and training terrorist elements on modern technologies and using them to harm national and public security.

THE FIRST TOPIC

Group E-Recruitment Metaverse Terrorist

It is important to realize that illegal online activities and cyber threats pose a serious challenge to both individuals and organizations, including terrorist groups as a potential source of cyber threats., However, we must remember that terrorist groups use diverse methods and tools for training, financing, making explosives, drawing, tactics, and planning terrorist operations, "The Metaverse as a Model." We discuss the electronic recruitment of terrorist groups for Metaverse's follows:

THE FIRST REQUIREMENT

What Is Metaverse Technology and the Impact of Technologies on Societal Security?

Bey one the world (Metaverse) is a term that refers to a virtual environment that resembles the real world, in which people can interact, exist, and create 3D content within using virtual characters (avatars). This concept has been depicted in many works of literature, movies, and games, and is gaining interest nowadays due to the advancement of technology and virtual reality and the concept of beyond the world raises a lot of discussions and expectations about the future of technology and social communication. This concept can include various applications and uses such as virtual games, distance education, e-commerce, social interaction, and even work and collaboration in virtual environments.

The metaverse world is a concept that includes augmented reality technology, virtual reality, and digital elements interwoven with the real world. In this new world, individuals can interact with a virtual environment that mixes real and digital elements, Augmented reality technologies allow people to see virtual objects embedded in the real-world using devices such as smartphones or smart glasses. This allows them to interact and enhance their experience with the environment around them (Orofino, 2022).

User avatars are digital interfaces that represent users' identity in the metaverse world. Individuals can customize their avatars with looks and descriptions that reflect their personality or preferences. They can also interact with other people's avatars and communicate with them, and the world of metaverse also features the application of financial technology such as cryptocurrency and non-fungible tokens (NFTs). NFTs), this creates a virtual economic foundation that enables trade and financial interactions within the digital world.

and Day by day, the world is moving towards a transition to Web 3,0, as it relies heavily on new and advanced technologies such as the development of cryptocurrencies, blockchain technology, decentralized applications, and decentralized file storage .And These basic technologies and components to develop a 3D experience in the new virtual world known as "Metaverse" comes with many advantages and benefits, but it also faces unique challenges and risk security, and we address it as follows:

First - the dangers of deep falsification technology through social networking sites and platforms:

- Deep faking is a technology of concern because it can lead to serious consequences, damage people's reputations or spread misleading information It affects community and family security And deceptive Through social networking applications Deepfakes are created by Training AI models on a wide range of images and videos Then those models are used to create fake videos that show that person saying or doing things they didn't actually say or do.

- Rename the deep fake to the term AI Deep Learning Algorithm which means, in Arabic, the deep learning algorithms of artificial intelligence, and these algorithms are distinguished by being able to solve any problem when we provide them with a huge amount of data on the matter (Eling & Wirfs, 2019).
- Referred to as deepfakes technology based on artificial intelligence that replaces the image of a face, voice, or both, with the face and voice of another person, so that the fake audio and video media appear as real (Hamid, 2022). Although it is a technology used in the film drama industry, the revolution in digital technology has enabled ordinary individuals to use this technology, including those who exploit it in abnormal behavior that harms individuals and societies. Politics has a large share of incitement, bullying, harassment, extortion, fraud, and fraud. The deep falsification of fake speeches delivered by leaders, unreal conversations between senior officials, and leaks that did not happen that changed the course of events in countries and their peoples.
- And among the negative uses of deepfakes is its use in election manipulation, political campaigns, or even in the manufacture of false news and rumors. Deepfakes is a major challenge to digital security systems, artificial intelligence, and technology in general, and requires effective solutions to combat this type of advanced forgery. And the deceiver (Raveena et al., 2015).
- Exposing children to harmful content: Deepfakes can be used to create fake videos and audio that contain harmful or inappropriate content that can affect children's behavior and mental health.
- Security risk: Deepfakes can be used to access sensitive information about children, which poses a security risk Great creation False scenes and circulation on sites Social communication with the aim of inflaming feelings and inciting violence and protests, and therefore, these actions can result in dangerous repercussions such as the outbreak of violence and riots and the exacerbation of conflicts and conflicts .Chokes Social and political, and its impact on security and economic stability to the state (Deep Fake Evidence, 2021).
- And it gets more serious Robots, spider squads, and virtual armies' tweet, blog, share, and click like" and recycle and spread fake news and misinformation her video The fake and fabricated T and among the users are those who believe and do not doubt, so they form an opinion and build a trend and the base of opinion expands affect the national security of countries.
    - In 2020 a video was created A deepfake of British actor Tom Hanks appears in it talking about the emerging corona virus, and it was circulated on the Internet (Farish, 2021).
    - In 2021 it was created Deepfakes of some famous people in India including the Prime Minister of India Narendra Modi have been circulating online.
    - In 2021, an app is launched In China which allows users to create deep fakes to their faces and share them across sites social media.
    - And at the beginning of the Russian invasion of Ukraine in March 2022 Pretonic and Zerbon, 2022). A fabricated video appeared(deepfake) Ukrainian President Volodymyr Zelensky on social media orders his citizens to lay down their arms Video clips fabricated using deepfake technology and the people to surrender to the Russian forces invading his country Moments later he posted The real Zelenskyy posted a video on Facebook showing the earlier message as fake.

o and It could be a sexual deepfake Negative impact on young men and women, when deepfakes are used to create fake pornographic content, this can lead to widespread circulation of this content on the Internet, exposing individuals to indecent scenes, and tarnishing their image and reputation This threat had a clear impact on many of the women who were targeted by artificial intelligence-enabled porn sites.

Second - Rumors on digital platforms and social media:

- Disinformation and rumors are widely used in media and psychological wars and are a powerful tool in shaping public opinion and provoking divisions and tensions in societies. Social media and the Internet to spread lies and rumors quickly and easily and amplify them through sensational headlines and pictures Influencing rumors fall under the concept war Mental should war and Shewa ideology ideological Which Aim ideas to control the minds of peoples.

- With the significant increase in the use of social networking sites, electronic platforms have become a fertile tool for spreading rumors and fake and false news. And Spreading rumors in times of crisis is a deadly disease and a betrayal against society and the nation It may be exaggerated and its content changed frequently, and this leads to misleading the public and creating chaos It may lead to the outbreak of violence and riots in societies or incite racism, hatred and incitement to terrorism It harms relations between states and societies Arabic (Fahad, n.d.).

- The speed of information circulation through social media contributes to spreading rumors, especially if the shared information is related to risky events or emergencies.

- Terrorist organizations and anti-state institutions use several advanced techniques to spread false news and content and This dissemination includes methods such as computers spread over social networks Automated Bots and Trolling by creating fake accounts on these sites and creating attractive headlines, including large numbers of users, and purchasing follow-up and reposting services social networking and crowdsourcing (OSCE, 2019).

- It is becoming more common using Internet borshch number of devices connected to the Internet, each running one or more bots And comes from traffic botnet from many IP addresses making it difficult to identify and block the source of malicious bot traffic And Boys can be used for a variety of purposes Spreading news on social media and electronic platforms quickly and in huge numbers Hacking, spam and espionage and hack for websites.

- Media: And they are used to publish Certain ideas, as well as fake accounts, in order to gain followers by themselves, by increasing social networks and increasing their complexity and It spreads fake news as it produces and distributes articles on a large scale and bots create fake accounts online which then gain followers, recognition and power Some are programmed to spread misinformation Fake news is often spread through unofficial news websites And from here enable sites Social networking spread all nations false In fact, fake news spreads quickly because it is usually designed to attract attention and galvanize emotions, which is why it often contains outlandish claims or stories that stir anger or fear. Anda bad bot can cause significant damage by collecting passwords, logging keystrokes, and even collecting financial information (Mustafa, 2021).

- Research from the Center for Informed Democracy and Social Cybersecurity at Carnegie University indicates Mellon notes that “the robots may account for between 45and 60% of accounts Twitter that discussCovid-19”AndMany of these are published the accounts misinformation users, and that9-15% of accounts Twitter, And about 60 million accounts on Facebook, are robots to spread false news (Al-Ahram newspaper, n.d.).

- The dangers of the dark webDark Web) in spread rumors:

- Where Displays 533 million accounts of Facebook in 2019 Blockage of phone numbers and datasets and Business Insider reported, from 106 duto(1)And 32 million users in the US, 11 million in the UK, and 6 million in Indian Hackers can Use them to impersonate people and commit fraud And its use in spreading false news and rumors on social networking sites: by operations (Web Traffic) Within certain sites that raise concern and public opinion with false and fake news, and those accounts that have been hacked are purchased through the (market)under the umbrella of the dark web Dark Web.

- And in general20203 million and 900 thousand card numbers were monitored stolen banking in the "deep internet", and leaking4 billion accounts to bear Data 1.3billion users a year2022 For Facebook and Twitter, which made that sensitive data vulnerable to theft and exchange on the Internet (Said, 2021).

- And here you are Terrorist organizations and various organizations use stolen accounts and hacked websites to fund and support their criminal activities terrorist and extremist and also to spread fake news And rumors as well These organizations also use botnets to create fake accounts that perform certain interactions and tweets on social networking sites with the aim of influencing users and distorting their views.

The researcher thinks that Spreading rumors and false news on the Internet is not random It is done in a systematic way and many people take advantage of this method to achieve their malicious goals Indeed, the circulation of rumors and false news on site social networking is a threat real national security globally.

THE SECOND REQUIREMENT

Crime Stories in the World of Virtual Reality "Metaverse"

The metaverse is a fictional world in which modern technology is used to create virtual reality environments. Although the virtual world can be a place for experience, adventure, and positive social interaction, it is not without some challenges and risks, including terrorist crimes., And virtual reality, people can exploit technology to carry out various terrorist acts. The virtual world may be used to recruit extremists, train them to carry out attacks, or even carry out cyber and disruptive attacks We address the main risks of virtual reality as follows:

- **Virtual espionage:** The virtual world can be exploited to spy on sensitive activities and information. Attackers can use the technology available in virtual reality to hack security systems and spy on companies, individuals, or even governments.
- **Advertising and promotion:** The virtual world can be used to promote extremist ideology and incite violence and terrorist crimes. Virtual platforms can be created to propagate and promote extremist ideologies and attract supporters.
- **Fraud and fraud:** The virtual world can be exploited to carry out fraudulent and fraudulent activities. Attackers can use virtual reality to create virtual reality social networks to lure individuals and perform fraudulent operations, such as stealing credit card information or hacking into bank accounts, (Major, 2022).
- **Violence and physical attacks:** The virtual world can be used to carry out acts of violence and physical attacks. Virtual environments that simulate real locations can be created and used to train for bombings, gun attacks, or even physical assaults (El Badry, 2021).

- **Privacy violations:** The virtual world can be exploited to violate users' privacy. There may be collection of personal information or spying on the private activities of individuals within the virtual world.

First – risks Metaverse Augmented reality associated with social networking sites and platforms:

- metaverse technology (Metaverse) is a new and advanced technology that aims to create a 3D virtual world in which users can interact and interact with virtual objects and people in a virtual world Virtual and augmented reality technology can be used for malicious purposes such as training terrorists and planning terrorist operations, in addition to propaganda and promotion of extremist ideas .And This technology can also be used to spread lies and disinformation and to covertly communicate between members of terrorist organizations (Khalifa, 2022).
- An example of the use of virtual and augmented reality technology in terrorist activities is that the "ISIS" group used augmented reality to prepare videos showing their terrorist operations in a realistic and terrifying way, which was used in recruitment and influencing the masses.
- The metaverse digital landscape is very active for cybercriminals. Whether they are exploiting old threats in new ways in a new virtual environment, using time-tested social engineering and phishing techniques, or even creating new technical attacks to monetize in new ways, the reality is that Increased activity of cybercriminals in this world And This increase stems from risks related to Ethereum DNS services, social engineering, exploiting fraudulent client services activities, massive cyberattacks, and the use of malicious smart contracts, (Hamid, n.d.).

Second - the development of the augmented reality of terrorist organizations through electronic platforms and social networking sites:

- The terrorist al-Qaeda organization used virtual reality techniques to train its fighters to fight, as the organization's media brigades provided videos showing fighters training in a virtual environment, and published videos showing fake footage of killings and targeting, and that was in the period from 2013 to 2015.
- In 2016, ISIS organizations launched a video game called "Prince of Martyrs", which includes virtual training for fighters in the use of weapons and the destruction of targets, including suicide bombings.
- In 2020, a report by the French Ministry of the Interior revealed that ISIS used electronic game applications on mobile phones to train its members to use weapons and film attacks.
- In 2019, a New Zealand gunman used virtual reality to train himself to carry out the terrorist attack he carried out in two mosques, killing 51 people.
- The extremist organizations use virtual reality technology to train Its elements are on the use of weapons and the implementation of terrorist operations, where the trainees can wear virtual reality glasses and take advantage of simulation techniques to train them in the manufacture of explosive devices, the dismantling and assembling of rifles, the manufacture of primitive drones and other various training patterns. Carrying out terrorist operations. This type of training and simulation is one of the tools used by extremist organizations to develop their subversive methods and increase the efficiency of their members in carrying out terrorist operations, (Said, n.d.).

- and It is considered Stealth and camouflage One of the most important strategies of terrorist groups is to hide their identities and carry out their operations without revealing their true identity. The use of virtual reality technologies such as Metaverse provides extremists and terrorists with an opportunity to disguise and camouflage further. By creating virtual personalities using avatars, any individual within the organization can represent himself without revealing his identity. This is used Virtual personalities to hide the identity of extremists and terrorists within the organization and facilitate communication and coordination between them in a safe and confidential manner. The use of modern technologies such as smart glasses allows extremists and terrorists to control their virtual personalities and employ them in terrorist activities without revealing their true identities, which increases the difficulty of detecting and trapping them by the security authorities.
- Metaverse and other similar Internet platforms are a fertile and active environment for extremist organizations, where these organizations can exploit advanced digital technologies to organize and train their members and exchange information and resources in secret. The use of encryption and complexity allows the effective concealment of members' identities and activities on these sites. Platforms and websites, (Khalifa, n.d.).
- Training and education of terrorists Metaverse may be used to provide training and education to terrorists on how to manufacture weapons and explosives and carry out terrorist attacks and This type of training can provide virtual reality and sophisticated simulations that help terrorists improve their skills and orient themselves more effectively.
- Planning and control: Terrorists can use metaverses to plan, monitor and reconnaissance potential targets And They can use available spatial and temporal data to analyze locations and identify the most vulnerable targets.

Third - Risks of Metaverse Technology to Public Health:

1. However, there are some potential public health risks when adopting Metaverse technology. These risks include the following:
2. **Social isolation:** Excessive focus on the virtual world and digital interaction may lead to social isolation in the real world and Individuals may forget to communicate and interact with others in real life and become overly immersed in the virtual world, which can negatively affect social relationships and mental health.
3. **Digital addiction:** Continuous and continuous interaction with technology may cause metaphysics in digital addiction And achieving exciting, stimulating and interactive experiences in the virtual world may lead to excessive dependence on this technology and difficulty in controlling use.
4. **Mental and physiological health:** The use of Metaverse technology may affect the mental and physiological health of individuals And Intense, realistic experiences in the virtual world may produce negative effects such as dizziness, nausea, and headaches. In addition, excessive reliance on technology may increase sleep problems and stress. And anxiety, (**Nanoel, 2021).**

Sees researcher risks sites Social communication on the security of societies may lead to the spread of internal violence sites Social communication is the dissemination of cultures, trends, and ideas that are not consistent with the values of society and may contradict them altogether, especially for groups of young people and young people who may not have sufficient immunity against being affected by these ideas, which may result in their alienation from society and the distance between them and it to a degree that may reach the point of hostility or estrangement by virtue of The ability of social networking sites to establish an alternative virtual world that raises sectarian, religious and tribal sensitivities and tensions that may threaten national cohesion and put it in front of serious risks. The ease of use, the ability to hide, camouflage, and networking, as well as the ability to communicate with a broad mass base easily and easily, is what helped extremist groups to take advantage of social networking sites and harness them to serve their destructive ideas, as it helped them achieve the element of recruitment in a large and wide manner.no About the ease of obtaining information, accessing databases, hacking government accounts and websites, and exploiting them in creating information terrorism, mobilizing and recruiting new terrorists.

Sees researcher that it by establishing the legislative framework Egyptian and Emirati Appropriate for cyber security, combating cybercrimes and protecting privacy "The Metaverse Model "With the participation of the concerned and experienced parties in the governmental and private sectors, with the guidance of expertise, experiences and relevant international programs., where is update the Legislation on those offenses may be prepared It is necessary regarding legal confrontation because these technical crimes are developing rapidly. Therefore, countries rely on the application of their laws to codify these penalties, but they need continuous development due to the high rates of Internet use, social communication, and the increasing seriousness of these crimes. The United Arab Emirates operates And Egypt strive To enhance the security of personal data and combat cybercrime and technical Through the adoption of legislation and policies that protect citizens and residents in the country, (Anwar, n.d.).

RESULTS

- Social media has become a societal force pressuring in favor of or against policy planners and decision-makers all over the world, as these means can prepare massive electronic crowds, in support of or rejection of any decision, and thus have become a major element in political equations within countries.
- Facebook and Twitter are among the most important social media that are used for interaction and coordination between terrorist organizations.to save it Changing virtual societies, which these groups benefit from in recruiting, coordinating and planning their operations terrorist, Hence, social media enables the spread of false claims, causing them to be promoted faster than the real news in reality, and fake news spreads quickly because it is usually designed to attract attention and attract emotions.
- It is possible that artificial intelligence can be used as a tool of psychological warfare in contemporary reality, through what is known as "deep falsification", through which a human image can be created based on intelligence algorithms. artificial, And Dar Al-Iftar confirmed that it is not permissible to use technology (deepfake- deepfakes) to fabricate video or audio clips of people using artificial intelligence to make them appear to be doing or saying something they did not actually do or say.
- Developed by the United Arab Emirates and Egypt Rumors Act Information technology challenges to be a deterrent against all those who wish to spread confusion and turn the facts around for personal goals, in order to cause havoc among the citizens.

RECOMMENDATIONS

- It is necessary for legislation to keep pace with recent developments in the world of technology and to include legal texts regulating electronic activities and punishing technical crimes in effective and deterrent ways. Revisiting existing laws could allow for new classifications of technology offenses to be included and penalties to be updated according to new threats.
- The crimes I mentioned (fraud, forgery, piracy, theft, impersonation, harassment, cyber terrorism, violation of privacy, abuse of others, and espionage) pose serious challenges in the digital world, and it is necessary that legislation be equipped to deal with them effectively.
- There is always a need to develop and improve laws to keep pace with technological developments and protect society from new threats, and continuous dialogue and cooperation with the various stakeholders is necessary to ensure the best results in this regard.
- Achieving a balance between protecting personal rights and freedoms and combating technical crimes is a challenge, and it is important for legislation to be clear and transparent and to ensure fair legal procedures and mechanisms to guarantee the rights of the accused.
- Much needed Policy reassessment cyber-Special face letters Hate to merge context with content, thus narrowing down Its scope to ban the most harmful cases posted across social media different, where Encrypted messages are dangerous implicitly, which may not be recognizable; Where may Some use hate code words, However, it is not included in the list of prohibited words on social networking sites.
- Training young people on how to safely use social networking sites through specialized courses supervised by experts and specialists Patriots And developing their awareness of the danger of the ideology spread by extremist and terrorist groups on these sites.
- crimes Technology Cal metaverse It is considered one of the serious and complex crimes as it is a transnational crime, and the latest technologies are used in it, and the perpetrators are hidden and outside the state in most cases, which requires confronting them with concerted efforts, both local and global, pointing out that these cases commit many crimes such as electronic fraud and defamation and terrorism and other crimes.
- Enhancing cooperation between all sectors in order to combat cyber-attack emerging in the cyber arena, and creating a common system that secures the information required to enhance proactive measures and procedures in order to protect data in all vital sectors, and achieve a balance between cybersecurity on the one hand and operational work on the other hand, in addition to strengthening proactive response strategies in the event of exposure to electronic attacks that disrupt business, and the need for better research Cyber security practices.
- Organizing intensive training courses in specialized technical centers to train policemen and judicial officers, innovative and important, to enhance their capabilities in combating and investigating crime. These courses can cover a range of technical and investigative topics and skills, such as: Information Technology and Digital Investigation and Evidence collection and analysis, including deleted data retrieval and smartphone analysis.
- Encouraging the promotion of research and study in the field of combating technical and informatics crimes and information technology is an important step to maintain digital security and develop specialized cadres. By promoting research and education in this field, the expertise and skills needed to combat and prevent technological crime and respond to security challenges can be developed.

REFERENCES

Dayani, R., Chabra, N., Kadina, T., & Kaushal, R. (2015). Rumor Detection in Twitter: An Analysis in Retrospect. In *2015 IEEE International Conference on Advanced Networks and Telecommunications Systems (ANTS)*. IEEE. 10.1109/ANTS.2015.7413660

Eling, M., & Wars, J. (2019). What are the actual costs of cyber risk events? *Eur. J. Opera. Res., 272*. 1109–1119.www.scopus.com

Essam, A. (2021). Role The United Nations in the fight against terrorism 2001-2020. The Arab Democratic Center for Strategic, Hunting and Political Studies, Cairo.

OSCE. (2019). *Understanding the Role of Social Communication, and Preventing Countering Violent Extremism Conducive to Terrorism*. OSCE Secretariat.

Babylonian, A. (2020). *Space security email*. Studies Institute Arabic, League of Arab States.

Al-Ahram newspaper. (2021). The private data of more than 533 million users was leaked. *Al-Ahram Newspaper*.

Majun, M. (2022). Incitement to hatred and violence in social networks. The Islamic Military Coalition to Combat Terrorism, Riyadh.

UAE. (2021). *National Program for Artificial Intelligence*. UAE. https://ai.gov.ae/wp-content/uploads/2021/07/AI-Deepfake-Guide-AR-2021.pdf

Fahd, W. (2022). *Studying Artificial Intelligence... Between Terrorist Tactics and National Strategies*. Trends Center for Research and Studies, Abu Dhabi, UAE. https://trendsresearch.org/ar/insight/ai-between-terrorist-actics-and-national-strategies/

Fahd, W. & El-Meadowy, W. (2022). Arbitrary search titled Strategic directions to confront extremism and takfiri thought, a study in the light of the Egyptian and Emirati experience. *Police Thought Journal*, Sharjah Police Research Center.

Fahd, W. & Mustafa, W. (2021). The effectiveness of chatbot technology "conversational bots", in institutions. *Journal of Media Research, Faculty of Mass Communication, Al-Azhar University*.

Farish, K. (2021). *Deepfakes and their impact on women*. Dacbeach Croft. https://www.dacbeachcroft.com/en/gb/articles/2021/august/deepfakes-and-their-impact-on-women/

Elisa Orofino, E. (2021). nanoelectronics warfare. *Lebanese National Defense Journal, 118*.

Orofino, E. (2022). *Online Radicalization: How to Detect and Deal with Extremist Content (United Kingdom Model)*. European Eye on Radicalization Report. https://eeradicalization.com/exploring-online-radicalization-how-to-spot-extremist-content-and-what-to-do-about-it/

Orofino, E. (2022). Rumors and Cybercrime Crimes in the Arab Emirates. *Journal of Fiqh and Legal Research,* Al-Azhar University, Cairo. https://jlr.journals.ekb.eg/article_251626_ec495d5801eb0c97219e5b22d07cc5ad.pdf https://digitalwellbeing.ae/ar/digital_laws_in_uae

Orofino, E. (2022). Digital counterfeiting and its impact on the authenticity of digital evidence in criminal cases, a comparative jurisprudence study. *Journal of Comparative Jurisprudence, Faculty of Sharia Law, Al-Azhar University, Cairo, 14.*

Orofino, E. (2021). International Security Confrontation of Criminal Activities Committed Through the Dark Web. *Public Security Magazine.*

Orofino, E. (2021). The Depths of the "Dark Internet", Hiring Killers and Abnormal Services in Exchange for Cryptocurrency. *Asharq Al-Awsat Newspaper, Al-Arab International Newspaper.*

Chapter 7
The Future of Cyber-Crimes and Cyber War in the Metaverse

Sameer Saharan
https://orcid.org/0000-0002-7487-6297
Mody University of Science and Technology, India

Shailja Singh
Mangalayatan University, Jabalpur, India

Ajay Kumar Bhandari
https://orcid.org/0009-0009-9400-1330
Amity School of Applied Sciences, Amity University, India

Bhuvnesh Yadav
Amity School of Applied Sciences, Amity University, India

ABSTRACT

The future of cybercrimes and cyber warfare in the metaverse is a topic of concern. Understanding the emerging landscape is crucial. With technological advancements and the pervasive influence of the metaverse, new cyber threats have emerged. This chapter provides an overview of challenges and ramifications associated with cybercrimes and cyber warfare in the metaverse. It explores evolving cyber threats in the metaverse, considering AI, machine learning, and quantum computing. Cybercrimes include virtual asset theft, identity theft, phishing, harassment, and online extortion. Cyber warfare in the metaverse involves state-sponsored attacks, espionage, information warfare, and manipulation of virtual defense systems. Robust cybersecurity measures, collaboration among stakeholders, and cyber literacy are essential to mitigate risks.

DOI: 10.4018/979-8-3693-0220-0.ch007

INTRODUCTION

The metaverse, a virtual reality space where individuals interact with each other and digital entities, rapidly evolves and expands. With its immense popularity and increasing integration into our daily lives, the metaverse has become a potential battleground for cyber warfare. Cyberwar in the metaverse refers to the utilization of cyber tactics and techniques to disrupt, manipulate, or infiltrate virtual environments, posing serious threats to individuals, organizations, and even nations.

BACKGROUND

The concept of the metaverse originated from science fiction, but recent technological advancements have brought it closer to reality. The convergence of virtual reality, augmented reality, artificial intelligence, and blockchain technology has paved the way for the development of immersive virtual worlds with vast social and economic implications. As the metaverse grows in complexity and user engagement, it becomes a lucrative target for cybercriminals and state-sponsored actors seeking to exploit vulnerabilities for personal gain or strategic purposes.

The Estonian cyber-attacks in 2007 were the inaugural instance of recognized cyber warfare, targeting the government, banks, media, and critical infrastructure. Leveraging Distributed Denial of Service (DDoS) techniques and malware, the attacks disrupted Estonia's computer networks, causing significant impacts on government services, banking, media, and public access to information. The incident exposed vulnerabilities in Estonia's cybersecurity defenses, serving as a catalyst for global awareness on the potential consequences of cyber-attacks on a nation's critical infrastructure. This event prompted governments worldwide to prioritize bolstering cybersecurity measures, leading to increased efforts and international cooperation in the face of evolving cyber threats. Since then, subsequent cyber warfare incidents globally have reinforced the imperative for continuous advancements in cybersecurity practices to mitigate future risks (Czosseck et al., 2013; Haataja, 2017; Herzog, 2011; Ottis, 2008).

Recent news highlights growing concerns about cyber warfare in the Metaverse, a virtual reality space where hackers and state-sponsored actors target virtual worlds, leading to disruptions, theft of assets, and privacy breaches (Dolata & Schwabe, 2023). These incidents underscore the pressing need for robust cybersecurity in the Metaverse (Chopra, 2021; Fouad, 2021; Smith et al., 2023). The articles emphasize the escalating frequency and sophistication of attacks on virtual reality platforms, presenting unique security challenges. National security implications are also noted, stressing collaborative efforts among governments and security agencies to protect virtual infrastructure and national interests. In light of these challenges, proactive measures, awareness, and strategic planning are crucial to ensure the security and integrity of the evolving Metaverse.

DIFFERENCE BETWEEN CYBER-CRIME AND CYBER WARFARE

Cybercrime and cyber warfare both are terms associated with malicious activities in the digital realm, but they differ in terms of scope, intent, and targets (Bernik, 2014). Here are the key differences between cybercrime and cyber warfare:

1. Scope: Cybercrime typically refers to illegal activities carried out by individuals or organized groups with the intent to gain unauthorized access, steal data, commit fraud, or disrupt computer systems for personal or financial gain (McGuire & Dowling, 2013). Cyber warfare, on the other hand, involves state-sponsored or politically motivated attacks aimed at disrupting or destroying critical infrastructure, compromising national security, or conducting espionage on a larger scale (Robinson et al., 2015).
2. Intent: The primary intent of cybercrime is usually financial gain or personal benefit. Cybercriminals may seek to exploit vulnerabilities for monetary rewards, such as stealing financial information, selling stolen data, or conducting ransomware attacks. In contrast, the primary intent of cyber warfare is to advance geopolitical objectives, exert influence, or inflict harm on rival nations. Cyber warfare may involve activities like espionage, sabotage, or disruption of vital systems to achieve political or military goals (Bernik, 2014).
3. Targets: Cybercrime can target individuals, businesses, organizations, or specific sectors, such as banking, e-commerce, or healthcare. Cybercriminals often focus on exploiting vulnerabilities in systems and networks to access valuable data or extort money (Sabillon et al., 2016). In contrast, cyber warfare typically targets critical infrastructure, government agencies, military systems, or key industries to cause significant damage, disrupting operations, or gaining strategic advantage in conflicts between nations (Robinson et al., 2015).
4. Actors: Cybercrime can be carried out by individuals or organized criminal groups who operate for personal gain. These actors may operate independently or collaborate in underground forums or hacking communities (Pastrana et al., 2018). Cyber warfare, however, involves state-sponsored or state-supported activities conducted by national intelligence agencies or military organizations. The scale and sophistication of cyber warfare operations often exceed those of individual cybercriminals (Bussolati, 2015).
5. Legal Framework: Cybercrime is generally recognized as illegal in most jurisdictions, and laws exist to prosecute and deter cybercriminal activities. Legal frameworks and law enforcement agencies focus on investigating and prosecuting cybercriminals, protecting victims, and enhancing cybersecurity measures (Calderoni, 2010). Cyber warfare, on the other hand, operates in a complex and often murky legal landscape. International laws and agreements regarding cyber warfare are still evolving, and the attribution of cyber-attacks to specific nation-states can be challenging (Pipyros et al., 2016).

SIGNIFICANCE

Analyzing cyber war in the metaverse holds significant importance due to several key reasons:

- Security Implications: The metaverse's interconnected nature and reliance on virtual assets and identities make it vulnerable to cyber threats. Understanding the potential risks and security implications of cyber warfare in the metaverse is crucial for developing effective defence strategies and safeguarding against attacks (Di Pietro & Cresci, 2021).

    1. Economic Impact: The metaverse has its digital economies, where users transact, trade virtual assets, and engage in online commerce. A cyber war targeting the metaverse could disrupt these

economies, resulting in financial losses, market instability, and erosion of trust. Analyzing the potential economic impact of cyber warfare in the metaverse helps policymakers and stakeholders devise mitigation measures and enhance resilience (Yoo et al., 2023).

2. Privacy and Personal Safety: Individuals engage with the metaverse using their personal information and avatars, blurring the boundaries between the virtual and physical worlds. Cyber warfare in the metaverse poses risks to privacy, personal safety, and identity theft. Understanding the implications of cyber-attacks on individuals' privacy rights and personal safety is vital for ensuring adequate protection (Wang et al., 2022).
3. National Security: The metaverse's growing influence raises concerns about national security. Cyber warfare in the metaverse can target critical infrastructure, government entities, and military operations. Analyzing the potential threats and vulnerabilities associated with cyber war in the metaverse is essential for national security agencies to devise robust defence strategies and policies (Wang et al., 2022).

The objective of this chapter is to examine the future implications of cyber-crimes and cyber warfare in the metaverse. It aims to explore the potential risks and challenges arising from the intersection of virtual reality, digital interactions, and criminal activities. The study will analyze emerging trends, technological advancements, and the evolving nature of cyber threats in the metaverse. Ultimately, it seeks to provide insights and recommendations to inform policy, security measures, and societal responses in the face of these evolving challenges.

THE METAVERSE: AN OVERVIEW

The metaverse refers to a virtual reality space or collective virtual universe where individuals interact with each other and digital entities in a shared online environment. It is a concept inspired by science fiction and represents a fully immersive and interconnected virtual world that blurs the boundaries between physical and digital realities (Laeeq, 2022; Mystakidis, 2022; Ning et al., 2023; Sparkes, 2021; Wang et al., 2022).

CHARACTERISTICS OF THE METAVERSE

The characteristics of the metaverse are the following (Ning et al., 2023; Wang et al., 2022) (Figure 1):

1. Immersive Virtual Environment: The metaverse provides users with an immersive virtual environment where they can engage in various activities, interact with other users, and explore digital landscapes realistically and interactively.
2. Shared Virtual Space: It is a shared virtual space where users from different locations can connect and interact in real time. They can communicate, collaborate, and engage in social interactions within the metaverse.
3. Interconnectedness: The metaverse is characterized by a high degree of interconnectedness. Users can navigate between different virtual environments, seamlessly transitioning from one digital realm to another.

Figure 1. Characteristics of the Metaverse

4. User-Created Content: The metaverse allows users to contribute to the virtual world by creating and sharing their own content, such as virtual objects, environments, and experiences. This user-generated content adds to the richness and diversity of the metaverse.
5. Virtual Economies: The metaverse often encompasses virtual economies where users can buy, sell, and trade virtual assets, currencies, and services. These economies can have real-world value and provide opportunities for entrepreneurship and commerce within the virtual realm.
6. Technological Advancements: The metaverse relies on advanced technologies, including virtual reality (VR), augmented reality (AR), artificial intelligence (AI), and blockchain, to create immersive experiences, facilitate interactions, and ensure security and authenticity within the virtual world.
7. Potential for Infinite Expansion: The metaverse has the potential for infinite expansion, with new virtual environments, experiences, and functionalities constantly being added and evolving.

In the Metaverse, a virtual environment refers to a digitally created space that users can explore, interact with, and inhabit. It is a simulated reality that replicates elements of the physical world or presents unique and fantastical realms. Virtual environments in the metaverse can vary widely in their design, theme, and purpose. These virtual environments are typically accessed through immersive technologies such as virtual reality (VR) or augmented reality (AR) devices, which enhance the user's sensory experience and create a sense of presence within the virtual space. Users can navigate through these environments, interact with objects and other users, and engage in various activities (Mystakidis, 2022). Virtual environments in the metaverse offer a multitude of possibilities. They can be designed to simulate real-world locations, such as virtual replicas of cities, historical landmarks, or natural landscapes. Alternatively, they can be imaginative and fantastical, featuring fictional worlds, futuristic settings, or virtual realms with unique laws of physics and possibilities. Within these virtual environments, users can engage in diverse activities, such as exploring virtual landscapes, attending virtual events and conferences, participating in multiplayer online games, socializing with other users, creating and manipulating virtual objects, and even conducting business transactions. Virtual environments play a pivotal role in creating the immersive and interactive nature of the metaverse. They provide users with a sense of presence, enabling them to feel as if they are physically present within the digital space. This immersive experience fosters a deeper level of engagement and facilitates social interactions, collaboration, and exploration. The design and development of virtual environments require expertise in areas such as computer graphics, 3D modelling, animation, physics simulation, and user interface design (Lee et al., 2021; Van der Land et al., 2011). These environments can be created by individuals, organizations, or entire communities within the metaverse, contributing to the vast and ever-expanding virtual landscape. Overall, virtual environments in the metaverse form the foundation for users' experiences and interactions. They offer a rich and diverse array of digital spaces where individuals can explore, socialize, learn, and create, blurring the boundaries between the physical and digital realms and opening up new horizons for immersive and interactive experiences.

CYBER THREATS IN THE METAVERSE

Cyber threats in the metaverse present a formidable challenge in the digital realm, necessitating a proactive and comprehensive approach to safeguarding the security and integrity of virtual environments. As the metaverse continues to expand and evolve, it becomes an enticing target for malicious actors seeking to exploit vulnerabilities and disrupt the immersive digital experiences of users. Some of the key cyber threats that exist within the metaverse are the following (Bernik, 2014; Bussolati, 2015; Calderoni, 2010; Chopra, 2021; Fouad, 2021; Pastrana et al., 2018; Pipyros et al., 2016; Robinson et al., 2015; Sabillon et al., 2016; Smith et al., 2023) (Figure 2):

1. Malware and Viruses: Malware and viruses, just like in the physical world, are major threats in the metaverse. They can enter the virtual environment through downloads, links, or compromised virtual objects, resulting in unauthorized access, data theft, or system compromise. To counter these threats, robust security measures like regular software updates, antivirus software, and user awareness are essential. Examples of malware and viruses commonly encountered in the metaverse, along with their roles, include:

    a. Ransomware: Encrypts virtual assets or accounts, demanding payment in virtual currency to restore access.
    b. Trojan Horse: Infiltrates the metaverse by disguising as legitimate software and can steal sensitive information or disrupt virtual environments.
    c. Botnets: Control networks of compromised devices and can be used for DDoS attacks, causing disruptions.
    d. Keyloggers: Record keystrokes to capture sensitive information, compromising virtual asset login details.
    e. Spyware: Collects information without user knowledge, compromising privacy and security.
    f. Worms: Self-replicating malware that can spread across virtual environments and devices, causing damage and stealing sensitive information.

These malware and viruses are a major concern in the metaverse, and understanding and defending against them are crucial for a safe virtual experience. Various studies and sources have contributed to this understanding, providing insights into the potential risks and their implications.

Figure 2. Cyber threats in Metaverse

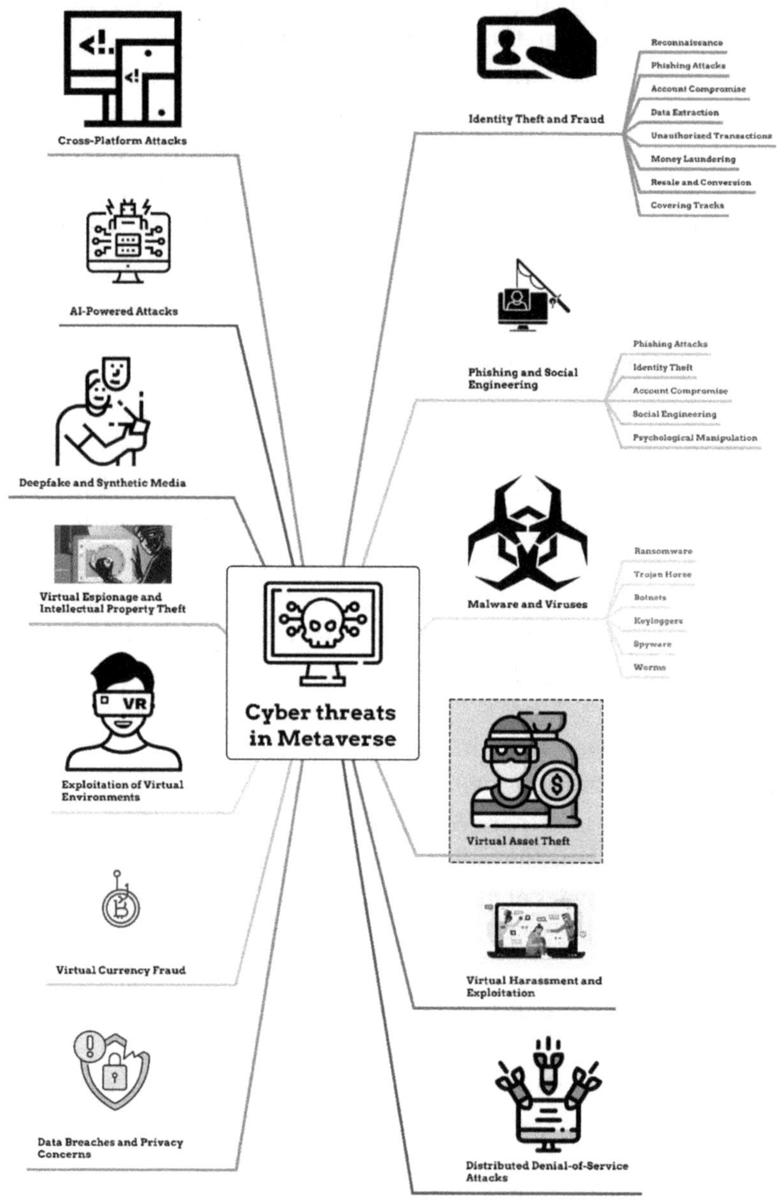

2. Phishing and Social Engineering: Phishing attacks are widespread in the metaverse and involve deceptive emails, messages, or social interactions aimed at tricking users into revealing sensitive information or engaging in malicious actions. Education and awareness programs are essential for helping users recognize and avoid such scams. Meanwhile, platform operators can implement security protocols to detect and mitigate phishing attempts. Key aspects of phishing and social engineering in the metaverse include:

a. Phishing Attacks: Malicious actors deceive users into disclosing sensitive information, such as login credentials or financial details, through virtual messages, emails, or fake websites, gaining unauthorized access to assets, user accounts, or data.
b. Identity Theft: Phishing attacks often target user identities, with cybercriminals impersonating trusted entities to deceive users into sharing personal information, which can be exploited for unauthorized access, financial fraud, or illicit activities.
c. Account Compromise: Phishing can lead to the compromise of user accounts, enabling attackers to steal virtual assets, manipulate transactions, or engage in unauthorized activities.
d. Social Engineering: Attackers manipulate users into divulging information or performing actions compromising security, exploiting trust, emotions, or lack of awareness.
e. Psychological Manipulation: Phishing and social engineering rely on psychological manipulation techniques, exploiting cognitive biases and emotions, which can be especially effective in immersive virtual environments.

3. Identity Theft and Fraud: In the metaverse, identity theft and fraud are significant threats. Cybercriminals gather information about potential targets, initiate phishing attacks to gain unauthorized access, compromise user accounts, extract personal information and virtual assets, conduct unauthorized transactions, and may engage in money laundering. They often resell or convert stolen assets and take steps to cover their tracks, using techniques like VPNs to avoid detection.
4. Virtual Asset Theft: The metaverse is replete with virtual assets, ranging from digital currencies and virtual goods to unique virtual properties. These assets can be lucrative targets for cybercriminals who seek to steal or exploit them for financial gain. Implementing secure transaction mechanisms, encrypted storage, and secure virtual property management systems can help mitigate the risk of virtual asset theft.
5. Virtual Harassment and Exploitation: The immersive and interactive nature of the metaverse can, unfortunately, give rise to virtual harassment, stalking, or exploitation. Cyberbullies and malicious individuals may target users, leading to emotional distress and harm. Strong community guidelines, reporting mechanisms, and moderation systems are crucial in maintaining a safe and inclusive metaverse environment.
6. Distributed Denial-of-Service (DDoS) Attacks: DDoS (Distributed Denial of Service) attacks in the metaverse aim to disrupt virtual platforms and services by overwhelming them with a flood of malicious traffic, rendering them inaccessible to users. These attacks can have significant consequences, including service outages, financial losses, and user frustration. Here's a summary of DDoS attacks in the metaverse:
   a. Preparation: Attackers identify vulnerable targets within the metaverse, such as gaming servers, virtual marketplaces, or social platforms. They assemble a botnet, a network of compromised devices, to launch the attack.
   b. Botnet Deployment: The botnet, comprising thousands or millions of compromised devices, is deployed to initiate the attack.
   c. Traffic Overload: Attackers direct the botnet to generate massive traffic toward the targeted metaverse services. This flood of traffic overwhelms resources, causing disruption.
   d. Service Disruption: DDoS attacks make metaverse services inaccessible or significantly degrade their performance, resulting in financial losses and user dissatisfaction.
   e. Duration and Variations: DDoS attacks can vary in duration, intensity, and techniques used. Some are short bursts, while others are prolonged assaults. Various attack types are employed.

  f. Mitigation and Defense: Mitigation strategies, like traffic filtering, rate limiting, and Content Delivery Networks, are used to defend against DDoS attacks. Real-time monitoring systems help identify and block malicious traffic.
  g. Evolving Threats: DDoS attacks in the metaverse continue to evolve with advancing technology. Attackers may use new techniques, like IoT-powered botnets or vulnerabilities in emerging virtual reality and augmented reality platforms. Staying vigilant and implementing robust security measures are essential to counter these evolving threats.

7. Data Breaches and Privacy Concerns: The metaverse collects vast amounts of user data, including personal information, transaction records, and behavioral patterns. Data breaches can lead to unauthorized access, exposure of sensitive information, and privacy violations. Strong data protection measures, encryption, secure data storage, and adherence to privacy regulations are essential to safeguard user data in the metaverse.
8. Virtual Currency Fraud: Virtual currencies are widely used in the metaverse for transactions and economic activities. However, cybercriminals may engage in fraudulent schemes such as fake virtual currency exchanges, Ponzi schemes, or scams targeting virtual currency holders. Implementing secure and regulated virtual currency systems, conducting thorough due diligence on virtual currency platforms, and educating users about potential risks can help mitigate this threat (Saad et al., 2019).
9. Exploitation of Virtual Environments: The dynamic and interactive nature of virtual environments can be exploited by cybercriminals. They may create malicious virtual objects or manipulate the virtual environment itself to gain unauthorized access, control systems, or disrupt user experiences. Stringent security measures, including secure coding practices, vulnerability assessments, and real-time monitoring, are essential to identify and mitigate such exploitations.
10. Virtual Espionage and Intellectual Property Theft: Within the metaverse, valuable intellectual property, designs, and creative content are generated. Cybercriminals may engage in virtual espionage, attempting to steal or replicate proprietary information, designs, or creations. Implementing robust access controls, encryption, and digital rights management systems can help protect intellectual property within the metaverse.
11. Deepfake and Synthetic Media: With advances in artificial intelligence and deep learning, the metaverse may witness the rise of deep fake and synthetic media, where realistic but manipulated content is created. This poses risks in terms of misinformation, identity theft, and reputational damage. Developing advanced detection algorithms, promoting media literacy, and encouraging user scepticism can help mitigate the impact of deepfake and synthetic media within the metaverse. Deepfake and synthetic media attacks in the metaverse refer to the malicious use of AI-generated content to deceive, manipulate, or spread misinformation within virtual environments. Here is an overview of the procedure and impact of such attacks:
  a. Generation of Synthetic Media: Attackers create or obtain AI-generated synthetic media, such as deepfake videos, audio recordings, or images, using advanced machine learning algorithms. These synthetic media are manipulated or fabricated to resemble real individuals or events, often to spread false information or mislead others.
  b. Distribution within the Metaverse: Attackers disseminate the synthetic media within virtual environments, such as social platforms, virtual reality experiences, or online communities. They may pose as trusted individuals or create fake accounts to spread the manipulated content widely and rapidly.

c. Misinformation and Deception: Synthetic media is designed to deceive and mislead viewers. Deepfake videos, for example, can portray individuals saying or doing things they never actually did, leading to the dissemination of false information or damaging reputations. Synthetic media attacks can be used for political propaganda, misinformation campaigns, identity theft, or even virtual harassment.
d. Amplification and Virality: Synthetic media attacks can quickly gain traction within the metaverse due to the viral nature of online sharing and the tendency of users to trust and share content without verification. The rapid spread of manipulated media can amplify the impact of the attack, potentially reaching a wide audience and causing significant harm.
e. Trust and Security Concerns: Deepfake and synthetic media attacks erode trust within virtual environments, undermining the authenticity and credibility of content and interactions. Users become increasingly wary of the veracity of information and the identities of other users, leading to a breakdown in trust and potentially disrupting social dynamics within the metaverse.
f. Countermeasures and Detection: Mitigating the risks of deepfake and synthetic media attacks requires robust countermeasures. This includes developing advanced detection algorithms and AI-based tools capable of identifying and flagging manipulated content. Platform operators and virtual environment providers can implement policies and guidelines to address the spread of synthetic media, while users can be educated about the risks and taught critical thinking skills to evaluate the authenticity of media content.
g. Legal and Ethical Considerations: Deepfake and synthetic media attacks raise significant legal and ethical concerns. Legislation may need to be developed or strengthened to address the creation, distribution, and misuse of synthetic media. Ethical considerations involve striking a balance between freedom of expression and protecting individuals' rights to privacy, reputation, and security within the metaverse.
h. Virtual Terrorism and Extremism: The metaverse can become a platform for promoting extremist ideologies, hate speech, or even acts of virtual terrorism. Such activities can have real-world consequences, including inciting violence or spreading radicalization. Implementing strict community guidelines, proactive moderation, and cooperation with law enforcement agencies are crucial in combating virtual terrorism and extremism.

12. AI-Powered Attacks: Artificial intelligence (AI) technologies can be leveraged by cybercriminals to enhance the effectiveness of their attacks within the metaverse. AI-powered attacks can automate the identification of vulnerabilities, generate sophisticated phishing campaigns, or launch targeted social engineering attacks. Developing AI-based defence mechanisms, employing anomaly detection algorithms, and advancing AI ethics and regulations are important in countering AI-powered cyber threats (Li et al., 2020).
13. Cross-Platform Attacks: The metaverse comprises multiple interconnected platforms and virtual environments. Cybercriminals may exploit vulnerabilities in one platform to launch attacks on other interconnected platforms or leverage information obtained from one platform to target users in another. Establishing secure APIs, enforcing strict data-sharing protocols, and conducting comprehensive security assessments across platforms can help mitigate cross-platform attacks (Sarkar et al., 2019).

CYBER WARFARE IN METAVERSE

1. State-sponsored attacks and espionage: State-sponsored attacks and espionage refer to cyber activities conducted by governments or state entities to gather intelligence, influencing foreign affairs, or advancing national interests (Datta, 2022; Izycki & Vianna, 2021). Here are some key aspects of state-sponsored attacks and espionage:

    a. Motivation: State-sponsored attacks and espionage are driven by political, economic, or military motives. Governments engage in these activities to gain strategic advantages, gather sensitive information, disrupt rival nations, or shape global events according to their interests.
    b. Advanced Capabilities: State-sponsored actors often possess significant resources and advanced cyber capabilities. They may have access to sophisticated hacking tools, intelligence agencies, and skilled personnel who can conduct targeted and covert operations.
    c. Intelligence Gathering: State-sponsored espionage involves infiltrating the computer networks of other nations, organizations, or entities to collect classified or sensitive information. This can include intellectual property, military plans, diplomatic communications, economic data, or technological advancements. The acquired intelligence helps shape a nation's policies, military strategies, and decision-making processes.
    d. Covert Operations: State-sponsored attacks can involve covert operations that aim to disrupt, sabotage, or manipulate critical infrastructure, government systems, or key industries. Such attacks may target energy grids, transportation networks, financial systems, or military infrastructure to create chaos, exert influence, or gain a strategic advantage.
    e. Attribution Challenges: Determining the exact source of a state-sponsored attack or espionage activity can be complex. State actors often employ sophisticated techniques to conceal their identities, such as utilizing proxy servers, employing false flag operations, or routing attacks through multiple compromised systems. This makes it challenging to attribute cyber attacks to specific nations with absolute certainty.
    f. Geopolitical Implications: State-sponsored attacks and espionage have significant geopolitical implications. They can strain international relationships, escalate tensions between nations, and impact global security. Such activities may lead to retaliatory measures, diplomatic conflicts, or the imposition of sanctions.
    g. International Norms and Agreements: The international community recognizes the need to address state-sponsored cyber activities. Efforts are being made to establish norms, agreements, and frameworks to deter and mitigate such actions. International organizations, including the United Nations and regional alliances, work towards establishing guidelines and rules to govern cyber behavior among nations.
    h. Countermeasures: Defending against state-sponsored attacks and espionage requires robust cybersecurity measures, intelligence sharing, and diplomatic efforts. Governments and organizations invest in cyber defences, incident response capabilities, threat intelligence sharing, and cooperation with law enforcement agencies to detect, prevent, and respond to such activities.

State-sponsored attacks and espionage pose significant challenges to national security, global stability, and the integrity of critical systems. Recognizing the existence of these activities and implementing proactive measures is crucial for protecting sensitive information, safeguarding infrastructure, and maintaining international relations in an increasingly interconnected and cyber-dependent world.

2. Information warfare and manipulation: The procedure of information warfare and manipulation in the metaverse involves various steps and tactics (Barbieri, 2021; Bolton, 2021; Ottis, 2008; Robinson et al., 2015). Here is a general outline of the procedure:
   a. Target Identification: The first step is to identify the target audience or individuals who are susceptible to manipulation. This can include social media users, online community members, or specific interest groups within the metaverse.
   b. Psychological Profiling: Once the target audience is identified, psychological profiling is conducted to understand their beliefs, values, preferences, and vulnerabilities. This helps in tailoring the manipulation tactics to exploit specific psychological triggers and biases.
   c. Creation of Manipulative Content: Manipulative content is created to influence the target audience. This can include the production of fake news articles, misleading videos, fabricated social media posts, or persuasive narratives designed to shape opinions or provoke emotional responses.
   d. Dissemination Strategies: Various dissemination strategies are employed to ensure the manipulation content reaches the target audience effectively. This can involve the use of social media bots, fake accounts, coordinated posting campaigns, or leveraging influential individuals or groups to amplify the reach and impact of the manipulative content.
   e. Amplification and Virality: Techniques such as social media algorithms, targeted advertising, or viral marketing strategies are used to maximize the visibility and spread of manipulative content. This helps in creating an illusion of credibility and generating a widespread impact.
   f. Exploitation of Echo Chambers: Manipulators often exploit echo chambers, where like-minded individuals gather and reinforce their existing beliefs and biases. By infiltrating these echo chambers and spreading tailored manipulative content, they can strengthen confirmation biases and create a sense of consensus among the targeted audience.
   g. Discrediting Opposing Views: Discrediting or undermining opposing viewpoints or credible sources of information is another tactic used in information warfare. This can involve spreading misinformation about credible sources, launching smear campaigns, or engaging in character assassinations to erode trust in alternative perspectives.
   h. Emotional Manipulation: Emotional manipulation techniques are employed to trigger specific emotions in the target audience. This can include playing on fears, exploiting cultural or social anxieties, or appealing to empathy and compassion to sway opinions and elicit desired reactions.
   i. Monitoring and Adaptation: Throughout the process, manipulators continuously monitor the impact of their tactics and adapt their strategies based on the responses and feedback received. They analyze engagement metrics, sentiment analysis, and other indicators to refine their approach and maximize their effectiveness.
   j. Reinforcement and Escalation: Once the manipulation tactics start to yield desired results, manipulators may reinforce the narrative, escalate the intensity of their campaigns, or initiate coordinated actions to further their objectives. This can include inciting online debates, organizing protests, or fostering polarization within the metaverse community.

3. Hacking of Virtual Defence Systems: The hacking of virtual defence systems in the metaverse involves a series of steps and techniques aimed at gaining unauthorized access and compromising the security measures in place. The procedure begins with reconnaissance, where the hacker gathers information about the system's vulnerabilities. They then conduct a vulnerability assessment to identify weaknesses and proceed to exploit them, often using software vulnerabilities, social engineering, or phishing techniques. Once inside, the hacker seeks to escalate privileges, deploy malware for persistence, and maintain stealth by evading security measures. They may exfiltrate or manipulate data, covering their tracks to avoid detection. However, it is crucial to note that hacking virtual defence systems is illegal and unethical, with severe legal consequences (Guo et al., 2022; Kang et al., 2021; Ko, 2020; Yeom et al., 2021).
4. Disruption of critical infrastructure: The disruption of critical infrastructure in the metaverse follows a systematic procedure designed to target and undermine essential systems. It begins with the selection of specific infrastructure, such as power grids, communication networks, and financial systems, which are crucial for the smooth functioning of virtual services. Extensive reconnaissance is conducted to gather detailed information about the target, including vulnerabilities and dependencies. A comprehensive vulnerability assessment follows, identifying weaknesses and potential entry points. By exploiting these vulnerabilities, the attacker gains unauthorized access and control. They deploy malicious payloads, such as malware or denial-of-service attacks, to disrupt the infrastructure's availability, integrity, or functionality. The attacker employs techniques to conceal their activities and evade detection, covering their tracks and encrypting communications. The objective is to cause sustained disruption, potentially establishing long-term persistence within the infrastructure for future attacks. It is essential to understand that the disruption of critical infrastructure is illegal, and unethical, and poses significant risks to public safety and societal well-being (Izycki & Vianna, 2021).

DETECTION OF CYBER-CRIME AND CYBER WARFARE IN THE METAVERSE

1. Incident Response Planning: Incident Response Planning plays a crucial role in detecting and responding to cybercrime or cyber warfare incidents. It involves the use of various software tools and technologies to facilitate effective incident detection, analysis, response, and recovery. Here are some examples of software commonly used in different phases of incident response:

    a. Security Information and Event Management (SIEM) tools: SIEM solutions, such as Splunk, IBM QRadar, or ArcSight, are used for real-time monitoring and correlation of security events and logs. They collect and analyze data from various sources, including network devices, servers, and applications, to detect and alert potential security incidents (Shinde & Kulkarni, 2021).

    b. Intrusion Detection/Prevention Systems (IDS/IPS): IDS/IPS tools, such as Snort, Suricata, or Cisco Firepower, help detect and prevent unauthorized access and malicious activities. They analyze network traffic and system logs to identify suspicious patterns, known attack signatures, or abnormal behavior indicative of cyber threats (Morgan, 2021).

c. Endpoint Detection and Response (EDR) solutions: EDR tools, like CrowdStrike Falcon, Carbon Black, or Symantec Endpoint Protection, provide real-time visibility into endpoints and detect and respond to advanced threats. They monitor system activities, analyze behavior, and use threat intelligence to identify and remediate potential cyber threats (Arfeen et al., 2021).
d. Forensic Analysis Tools: Software tools like EnCase, Forensic Toolkit (FTK), or Autopsy are used for digital forensic analysis during incident investigations. These tools enable investigators to collect, analyze, and interpret evidence from compromised systems, logs, memory dumps, and other artefacts to reconstruct the incident and identify the attacker's techniques (Saharan & Yadav, 2022).
e. Vulnerability Assessment and Management Tools: Vulnerability assessment tools like Nessus, OpenVAS, or Qualys help identify and prioritize vulnerabilities in systems and networks. They scan for known vulnerabilities and misconfigurations, allowing organizations to patch or mitigate weaknesses before they are exploited (Upadhyay & Sampalli, 2020).
f. Threat Intelligence Platforms: Threat intelligence platforms, such as Anomali, Recorded Future, or ThreatConnect, provide access to comprehensive threat intelligence feeds, indicators of compromise, and contextual information about emerging threats. This information helps incident response teams stay updated on the latest attack trends and attribute incidents to specific threat actors (Samtani et al., 2020).
g. Security Orchestration, Automation, and Response (SOAR) Platforms: SOAR platforms, like Demisto, Swimlane, or Splunk Phantom, automate and streamline incident response processes. They integrate with various security tools, orchestrate workflows, and automate response actions to improve incident response efficiency and consistency (Islam et al., 2020).

The selection of specific software depends on an organization's requirements, budget, and technical capabilities. It is essential to choose tools that integrate well, provide the necessary functionality, and align with the organization's incident response strategy and goals.

2. Intrusion Detection Systems (IDS): IDS play a crucial role in detecting and preventing cyber warfare attacks. They monitor network traffic and systems for suspicious activities, unauthorized access attempts, and known attack signatures (Gümüşbaş et al., 2020). Here are some popular IDS software examples used in the field of cyber warfare:
   a. Snort: Snort is an open-source IDS that uses signature-based detection to identify and alert network-based attacks. It can detect various types of attacks, including network scanning, malware, and exploit attempts. Snort has a large community of users and offers flexibility for customization.
   b. Suricata: Suricata is an open-source IDS and Intrusion Prevention System (IPS) that provides real-time network traffic analysis. It can detect and prevent a wide range of threats, including network-based attacks, malware, and suspicious behaviors. Suricata supports multi-threading and high-speed packet processing.
   c. Bro/Zeek: Bro, now known as Zeek, is an open-source network security monitoring tool that functions as an IDS. It provides detailed network traffic analysis and can identify and log various types of network-based attacks. Bro/Zeek offers powerful scripting capabilities for customizing detection and analysis.

   d. Snorby: Snorby is a web-based front-end for managing and analyzing Snort alerts. It provides a user-friendly interface to view and investigate IDS alerts, generate reports, and perform data analysis. Snorby simplifies the management and monitoring of Snort IDS deployments.
   e. Suricata-IDS Management System (SIMS): SIMS is a web-based management system for Suricata IDS. It provides centralized monitoring, configuration management, and reporting capabilities for Suricata deployments. SIMS streamlines the management and administration of Suricata IDS sensors.
   f. Cisco Firepower: Cisco Firepower is a commercial IDS/IPS solution that offers advanced threat detection and prevention capabilities. It combines network-based IDS/IPS with additional security features, such as firewalling, URL filtering, and advanced malware protection. Cisco Firepower provides comprehensive security coverage for enterprise environments.
   g. McAfee Intrusion Prevention System (IPS): McAfee IPS is a commercial IDS/IPS solution that offers real-time threat detection and prevention capabilities. It uses signature-based and behavioral-based analysis to detect and block network-based attacks. McAfee IPS integrates with other McAfee security solutions for comprehensive threat management.
3. Log analysis: Log analysis is a critical component in detecting, investigating, and mitigating cyber warfare and cybercrime activities. Several software tools are available to aid in log analysis, providing features such as log collection, normalization, correlation, and visualization. Popular examples include Splunk, an advanced log management and analysis platform that offers real-time indexing, searching, and visualization of log data. Elastic Stack, an open-source solution comprising Elasticsearch, Logstash, and Kibana, provides scalability, real-time monitoring, and powerful search capabilities. Graylog, another open-source platform, enables log aggregation, alerting, and customizable dashboards. Commercial options include LogRhythm, offering real-time log monitoring, correlation, and automated response workflows, and IBM QRadar, a SIEM platform with real-time monitoring, correlation, and advanced threat intelligence. McAfee Enterprise Security Manager (ESM) integrates log collection, analysis, and correlation for comprehensive threat detection and response. These software tools empower organizations to collect, analyze, and visualize log data from various sources, aiding in the identification and response to cyber threats in the metaverse (Saharan & Yadav, 2022; Shinde & Kulkarni, 2021).
4. Malware analysis: In the realm of cyber warfare, understanding malicious software is paramount, and various software tools and frameworks assist in malware analysis. Notable tools include:
   a. IDA Pro: An interactive disassembler and debugger, widely used to dissect malware assembly code. It features disassembly, graphing, and data cross-referencing for unraveling malware functionality and logic.
   b. OllyDbg: A debugger and disassembler facilitating dynamic analysis of executable files. It allows researchers to set breakpoints, inspect registers and memory, and track code execution, aiding in identifying runtime behavior, analyzing API calls, and uncovering vulnerabilities.
   c. Ghidra: An open-source software reverse engineering framework developed by the NSA, assisting in binary file analysis and decompilation. Ghidra helps analysts understand malware structure and logic.
   d. Cuckoo Sandbox: For automated malware analysis, Cuckoo Sandbox executes suspicious files in a controlled environment, monitoring behavior and generating detailed reports. It aids in understanding the impact and behavior of malware.

e. YARA: A pattern-matching tool used to classify and identify malware based on predefined rules. Analysts create custom rulesets to detect specific malware characteristics or behaviors.
f. VirusTotal: An online platform for scanning files and URLs using multiple antivirus engines and analysis tools. Analysts can upload suspicious files to obtain comprehensive results and information about their reputation and detection rates.

These software tools, including IDA Pro, OllyDbg, Ghidra, Cuckoo Sandbox, YARA, and VirusTotal, are indispensable for experts in their efforts to effectively combat cyber threats by dissecting and understanding malicious software (van Liebergen et al., 2023).

5. Endpoint forensics: Endpoint forensics is a critical component in investigating cyber warfare incidents, focusing on collecting and analyzing digital evidence from devices like computers and mobile devices. Several software tools assist in endpoint forensics for identifying and analyzing potential cyber warfare activities. Notable examples include:

a. EnCase Endpoint Investigator: This tool aids forensic analysts in collecting and examining evidence from endpoint devices, enabling deep analysis of system artifacts and event reconstruction.
b. SANS SIFT (SANS Investigative Forensic Toolkit): An open-source toolkit designed for digital forensics and incident response, offering disk imaging, memory analysis, and log analysis tools.
c. Volatility: A widely-used open-source memory forensics framework that extracts and analyzes volatile data from device memory to uncover evidence of malicious activities.
d. Autopsy: An open-source digital forensics platform with a user-friendly interface, facilitating endpoint analysis with features like disk imaging, keyword searching, and timeline analysis.
e. FTK (Forensic Toolkit): A comprehensive digital forensics software suite with tools for endpoint analysis, data recovery, keyword searching, file carving, and email analysis.
f. OS Forensics: Focused on extracting and analyzing artifacts from endpoint devices, it offers features for disk imaging, file searching, and registry analysis, aiding in identifying cyber warfare evidence and potential threat actors.

These software tools empower forensic analysts to collect and analyze digital evidence, helping reconstruct events and identify the tactics, techniques, and procedures employed by threat actors in cyber warfare scenarios (Saharan & Yadav, 2022).

6. Memory analysis: Memory analysis is a critical component of investigating cyber-attacks in the metaverse. It enables analysts to extract and examine volatile data from computer memory, providing valuable insights into attackers' techniques and activities. Various tools, such as Volatility and Rekall, offer comprehensive capabilities for memory analysis, while commercial tools like Redline and Mandiant Memoryze provide advanced features. Lightweight tools like DumpIt simplify memory capture. These tools empower analysts to identify malicious processes, detect hidden malware, analyze network connections, and gain insights into attackers' activities. The knowledge gained from memory analysis is crucial for timely incident response and helps mitigate cyber threats in the ever-evolving metaverse environment (Pagani et al., 2019; Paul Joseph & Norman, 2020).

FUTURE ASPECT OF CYBER-CRIME IN METAVERSE

The future of cybercrime in the metaverse is a complex and evolving landscape. While it's challenging to predict with certainty, several trends and areas of concern are likely to shape the future of cybercrime in the metaverse:

1. Deepfakes and Synthetic Media: As artificial intelligence and deep learning technologies advance, the creation and dissemination of deepfake content and synthetic media may become more sophisticated. This could lead to more convincing and damaging instances of misinformation, identity theft, and reputational harm.
2. Financial Cybercrimes: With the rise of virtual economies and the potential for real financial transactions within the metaverse, cybercriminals may increasingly target digital assets, virtual currencies, and financial systems. This includes theft, fraud, and money laundering within the metaverse.
3. Virtual Property Theft: As users invest in virtual real estate, assets, and collectibles, cybercriminals may target these valuable digital possessions. The theft and illicit trade of virtual property could become a lucrative criminal enterprise.
4. Virtual Extortion and Ransomware: Cybercriminals might employ virtual extortion tactics, including threats to disrupt or destroy virtual property or assets unless a ransom is paid in virtual currency.
5. Identity Theft and Privacy Invasion: The metaverse's interconnected nature may provide cybercriminals with more opportunities to steal user identities and invade their privacy. This could lead to personal data breaches, account hijacking, and more sophisticated forms of social engineering.
6. DDoS Attacks: As metaverse platforms and services become more prevalent, DDoS attacks could increase in frequency and sophistication, impacting the availability of virtual experiences.
7. Exploitation of Emerging Technologies: As new technologies are integrated into the metaverse, cybercriminals may exploit vulnerabilities in augmented reality, virtual reality, Internet of Things (IoT) devices, and other emerging technologies, potentially leading to novel forms of cyberattacks.
8. Regulatory and Legal Challenges: As the metaverse blurs the lines between virtual and physical spaces, regulatory and legal frameworks may struggle to keep up with the novel challenges posed by cybercrime in this environment.
9. Evolving Security Measures: To combat these threats, cybersecurity measures will need to adapt and evolve. This includes advanced intrusion detection systems, behavioral analysis, AI-driven security, and blockchain-based security solutions to protect virtual assets.
10. Media Literacy and User Education: Encouraging media literacy and educating metaverse users about the risks of cybercrime will be crucial. Users must develop critical thinking skills to assess the authenticity of content and recognize potential threats.

In the face of these challenges, collaboration between metaverse platform operators, law enforcement agencies, cybersecurity experts, and users will be vital to enhance security and create a safer virtual environment. As the metaverse continues to evolve, staying vigilant and proactive in addressing emerging cyber threats will be key to its long-term success and safety.

TECHNOLOGICAL ADVANCEMENTS AND SOLUTIONS

The metaverse presents a unique and dynamic environment with its own set of cybersecurity challenges. To secure the metaverse and protect against cybercrimes and cyber warfare, various software tools and technologies can be employed. Here is a brief overview of key tools and technologies for enhancing metaverse security:

1. Antivirus and Anti-Malware Software: These tools are crucial for detecting and preventing known malware and malicious activities. They offer real-time protection and should be regularly updated to guard against evolving threats.
2. Firewall Systems: Firewalls act as a protective barrier, monitoring and controlling network traffic, and preventing unauthorized access. They are essential for safeguarding the virtual environment from external threats.
3. Encryption Tools: Encryption software is fundamental for securing data within the metaverse, ensuring that sensitive information remains confidential even if intercepted.
4. Intrusion Detection and Prevention Systems (IDPS): IDPS software continuously monitors network traffic, detecting and responding to potential threats, thereby minimizing the risk of cybercrimes and unauthorized intrusions.
5. Virtual Private Networks (VPNs): VPNs create secure and encrypted connections between users and the metaverse, protecting data privacy and mitigating eavesdropping.
6. User Authentication and Access Control: Robust authentication mechanisms, such as multi-factor and biometric authentication, enhance security, and access control ensures that only authorized users have access to sensitive resources.
7. Security Information and Event Management (SIEM) Systems: SIEM software collects and analyzes log data from various metaverse platforms, enabling real-time threat detection and proactive incident response.
8. Threat Intelligence Platforms: These platforms help organizations stay informed about the latest threats specific to the metaverse, assisting in implementing timely countermeasures.
9. Incident Response and Forensic Tools: In the event of a security incident or cybercrime, these tools are essential for investigation, evidence collection, and recovery, while ensuring the chain of custody is preserved.

By utilizing these tools and technologies, the metaverse can establish a robust security framework to defend against cybercrimes and cyber warfare. However, it's crucial to adapt to evolving threats and continue developing innovative security solutions to safeguard this dynamic digital realm.

METAVERSE AGAINST CYBER-CRIME

Preventing cybercrimes using the metaverse involves leveraging the unique capabilities of virtual environments to enhance security. Here are some strategies for preventing cybercrimes within the metaverse:

1. Blockchain-Based Security: Implement blockchain technology for secure user authentication, data integrity, and transaction tracking. Blockchain's decentralized nature can help prevent identity theft and fraud.
2. Digital Identity Management: Develop robust digital identity management systems to ensure that users are who they claim to be. Biometrics, secure user profiles, and digital certificates can enhance identity verification.
3. Encryption and Secure Communication: Use end-to-end encryption for all communications within the metaverse to protect user data and conversations from eavesdropping.
4. Virtual Private Networks (VPNs): Encourage the use of VPNs to anonymize user connections and protect their privacy. VPNs can make it more challenging for cybercriminals to track users.
5. Secure Transactions: Implement secure payment and transaction mechanisms for virtual assets and currencies. Ensure that financial transactions are protected from theft and fraud.
6. AI-Driven Threat Detection: Utilize artificial intelligence and machine learning to monitor user activities and identify suspicious behavior or cyber threats in real-time.
7. User Education: Conduct user awareness programs within the metaverse to educate users about potential cyber threats, safe online practices, and how to recognize phishing attempts and scams.
8. User Reporting Systems: Establish easy-to-use reporting mechanisms for users to report suspicious activities, cybercrimes, or potential security vulnerabilities.
9. Collaborative Security: Foster collaboration among virtual world operators, security experts, and law enforcement agencies to share threat intelligence and collaborate on security measures.
10. Cross-Platform Security: Ensure consistent security measures across different platforms and devices within the metaverse. Cybersecurity should not vary significantly from one virtual environment to another.
11. Regular Updates and Patches: Maintain and update the metaverse's software and security protocols to patch vulnerabilities and protect against emerging threats.
12. Geofencing and Access Controls: Implement geofencing and access controls to restrict user access to specific virtual areas, safeguard sensitive content, and protect against unauthorized entry.
13. Virtual Environment Monitoring: Continuously monitor the metaverse for potential threats, vulnerabilities, or irregular activities, allowing for proactive responses.
14. Community Guidelines and Moderation: Enforce community guidelines and employ proactive content moderation to maintain a safe and respectful virtual environment.
15. Legal Frameworks: Work with governments to establish legal frameworks and regulations specific to the metaverse, allowing for prosecution and deterrence of cybercriminals.
16. Secure Development Practices: Encourage developers to follow secure coding practices and consider cybersecurity in the design and development of virtual platforms and applications.

Preventing cybercrimes using the metaverse requires a combination of technological solutions, user awareness, and regulatory measures to create a secure and trustworthy digital space. It's essential to remain vigilant and adapt to evolving cyber threats in the dynamic virtual environment.

SUMMARY

The future of cybercrimes and cyber warfare in the metaverse is a complex and evolving landscape, fraught with significant challenges and risks. This chapter provides a comprehensive analysis of the potential threats, impacts, and countermeasures associated with cyber activities in the metaverse. It underscores the metaverse's role as a transformative virtual reality space, transcending traditional boundaries, and the rapid advancements in immersive technologies. The chapter delves into various types of cyber threats, real-world examples, and their potential consequences, emphasizing the need for proactive measures and advanced technologies for detection and response. It also explores state-sponsored attacks, information warfare, and the geopolitical implications of cyber conflicts within the virtual realm. Lastly, the chapter underscores the importance of robust cybersecurity measures, ethical considerations, and international cooperation to ensure the security and resilience of virtual environments in the face of evolving cyber threats.

In conclusion, this chapter provides a comprehensive and detailed examination of the future of cybercrimes and cyber warfare in the metaverse. It highlights the evolving nature of threats, the potential impacts on individuals and societies, and the essential steps needed to safeguard the metaverse from malicious activities. By understanding the challenges and adopting proactive measures, we can navigate the virtual landscape with greater resilience and security.

REFERENCES

Arfeen, A., Ahmed, S., Khan, M. A., & Jafri, S. F. A. (2021). Endpoint Detection & Response: A Malware Identification Solution. *2021 International Conference on Cyber Warfare and Security (ICCWS)*. Semantic Scholar.

Bernik, I. (2014). *Cybercrime and cyber warfare*. John Wiley & Sons. doi:10.1002/9781118898604

Bolton, D. (2021). Targeting ontological security: Information warfare in the modern age. *Political Psychology*, *42*(1), 127–142. doi:10.1111/pops.12691

Bussolati, N. (2015). The Rise of Non-State Actors in Cyberwarfare: Cyber War: Law and Ethics for Virtual Conflicts. Oxford University Press. doi:10.1093/acprof:oso/9780198717492.003.0007

Calderoni, F. (2010). The European legal framework on cybercrime: Striving for an effective implementation. *Crime, Law, and Social Change*, *54*(5), 339–357. doi:10.100710611-010-9261-6

Chopra, A. (2021). Cyberattack-Intangible Damages in a Virtual World: Property Insurance Companies Declare War on Cyber-Attack Insurance Claims. *Ohio St. LJ*, *82*, 121.

Czosseck, C., Ottis, R., & Talihärm, A.-M. (2013). Estonia after the 2007 cyber attacks: Legal, strategic and organisational changes in cyber security. *Case studies in information warfare and security: For researchers, teachers and students, 72*.

Datta, P. (2022). Hannibal at the gates: Cyberwarfare & the Solarwinds sunburst hack. *Journal of Information Technology Teaching Cases*, *12*(2), 115–120. doi:10.1177/2043886921993126

Di Pietro, R., & Cresci, S. (2021). Metaverse: security and privacy issues. *2021 Third IEEE International Conference on Trust, Privacy and Security in Intelligent Systems and Applications (TPS-ISA)*. IEEE.

Dolata, M., & Schwabe, G. (2023). What is the Metaverse and who seeks to define it? Mapping the site of social construction. *Journal of Information Technology*, 02683962231159927.

Fouad, N. S. (2021). Securing higher education against cyberthreats: From an institutional risk to a national policy challenge. *Journal of Cyber Policy*, *6*(2), 137–154. doi:10.1080/23738871.2021.1973526

Gümüşbaş, D., Yıldırım, T., Genovese, A., & Scotti, F. (2020). A comprehensive survey of databases and deep learning methods for cybersecurity and intrusion detection systems. *IEEE Systems Journal*, *15*(2), 1717–1731. doi:10.1109/JSYST.2020.2992966

Guo, W., Xu, J., Pei, Y., Yin, L., Jiang, C., & Ge, N. (2022). A distributed collaborative entrance Defense framework against DDoS attacks on satellite internet. *IEEE Internet of Things Journal*, *9*(17), 15497–15510. doi:10.1109/JIOT.2022.3176121

Haataja, S. (2017). The 2007 cyber attacks against Estonia and international law on the use of force: An informational approach. *Law, Innovation and Technology*, *9*(2), 159–189. doi:10.1080/17579961.2017.1377914

Herzog, S. (2011). Revisiting the Estonian cyber attacks: Digital threats and multinational responses. *Journal of Strategic Security*, *4*(2), 49–60. doi:10.5038/1944-0472.4.2.3

Islam, C., Babar, M. A., & Nepal, S. (2020). *Architecture-centric support for integrating security tools in a security orchestration platform*. Software Architecture: 14th European Conference, ECSA 2020, L'Aquila, Italy.10.1007/978-3-030-58923-3_11

Laeeq, K. (2022). *Metaverse: why, how and what*. How and What.

Lee, L.-H., Braud, T., Zhou, P., Wang, L., Xu, D., Lin, Z., Kumar, A., Bermejo, C., & Hui, P. (2021). All one needs to know about metaverse: A complete survey on technological singularity, virtual ecosystem, and research agenda. *arXiv preprint arXiv:2110.05352*.

Li, Y., Yang, X., Sun, P., Qi, H., & Lyu, S. (2020). Celeb-df: A large-scale challenging dataset for deepfake forensics. *Proceedings of the IEEE/CVF conference on computer vision and pattern recognition*. IEEE.

McGuire, M., & Dowling, S. (2013). Cyber crime: A review of the evidence. *Summary of key findings and implications. Home Office*. Research Reports (Montgomery), 75, 1–35.

Morgan, R. A. (2021). *Exploring the Feasibility of Developing a Customized IDS/IPS Security Control for Computer Network Security*. Colorado Technical University.

Mystakidis, S. (2022). Metaverse. *Encyclopedia*, *2*(1), 486–497. doi:10.3390/encyclopedia2010031

Ning, H., Wang, H., Lin, Y., Wang, W., Dhelim, S., Farha, F., Ding, J., & Daneshmand, M. (2023). A Survey on the Metaverse: The State-of-the-Art, Technologies, Applications, and Challenges. *IEEE Internet of Things Journal*.

Ottis, R. (2008). Analysis of the 2007 cyber attacks against Estonia from the information warfare perspective. Proceedings of the 7th European Conference on Information Warfare,.

Pagani, F., Fedorov, O., & Balzarotti, D. (2019). Introducing the temporal dimension to memory forensics. *ACM Transactions on Privacy and Security (TOPS), 22*(2), 1-21

Pastrana, S., Hutchings, A., Caines, A., & Buttery, P. (2018). *Characterizing eve: Analysing cybercrime actors in a large underground forum.* Research in Attacks, Intrusions, and Defenses: *21st International Symposium, RAID 2018*, Heraklion, Crete, Greece.

Pipyros, K., Mitrou, L., Gritzalis, D., & Apostolopoulos, T. (2016). Cyberoperations and international humanitarian law: A review of obstacles in applying international law rules in cyber warfare. *Information & Computer Security.*

Robinson, M., Jones, K., & Janicke, H. (2015). Cyber warfare: Issues and challenges. *Computers & Security*, *49*, 70–94. doi:10.1016/j.cose.2014.11.007

Saad, M., Njilla, L., Kamhoua, C., Kim, J., Nyang, D., & Mohaisen, A. (2019). Mempool optimization for defending against DDoS attacks in PoW-based blockchain systems. *2019 IEEE international conference on blockchain and cryptocurrency (ICBC).* IEEE.

Sabillon, R., Cano, J. J., Cavaller Reyes, V., & Serra Ruiz, J. (2016). Cybercrime and cybercriminals: A comprehensive study. *International Journal of Computer Networks and Communications Security, 2016, 4(6).*

Saharan, S., & Yadav, B. (2022). Digital and cyber forensics: A contemporary evolution in forensic sciences. In Crime Scene Management within Forensic Science: Forensic Techniques for Criminal Investigations (pp. 267-294). Springer. doi:10.1007/978-981-16-6683-4_11

Samtani, S., Abate, M., Benjamin, V., & Li, W. (2020). Cybersecurity as an industry: A cyber threat intelligence perspective. The Palgrave Handbook of International Cybercrime and Cyberdeviance. Palgrave.

Shinde, N., & Kulkarni, P. (2021). Cyber incident response and planning: a flexible approach. *Computer Fraud & Security*, *2021*(1), 14–19.

Smith, K. T., Smith, L. M., Burger, M., & Boyle, E. S. (2023). Cyber terrorism cases and stock market valuation effects. *Information and Computer Security*, *31*(4), 385–403. doi:10.1108/ICS-09-2022-0147

Sparkes, M. (2021). *What is a metaverse.* Elsevier. doi:10.1016/S0262-4079(21)01450-0

Upadhyay, D., & Sampalli, S. (2020). SCADA (Supervisory Control and Data Acquisition) systems: Vulnerability assessment and security recommendations. *Computers & Security*, *89*, 101666. doi:10.1016/j.cose.2019.101666

Van der Land, S., Schouten, A., & Feldberg, F. (2011). Modeling the metaverse: A theoretical model of effective team collaboration in 3D virtual environments. *Journal of Virtual Worlds Research*, *4*(3). doi:10.4101/jvwr.v4i3.6126

Wang, Y., Su, Z., Zhang, N., Xing, R., Liu, D., Luan, T. H., & Shen, X. (2022). A survey on metaverse: Fundamentals, security, and privacy. *IEEE Communications Surveys & Tutorials*. IEEE. 10.1007/978-3-031-35504-2_8

Yeom, S., Shin, D., & Shin, D. (2021). Scenario-based cyber attack· defense education system on virtual machines integrated by web technologies for protection of multimedia contents in a network. *Multimedia Tools and Applications*, *80*(26-27), 34085–34101. doi:10.100711042-019-08583-0

Yoo, K., Welden, R., Hewett, K., & Haenlein, M. (2023). The merchants of meta: A research agenda to understand the future of retailing in the metaverse. *Journal of Retailing*, *99*(2), 173–192. doi:10.1016/j.jretai.2023.02.002

Chapter 8
A Prelude to Cybersecurity Challenges in the Metaverse

Shashwath Bhaskar
https://orcid.org/0009-0009-7038-8948
VIT Bhopal University, India

Aiesha Kuna
https://orcid.org/0009-0007-6953-3082
VIT Bhopal University, India

Akshaya Jayakumar
https://orcid.org/0009-0004-6606-5939
VIT Bhopal University, India

D. Lakshmi
https://orcid.org/0000-0003-4018-1208
VIT Bhopal University, India

ABSTRACT

The metaverse represents a transformative concept that has amassed substantial attention in recent years, with big corporations vying to gain hegemony over this domain. While revolutionizing the way we interact with and experience our environment, the metaverse unlocks a vast potential for cyber criminals and nation-states to take advantage of the present voids in its security. By analyzing existing literature and emerging trends, the authors delve into the uncharted territory of the metaverse, examining the ways in which users' digital avatars and assets are at risk- including poor security of NFTs, the scope for financial fraud, the dark verse, and social engineering, among other issues. This chapter provides insight into the real-world implications of cyber-attacks in the metaverse and examines the legal and ethical challenges of regulating cyber activity in virtual environments so that Law Enforcement Agencies, planners, and companies can navigate this field to create a safe virtual world for all.

DOI: 10.4018/979-8-3693-0220-0.ch008

INTRODUCTION

Widening up the horizons of the world as we know it, Extended Reality (XR) or cross reality is a collective term used to refer to all kinds of immersive technologies that rely on the use of spatial computing which facilitates and optimizes actions in these systems as defined by *Qamar* (2023). Extended Reality allows us to merge the physical and virtual worlds, seamlessly encompassing concepts of technologies like Virtual Reality (VR), Augmented Reality (AR), Mixed Reality (MR) and the Metaverse. As days pass, the use of XR devices is becoming more widespread and ingrained into our day-to-day lives. From the military to e-commerce, XR finds applications in various forms, providing a much more realistic way to interact with the virtual world; conversely even a much less real way to interact with the physical world. Immersive technology first began to be developed around the 1960s, when the first headset was created by a scientist named Ivan Sutherland, as stated by *Marr* (2022). In 1975, Myron Krueger implemented a combination of video cameras and projectors to build a VR world known as a 'Videoplace'. This research then observed rapid development and a variety of XR applications started to become available for iOS, Android, Windows, and Mac operating systems. The term XR then started to be popularized and after 2010 various industries began to establish their XR product lines globally according to *Mordor Intelligence* (2021). Both AR and VR technologies are said to be the backbone of the immersive tech space. Figure 1 shows the development of AR, which began in the 1960s, and Figure 2 shows the events in the innovative space that led to what VR is today.

Notable companies that took a dip into the massive prospects of XR include Facebook, Sony, Samsung and Google. Now standing at the pinnacle of the progression of immersive technologies is the metaverse- a term not unfamiliar to most.

The term "metaverse" was coined by Neil Stevenson for his 1992 cyberpunk novel, 'Snow Crash' *Numaan Huq et. al.* (2022). Stevenson's metaverse was a virtual place where characters could go to escape a dreary totalitarian reality. The protagonist, Hiro, navigates a VR world through an avatar- making

Figure 1. History of research and development in augmented reality

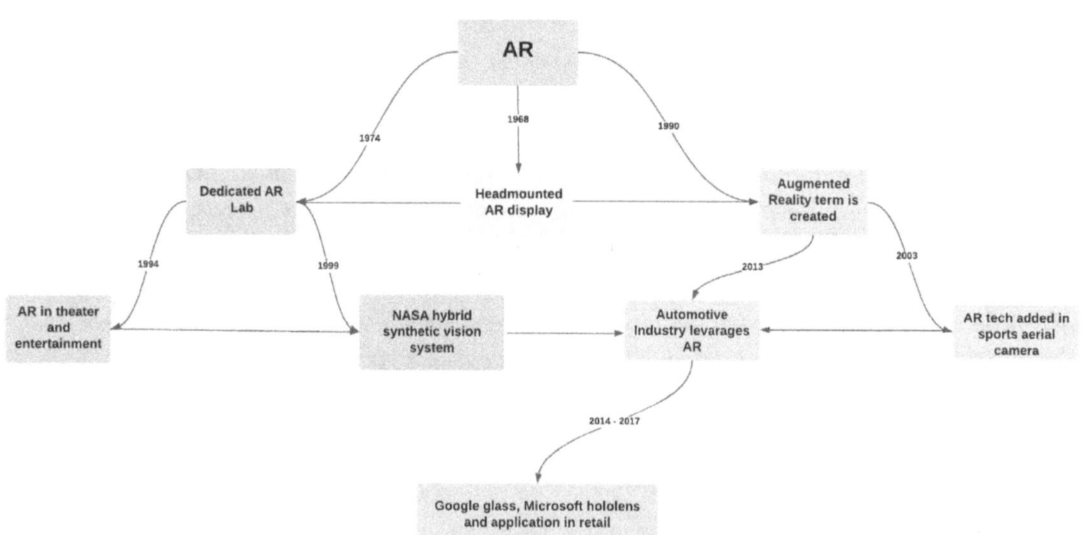

Figure 2. History of research and development in virtual reality

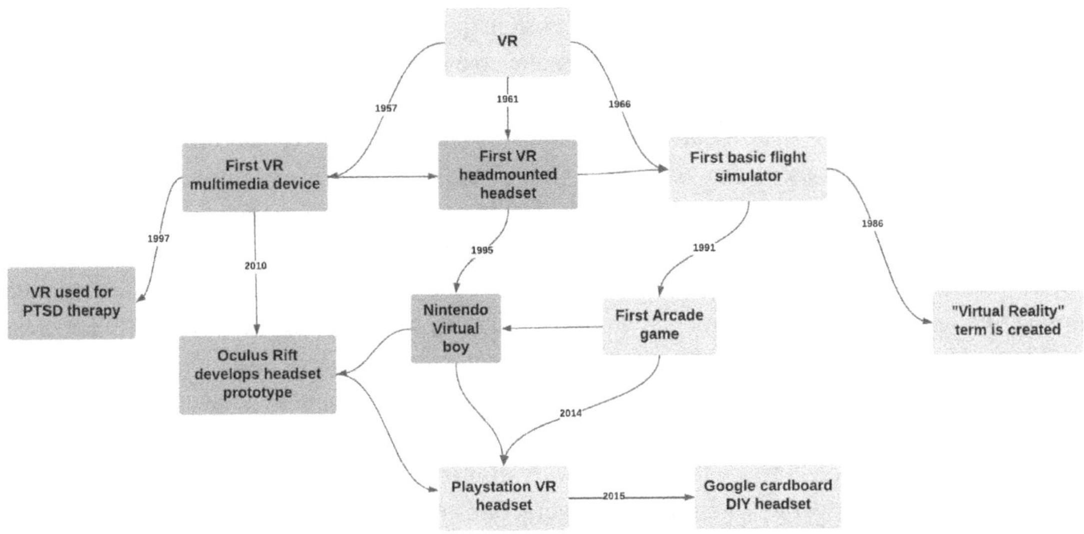

Figure 3. Evolution of the metaverse

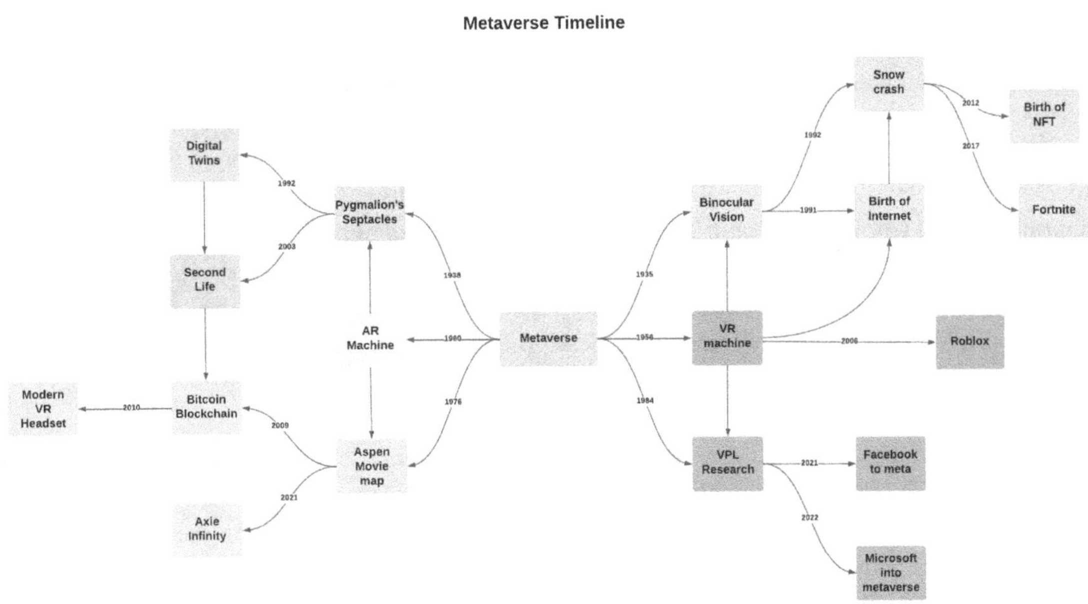

purchases, socializing, and even defeating real-world enemies within this world, explain *Rabindra Ratan et. al.* (2021). The doodles of Stevenson's imagination took shape in the age of ubiquitous computing, as countless aspects of this dreamed "metaverse" now exist in the present world, and act as a blueprint for the development of the metaverse. The concept of the metaverse is still quite abstract, with its definition and purpose differing from organization to organization. A widely accepted general definition as curated by *Numaan Huq et. al.* (2022) is- "The metaverse is a cloud distributed, multi-vendor, immersive-interactive operating environment that users can access through different categories of connected devices (both static and mobile). It uses Web 2.0 and Web 3.0 technologies to provide an interactive layer on top of the existing internet. As proposed, it is an open platform for working and playing inside a VR/AR/MR/XR environment based on *Stylinos Mystakidis*(2022). This concept is comparable to existing Massively Multiplayer Online Role-Playing Game (MMORPG) platforms, but while each MMORPG represents a proprietary single virtual world, the metaverse will allow players to seamlessly move between virtual spaces together with their virtual assets." A good example of the experimental metaverse is 'Second Life', an online multimedia platform wherein we create an avatar for ourselves and explore a virtual world. The metaverse aims to create a space that successfully digitizes the physical world to be replicated in a mirrored cloud-supported world, where normal interactions and transactions just like those in real life may take place in a metaphysical or non-physical online environment. Figure 3 depicts the timeline, or history, of events that led to the development of the metaverse. It shows the progress in both AR and VR technology, whose combined development has led to progress in the metaverse. *Stylinos Mystakidis*(2022)

OPPORTUNITIES

One of the key characteristics of the metaverse lies in its promise to remain decentralized and crowd-oriented, which stands to imply that there will likely never be an "end goal" or master plan for the metaverse. Rather, it is a utopian fantasy panning out in a speedily-developing path, bringing together various technical elements to construct highly realistic interactive virtual environments. The key building blocks of this new verse include Blockchain, Artificial Intelligence and Machine Learning, Cloud Computing, Spatial Computing, Natural Language Processing and 5G. It is also believed that Web 3.0, being inclusive of technologies like blockchain and peer-to-peer networks, is a major key to uplifting the potential of the metaverse given its portability and safety measures. Not only is the deployment of the metaverse a big step towards a more futuristic world, but it also opens up a wide range of prospects for use in various domains. *Awadallah et. al.* (2023)

1. Gaming: The gaming industry has already undergone major revolution with improvements in the field of AR/VR. This development continues to be carried forward with the metaverse, with more and more elements of realism being added to in-game experiences, making them more natural to play. Graphics and visuals are on an upward curve, becoming more breathtaking by the day. We are sitting on a gold mine in the form of gaming in the metaverse - with the market expected to surpass $660 billion within the decade.
2. Education: Utilizing the metaverse space, we would be able to create highly interactive and engaging environments to promote education in the fields of anatomy, biology, geography, chemistry and even arts and culture. It promotes easier absorption of information and also keeps a student's attention. AR and VR tools like Google Arts & Culture allow users to tour through 3D virtual

spaces of some of the world's most popular museums, enjoy viewing ballet up close or even travel abroad, all without stepping out of the classroom. Tugtekin (2023)

3. Retail: The whole experience of e-commerce, or even regular shopping, can be made a whole lot more enjoyable by use of the metaverse. Buyers may be allowed to inspect and analyze an item virtually in real time via their avatars or even on their real-world counterparts through AR technology within the metaverse. This promotion of retailers online would up the scope of brands to attract customers and invite them to try out their products from the comfort of a virtual space, ultimately acting as incentive to make a purchase. Since the metaverse is built to allow virtual transactions to reflect in the real world, it would not just be a matter of making a simple 'in-game purchase' of sorts, but rather could also be a purchase for a physical item.
4. Healthcare and Medicine: Within the medical field, AR/VR and the metaverse broaden up the options available to provide a better understanding of the human body, its ailments and their subsequent cures. A patient's vital signs may be monitored effectively in a virtual environment. Metaverse allows patients to be more involved in the process of their treatment, bridging the gap between doctor and patient like never before. The doctor may provide the patient with a 3D clinical application that can be used to monitor their weight, blood pressure etc. constantly. With the advancement of technology, doctors are also able to learn to perform surgery in a virtual environment to be prepared for the real thing, and models of AI & ML may even analyze a patient's current conditions to make educated guesses on what their problem might be, greatly helping the doctor with the diagnosis process.
5. Social Media: In 2021, Social Networking Sites (SNS) giant FaceBook proudly announced its name change to 'Meta', which served as a hint to showcase the prospect of the metaverse's implementation in the social sector as referenced from Jaipong (2023). On the significance of the name change, Meta CEO Mark Zuckerberg said, "Today we are seen as a social media company, but in our DNA we are a company that builds technology to connect people, and the metaverse is the next frontier just like social networking was when we got started" - Meta (2021). Likewise, a bunch of major tech companies are currently investing in developing tools and their own adaptations of the metaverse so as not to fall behind on the race for domination in what is undoubtedly the next big thing.
6. Entertainment: Filmmakers and any kind of artists within the entertainment industry are also geared up to take advantage of the metaverse's global and immersive nature. This mode of entertainment is especially gaining favor among the younger consumers, who are expected to be a major factor in the growth of the metaverse. Movie screenings and promotions can be arranged within the metaverse, even arranging virtual meet-and-greets between the cast and their fans. Similarly, several pop stars like Ariana Grande, Justin Bieber, Travis Scott and Marshmello have also made use of the metaverse environment through the likes of Fortnite and other metaverse-type applications to arrange e-concerts and related events for their fans.
7. Digital locations: The metaverse is basically creating spaces overlaid over the world as we know it- making room for the "building" of real estate within it. Early investors are already scoping out prospective properties in the metaverse like concert halls, shopping malls and even private properties. These locations could also correspond to some sort of physical location, requiring you to be a certain degree of closeness to it in order to interact or enter the space. For example, a restaurant could use Web 3.0 technology to set up a store in the metaverse where the user can virtually enter the restaurant and place an order using or earning loyalty points that are digitally tracked by the

company. Customers working or playing in that digital space may even place an order for a real-world pickup or delivery, should they be close enough. Internet publishing company Parade, which has "metaverse" listed as its headquarters on its Linkedin page, is also attempting to move the farmer's market concept into the metaverse- claiming to be the first "MetaMarket" the metaverse has to offer- accommodating 500 customers as digital avatars, who can talk with each other, visit vendors and buy products.

FOCUS OF THE STUDY

Although the deployment of the metaverse brings forward endless opportunities in various fields as discussed in the previous section, this development also subsequently can be considered to be opening a Pandora's Box- introducing revolutionary methods of crime which may prove challenging to deter. In this chapter, we will analyze the potential holes in the security of the metaverse to predict the possible crimes that it may be vulnerable to and therefore conceive some possible prevention methods.

CYBERCRIMES

With the rapid advancements in technology, it is becoming an irreplaceable part of our daily life and work. The internet has become an integral part of how we connect with individuals, businesses and governments worldwide. The difficulty of differentiating between real and virtual life with the development of the metaverse has made us more vulnerable to cybercrimes.

Cybercrimes are illegal activities being carried out with the use of digital devices, often targeting computer systems, networks and individuals with various malicious intents. It comprises various crimes like hacking into unauthorized computer systems, online financial fraud, data theft, online harassment, and spreading malware or ransomware.

The threat posed by cybercrimes is significant because of the anonymity and the worldwide reach the internet gives access to and presents numerous challenges to individuals, organizations and governments. The perpetrators have the ability to engage in criminal activities from anywhere on the globe, posing challenges in their detection and capture. The anonymity enables criminals to form an intricate network of miscreants who collaborate to execute sophisticated attacks based on *Seigfried-Spellar et. al.*(2022).

The evolution of computer systems and networks has considerably aided the growth of cybercrime. Crimes can be classified into five groups based on the primary functions of computer systems and networks.

1. Crimes where the computer or the network is used in criminal activity as a tool
2. Crimes in which the crime has taken place through the means of a computer or network
3. Crimes where the target of a crime is a computer system or a network
4. Old book crimes which are made possible using computers or networks
5. Additional information offenses.

Figure 4 represents the different types of cybercrimes classified based on the part the computer system or network plays and some examples of each like DOS attacks, Identity theft, Copyright, Online gambling, stealing of trade secrets etc based *Zhang Y. et. al.*(2012).

Figure 4. Classification of cybercrimes and their examples

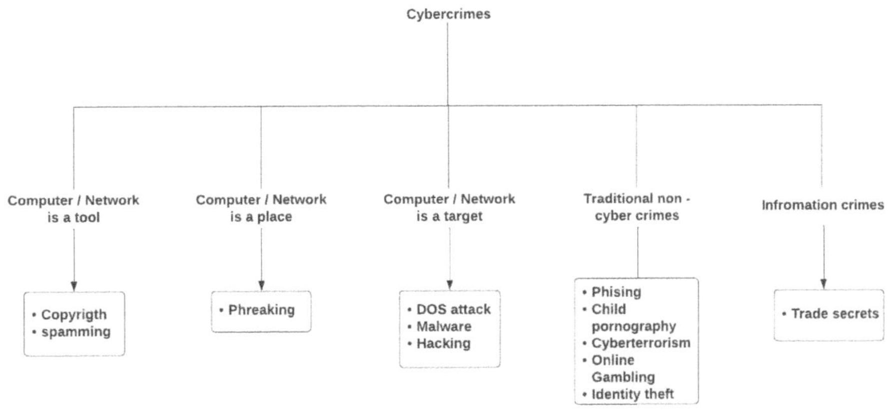

Cyber Warfare

In this era, battlegrounds are not limited to the traditional physical space between warring nation-states. The rise of technology and worldwide connectedness has given birth to a new dimension of conflict: cyberwarfare. Cyberwarfare is the use of cyberattacks with a war-like intent. Cyberwar is the scenario where two nations declare war, but their conflict is solely conducted through cyber warfare.

Unlike traditional warfare, cyberwarfare takes place in the intangible realm of cyberspace, where acts can have far-reaching effects on a country's security, economy, and society. It entails the deliberate exploitation of digital weaknesses, the creation of sophisticated malware and hacking tools, and the use of strategic tactics to disrupt or outwit an opponent.

Cyberwarfare motivations might vary greatly. Nation-states use cyberwarfare to achieve strategic goals such as intelligence gathering, political influence, economic benefit, or even sabotage. Non-state actors, such as hacktivist groups or cybercriminal organizations and terrorist institutions, may also participate in cyberwarfare to achieve their own ideological or financial agendas based on *Josh Baughman*(2022).

The techniques involved in cyberwarfare keep on evolving. Offensive Cyber attack operations can involve various tactics, consisting -

1. Cyber Espionage: State-sponsored cyber actors engage in espionage activities to acquire intelligence, steal sensitive information, or gain insight into the capabilities and intentions of an enemy.
2. DoS and DDoS attacks try to disrupt or destroy targeted systems, networks, or websites by flooding them with traffic or exploiting flaws in their infrastructure.
3. Manipulation and Destruction of Data: Cyberwarfare can entail modifying or destroying vital data, jeopardizing the integrity of information systems, and undermining an adversary's decision-making processes.
4. Malware and Advanced Persistent Threats (APTs): Advanced malware and APTs are used in cyberwarfare to gain unauthorized access to networks, sustain persistence, and carry out espionage or sabotage activities.

5. Offensive cyber operations: Nation-states may use offensive cyber capabilities to cripple an adversary's essential infrastructure, disrupt military command and control systems, or sabotage key targets. *Michael Robinson et al.*(2015) , *El Gataa et. al.*(2022)

POSSIBLE THREATS

NFTs

A Non-Fungible Token (NFT) is a type of cryptocurrency that involves the storage of a unit of data in the form of hashes or links to digital files of photos, audio, text, videos or other media stored in a blockchain and governed by smart contracts of Ethereum which give it a unique identity *David Vindal - Tomás(2022)*. Ethereum is a cryptocurrency, like bitcoin or dogecoin- but its blockchain additionally keeps track of who is holding and trading NFTs. A creator can easily demonstrate the existence and ownership of digital assets in the form of videos, images, arts, event tickets, etc. by using NFTs on smart contracts (in Ethereum), Wang et. al. (2021) explain. Additionally, the creator can earn royalties each time a successful trade on any NFT market is made or by peer-to-peer exchanging. NFTs are expected to become a potential Intellectual Property (IP) protection solution due to their high liquidity, ease of interoperability and full-history tradability. *Sara Qamar et. al.*(2023)

Being considered as the most reliable (and pretty much only) candidate to establish and enable ownership of digital assets in the metaverse, the highest sale boasted by an NFT so far is a whopping $91.8M for Pak's Merge. However, there is no legal foundation governing the ownership and verification of the public certificate of authenticity of NFTs. Security threats and concerns usage of NFTs in the metaverse raise include-

- Integrity Issues: NFTs are susceptible to ransom and similar criminal attacks as they do regulate ownership of data, but don't provide a particular location to store these assets. NFT files may be encrypted via ransomware attacks in such a way that the owner would still retain ownership over it but would be unable to access the data assets unless they succumb to paying a ransom fee. *Abeer M Awadallah et. al.*(20, 23)
- NFTs are vulnerable to blockchain hijacking attacks as they are verified using blockchain technology. Smaller blockchains are also open to Sybil attacks- the attacker can manipulate NFT ownership verification by controlling more than 50% of the peer nodes that are responsible for checking transactions. Further, NFT ownership may not be upheld by the metaverse space as there is no legal framework in place binding it to do so.
- IPFS: The assets verified by NFTs are usually stored on the InterPlanetary File System (IPFS) where the owner is required to pay a fee of some amount in order to "pin" or store the asset. However, the "pin" service provider may remove the asset if the fee is not paid in periods, therefore resulting in loss in assets.
- NFT artwork may present itself differently on different IP addresses and user agents. As demonstrated by security researcher Moxie Marlinspike, NFT artwork could be falsified by being displayed differently based on who was looking at it, as the assets were stored in a common central storage.

- Phishing: While the actual content of an NFT cannot be changed, the data file download links may be tampered with to further phishing, spear phishing attacks or even drive-by downloads as the popularity-and subsequently trust- in NFTs increases.
- Fraudulent brokers: It is estimated that a fee may be associated with transferring digital assets across diverse metaverse environments. Moreover, incompatible assets would necessitate a process of "conversion" to facilitate their movement from one virtual space to another. This scenario opens avenues for potential exploitation by malicious entities preying on individuals employing asset brokers, or even imposters posing as reputable brokers to deceive and defraud unsuspecting individuals.
- Forgery: Changing up a few data values from the original, NFTs may also be duplicated to resemble an existing artwork and the data files may be sold to a new buyer. This could very well prove effective if the counterfeit has an almost similar hash value and appears to be nearly the same.

The Darkverse

The darkverse is a manifestation of the dark web within the metaverse. The pseudo-physical nature of the metaverse presents the darkverse as a bigger security threat than the pre-existing dark web, which if nothing else was at least limited to simply cyberspaces bound to a computer screen. It replicates a surreptitious physical meeting with the added benefit of online open discussion forums and criminal forums that cannot be traced. Threats that the metaverse may be subject to in light of the darkverse are:

- Although it may provide a safe space to speak out against oppressive or restrictive governments or entities, the untraceable and anonymous nature of the darkverse acts as a breeding ground to facilitate illicit or criminal activities.
- Underground marketplaces: The metaverse could house various safehouses and marketplaces for criminal organizations to conduct illegal activities and trades hidden in plain sight. As it is possible to deem a space in the metaverse inaccessible without possession of a special token for authentication, even if Law Enforcement Agencies (LEA) had an idea about these spaces, they wouldn't be able to infiltrate them without having obtained these tokens, which could prove difficult if not impossible.
- An aspect of the metaverse states that some spaces may only be accessed by being present in a certain physical location. This acts as an added layer of security for any potential criminal organization conducting malicious activities within the metaverse as they wouldn't be encountered easily.
- LEA would be unable to access and intercept any proximity-based communication taking place between individuals or groups within the metaverse. This means that users intending to have conversations relating to any illegal trades or any sort of crime, while it would have instantly pinged on LEA threat radars had the conversation taken place in a regular chatroom, may not be detected in the metaverse if the users enable geolocation-based or proximity-based messaging.
- Identifying and regulating the distribution of child pornography or sexual assault is difficult enough as is on the dark web, but with the introduction of the darkverse there is a risk of significant increase in the number of these crimes committed as there is no method for LEA to monitor this activity or effectively track down the offenders in place yet. *Sara Qamar et. al.(2023)*

Financial Fraud

Cybercrime in banks is the act of getting budgetary pick up through profit-driven criminal action- including avatar extortion, ransomware attacks, mail, and endeavors to take budgetary accounts, credit cards, or other installment card data. In other words: Monetary cybercrime incorporates processes such as taking installment card data, picking up budgetary accounts to start unauthorized exchanges, blackmail, avatar extortion to apply for monetary items, and so on. *Sara Qamar et. al.*(2023)

"Nowadays the term "hacker" slowly disappears from the threat landscape and we see an increase of "criminals" who follow the same paths as always, the only difference being they are now cybercriminals. To avoid becoming a victim of financial cybercrime, you must understand that technology will react to the decisions you make–it cannot make decisions for you," – Adrian Constantin Stanila, Head of Cyber Security Incident Response team in Visma *Arkvik*, (2021).

We have all gotten the well-known mail where a few Nigerian rulers have kicked the bucket and their counselors are presently reaching you, the sole beneficiary, to send over a stack of cash to you. Different social building procedures are most frequently utilized to control casualties into giving private data. Other well-known tricks are Bitcoin tricks or cherish tricks, where individuals are focused on through fake profiles on dating sites or prevalent social media sites to strike up connections, driving to the scammer inquiring for cash exchanges and misusing the victim's feelings. *Abeer M Awadallah et. al.*(2023)

The results of an effective attack can be disastrous and have annihilating impacts on a company. It may affect the full economy of the company and indeed lead to liquidation in the most severe cases, particularly in the event that the company is small. Reputational damage within the eyes of partners, clients, and the common public is additionally a terrible result.

When it comes to individuals, they may experience having their accounts purged, reserve funds stolen, and subscriptions or loans taken up in their name after having their identity stolen.

Living, working, and playing in a substitute reality requires stores, and within the metaverse, this is facilitated by crypto-assets. Crypto resources are advanced representations of possessions which will be exchanged and stored digitally, using blockchain. *David Vindal - Tomás*(2022)

The various sorts of money related wrongdoing within the metaverse include-

- Phishing and fraud scams: One of the foremost common dangers is the different sorts of phishing and extortion tricks that occur. An effective strategy utilized by cybercriminals is social building. Abusing individuals' mental vulnerabilities online is already common, and has now become a major challenge within the metaverse as well. Attackers can impersonate verified metaverse personalities - for example by picking up control of well-known social media accounts or even mimicking trusted avatars within the metaverse, scammers may deceive individuals within the community to press on a phishing link or to send funds to the scammers' wallet.
- Code exploits: Another way to take people's crypto resources is by using malware that targets computerized wallets. Cyber blackmail and ransomware are infamous and exceptionally profitable cybercrime threats, and they pose a genuine concern within the metaverse as well, considering how the metaverse is built on digital finances.
- Wash trading: Wash Trading refers to the illegal exchange of NFTs in which the buyer and seller are the same. This is done to drive up the price of an asset. We would be unable to monitor whether a transaction is genuinely between two different parties or not, because of which wash trading is predicted to be a major threat to the economical balance within the metaverse. *Von Wachter et.*

al. (2022) estimate that as of now about 0.3% of all suspicious NFT trades may be connected to a case of wash trading.
- Money laundering, tax evasion, and fear monger financing: From the point of view of the culprit, cash washing or money laundering serves to conceal the unlawful beginning of a payment. The metaverse can be utilized as a channel to wash illegal reserves, whether they stem from real-world or crypto-based crime. *Numaan Huq(2022)*

Privacy Issues

Based on the advance and vista of the metaverse, we analyze the existing security and security issues in the metaverse based on *Sara Qamar et. al.(2023)*-

- Socialization-Related Security and Protection Issues and Solutions: In the metaverse, clients can interact with each other through the web, which implies the Internet serves as the spine for communication and associations. The metaverse also suffers from all the network-related security and protection issues that social networks in general are exposed to.
- Security Issues and Solutions: Online services' interactivity permits rogue programmers to extract information through injection attacks. To avoid this, end-user gadgets ought to approve client input, permit negligibly favored accounts, and run SQL Server with minimal privileges. Man-in-the-middle attack compromise the secrecy, astuteness, and accessibility of the framework. Solid confirmation and cryptographic protocols are essential for protecting information validity and guaranteeing information accessibility. Attack detection protocols screen the system and anticipate attacks. Cross-Site Scripting (XSS) attacks can inject virulent JavaScript code into websites, and web intermediaries with XSS location calculations can moderate endeavors. Profound learning models have moved forward detection exactness and effectiveness.

Some of the main security issues within the metaverse that businesses and their clients should be mindful of include based on *Abeer M Awadallah et. al.*(2023)-

- Need for security regulations
- Unchecked user information collection
- Users' information rights and ownership
- Interpreting current controls within the metaverse world
- User-to-user protection
- Minors' security concerns.

Cyber-Physical Threats

The Spatial Web refers to a computing experience presented in a 3D space. The metaverse presents an interactive layer over the physical world fuelled by Web3.0 and Spatial Web technologies. It is a conglomeration of the cyber and IoT worlds. This raises various cyber-physical threats and concerns-

- Smart contracts, which will act as the basis for countless automations in the metaverse, are susceptible to hacking or counterfeiting- potentially allowing a criminal to steal virtual assets (which would normally be delivered to a physical address).
- More aspects of our daily life and environment are bared to cyber attacks with the introduction of new classes of IoT and IIoT devices.
- The metaverse boasts a newfound level of entity-user communication, like a user using metaverse-enabled AR glasses gaining the ability to interact with smart city infrastructure. This opens up space for Man-in-the-Middle (MitM) attacks, illegal access to spaces and infrastructure that was otherwise not open to the public, etc. and similar new means for criminals to exploit the users of the metaverse.
- A Digital Twin is the virtual counterpart of a pre-existing physical object- be it a product, system or process. A significant number of Critical Infrastructure (CI) facilities would host digital twins in the metaverse to ensure ease in operations and remote work; however, this may also leave the CI facilities vulnerable to cyber attacks within the metaverse. *Yuntao Wang et. al.*(2022)
- Though location-based pricing is already the norm for most virtual asset distribution services, this may be manipulated in the metaverse for criminals to lure users towards the darkverse or other unlawful spaces within the metaverse under the guise of availing a hefty discount. Unsuspecting customers may even get scammed entirely.
- Still in its infancy, the metaverse still has ambiguous laws held in place for its function, and is not entirely tightly bound. *TEODOROV* (2023) raises the concern that this means that there isn't a formal definition or structured method to deal with serious crimes of a cyber-physical nature- like sexual assault, romance scams or even bullying in the metaverse. Since the metaverse may be accessed by one user under multiple names or identities, with their real identity well hidden, it is difficult for LEA to detect let alone punish violent crimes within cyberspace. However, the victim still suffers quite extremely from these crimes, and therefore even a virtual crime has physical or real-world implications.
- Since most businesses will have some presence in the metaverse, and some businesses may be entirely located there, it is crucial to ensure that the buildings housing these headquarters are secure and that any data contained within them is protected. Cyber-physical security will be required to ensure safety of these buildings to ensure that the buildings housing these headquarters are secure and that any data contained within them is protected. *Numaan Huq*(2022)

VR/AR/Extended Reality Threats

As the world eagerly stands by to witness how Extended Reality (XR) and Virtual Reality (VR) will modify the way we play, learn, work out, travel, shop and more, it's time to arrange for the worst-case scenario. AR Headsets are exciting, but they offer modern ways to extort information and alter the associations between the human and computerized universes. With Facebook presenting Meta and Virtual Reality, a modern wave of concerns and evaluations has arisen. Some of the AR security concerns and questions are based on *Yang-Wang Chow* (2023) -

- It is essential to affirm one's character within the genuine world, but the key issue in the metaverse is approving voice, facial highlights, and video recordings utilizing avatars. The metaverse is primarily a virtual community of individuals that interact through AR and VR gear.

- This brings up existing issues in a modern light, such as deceiving individuals into giving out their individual data through social engineering methods, identity theft utilizing biometric information, and so on. Another conceivable ambush we see here is the dissent of service, in which individuals who depend on AR shows for their occupations are abruptly disconnected from the stream of information they're getting. *Awadallah et. al.* (2023)
- Graphics and data are superimposed over the real environment in extended reality. Gamers, retailers, designers, and experts will make real-world choices based on the data advertised by AR applications.

Virtual reality (VR) privacy concerns are-

- Ransomware: Attackers may be able to inject malware into VR platforms to trick users into revealing personal information. Similar to AR, this opens the door to ransomware attacks, destroying systems before hostile attackers can demand ransom.
- Fake Identity: Machine learning algorithms make it possible to manipulate sounds and moves in ways that make them look real. Suppose a hacker has access to the motion tracking data of a VR headset. This can be exploited to create digital clones (also known as deep fakes) to weaken VR security. This can then be superimposed on other people's virtual reality experiences to launch social engineering attacks.
- Restrictions on external connections: Cybersecurity concerns aside, one of the biggest risks of VR is that it completely cuts off the user's audiovisual connection to the outside world. It is always important to first assess the physical security of your environment. This also applies to augmented reality. Especially in more immersive contexts, users need to maintain a strong awareness of their surroundings. *Numaan Huq*(2022) *Yang-Wang Chow* (2023)

Social Engineering in the Metaverse

Before we get into how social engineering works in the metaverse we need to know about social engineering and what are the different ways criminals use it to gain access into an organization or scam individuals.

Social engineering is a technique for influencing and misleading individuals or groups in order to obtain unauthorized access to sensitive information, commit malevolent acts, or affect their behavior. It is a non-technical strategy that depends on human psychology, trust, and weaknesses rather than software or hardware flaws. The goal of social engineering is to manipulate people into giving out crucial information, and financial data, or granting access to unauthorized systems for mandatory gain usually. It uses basic human qualities like curiosity, trust, helpfulness, or fear to persuade others to do things that benefit the attacker. *Siddiqi MA et. al.*(2022)

The threat scenarios and security concerns that may occur in the metaverse relating to social engineering are-

- Accurate sentiment analysis: In the metaverse, operators would be able to analyze personal data like eye tracking, body tracking, voice intonation, and more to comprehend user's feelings and sentiments. This capacity is comparable to what politicians use to measure public sentiment during elections. The fear here is that this data may be used to control individuals by presenting tailored narratives or information that corresponds with their thoughts, affecting their beliefs and judgements.*Yuntao Wang et. al.*(2022)

- Targeted narrative and persuasion: Criminals or state actors may target certain groups of people in the metaverse who are vulnerable to or sensitive to certain themes. They may convince and manipulate these groups by recognising them and delivering customized narratives or stories to them. This strategy may be used to effectively influence people's behavior and activities by exploiting their anxieties or fears.
- Deep forgeries and manipulation: Deep forgeries use artificial intelligence algorithms to create very realistic and fraudulent material. Deep forgeries might be used in the metaverse to mix synthesized speech with visual components, allowing for sophisticated manipulation and persuasion. This offers a considerable concern since individuals may be misled by convincing audio-visual information, leading to possible criminal or destructive behavior.
- Impersonate within the metaverse: Criminals can infiltrate a metaverse realm and mimic legitimate avatars, such as those representing a firm, organization, or even the government. They can misdirect people within the space by adopting these identities. This can result in a variety of malevolent acts, such as disseminating misleading information, duping people into giving sensitive data or engaging in fraudulent transactions, or generating a poor opinion of the impersonated organization through disruptive or damaging behavior.
- Impersonation for competitive mischief: Similarly, thieves can employ impersonated avatars to join a competitor's metaverse region and disrupt it. They can damage the reputation of the targeted firm by producing trouble or participating in improper behavior. This has the potential to harm the company's image, consumer trust, and overall commercial performance.
- Impersonation of service providers: Within the metaverse, criminals may imitate reputable service providers such as physicians. They can provide incorrect medical advice to patients in exchange for cash, taking advantage of the trust and vulnerability of those seeking help. This type of impersonation to commit fraud is not confined to the metaverse, although the anonymity and immersive quality of the virtual world can help. *Numaan Huq*(2022)

Traditional IT Attacks

Traditional IT assaults relate to a variety of hostile acts that have long been popular in the realm of information technology. These assaults usually target computer systems, networks, software, and people in order to gain unauthorized access, cause damage, steal sensitive information, or disrupt operations. Understanding conventional IT assaults is critical for establishing successful cybersecurity defenses. Some of the issues that may arise in the metaverse are-

- DDoS extortion attacks: Distributed Denial of Service (DDoS) attacks represent a serious danger to the metaverse. Multiple hacked computers or devices are used in a DDoS assault to flood a target system or network with huge amounts of traffic, surpassing its capacity and creating service outages. Such assaults on metaverse platforms may be launched by malicious bodies in order to extract money from the organizations that manage them. Because maintaining the metaverse infrastructure is costly and downtime can result in large financial losses, organizations may be forced to pay the attackers to cease the DDoS assaults and assure uninterrupted service. This emphasizes the significance of putting in place strong DDoS prevention methods to defend the metaverse infrastructure.

- Ransomware Attacks: Ransomware attacks can target Metaverse platforms, just like any other digital system. Hackers obtain unauthorized access to servers or data storage systems and encrypt the data, making it unavailable to legitimate owners. In exchange for decrypting the data and restoring access, the attackers want a ransom payment. Because the metaverse may include sensitive user or company data, ransomware attacks are a big problem. To reduce the likelihood of ransomware attacks, it emphasizes the importance of robust security measures such as frequent backups, network segmentation, and user awareness training.
- Vulnerabilities in IoT Devices: It is predicted that the metaverse will interface with numerous Internet of Things (IoT) devices to allow cyber-physical Augmented Reality (AR) interactions. This, however, presents the possibility of discovering exposed and vulnerable IoT devices on the metaverse internet. Malicious actors can use tools like Shodan, an internet scanning engine, to locate and target these devices, exploiting any vulnerabilities they may have. To solve this, tight security measures for IoT devices, such as frequent firmware upgrades, robust authentication, and encryption, should be introduced to reduce the danger of unauthorized access and potential compromise. *Yuntao Wang et. al.*(2022)
- Cloud-specific attacks: If the metaverse relies on existing technology and cloud infrastructure, it may be vulnerable to cloud-specific attacks. These attacks target weaknesses in cloud services and platforms, such as misconfigurations, lax access constraints, or insufficient data security mechanisms. Cybercriminals might use techniques like data breaches, privilege escalation, or server hijacking to undermine the metaverse infrastructure. To reduce these threats, organizations must use strong security practices while adopting and configuring cloud services, such as strong authentication procedures, encryption, and constant monitoring. *Pooja Kumari et. al.*(2022), *Numaan Huq*(2022)

Miscellaneous Threats and Issues

Besides the easily categorized safety concerns in the metaverse, there are a few more threats that we are vulnerable to of various kinds. These miscellaneous threats include-

- Security and Information Security: The collection and utilization of individual information inside the metaverse can raise concerns around protection and information security. Clients may stress almost their individual data being gotten to, shared, or abused without their consent.
- Cybercrime and Hacking: Similar to any advanced stage, the metaverse is powerless to cybercriminal exercises such as hacking, phishing, identity theft, and scams. Malicious individuals may endeavor to misuse vulnerabilities within the framework of the metaverse to pick up unauthorized information or control the virtual environment.
- Mental Property Encroachment: The metaverse can raise copyright and trademark encroachment issues, as clients make and share virtual objects, avatars, and situations. Securing mental property rights tends to get challenging, and debates may be sparked over proprietorship and utilization rights.

- Badgering and Bullying: The anonymity given by the metaverse can encourage people to engage in badgering, bullying, or other shapes of misconduct. This could hurt users' mental well-being and general experience inside the virtual world.
- Virtual Economy and Budgetary Extortion: With the development of virtual monetary forms and economies inside the metaverse, there's a potential for budgetary extortion, counting tricks, Ponzi plans, and cash washing. Clients may face dangers related to virtual resource robbery or unauthorized transactions.
- Habit and Wellbeing Concerns: Investing unreasonable amounts of time within the metaverse can lead to enslavement and disregard of real-life obligations. Furthermore, prolonged usage of virtual reality headsets may have health implications such as eye strain, motion affliction, and disorientation. *Numaan Huq*(2022), *Yuntao Wang et. al.*(2022)

CYBERWARFARE IN THE METAVERSE

With the tremendous and bombarding amounts of investment by nation-states in the development of the metaverse, it is very evident that the future of conflict is not just economic sanctions and traditional cyberwars but also full fledged wars in virtual spaces. *El Gataa et. al.(2022)*

In the coming years, with the development of the metaverse, militaries will not only use it to wage cyberwars but also use it to train their armies about different war scenarios, which will cost a lot more and also be dangerous to recreate in real life, along with testing and studying new weaponry and military strategies.

While the metaverse, in its current conceptual form, is largely focused on producing virtual experiences and interactions, cyber warfare tactics and methods might be applied in a metaverse-like environment. Here are a few examples of hypothetical scenarios:

1. Virtual Espionage: In the same way that intelligence agencies use traditional espionage to obtain information, operatives in a metaverse may enter virtual spaces and communities to gather sensitive data, control events, or spy on specific persons or organizations.
2. Virtual attack: Cyber attackers might conduct virtual assaults by exploiting weaknesses in the metaverse's infrastructure, such as software platforms, servers, or user interfaces. These assaults might interrupt services, steal virtual assets, or propagate malware throughout the metaverse ecosystem.
3. Identity Theft and Impersonation: In a metaverse where individuals build avatars to represent themselves, bad actors might deceive and influence other users by engaging in identity theft and impersonation. This might result in many types of social engineering assaults, fraud, or even reputational harm.
4. Manipulation of Virtual Currencies: If a metaverse incorporates virtual currencies or economies, cybercriminals may seek to exploit or manipulate those systems. They might use fraud, money laundering, or hacking in order to obtain an unfair edge or destabilize the virtual economy.

It is crucial to emphasize that these possibilities are theoretical, as the notion of the metaverse is still in its infancy, and its practical implementation and possible security concerns are not completely known. However, as virtual worlds and networked digital experiences expand, it becomes increasingly important to address cybersecurity risks in order to preserve the metaverse's safety and integrity.*El Gataa et. al.(2022)*

Please remember that this section is based on current knowledge of the metaverse and cyberwarfare. Future advances and real-world occurrences may alter the structure of these notions.

USE CASES AND THREATS

The metaverse houses infinite possibilities for applications in various domains. However, each of these use cases come with their own share of concerns for safety and probability of crimes. Table 1 shows the various scenarios in the metaverse and possible cybercrimes. *Numaan Huq*(2022)

Table 1. Scenarios in the Metaverse and possible cybercrimes

Metaverse use case	Threats
1. Social Media	
Social Media Influencers are rapidly picking up in popularity, amassing millions of followers worldwide on their respective platforms. The expansion of the metaverse stands to further their influence over the masses, taking on a greater role. Fans would be able to communicate or follow their idols in real time, even holding virtual fanmeets. Influencers would also be able to set up advertisements, sponsorships, product placements or even just regular documentation of their experiences in the form of interactive VR videos.	**Privacy-** Influencers may be more vulnerable to stalkers and creeps, considering that the metaverse may make it easier to track their location using their avatars. **Social Engineering-** Their avatars may be duplicated, and the user may be profiled by their data to accurately impersonate them, in turn misleading or scamming their fans. This may even lead to damaging of the user's reputation. **Financial Fraud-** Since criminals would have the added advantage of anonymous avatars, it would be easier for them to commit fraud- especially under the guise of being a popular influencer.
2. Advertising	
The metaverse will be heavily trafficked with advertisements, with companies already giving us a glimpse into this prospect by in-game advertisements in games like Cyberpunk 2077 as well as movies like Blade Runner. We are sitting on a virtual gold mine of sorts with respect to the advertisement industry. As the virtual world is independent of the rules of physics, we may even paint the entire sky in advertisements if we want to. A users' avatar may be anonymous, but its activity can be tracked and profiled to show relevant advertisements.	**Financial Fraud-** Fake advertisements and endorsements are bound to inflate the value of digital assets, resulting in increase in pump-and-dump schemes. **Privacy-** There is expected to be unregulated sharing of data with third-party organizations, which includes personal information. **VR/AR/MR/XR Threats-** If the advertisements remain unregulated, some may even lead users to unsafe locations.
3. Publishing Industry	
Digitization across the world has abolished the need for traditional libraries and caused them to see a great decline in visitors, since all information has been made digital and easily accessible. With the metaverse, however, we would see libraries make a comeback in the form of digital libraries for users to explore. These libraries will house digital copies of books, audio files and video files. They may even contain VR books or VR videos to experience.	**VR/AR/MR/XR Threats-** The propagation of fake news- which is already a major problem in our society- would be made easier. It is dangerous if an organization or criminal chooses to target a vulnerable user and display this sort of news to them on a sensitive topic. There could be mass rioting in extreme cases. **Miscellaneous-** Copyright infringement will prove difficult to track within the metaverse as there is currently no mechanism to monitor it nor is there a firm set of laws governing it within the jurisdiction of copyrights.
4. Training	
By allowing students to explore and understand concepts in 3D, the metaverse helps them indulge their curiosity. Exploring the pyramids, assembling various things, and many more can be an example. Metaverses enhance education, training, and simulation in general. It brings a good user experience, resulting in a more accurate simulation of topics, allowing users to work on it like an actual event instead of sitting in a simulation. Smaili (2022).	**Privacy -** Metaverse space operators can track users indefinitely and intrude on users' privacy. **Social Engineering -** To sway the groups, criminals will choose to target the ones that are the most vulnerable and sensitive to a particular issue. Cyber-physical worlds can be profoundly affected by visuals and speech
5. Art	
In the metaverse, artists have the liberty and freedom to create intricate art since there are no physical laws that govern the physical world in the metaverse unless added otherwise.	**NFTs –** Cybercriminals will use NFTs as targets for ransomware attacks in the metaverse. **Financial Fraud –** Criminals can gain profit by selling forged artwork in the metaverse. **VR/AR/MR/XR Threats –** There will be fake metaverse galleries that display and sell counterfeit artwork.

continued on following page

Table 1. Continued

Metaverse use case	Threats
6. Shopping	
Metaverse will reinvent the shopping experience by having mega malls, where all the major brands will be present in the form of virtual overlays (which will provide customers with extra information like sales, customization options, and many more) and digital storefronts (especially for E-commerce retailers like Amazon and Alibaba), where users will be able to visit, browse and shop in all these malls, and the customers will have a fully-abled avatar on which they can try on their clothes.	**NFTs -** Users will need a broker to handle asset exchanges; there will be a fee to move digital assets across metaverse worlds. Payment or banking information can be stolen from users by criminals pretending to be brokers. **Financial Fraud –** Fake businesses can pose as legitimate vendors and offer counterfeit goods. **VR/AR/MR/XR Threats -** Cybercriminals will duplicate the real-world store's digital twins in another metaverse space and defraud customers using them.
7. Experiences industry	
In the metaverse, users will be able to feel things physically with full-body actuator suits. Touching an object, feeling a push, feeling a jump, and experiencing the elements are all possible for them. It was explored in the movie version of Ready Player One to combine a full-body suit with an omnidirectional treadmill. There is potential for these to be a replacement for theme parks and other similar entertainment industries.	**Cyber-Physical Threats –** Infections caused by malicious code embedded in body suits can cause malfunctions and endanger users. In a suit, for example, bypassing the cooling mechanism and making it unbearably hot; intensifying burns or enhancing pain thresholds; triggering epilepsy or seizures by stroboscopic light effects in the headset. **VR/AR/MR/XR Threats –** Access to body suits allows criminals to monitor users' behavior. **Privacy –** Biometric data that can be misused, such as that related to health, will be accessible through the suits.
8. Critical Infrastructure	
Hydroelectric factories (or any critical structures) can move virtually inside digital twins using the metaverse. All the important outfits and detectors in the factory are network connected. Their values can be visually read in the metaverse digital twin, and corrective or conservation conduct taken. The digital binary gives the workers a physical sense of the actual factory and its outfit placement versus simply viewing readings on a control panel and looking at CCTV images. Third-party contractors can also ever work inside the digital twin of the hydro factory, which significantly reduces trips and increases effectiveness.	**Cyber-Physical Threats –** A criminal can exploit the digital twin of a power plant to gain unlawful access to its internal systems and ICS/SCADA environment. **Traditional IT Attacks –** Since the digital twin runs on IT infrastructure, criminals exploit everyday IT attacks. Brute forcing, vulnerability exploitation, and ransomware are examples of IT attacks that we see everyday. **VR/AR/MR/XR Threats –** Using a site's digital blueprints, criminals can plot their attacks or plan their exits and entrances.
9. IIoT	
Some jobs can move from the real world into the metaverse, where cyber-physical interaction exists. For example, industrial equipment can now be operated by specialist operators thousands of miles away without needing special simulators because all the equipment is connected and accessible via custom metaverse space interfaces. Another example: security guards can do their job monitoring a physical world facility via the metaverse. The guards can use sensors and CCTVs built into the physical space by interacting with a digital twin in the metaverse. The digital twin gives them the physical feel of the facility and reduces the need for hourly foot patrolling.	**Cyber-Physical Threats –** Culprits can launch MitM attacks between artificial outfit and the remote drivers. **Traditional IT Attacks –** Traditional IT attacks, similar to vulnerability exploitation, can be used to gain access to artificial outfit. Because everything in the metaverse is connected, side movement will also be easy after the original entry **VR/AR/MR/XR Threats –** Culprits can pre plan physical attacks if they ever get access to a digital twin of the point. This can be via icon appropriations, or by penetrating raw information exposed to the metaverse.

SAFETY MEASURES

As we all know, "Precaution is better than cure." and in the ever-changing metaverse world, safeguarding against cybercrime is critical. Here are several precautions that may be taken:

- Secure Authentication: To prevent unauthorized access to user accounts, employ strong authentication systems such as Two-Factor Authentication (2FA) or biometric authentication.
- Encryption: Use end-to-end encryption for metaverse connections to safeguard sensitive data from interception by unauthorized parties.
- Secure Development Practises: When designing metaverse apps and platforms, use secure coding practices. Update and patch software on a regular basis to resolve vulnerabilities.
- User Education: Inform users about possible threats and safe internet practices. Teach children the value of using strong, unique passwords, avoiding questionable links, and exercising caution when providing personal information.

- Virtual Asset Security: Implement stringent security measures for virtual assets such as digital currency and virtual items. To provide transparency and prevent unauthorized transactions, use blockchain technology or other secure decentralized systems. *David Vindal - Tomás* (2022).
- Monitoring in Real-Time: Use modern monitoring systems to detect and respond to cyber threats in real-time. This may entail the use of machine learning algorithms to detect suspicious activity and potential security breaches.
- Establish explicit reporting methods to allow users to report cybercrime or questionable activity. Investigate and respond to reported situations as soon as possible.
- Legal Framework: Create and implement relevant legal frameworks and rules to combat cybercrime in the metaverse. This might involve data security, digital currency, and online fraud legislation.
- Collaboration: Encourage collaboration across metaverse platforms, developers, and security professionals in order to exchange threat intelligence and build standardized security measures.

LIMITATIONS

The metaverse is still in its early stages of development. This means that there is limited data available on cyber threats in this space. For example, we do not yet know how common cybercrimes and cyberwars are in the metaverse, or what the most common types of attacks are. This makes it difficult to assess the full scope of the problem and develop effective mitigation strategies.

The metaverse is a complicated and ever-changing ecosystem. As a result, predicting how cyber threats will grow in the future is challenging. We don't know, for example, how emerging technologies like artificial intelligence and blockchain will be utilized to perpetrate cybercrime and cyberwarfare in the metaverse. This makes long-term preventative methods harder to create. The study paper concentrates on a specific sort of cybercrime or cyberwarfare. As a result, the study may not address other forms of cyber danger that may arise in the metaverse. This research paper may rely on a small number of sources. This implies that the article may not provide a thorough picture of the metaverse's cyber threat landscape.

CONCLUSION

The definition of the metaverse continues to evolve and solidify further each day, as of now still being an abstract concept. It embodies a modern-day utopian fantasy, encompassing the finally materializing visions of our predecessors. The possibilities of the metaverse are boundless, with wide-reaching roots trenched deeply in many aspects of our day-to-day life including medicine, entertainment, social media, travel, education and retail. Perhaps due to this very versatility and range the metaverse has caught the eye of most major corporations- with investments of over $50 billion pouring in, mention *Huang et. al.* (2022). Further, this market is set to present an $800 billion dollar opportunity, according to Bloomberg Intelligence. And while the prospective is exciting, the reality is that the effective deployment of the metaverse is destined to face pushback from the widespread smartphone ecosystem, amassing 6 billion users and counting. For the initial stages, deployment and acceptance is expected in the first world countries which are already highly developed and possess well-established telecommunication networks as well as a projected user base which would be able to afford the hardware necessary for accessing the metaverse- which carries quite a hefty price. However, as in the case of smartphones, it is predicted that this technology will slowly be adapted the world over as it progressively becomes universally supported and more affordable for all sections of society.

On the other hand, the evolution of the metaverse and its subsequent acceptance is also bound to raise various issues on its journey of materialization. In the previous sections, we've taken a glance at the possible security threats we might expect in the metaverse, of which the five most concerning would be-

- NFTs will be the major source of transactions and widely used as tokens to regulate ownership of digital assets. They are vulnerable to fraud, duplication, ransome and other threats.
- The darkverse opens up opportunities for illegal activities and crime to take place within the metaverse. It would also make it difficult for LEA to track down the perpetrators or infiltrate spaces.
- Property within the metaverse or NFTs can be used for money laundering.
- The metaverse poses privacy concerns as with evolving technologies, we are always being monitored. The tracking and usage of user data without their knowledge or primary consent- including that used for social profiling- would run rampant.
- Malicious bodies may attempt to influence vulnerable groups of people with certain narratives on sensitive topics.

While the possibilities of crime are concerning, the metaverse is a huge project requiring resources which cannot be obtained by a single company or organization. With the backing of all major corporations, the metaverse may be shaped as per our requirements and hopes- realistically, though, we can expect that the metaverse we have envisioned isn't possible to attain, and the definition of the metaverse will be modulated to fit our finite possibilities. Considering the fact that the metaverse is already attracting large investments, now is a good time to begin the development of security models for the metaverse. Although doing so will prove challenging as it is not easy to envision potential threats within a system which has not been built yet, acting early and attempting to create security guidelines on the basis of these possibilities would give us an edge over the prospective criminals and also would help us protect the future metaverse as well as metaverse-like applications.

REFERENCES

Arkvik, I. (2021). What is financial cybercrime and how to prevent it. VISMA.

Awadallah, A. M., Damiani, E., Zemerly, J., & Yeun, C. Y. 2023, March. Identity Threats in the Metaverse and Future Research Opportunities. In *2023 International Conference on Business Analytics for Technology and Security (ICBATS)* (pp. 1-6). IEEE. 10.1109/ICBATS57792.2023.10111122

Baughman, J. (2022). Enter the Battleverse: China's Metaverse War. *Military Cyber Affairs: 5*(1).

Chow, Y. W., Susilo, W., Li, Y., Li, N., & Nguyen, C. (2022). Visualization and Cybersecurity in the Metaverse: A Survey. *Journal of Imaging*, *9*(1), 11. doi:10.3390/jimaging9010011 PMID:36662109

El Gataa, I. (2022). *Non-state actors & cyber-warfare.*

Huang, J., Sun, P., & Zhang, W. 2022, March. Analysis of the Future Prospects for the Metaverse. In *2022 7th International Conference on Financial Innovation and Economic Development (ICFIED 2022)* (pp. 1899-1904). Atlantis Press. 10.2991/aebmr.k.220307.312

Huq, N., Reyes, R., Lin, P., & Swimmer, M. (2022). *Cybersecurity Threats Against the Internet of Experiences*. Trend Micro Res.

Jaipong, P., Siripipattanakul, S., Sriboonruang, P., Sitthipon, T., Jaipong, P., Siripipattanakul, S., & Sitthipon, T. (2023). A Review of Metaverse and Cybersecurity in the Digital Era. *International Journal of Computing Sciences Research*, *7*, 1125–1132. doi:10.25147/ijcsr.2017.001.1.122

Kumari, P., & Jain, A. K. (2023). A comprehensive study of DDoS attacks over IoT network and their countermeasures. *Computers & Security, 127.*

Marr, B. (2022). *The fascinating history and evolution of Extended Reality (XR) – covering AR*. VR and MR.

Meta. (2021). *Introducing Meta: A Social Technology Company*. Meta.

Mystakidis, S. (2022). Metaverse. *Encyclopedia*, *2*(1), 486–497. doi:10.3390/encyclopedia2010031

Qamar, S., Anwar, Z., & Afzal, M. (2023). A systematic threat analysis and defense strategies for the metaverse and extended reality systems. *Computers & Security*, *128*, 103127. doi:10.1016/j.cose.2023.103127

Ratan, R. & Lei, Y. (2021). *What is the metaverse? 2 media and information experts explain*. Down to Earth.

Robinson, M., Jones, K., & Janicke, H. (2015). Cyber warfare: Issues and challenges. *Computers & Security*, *49*, 70–94. doi:10.1016/j.cose.2014.11.007

Seigfried-Spellar, K. C., Holt, T. J., & Bossler, A. M. (2022). *Cybercrime and Digital Forensics: An Introduction. (n.p.)*. Taylor & Francis.

Siddiqi, M. A., Pak, W., & Siddiqi, M. A. (2022). A Study on the Psychology of Social Engineering-Based Cyberattacks and Existing Countermeasures. *Applied Sciences (Basel, Switzerland)*, *12*(12), 6042. doi:10.3390/app12126042

Smaili, N., & de Rancourt-Raymond, A. (2022). Metaverse: Welcome to the new fraud marketplace. *Journal of Financial Crime*. Advance online publication. doi:10.1108/JFC-06-2022-0124

Teodorov., A.V. (2023). Cybercrimes in the Metaverse: Challenges and Solutions. In *Proceedings of the International Conference on Cybersecurity and Cybercrime-2023* (pp. 209-215). Asociatia Romana pentru Asigurarea Securitatii Informatiei.

Tugtekin, U. (2023). The Dark Side of Metaverse Learning Environments: Potential Threats and Risk Factors. In Shaping the Future of Online Learning: Education in the Metaverse (pp. 57-67). IGI Global.

Vidal-Tomás, D. (2022). The new crypto niche: NFTs, play-to-earn, and metaverse tokens. *Finance Research Letters*, *47*, 102742. doi:10.1016/j.frl.2022.102742 von Wachter, V., Jensen, J. R., Regner, F., & Ross, O. 2022. NFT wash trading: Quantifying suspicious behaviour in NFT markets. *arXiv preprint arXiv:2202.03866.*

Wang, F. Y., Tang, Y., & Werbos, P. J. (2023). Guest editorial: cyber–physical–social intelligence: toward metaverse-based smart societies of 6I and 6S. *IEEE Transactions on Systems, Man, and Cybernetics. Systems*, *53*(4), 2018–2024. doi:10.1109/TSMC.2023.3243558

Wang, Q., Li, R., Wang, Q., & Chen, S. 2021. Non-Fungible Token (NFT): Overview, evaluation, opportunities and challenges. *arXiv preprint arXiv:2105.07447.*

Wang, Y., Su, Z., Zhang, N., Xing, R., Liu, D., Luan, T. H., & Shen, X. (2022). A survey on metaverse: Fundamentals, security, and privacy. *IEEE Communications Surveys and Tutorials.*

Wu, J., Lin, K., Lin, D., Zheng, Z., Huang, H., & Zheng, Z. (2023). Financial Crimes in Web3-empowered Metaverse: Taxonomy, Countermeasures, and Opportunities. *IEEE Open Journal of the Computer Society*, *4*, 37–49. doi:10.1109/OJCS.2023.3245801

Zhang, Y., Xiao, Y., Ghaboosi, K., Zhang, J., & Deng, H. (2012). A survey of cyber crimes. *Security and Communication Networks*, *5*(4), 422–437. doi:10.1002ec.331

Chapter 9
Potential Threats:
Extremism and Terrorism in the Metaverse

Ehab Khalifa
Future for Advanced Research and Studies, UAE

ABSTRACT

Throughout history, terrorism has adeptly leveraged technological advancements to further its ominous objectives. As societies have evolved, so too have the methods employed by extremists. From the early utilization of print media to spread propaganda, to the more recent harnessing of social media platforms for recruitment and radicalization, terrorist groups have consistently exploited the cutting edge of available technology. Now, with the dawn of the Metaverse, terrorism is about to be at another pivotal intersection. This digital realm, characterized by immersive virtual environments and complex interactivity, offers a new frontier for these malevolent actors. The metaverse not only provides concealed platforms for communication and coordination, but also introduces potential grounds for training, recruitment, and even virtual staging of attacks. As we venture deeper into this digital epoch, it's imperative that we remain vigilant, recognizing that as technology advances, so too will the tactics of those intent on using it for harm.

INTRODUCTION

The world is about to live a completely virtual life through "The Metaverse", a kind of universe where human interactions are undertaken neither face-to-face nor digitally, but in ways that combine properties of the real, physical world with properties of the internet and smart technology, adding to them other elements. The result would be a new world, or, to be more accurate, new worlds, this boundless landscapes and anonymity could offer a haven for radical ideologies and extremist activities.

Each of these new worlds in the Metaverse would try hard to distinguish itself from the other worlds by promoting difference and uniqueness, in order to present itself as the best and most successful type of models. They would have its own citizens, constitution, and laws which have nothing to do with the laws of the real world. As a result, it would fall a prey to extremism, which would, consequently, give rise to new forms of religious fanaticism, chauvinism and racism.

DOI: 10.4018/979-8-3693-0220-0.ch009

Even worse, people with radical ideas and beliefs may join hands, forming groups that would practice cult-like rituals in temples that would be founded by the members of these groups, in such a situation, radicalism looms large; inhabitants of the metaverse are more than likely to adopt extremist patterns of thinking, or even become terrorists.

Furthermore, the metaverse's darker corners might evolve in ways reminiscent of today's dark web. As people grapple with virtual addictions and as digital theft, fraud, and harassment manifest in novel forms, there's an increased risk that extremist organizations would exploit these platforms. Especially worrisome is the potential for terror outfits with ideological and religious motivations to employ the metaverse as a recruiting ground, communication hub, and even a training camp for real-world atrocities.

In the light of the foregoing, this chapter sheds light on the metaverse as a concept, with special focus on the ways in which extremist and terrorist organizations would use it for purposes of communicating, recruiting, financing and training, in an attempt to raise awareness of the potential dangers of the metaverse so that they can be avoided.

This chapter is a desktop research study, seeks to explore the potential uses of the metaverse by extremists and terrorists, this could be through defining the concept of the metaverse first, then exploring the possible applications for the extremists and terrorists in the metaverse, with a focus of the most likely uses for the terrorist groups.

The Definition of the Metaverse

In Connect 2021, the Facebook annual conference for the year 2021, Mark Zukerberg announced that he has changed the name of his company to Meta (Connect, 2021), thus revolutionizing the world's largest social network and adopting a new strategy based on what can be called 'the metaverse industry'. Just like Alphabet became the parent company of Google, Facebook became one of the companies that Meta owns. As a result of the outbreak of COVID19, the internet gained more importance as the main means of communication in the areas of education, work, medicine, shopping, etc., which stimulated much thinking about the future of the internet in general as well as about the future of human communication, which mostly takes place in cyberspace, through social networks. Questions arose about future developments in human communication and developments in the nature and usage of the internet. One of the most important questions asked at that time was: will it be possible for humans to be transferred to the internet so that they can inhabit it instead of watching it through computers and smart phones? If the answer was yes, what kind of technology would be used for fulfilling this purpose? These questions, among others, were associated with the feeling that internet needs to be revolutionized.

As for the term 'Metaverse', it was first used by Neal Stephenson in the sci-fi novel *Snow Crash* (1992) (Levy & Stephenson, 2022). The word combines 'Meta', Facebook's new name which means 'beyond', with 'verse', short for 'universe', to denote a universe beyond the world we know and live in.

It is interesting that Stephenson uses the term pejoratively as a reference to the virtual world owned by despotic companies that enslave the end users of technology, which is not far from the truth of technology companies, which regard their clients as commodities.

However, it is worth noting that Zukerberg was not the first to develop the metaverse technology. In fact, this technology had been around before Zukerbeg came up with the name. One of its most famous examples is the augmented-reality game called Pokemon Go, which can be considered a prototype of the metaverse (Patel, 2021).

The word 'metaverse' denotes infinite virtual worlds that can be created in the internet, just like the worlds depicted in the movie called *Ready Player One* (2018). The movie predicted what the world would be like in 2045, but it seems that the predictions of the movie makers would come true much sooner. It would not be long before all human interactions would take place through AR glasses and VR glasses supported by 5G networks. This trinity would actually be the key to the metaverse.

Instead of accessing this new world through computers and smart phones, we would use VR glasses to enter it. These glasses, which are currently used in video games, would be redesigned so that they can replace smart phones, as they would be connected to the internet and they would merge with augmented reality technologies so that once you look at something, you can see every piece of information about it before your very eyes. In other words, VR technology, which uses a computer-generated environment, wuold be combined with augmented reality technology, which uses a real world environment, the outcome being a mixed world-namely, the metaverse.

All human interactions taking place in the metaverse would be three-dimensional. In other words, they would be carried out in an artificial environment which is a simulation of the real world. People would be present in this environment in flesh and blood, making things happen through their actual actions and movements, rather than through keyboards and video cameras. This is why it was necessary to come up with a remarkably powerful medium capable of transferring huge amounts of data in real time, so that the metaverse would be a real world. This development in VR glasses is similar to a great extent to the developments in the area of smart phones. In 2007, Steve Jobs developed what came to be known as the iPhone, which is a combination of the ordinary telephone and the IPod, connected to the internet. Many developments followed, revolutionizing human interaction in a relatively short time. This would be the same for VR glasses, too. Just like smart phones gave us access to the internet, VR glasses would give us access to the metaverse.

Other factors that would accelerate the shift towards VR glasses is the popularity of social networks and 5G networks, and the remarkable developments in the areas of virtual reality, augmented reality and the internet of things. These developments have provided the environment necessary for using metaverse technology on a wider scale.

Though the internet has always been utilized by extremist and terrorist organizations, terrorists have always find it difficult to make use of the full potential of the internet because there have always been boundaries between internet users, i.e. computer monitors and keyboards. The metaverse, however, may help terrorists overcome this problem because for the first time internet users would be able to interact face to face, with nothing whatsoever to separate them.

Different Types of Social Extremism

The metaverse can be a safe haven for those suffering from the harsh realities of our world. People suffering from psychological problems, family problems or work problems could seek refuge in it. Similarly, people living in war- infested or corruption-infested countries could retreat to it. Some people may even resort to it out of boredom, or to achieve their dreams which they cannot fulfill in the real world. Gradually, people would tend to spend most of their time in the metaverse, leaving it only to go to sleep every night. Thus, human life would be reduced to no more than a kind of interaction carried out via VR glasses. People would be busy building their own ideal worlds, where there would be no such thing as problems or cares, and where the wildest dreams could easily be achieved, and where friends would abound and enemies would be nowhere to be found. As a result, users would have no time for building human civilization and making the world a better place.

The metaverse, tangible yet unreal, would be the center of human life. It would be as if people were able to write a novel full of happy incidents and to live inside that novel; expectedly, they would become addicted to this novel, and unwilling to leave it, since leaving it would mean that they would have to face the real world with all its problems and misery. When utmost gratification of their desires would be reached, people would be hungry for more, and so they would seek other kinds of pleasures, equally materialistic.

People would think that they "own" the metaverse, but one day they would wake up to the catastrophic fact that it is the metaverse that owns them, and that they are but prisoners in the metaverse, just like Neal Stephenson predicted; they would be able neither to leave their artificial world nor to return to their old, real world. Gradually, the lives of the metaverse users would turn into a nightmare, and they themselves would turn into extremists who do not care about their real houses or cities, or to the real world in general; they would, instead, dedicate all their efforts to create an imaginary paradise in a virtual world where they would spend most of their time, only taking off their VR glasses at bedtime.

In other words, people would want nothing to do with the real world. They would avoid life by living in the metaverse where they could be anything and do anything. This lifestyle is not very different from the lifestyle of those who, in today's world, never leave their mobile phones except when going to bed. The same escapist attitude can be detected in both cases.

This may be convenient for depressed people with suicidal tendencies, as living in the metaverse would be an alternative to taking their own lives, but what would life on earth be like if people shied away from facing their responsibilities and decided to surrender by retreating to a virtual world where anything and everything is achievable, instead of persevering with the attempt to make things better?

If it were possible to create infinite worlds in the metaverse, this means that infinite patterns of human interaction would arise. Perhaps this is what Meta meant when it designated the infinity symbol as its slogan. People would live in the worlds of the metaverse either as themselves or using avatars, oscillating between their real personalities and the personalities they wish they had in real life. This hybrid kind of identity would bring about several patterns of interaction which would affect, and be affected by, one another.

People may go so far as to choose to interact with the dead, through reviving their dead relatives and friends in the form of virtual characters. This could be achieved by using all the digital data specific to the dead person, such as images, videos, voiceprint and personal data. Using the data, an AI system would create a virtual character representing the dead person, which would live in the metaverse and interact with those who used to love him/her in real life.

People suffering from terminal diseases may decide to create virtual versions of themselves which would survive them, granting them some sort of immortality. Thus, the metaverse could be a world where no one would die, a world where people could fulfill their wildest dreams and satisfy their slightest whims without leaving their couches.

Fearful as they are, these changes would inevitably occur, because the way to them has already been paved; people work, learn and do shopping via the internet in today's world, so internet dependency is not something strange or new to most, if not all, of us. This particularly applies to the younger generations; most children and teenagers tend to spend most of their free time browsing the internet instead of pursuing such traditional hobbies as drawing, painting, playing sports, etc.

As the metaverse would provide limitless opportunities, it is not unlikely that some people would seek to revive dreams of caliphate in its virtual space. We have already seen ISIS's "virtual caliphate". Extremists may go so far as to create their own state which they failed to establish in reality. They may create governments, choose ministers, and recruit volunteers who may be true believers in the extremists' subversive ideas or simply people who are thirsty for wreaking havoc. The extremists may use the metaverse as their training ground, engaging in virtual drills that would then be 'translated' into real terrorist attacks in the real world. They may also use the metaverse for the purposes of propaganda or for financing their activities, etc. It is useful here to remember that terrorists have always made use of technological developments; the metaverse, therefore, would not be an exception to the rule. This time, however, the consequences would be more serious than ever before.

Terrorists' Uses of the Metaverse

Terrorist organizations have always sought to utilize smart technologies so that they can achieve their destructive aims and disseminate their traditional ideas in ways that do not lag behind the rapid technological developments characteristic of our times.

They used cassette tapes and video tapes to deliver their messages to the world when these were the latest technology, then they echoed the shift towards internet forums and blogs, then came the age of social networks and smart phone applications, and terrorists were quick to make use of these in furthering their causes.

Chat rooms and social network games are now used for recruit those who may be potential terrorists. Terrorist attacks have also changed a lot. Explosive belts and motorcycle bombs have given way to cyberattacks and drone attacks. Makeshift weapons and improvised firearms are also giving way to 3D-printed weapons and firearms. For communication, terrorist organizations make use of the encryption potential of virtual private networks (VPN), proxy servers, and the dark web, which guarantees high degrees of security. Last but not least, they depend on crypto and like virtual currencies for financing their activities.

In short, technology has become one of the major weapons of terrorists, especially these kinds of technology which can be used for civil purposes and military purposes at the same time. A case in point is the drone; it can be used for such peaceful purposes as taking pictures, entertainment, etc. but can also be used for launching attacks. Technological developments have given rise to new patterns and types of terrorism. One of these is the so-called 'lone wolf terrorism', where the terrorist uses the internet for familiarizing himself with extremist ideas and for learning how to make weapons, but he shies away from identifying with any terrorist organization, preferring to work alone.

The metaverse would also be used by terrorist organizations just like any other technological development. It would be used for such purposes as training terrorists, preparing simulations of terrorist attacks, spreading propaganda, and communicating with other terrorists. As Tech Companies have pledged to guarantee the privacy of the metaverse users, the task of security apparatuses combating terrorism would be extremely difficult.

Following is a discussion, there are 10 possible main purposes for which terrorists are expected to use the metaverse. These are:

Propaganda

Usually extremist organizations try to use all kinds of media to disseminate their subversive ideas and beliefs. It comes as no surprise, therefore, that terrorists and extremists would make use of the metaverse just as they used cassette tapes and the internet. One of the main purposes for which extremist organizations would use the metaverse would be propaganda, which would take new forms and dimensions as a result of all the possibilities that the metaverse would offer.

VR videos may be made with the aim of disseminating certain ideological beliefs, giving explanations for certain behaviors, or promoting certain destructive activities. Not only would extremists use chat rooms to talk to people and recruit them openly and straightforwardly, but they may also invite them to virtual religious gathering where they could explain their goals and activities to them.

The possibilities are actually limitless; even VR games may be used for promoting extremist agendas. Extremists may even reenact certain moments which have strong emotive power so as to shock their opponents and to arouse the enthusiasm of like-minded users. They may, for instance, reenact past triumphs in their history, such as the 9/11 attacks or the November 2015 Paris attacks. They may also seek to use purely humanitarian causes for their own advantage, reenacting, for example, scenes representing the Palestinians' struggle for freedom, so that their sympathetic attitude with the Palestinians would give them credibility and lead other users to lend them an ear.

Communication

The metaverse would be a safe haven for extremists and terrorists wishing to communicate with one another, simply because it guarantees decentralization, provides avatars that can be used to conceal identity, and offers utmost privacy and secrecy of communications through encryption. This makes it extremely difficult, if not impossible, to track the terrorists' locations, especially if these terrorists used VPN or applications that would conceal their digital footprint.

Therefore, the metaverse may be used by terrorist organizations to send instructions to the members before a terrorist attack. It may also be used to accommodate some sort of central command that would manage worldwide terrorist networks and coordinate with terrorists all over the world.

Even worse, a virtual caliphate may be established, just like the one which was announced by ISIS so that leaders of the organization could pledge allegiance, or rather "virtual" allegiance, to the caliph online. The leaders all over the world made videos in which they swore allegiance to ISIS, and then posted them on the internet. A similar scenario could occur with the metaverse; the leaders' avatars could meet the caliph's to swear allegiance to him face-to-face, so to speak, as if all this was happening in reality and not on the internet.

Leaders of terrorist organizations could also use augmented reality technologies to send orders and instructions to terrorists in theaters of operations in the form of arrows and other symbols that could be only understood by these terrorists. These arrows and symbols may even be used to identify the places that are supposed to be targeted or the people who are supposed to be assassinated in the real world.

Recruiting

In addition to the aforementioned purposes, the metaverse can be used for recruiting youth through directly or indirectly contacting would-be terrorists. This can take place during encrypted chats or in restricted chat rooms, which would be a safe space for terrorist organizations, providing them with easy access to potential recruits (Denning, 2010).

The metaverse may be particularly useful for recruiting adolescents, who would be among the major users of the metaverse, because of its great entertainment potential. Virtual applications and games can be used by terrorist organizations to attract teenagers and youth lacking in awareness. Subversive ideas could be easily instilled in adolescents in such case.

For instance, there may create a game similar to Fortnite, featuring a terrorist training for an attack inside the metaverse. The player would be able to plan for an attack. S/he may also be trained, in the game, to use weapons, choose a target, disguise himself/herself, or even carry out a suicide bombing. Thus, games can be used for creating a generation of highly trained terrorists (**UNODC**, 2012).

Financing

Extremist organizations depend on several sources for financing their activities. For instance, members of the organizations can provide the required money themselves. In addition, they can depend on such activities as drug trafficking, people smuggling, and arms trade. They may even found charities as a cover for their activities, and accept donations under the false pretense of using them to help the poor or to support humanitarian causes. Last but not least, they may have online fundraising events, making it possible for users to donate money through crypto transactions.

The metaverse could also be used for financing terrorist activities. Terrorists could create virtual rooms and sites within it where they could urge other users to donate. As the metaverse is characterized by decentralization, things could get more complicated. Blockchain, crypto currency and NFTs are among the building blocks of the metaverse.

Actually, having a crypto wallet would be a prerequisite for entering the metaverse. Besides, users would have to keep their digital investments if they want to enter the metaverse. As it is impossible to uncover the real identities of users in the metaverse, and as there is no central system governing the Blockchain system, terrorists may be encouraged to come up with new, easier methods to finance their activities. They may, for instance, start to buy and sell crypto currencies, or to ask their metaverse followers for money (Council of the European Union, 2022).

Extremist organizations already conduct cyberattacks. Similarly, they may conduct cyberattacks on individuals, banks and companies in the metaverse, and transfer money to their own bank accounts all over the world. They could also use the metaverse for E- commerce purposes, which would be convenient to them, because with all the privacy that the metaverse would guarantee it would be almost impossible to track them.

Training

The internet is gaining great popularity with terrorists that need a safe space where they can train, especially lone wolves. In this respect, YouTube and Dailymotion videos are particularly useful. In addition, lone wolves and co also make use of closed and secret groups on social networks, where information on how to make bombs and explosive devices is available, as well as information on how to use firearms and dangerous chemicals, and how to carry out terrorist attacks. Thus, the internet can, in a way, be a virtual training platform for terrorists, be they lone wolves or members of extremist organizations.

The nature of the metaverse would make it even more suited for training purposes as far as terrorists are concerned, simply because one of the main functions of the metaverse is training people, or, in other words, to help them develop their skills through augmented reality technologies. Therefore, the metaverse can be used for carrying out simulations of terrorist attacks, so that would-be terrorists could learn how to fly planes or drones, how to make explosives and weapons, how to aim and shoot, or how to kidnap people and take them hostages (Senno, 2022), etc.

Even worse, simulations of complete terrorist attacks that include the tiniest details pertaining to the theater of operations, the timing, the movements of the people involved, etc. could be carried out in the metaverse. Thus, the metaverse would provide extremists with opportunities to learn more innovative and effective methods of planning and training for terrorist attacks. It may even help them come up with alternative plans and emergency strategies.

Collecting Information

The metaverse could provide terrorist organizations with the means necessary for collecting information that would help them carry out terrorist attacks. It could provide them with information about how targeted buildings look in real life, through 3D maps and 4D maps which would include virtual versions of the buildings (i.e. government offices, companies, etc.). This would make it possible for them to walk in these buildings and study entrances and exits.

Furthermore, if people who terrorists would target (police officers, army officers, etc.) had avatars that are close imitations of their real selves, that would make it easy for terrorists to learn a lot about their victims from the metaverse. For instance, they could have access to information about the victims' identities, friends, relatives, wives, children, etc., not to mention information about the place of their houses and their usual whereabouts. They would also be able to acquire information about the victim's date of birth, education, graduation year, in addition to any kind of information the victim would choose to include in his metaverse personal profile.

Disguise and Camouflage

The metaverse would guarantee a high degree of privacy. Anyone would be able to create an avatar for himself/herself to conceal his/her identity. Terrorists could make use of such avatars so that they could communicate inside and outside their terrorist organizations without being identified. In other words, avatars could be used the same way code names are used; code names, in other words, would develop into avatars which terrorists would control via VR glasses.

Reviving Famous Leaders of Terrorist Groups

AI-supported metaverse technologies could be used for creating virtual avatars representing famous leaders of terrorist groups who were assassinated, such as Osama bin Laden, Ayaman al-Zawahiri or Abu Bakr al-Baghdadi, etc. Terrorists could meet these "virtual" leaders in virtual mosques, caves, or even parks, to listen to them delivering their typical fiery speeches. Thus, the metaverse could be used for reviving extremist thoughts and raise terrorists' morale (Elson, Doctor, and Hunter, 2022).

Creating New Targets for Terrorists

The metaverse would be a close virtual imitation of life with all its details and activities. All kinds of celebrations would be held when new companies, government buildings, roads, etc. are built. Festivals would be held, and memorials would be established, just like in real life. Such celebrations and festivals could be targeted by terrorists. For instance, concerts of famous singers and celebrations of national holidays may be regarded by terrorists as opportunities to conduct terrorist attacks which would be similar to the cyberattacks they launch on government websites. Such attacks may paralyze the metaverse or parts of it, or make it impossible to reach certain places in it, where the celebrations are held, or cause the concerts to stop, etc., (Weimann and Dimant, 2023).

Psychological Warfare

The propaganda used by terrorist organizations are no longer restricted to disseminating information, true or false; it now includes waging psychological warfare which spreads feelings of doubt and distrust in societies, thus enabling terrorists to win their battles easily and without having to face any kind of resistance from people and without having to be in direct confrontation with the authorities. This is what ISIS used to do. ISIS leaders used to achieve victory by arousing fear, through broadcasting their violent activities. When people saw them slaughter their victims, torture them, burn their houses, etc. they were always quick to leave their houses and run away, and so ISIS was always able to take their lands almost effortlessly.

As the metaverse would be based on highly advanced technologies that make it easy to create very accurate simulations of real-life situations, psychological warfare would be even fiercer and more effective than ever before. Technology would help manipulate people on a much larger scale, and in new ways that would revolutionize psychological warfare. Therefore, fear, pure fear, would become unprecedented, which would, in turn, mean easier victories as far as terrorists are concerned.

The Darkverse and the Dark Rooms

The Darknet has provided extremist organizations with an escape from counter-terrorism authorities which used to close terrorist accounts and websites or even hack them. The Darknet has enabled these terrorist organizations to carry out such activities as communicating, recruiting, raising funds, and doing illegal trade with utmost secrecy and privacy.

Though it has always been believed that terrorist organizations use the Darknet, evidence was lacking until US National Security Agency could, in August 2013, intercept encrypted communications between Qaeda leaders Ayman al-Zawahiri and Nasir al-Wyhayshi (Mccormick, 2013).

Similarly, there could be a 'Darkverse', so to speak, inside the metaverse, where members of terrorist organizations would secretly arrange terrorist attacks, practice making explosives, sell and buy firearms and co, or even do illegal trade and launder money. Following is a brief discussion of the ways in which terrorist organizations may use the Darkverse:

1. **Stealth:** If security apparatuses could cooperate with the metaverse developers so that the content published in the metaverse could be censored, terrorists may resort to the Darkverse where they would create secret, encrypted networks that would make it easy to exchange subversive content.

2. **Communicating**: Extremist organizations have already used the Darknet and encrypted messaging applications and chat rooms in video games as we have earlier explained. Similarly, they could use the Darkverse for communicating and exchanging instructions in the form of encrypted messages.
3. **Recruiting**: The metaverse per se could be used for preliminary communications between extremist organizations on the one hand and recruits on the other hand, but more 'serious' information such as how to join the organizations would be exchanged in the dark rooms of the Darkverse, let alone instructions.
4. **Financing**: Generally speaking, terrorists use crypto currencies so that they can carry out transactions and collect money for terrorist attacks. As NFTs are among the building blocks of the metaverse, this means that the Darkverse could be a safer environment as far as these organizations are concerned, because it would make it possible to interact 'under cover', so to speak, without being tracked.

CONCLUSION

Technology is usually a double-edged weapon. It can be useful for people as it can make their lives easier and safer, but it can also be a source of annoyance. As the metaverse is an unprecedented revolution-together with the AI revolution and such smart technologies as the internet of things, the Blockchain, etc. – it is expected to revolutionize almost every area of human life. While it can be used for useful purposes, it can also be used to cause harm. Therefore, it is necessary to come up with a strategy that determines and defines ways of using the metaverse. In addition, it is important to decide which areas the metaverse would be used in and which areas it must not be used in. Furthermore, it is very important to accurately define the nature of the relationship between governments on the one hand and the companies which would develop the metaverse on the other hand, so that the governments would censor the metaverse, and citizens would not use it for criminal purposes.

There is still a chance to avoid the disadvantages of the metaverse, especially as this technology is still being developed. It is possible to design the metaverse from the outset so that it cannot be used by terrorist and extremist organizations. Thus, it is necessary for developer companies, the civil society, government and security apparatuses to work together to arrive at criteria that would guarantee safe use and limit the risks of using the metaverse it for terrorist purposes to a minimum.

The gap between societies which would occur as a result of creating the metaverse should be taken into consideration. It is expected that rich societies which can afford this new technology and develop it to make the best use of it would be more capable to avoid the risks of using the metaverse than the poor countries which do not have the funds and technology necessary for countering the negative sides of it. That would widen the gap between rich countries and poor countries, which would eventually mean that extremist thoughts would spread in poor countries, which would, in turn, affect people inside and outside the metaverse all alike.

REFERENCES

Council of the European Union. (2022). *The Metaverse in the Context of the Fight Against Terrorism.* EU. https://data.consilium.europa.eu/doc/document/ST-9292-2022-INIT/en/pdf

Denning, D. E. (2010). Terror's web: how the Internet is transforming terrorism. In Y. Jewkes & M. Yar (Eds.), *Handbook of Internet Crime* (pp. 194–213). Willan Publishing.

Elson, J., Doctor, A., & Hunter, S. (2022). The metaverse offers a future full of potential – for terrorists and extremists. *The Conversation*. https://theconversation.com/themetaverse-offers-a-future-full-of-potential-for-terrorists-and-extremists-too-173622

Levy, S. (2022). Neal Stephenson Named the Metaverse. Now, He's Building It. *Wired*. https://www.wired.com/story/plaintext-neal-stephenson-named-the-metaverse-now-hes-building-it/

Mccormick, T. Y. (2013). The Darknet: A Short History. *Foreign Policy*.

Meta. (2021). *Our vision for the metaverse*. Meta. https://tech.fb.com/ar-vr/2021/10/connect-2021-our-vision-for-the-metaverse/

Patel, N. (2021). The metaverse is already here — and it's full of Pokemon, says Niantic CEO John Hanke. *The Verge*. https://www.theverge.com/22832490/niantic-ceo-john-hanke-metaverse-pokemon-go-ar-vr-podcast-decoder-interview

Senno, S. (2022). *The Metaverse, an opportunity for society or terrorism?* AMISTADES report. https://en.amistades.info/post/metaverse-an-opportunity-for-society-or-terrorism

UN. (2012). *The use of the Internet for terrorist purposes*. UNODC. https://www.unodc.org/documents/terrorism/Publications/Use_of_Internet_for_Terrorist_Purposes/ebook_use_of_the_internet_for_terrorist_purposes.pdf

Weimann, G., & Dimant, R. (2023). The Metaverse and Terrorism: Threats and Challenges. *Prespectives on terrorism, 17*(2). https://pt.icct.nl/sites/default/files/2023-06/PT%20-%20Vol%20XVII%2C%20Issue%20II%20-%20June%202023%20A5.pdf

Chapter 10
Metaverse Forensics: A Preliminary Analysis of Opportunities and Challenges

Faouzi Kamoun
https://orcid.org/0000-0002-3740-1452
ESPRIT, Tunisia

Zainab Khalid
National University of Sciences and Technology, Pakistan

Farkhund Iqbal
Zayed University, UAE

Richard Ikuesan
https://orcid.org/0000-0001-7355-2314
Zayed University, UAE

Siem Zeresenay
Zayed University, UAE

Sened Abraham
Zayed University, UAE

ABSTRACT

The metaverse is poised to offer an immersive virtual environment for people to meet, socialize, collaborate, play, and conduct business transactions. Although the metaverse has not yet reached its full maturity, it has already been misused to launch illegal activities that can jeopardize the safety and well-being of individuals, and cause harm to organizations. Despite its increased importance, "metaverse forensics" remains an unexplored research topic. This chapter starts by reviewing the state-of-the-art research related to metaverse cybersecurity threats and underlying ethical, privacy, and legal issues. It then presents the results of a forensic investigation analysis performed on the VRChat and AltspaceVR metaverse platforms. The authors present new insights into metaverse forensics in terms of accessing digital containers and retrieving useful information for forensic investigators. Additionally, they highlight the primary obstacles encountered in metaverse digital forensic investigations and put forth recommendations for future research directions.

DOI: 10.4018/979-8-3693-0220-0.ch010

INTRODUCTION

The metaverse has brought major changes to the way we socialize and interact with each other. It has emerged as a potential new catalyst for innovation bringing a new breed of business models, products, and services into a rich marketplace. During the first ten months of 2021, the metaverse industry received over US$10 billion in venture capital funding (Kunthara, 2021). The public offering by Roblox at the beginning of 2021 signaled the beginning of a new wave of social engagements in the metaverse. In fact, many big events have been organized including birthday parties, concerts, egg hunt contests, and a tie-in with Gucci in celebration of its 100th anniversary, among many others (Garon, 2022). Snapchat's 3D bitmoji feature, introduced in July 2021, enabled users to create avatars for augmented reality, thus uplifting user experience (Garon, 2022). In October 2021, Facebook announced that it was changing its brand name to Meta and declared the metaverse to be the future of an embodied Internet where people will be inside rather than just looking at it (Mackenzie, 2022). This vision reflects a migration of the Internet from Web 2.0 towards Web 3.0 whereby the presence of a decentralized online platform allows users to own and control the assets they create. Microsoft envisages an "enterprise metaverse" where business gatherings and classrooms will take place in the form of immersive avatar-based online interactions. The metaverse offers a perpetual, persistent, and immersive multiuser virtual environment, enabling seamless embodied user interactions in real-time and dynamic trading of artificial artifacts (Mystakidis, 2022). With the premise of mixed reality, the metaverse is poised to perfectly blend the digital and the real worlds so that they become impossible to tell apart (Reid, 2021). As a massive aggregator of technologies, applications, and end-users, the metaverse is on the verge of acquiring the quality of a singleton, an attribute for a fast-emerging technological trend that, at a point in time, seems uncontrollable and irreversible, resulting in unforeseen social and legal ramifications (Di Pietro & Cresci, 2022).

The term metaverse was first introduced in 1992 in a Neal Stephenson novel titled – Snow Crash. Neal presented the metaverse as a Virtual Reality (VR) environment based on the Internet and Augmented Reality (AR), using avatars and software agents (Joshua, 2017). The novel was later portrayed in the science fiction movie Ready Player One (Sparkes, 2021). Today, the metaverse is depicted as an integrated immersive ecosystem from the modern Internet that uses VR headsets, haptic gloves and suits, AR glasses, blockchain technology, holograms, Brain-Computer Interface (BCI) technologies, and avatars to seamlessly bring together the physical and the virtual worlds, enabling people to interact through avatars in the context of 3D virtual shared experiences (Braud et al, 2021). What differentiates the metaverse from traditional online platforms is the immersive user experience where the boundary between the physical and the virtual world is blurred. In other words, the metaverse projects the physical person into a virtual avatar capable of interacting with other persons, embodied into avatars, in various forms of cooperative or competitive activities. Some popular Massively Multiplayer Online Role-Playing games (MMORPGs) such as Second Life (SL) are hosting more than 11 million residents (Leenes, 2007).

The metaverse has ignited innovative business models across diverse application domains such as retail, leisure and hospitality, gaming, tourism, health, education, luxury fashion, marketing, logistics, education, manufacturing, warehouse management, sport, fitness, military, and social networks. An increasing number of tech giants such as Facebook, Microsoft, Amazon, Snap Inc, and NVIDIA have already showcased, via huge investments and many acquisitions, their desire to conquer the world of the metaverse. The adoption and diffusion of metaverse services have also been facilitated by the integration of blockchain and virtual currencies, in addition to the decline in physical social activities during the covid-19 pandemic.

Like most social networking platforms, the metaverse will rely on monetizing the collected user data and the digital crumble left behind while interacting with the platform as the main price to be paid in return for free access. At the same time, the metaverse has also raised new concerns related to ethics, data privacy, cyber security, regulations, personal safety, mental health, and well-being. In particular, the metaverse has become an appealing target for cybercriminals with a new emerging breed of violations such as virtual espionage and virtual stalking (Leenes, 2007). The metaverse has also been exploited as a virtual channel of misconduct whereby avatars have been reported to sexually harass other avatars (Hu et al, 2021). Several mechanisms have been proposed to enforce the privacy of metaverse users' data and interactions. Among these we can cite (1) the adoption of Privacy-Enhancing Technologies (PETs) to obfuscate private data from the sensors before sharing it with cloud services, (2) the reliance on secondary avatars to hide the real avatar and the associated Personally Identifiable Information (PII), (3) the activation of privacy bubbles to restrict other avatars outside the bubble from visually accessing or spying on one's avatar, and (4) the adoption of a distributed ledger on Blockchain to record, share and synchronize metaverse-related data and transactions (Fernandez & Hui, 2022).

In addition to the alluring temptation of stealing PII, the presence of crypto assets such as cryptocurrencies and metaverse Non-Fungible Tokens (NFTs) such as virtual avatars, real estate, and other virtual properties and assets has further captivated the interest of hackers in the metaverse due to the potential financial incentives. Through its seamless adoption of cryptocurrencies, the metaverse is also poised to join the rest of the online realm as a money laundering haven for criminals. When misused, the metaverse can also promote online scams, fraud, and bullying (Dwivedi et al, 2022).

A key success factor for metaverse platforms is the capability to provide users with a realistic and immersive experience, which often requires the continuous sensing of biometric data whose unauthorized access can pose a threat to users' privacy, security, and even safety (Katterbauer et al, 2022).

The lack of clear governance, policies, and regulations over the metaverse, as it spans two worlds (physical and virtual), as well as potentially many countries and jurisdictions, remains a serious concern. For instance, a user can exploit the supposed anonymity of avatars in the metaverse to hide behind his avatar and indulge in illegal actions.

This chapter aims to shed light on the unique forensic aspects of the metaverse by presenting, to the best of our knowledge, the first forensic study associated with the metaverse. The potential disruptive impact brought by the metaverse calls for forensic investigators to rethink the applicability of current digital forensic methods and tools and to explore new approaches to extract digital evidence that can be used as evidence in civil and criminal lawsuits.

The main objectives of this contribution are fourfold:

- Synthesize the state of the art in metaverse cyberthreats research and associated privacy and legal issues.
- Draw the attention of researchers to the key challenges of metaverse forensics and seek a better understanding of some of these challenges through case studies related to VRChat and AltspaceVR.
- Present a metaverse forensic investigation procedure that can guide future research.
- Provide some preliminary results on metaverse forensics including the ability to access disk space and memory dump artifacts.

The remainder of this chapter is organized as follows. Section 2 provides background information detailing the development of the metaverse and the concerns that it raised. Section 3 discusses the state-of-the-art research on metaverse cybersecurity threats and associated ethical and privacy concerns. Section 4 exposes some legal issues and dilemmas that surfaced with the usage of avatars in the metaverse, while section 5 provides concrete examples of reported metaverse offences. Section 6 details the experiments and results of our forensic investigations of two renowned metaverse platforms, namely VRChat and AltspaceVR. Finally, Section 7 provides a summary of the main findings of this study and some suggestions for future research.

BACKGROUND

The metaverse aims to leverage Virtual Reality (VR), Augmented Reality (AR), Mixed Reality (MR), Extended Reality (XR), and other technologies to expand the physical world, enabling people to interact within real and simulated environments with the assistance of Head-Mounted Displays (HMDs), avatars, and holograms (Dwivedi et al, 2022). Users participate in the virtual metaverse world through digital avatars. These avatars represent the virtual incarnations of metaverse users and are expected to have the same legal authority in the metaverse as a citizen's legal rights in the real world. The degree of immersion in the virtual metaverse has been accentuated thanks to the introduction of full-body haptic bodysuits such as Teslasuit or Holosuit that are capable of tracking users' motions, providing real-time haptic feedback and extracting transcended biometrics (Gadekallu et al, 2022). Thanks to recent advances in BCI research, it will be possible to combine brain-sensing technology with Artificial Intelligence (AI) algorithms to translate brain waves emanating from cognitive activity into direct digital commands, making it easier for end-users to interact with the metaverse. Already, many immersive VR environments, such as SL, Sandbox, Roblox, ZEPETO, AltspaceVR, Epic Games, Decentraland, Fortnite, Omniverse, Snapchat, Cryptovoxels, and VRChat have provided us with sneak previews of the potential opportunities and challenges of upcoming metaverse platforms (Dwivedi et al, 2022). Companies such as Meta, Microsoft, Nvidia, and Alphabet are investing billions in support of the metaverse ecosystem.

Various enabling technologies are brought together to represent the building blocks of the metaverse. These include Blockchain, AR, VR, 3D virtual and physical technologies (including holograms), advanced graphics and processors, AI, Internet of Things (IoT), Digital Twin (DT), 5/6G networking, Software-Defined Networking (SDN), cloud and fog computing, and NFTs. Further, to standardize, harmonize and synchronize the information exchange between and among the virtual and the real world, two main international standards have emerged, namely MPEG-V (ISO/IEC 23005, 2020) and IEEE 2888.x (IEEE 2888.x, 2023). These standards are expected to resolve most of the compatibility and interoperability issues between the virtual and the physical worlds.

The metaverse has enabled a diverse range of applications including gaming, social interactions (virtual living, shopping, dating, chatting, and traveling), online collaborations, 3D simulation and design, and content generation (Wang et al, 2022). The growing trend in the adoption of the metaverse as a virtual office environment (via platforms such as Horizon Workroom and Microsoft mesh) has raised privacy and security concerns among employees and employers alike as the threats of spying, intrusions, and snooping remain plausible (Wang et al, 2022).

Figure 1 depicts the high-level architecture of a metaverse ecosystem. As may be seen, it consists of two entities: end-users and a metaverse platform. The end-users can access the services provided by the platform using a variety of access devices including smartphones, HMDs, PCs, laptops, or other IoT-connected/wearable devices such as headsets, helmets, and haptic gloves. A user can create one or more

Figure 1. Overview of metaverse architecture
(adapted from (Dwivedi et al, 2022))

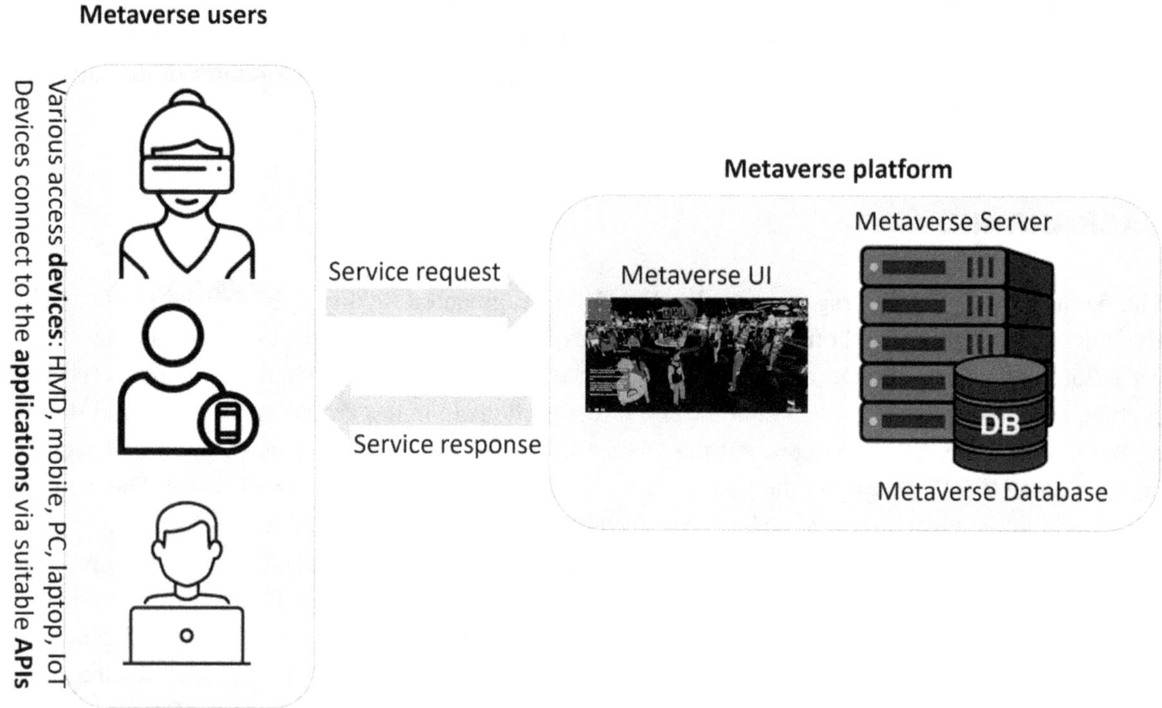

digital avatars that can take the shape and look of a human being, animal, imaginary/fantasy creature, etc. The metaverse access devices can store sensitive personal information. For instance, conversation records can be retrieved from metaverse headsets equipped with live microphones, while video recordings can be retrieved from HMDs with always-on cameras (Dwivedi et al, 2022). Furthermore, it is possible to exploit eye-tracking technology to retrieve what the player looked at or completely hijack wearable devices (Wang et al, 2022; Fineman & Lewis, 2018). Access devices like VR headsets and wearable devices convert raw sensory data into telemetry information to be consumed by the VR application via suitable APIs. In response to the received telemetry data, the VR application responds with visual stimuli to the player which is under total control of the application (Nair et al, 2022).

Users interact in real-time with the platform using secured wireless communication. They can play games, engage in virtual social interactions with other participants, collaborate, conduct purchase transactions, etc. On the platform's side, the users' interactions generate two types of data: static and dynamic. Static data include, for example, account and personal information to use the service (e.g., email address, phone number), and avatar information, while dynamic data include behavior and biometric information (e.g., location, gender, facial expressions, eye movement, body movement, physiological responses, hand gestures), among others. Equipped with smart wearable devices, users can manipulate their avatars and interact with other avatars by making use of the latest advancements in Human-Computer Interaction (HCI), XR, and BCIs. Most of the data shared on the platform are sensitive by nature. For instance, voice and video recordings associated with intimate avatar virtual interactions, and corporate secrets shared among avatar co-workers can be the target of cybercriminals (Dwivedi et al, 2022). Big data collected from users to provide precision motion tracking, high-fidelity animation, and immersive experiences embeds a wealth of physical and psychological information that can maliciously be exploited to infer medical conditions, mental disorders, personality, emotion, and personal identity (Buck & McDonnell, 2022). This data can be misused to manipulate users psychologically and compel them to participate in situations they would typically decline to engage in. Miller et al (2022) found that five minutes of video motion tracking data collected from HMD was sufficient to identify a user with 95% accuracy. It is also observed that some of the personal data collected from wearable devices and transmitted through encrypted wired and wireless communication channels can be disclosed by eavesdropping, differential attacks, and advanced inference strikes (Wang et al, 2022).

The interaction between the virtual and the real realms creates specific privacy issues, especially when the boundary between real and virtual lives becomes both shallow and permeable (Leenes, 2007). For instance, the risk associated with the privacy of user data and behavior in the metaverse can easily spill over offline (in the real world) to cause harm, fraud, and extortion, especially with social engineering attacks (Di Pietro & Cresci, 2022).

The potential illegitimate uses of the metaverse led many lawmakers, civil groups, law enforcement agencies, and governments to express their concern over the potential unlawful and criminal usage of these platforms. This concern is further amplified by the fact that the metaverse is projected to become a pervasive environment devoid of self-governance or self-regulation. The potential misuse of the metaverse to launch illegal or criminal activities calls for forensic analysts to pay special attention to the forensic aspects of these platforms.

LITERATURE REVIEW

Related work to metaverse forensics is very scarce, albeit some researchers have tried to explore the privacy risks of the metaverse. Among the noticeable contributions in this regard is the experimental study conducted by Nair et al (2022). The authors showcased how attackers can use an adversarial program to extract and infer from VR devices the personal attributes of "anonymous" volunteering participants playing an "escape room" VR game. Among these attributes are personal information related to biometrics, demographics (e.g., gender, ethnicity), geolocation, and VR device specifications.

Many studies (e.g., (Dailybrief, 2022)) have raised concerns that metaverse adoption will most likely amplify cybersecurity risks with data and identity theft, ransomware, and disinformation campaigns becoming more personalized and destructive. Among the most cited metaverse security concerns are (1) identity management, (2) DDoS attacks, (3) device vulnerability, and (4) data explosion and exploitation (Kasiyanto & Kilinc, 2022).

Other studies (e.g., (Gulthane et al, 2019; Lim et al, 2022; Liu et al, 2019; Miller et al, 2020; Valluripally et al, 2020)) explored the applicability of traditional cybersecurity attack vectors in VR learning environments with a special emphasis on assessing the privacy risks in VR environments.

Falchuk et al (2018) highlighted the risks of using social engineering attacks to track digital footprints and digital breadcrumbs that can reveal personal sensitive information about metaverse users such as location, shopping preferences, credit card numbers, social security identity numbers, and mother's maiden names. Among the proposed countermeasures are (1) the creation of a mannequin or multiple clones of one's avatar to hide one's activities in the metaverse, (2) reserving an instance of a private metaverse space for the exclusive use of one's avatar, and (3) enabling some evasion features such as teleportation, invisibility or other forms of disguise and masquerade (Falchuk et al, 2018). Ironically, these countermeasures can be used as methods for metaverse anti-forensics, as well.

In their discussions of the lack of social privacy in the metaverse, Ning et al (2021) argued that traditional privacy control and preservation mechanisms in the real world are not transposable to the metaverse. They cited the example of Bob's avatar following Alice's avatar as she is shopping in a virtual mall in the social metaverse, recording her digital footprints such as purchased items, conversations, and visited stores. This information can be exploited subsequently to conduct a social engineering attack in the real world.

Casey et al (2021) demonstrated how VR handsets can be the subject of a "Human Joystick Attack", whereby hackers can potentially disorient immersed users, activate their HMD camera without their knowledge, cover their field of vision with superimposed images, and modify their perception of the virtual environment to push them to physically move to potentially dangerous locations. The hijacking of a VR/AR handset can potentially enable hackers to steal user profiles and misappropriately use the stolen digital avatars in the metaverse (IT-online, 2022).

Gadekallu et al (2022) reviewed the data privacy and security issues in the metaverse and highlighted how distributed ledger technology in blockchain can play an important role in tracing the integrity of the metaverse data and in validating the authenticity of the virtual transaction records. They showed how blockchain can enforce the preservation of metaverse data using private and public key infrastructures. They also cited the main drawbacks of blockchain in the metaverse, namely higher transaction processing time and limited scalability.

Leenes (2007) focused on the privacy issues pertaining to the SL platform. He raised concerns about the default settings of the gaming platform that favor openness and transparency at the expense of user anonymity and privacy. For instance, the default setting of a "third person perspective" allows an SL player to use his camera to discreetly spy on other avatars' interactions or to indulge in other forms of virtual stalking by secretly attaching a camera to another avatar. In addition, it is possible to right-click on a particular avatar or perform a search operation to retrieve profile information that was made public (e.g., data of birth, photo, website of interests, virtual interests, etc.). When a resident in Second Life engages in a voice chat with another resident, this conversation becomes observable to other players within a radius of about 20 meters. SL has also introduced gadgets that can transpose users' behavior in the metaverse into the real world. This is, for instance, the case of the free SLstats wristwatch that can report the location of the watch wearer and any other nearby avatar to a database hosted on SLStats.com, which is within the reach of the Google search engine. This is yet another evidence of how personal information can escape from the virtual towards the real world.

Wang et al (2022) considered service trust issues associated with User Generated Content (UGC) and virtual object trading in the metaverse, citing potential fraud risks associated with virtual objects' authenticity and trustworthiness. They showcased the potential exploitation of vulnerabilities in metaverse systems to undermine service trust by citing the attack against Paraluni, a metaverse financial project on the Binance Smart Chain (BSC). In this case, hackers exploited reentrancy vulnerability in smart contracts to steal $1.7 million in 2022. The authors discussed the security and privacy threats behind the metaverse and then attempted to explore some potential countermeasures.

Bertino and Islam (2017) showcased how personal information (e.g., metaverse users' profiles) stored in metaverse cloud/edge servers can also be the subject of differential attacks or Denial-of-Service (DoS) attacks. Bono et al (2009) conducted two case studies (SL and Anarchy Online) and demonstrated how it is practically possible to compromise and hijack players' devices such as laptops.

Lee et al (2021) focused on WebVR, a JavaScript programming interface that enables 3D VR presentation on HTML browsers. WebVR websites enable immersive virtual world experiences. The authors identified three main security threats imposed by third-party WebVR ads, anmely:

- Gaze and controller cursor-jacking attacks that can introduce fake gaze and controller cursors (new input channels from HMDs and VR controllers, respectively) into VR scenes to incite users into clicking on promotional VR material.
- Blind spot tracking attack that places promotional virtual items in the opposite direction of a user's current line of sight.
- Abuse of an auxiliary display (e.g., laptop/desktop) attack that takes advantage of the inability of users to view the main display when they wear the HMD by displaying diverse ad impressions or videos to maximize ad view counts.

Bermego and Hui (2022) discussed the lack of governance on metaverse platforms and provided several alternatives to address this issue including the usage of metaverse moderators, self-governing metaverse communities, AI-powered automation tools to detect abuses, embedding privacy in the software code of the metaverse solution (e.g., avatar privacy bubbles), and punitive sanctions against avatar misbehaviors, among others.

Mackenzie (2022) refuted the 'old wine in new bottles' argument when it comes to describing the relationship between offline cybercrimes and their online counterparts. He maintained the vision that cybercrimes in the metaverse will be a hybrid mix of new problems and new forms of scams with old, déjà vu problems. In particular, he maintained that the criminology of cryptocurrency is a seminal step toward criminology in the metaverse. The metaverse can turn into the favorite place of contemporary crypto finance scams where grey economic activities will take place in a virtual world and be concealed to some extent from the scrutiny of public authorities. The likelihood of police or other law enforcement agencies conducting investigations into crypto scammers operating within the metaverse is minimal (Mackenzie, 2022). Put simply, from a legal perspective, the metaverse has created a new space where existing laws would be incompatible (Kasiyanto & Kilinc, 2022)

Huq et al. (2022) asserted that predicting cybersecurity threats in the metaverse realm is challenging as the metaverse is still in its early evolutionary state. However, they identified nine broad categories of current and potential threats as shown in Table 1.

To the best of our knowledge, our study is the first reported contribution that aimed to explore the unexplored realm of metaverse forensics, albeit the claim of Jeon et al (2022) that digital forensics cannot be used in metaverse space and that it is not possible to assess the extent of damage and track malicious users in the metaverse. More specifically, this chapter aims to enhance our understanding of metaverse forensics by drawing the attention of forensic investigators and researchers to some peculiar challenges associated with this research field. We will present a metaverse forensic investigation procedure and provide some new results of a metaverse forensic investigation taking VRChat and AltspaceVR as case studies.

Table 1. Metaverse cybersecurity threats (Huq et al, 2022)

Application area	Threats
Digital twins in critical infrastructure facilities (e.g. power plants)	Cyber-physical threats via digital twin exploits. Traditional IT attacks (brute forcing, vulnerability exploitation, ransomware). VR/AR/MR/XR threats.
IoT devices controlled via custom metaverse space interfaces	Man-in-the-middle attacks, avatar takeovers.
Social media	Avatar spies, criminals hiding behind avatars to commit financial fraud. Social engineering.
Advertising	Unauthorized sharing of user data. Financial fraud (e.g., pump-and-dump schemes for digital assets, fake ads, fake recommendations, endorsements, etc.) Selling scams or cheats of a digital product.
Shopping	Stealing payment and banking information (e.g. via broker impersonation)
Art	NFT ransomware. Sale of counterfeit or stolen artwork.
Education	Invasive tracking of user activities. Social engineering attacks.
Publishing (e.g., virtual digital libraries)	Copyright infringements Fake news
Immersive entertainment	Malware hidden in body suits to cause physical harm, steal biometric data or monitor user's actions

LEGAL ISSUES WITH AVATARS IN THE METAVERSE

In this section, we present some legal issues surrounding the usage of the avatar of a real-life person in the metaverse with the main objective to infer potential implications for metaverse forensic investigations. Most of these discussions are derived from the noteworthy recent contribution of Cheong (2022). We refer interested readers to the above-mentioned contribution and the references cited therein for a comprehensive review of the potential harms that avatars could cause in the metaverse, and which can potentially spread to the real world.

Governance is a key issue in the metaverse where the rules that prevail are limited to "terms of uses", and community standards and codes supported by the platform owners (Kasiyanto & Kilinc, 2022). The Terms of Services (ToS) and the Community Standards (CS) of most metaverse platforms require first-time registering users to provide accurate information about their real name, gender, date of birth, country of residence, and in certain cases payment data. This information is typically made available to the metaverse owner only, unless the user chooses to share it with other users during virtual conversations or if he chooses to include it in his public profile.

Kasiyanto and Kilinc (2022) elaborated on the legal conundrums of the metaverse, highlighting the legal issues associated with "virtual property laws", privacy and data protection, smart contract laws, monetary and payment system laws, regulations of crypto assets, tax law, and criminal law. Criminal activities in the metaverse can take many forms such as stalking, assault, abusive conduct, kidnapping, intellectual property law violations, financial frauds, and scams.

While interacting in the metaverse, avatars can affect (a) other avatars, (b) metaverse virtual infrastructures, (c) the real people behind other avatars, or (d) third parties in the real world (Cheong, 2022).

Such interaction can potentially lead to harm which could be confined within the metaverse or outspread to the real world, in which cases liability can be imposed on the responsible avatar, the owners of the metaverse platform, or the real person behind the avatar (Cheong, 2022; Lavoie et al, 2021). Cheong (2022) identified four scenarios through which the imposition of liability requires the identification of the real person behind a wrongdoer avatar, namely fraud, defamation, identity theft, and crime. Digital forensics might play a role in establishing such an association between the wrongdoer's virtual avatar and its "owner".

The Guardian reported a criminal case that illustrates how porous is the boundary between the real world and the virtual world and how the leakage between the two can have damaging consequences (Satanage, 2007). In this case, a factory worker was accused of killing a colleague because of a 'love triangle' involving a cyber relationship on SL, one of the proto-metaverse experiences (Murray, 2022).

Cheong (2022) highlighted several legal issues associated with the misuse of avatars in the metaverse and the underpinning questions related to avatar rights and liabilities in the metaverse. For instance, are avatars responsible for their actions in the metaverse? Should they be granted a legal personality in the metaverse? Do avatars have the rights to be protected against other avatar assaults in the metaverse? What legal recourse can be pursued against an offending avatar that has caused harm to other avatars or to the individuals controlling them? What would happen if the future generation of avatars acquire AI capabilities and be able to make their own decisions, bypassing the real persons behind them? How to handle liability issues in case of avatar hijacking (e.g., through identity theft)? What happens if an avatar becomes infected with a virus and commits a crime in the metaverse? Cheong (2022) suggested that:

- At least all avatars in the metaverse should be subject to formal registration, the same way a company is incorporated, meaning that each avatar shall be granted a separate legal personality, and
- The anonymity of avatars should be relinquished in cases of significant legal infractions.

SPECIFIC METAVERSE INCIDENTS AND OFFENCES

Undoubtedly, the metaverse is poised to offer an exciting new level of immersive experience and social interaction. However, it has also opened the door for cyberbullying, cyberstalking, and cybercrimes to take place in the virtual world whilst projecting back onto the victim's real world. The metaverse combines multiple entwined technologies and blurs the line between the real and virtual realms, resulting in an expanded attack surface that hackers can exploit. This creates a situation where vulnerabilities in the virtual world can be used to harm users in the physical world (Dwivedi et al, 2022). Leenes (2007) demonstrated how the user functionality in Second Life (SL) which allows the creation of unverifiable alternate accounts (Alts), separate from the primary avatar's identity, creates opportunities to exploit anonymity to engage in disruptive behaviors such as trolling, flaming, and spamming.

While researchers are still trying to better grasp the potential cybersecurity threats and privacy-violation vulnerabilities on the metaverse, many worrisome incidents and offenses committed on metaverse platforms have recently been reported. These include personal harassment, sexualization of avatar interactions, data exploitation, and unlawful gambling (Dwivedi et al, 2022). A recent study by the Centre for Countering Digital Hate (CCDH) conducted on Facebook metaverse revealed the presence of many predators and found that users were exposed to abusive behavior (such as bullying, racism, and exposure to harmful and sexual content) every seven minutes (CCDH, 2022). Another empirical study conducted by Statista revealed other metaverse concerns related to users' addiction to simulated reality, privacy issues, and mental health problems (Statista, 2022).

In a widely publicized cybersecurity incident in the metaverse, hackers successfully launched a ransomware attack against the Roblox metaverse gaming system, asking users to grant them in-game Robux virtual currency in exchange for the decryptor (Wang et al, 2022).

Interpol's 2022 global crime trend report anticipates that the metaverse will intensify the already concerning frequency of cyberattacks, amplifying the risks associated with child abuse, personal data theft, money laundering, fraud, counterfeiting, and sexual assault (Barr, 2022).

There have been several reported incidents of cyberbullying in metaverse platforms. The USA Today (Shen, 2022) reported the case of a woman who claimed to have been verbally and sexually assaulted while playing the virtual game "Horizon Worlds", developed by Meta. According to the claimant, she witnessed 3-4 male avatars, with male voices, virtually assaulting her avatar. Another case of sexual harassment was reported by a female beta tester for the Horizon Worlds Meta platform whose avatar was groped by a stranger. Meta's internal review of the case suggested that the beta tester should have used the "Safe Zone" tool which creates a protective bubble that users can activate when feeling threatened. When the safe zone is activated on a given avatar, no other avatars can interact in any way with it (Basu, 2022).

In another incident, the New York Times reported a case of a cyberbullying incident that happened on the Population One platform (acquired lately by Meta) whereby a player's avatar approached a female player's avatar and engaged in indecent acts against her avatar (Frenkel & Browning, 2021).

Another incident occurred wherein a woman experienced a virtual assault while engaged in the QuiVR virtual game. In this case, an avatar under the nickname BigBro442 made explicit gestures toward her avatar. Despite the woman's attempts to distance her avatar, the offending avatar persistently pursued and chased her avatar (Time, 2016).

In another (yet controversial) case, a Russian teenager was sentenced by a Siberian military court to five years in prison for alleged "training for terrorist activities" because he attempted to blow up a virtual building of the FSB security service in the virtual online game Minecraft (Euronews, 2022). This has led many researchers to warn against the potential abuse of the metaverse space by terrorists and online extremists who could exploit it for recruitment, training, coordination, and planning of attacks (Elson et al, 2022; Debuire, 2022). Huq et al (2022) refer to the "darkverse" (in analogy to the dark web) to describe the hidden clandestine universe inside the metaverse which can serve as a haven for criminals to carry out unlawful or illicit activities while being shielded from the monitoring of Law Enforcement Agencies (LEA).

Leenes (2007) highlighted the controversial legal usage of virtual detective agencies in the SL virtual space, such as those run by Markie McDonald for covert operations, surveillance, and spying. He reported the case of an SL female user who hired the agency to set up a "honey trap" to uncover the potential infidelity of a male acquaintance in the metaverse world.

A notable metaverse incident came to light when the user data stored on a server database of the SL virtual platform was compromised, causing the disclosure of unencrypted usernames and addresses, as well as encrypted payment details and passwords (Techcrunch, 2006).

Cyberattacks were also able to breach the security of blockchain-based NFT marketplaces that are commonly present across many metaverse platforms. For instance, OpenSea, a peer-to-peer marketplace for NFTs, had to endure a loss of $1.7 million when the accounts of 17 users were hacked through phishing attacks that exploited a loophole in the smart contract software (Threatpost, 2022).

METAVERSE FORENSIC INVESTIGATION

Metaverse digital forensics involves identifying, extracting, aggregating, and analyzing digital evidence that can span both the virtual as well as the real world. To further research in metaverse forensics, two case studies i.e., scenarios of test user(s) playing a metaverse game and being subjected to simulated bullying instances, are presented. These case studies are limited to performing metaverse investigation on two platforms, namely VRChat and AltspaceVR, with the main objective of extracting as much forensically relevant information as possible to support the investigation process. The first VRChat case study involved a test user interacting in the metaverse via a VR headset, while the second AltspaceVR case study involved a test user with just a PC, interacting with another user who was equipped with a VR headset. The scope of the forensic analysis included physical end devices and sensors owned by the victim of bullying/harassment i.e., the host computer(s)/smartphone(s), and VR headset(s). Based on the six cardinal points of investigation (5W+1H), our metaverse forensics investigation aimed to address the following questions:

- What happened? (Nature of the offense)
- Where did it happen? (Virtual and physical location of the offense, including VR headset geospatial telemetry data)
- When did it happen? (Time and date)
- Who was involved? (The avatars and the associated users)
- Why did it happen? (Reason or motive of the offense)
- How did it happen? (Manner, methods, and devices used in the offense)

ETHICAL CONSIDERATIONS

As with any research that involves human subjects, diligent efforts have been made to ensure that the rights and well-being of the involved participants are adequately safeguarded. The main identified ethical risks are associated with (1) potential physical/emotional discomfort and/or exhaustion from using the VR devices, (2) potential distress due to the discomfort in disclosing personal information, and (3) potential breach of the participants' personal data. We have taken several precautionary measures to address these concerns:

- We have fully adhered to the guidelines set by the ESPRIT Research Ethics Committee on the usage of human subjects in research by demonstrating full respect for the rights of the participants, while addressing all the potential concerns related to confidentiality, informed consent, and conflicts of interest.
- We have obtained written informed consent from all participants. Prior to that, we conducted an orientation session to explain to the participants the research objectives, their roles, the assigned tasks, the risks and benefits associated with the experiments, and the privacy mechanisms put in place to safeguard their personal data and to request whether they wish to participate. We also informed the participants about the nature of data that might be collected and gave them the option to withdraw from the experimental study at any time.

- We provided high-fidelity VR headsets and powerful gaming consoles to the participants to mitigate the risk of VR sickness.
- We anonymized all collected data to that it cannot be traced back to a particular individual.
- All participants in the experiments used fictitious online aliases.

Case Study #1: VRChat Forensic Investigation

VRChat is a virtual reality social platform where people from around the world engage in conversations, interact, and socialize in near real-time. Users can explore virtual worlds, customize their avatars with several preferences and represent themselves in the metaverse. Users can build and design their virtual worlds, where unique avatars are tailored, engaging users in immersive experiences such as playing interactive games and sharing content.

As an interconnected and complex digital realm, conducting digital forensics on the metaverse can be challenging. In this first case study, a scenario is analyzed where simulated bullying activities are examined in the VRChat platform. This study aims to provide insights into the unique aspects of metaverse forensics and extract digital evidence/artifacts from the virtual environment to support the case. To simulate an authentic scenario, we created sterile accounts with new usernames and passwords on two different VR headsets: HTC Vive, and Meta Quest 2.

Scenario

Users are first required to create an account or log in with a gaming or distribution platform such as Steam. The application can be downloaded on the Steam platform for free and it is directly available on the Oculus store supporting Quest headsets (i.e., Oculus Quest 2). When a user logs in successfully, virtual instances can be created where multiple users join to interact with each other. Invitations can be sent to friends or people online to join private or public rooms and may engage in several activities including voice conversations, chat rooms, playing games, etc.

To examine interactions within a scheduled private VRChat room, we established a specific scenario incorporating two users who were equipped with distinct VR headsets. User A used an HTC Vive and User B used a Meta Quest 2. The objective was to assess their virtual interactions and gather forensic artifacts for analysis.

User A and User B, who had previously connected as friends, decided to meet in a private VRChat room created by User A. User A sent a chat invite to User B to join him in his home world. During their

Figure 2. VRChat interface

interaction, both users had audio and video conversations, shared virtual objects, and engaged in virtual gestures and movements. The private room provided them with a secluded environment for their interaction.

After the interaction concluded, User A and User B logged out of VRChat. The next step involved the forensic analysis of the headsets.

Experimental Setup

The necessary hardware equipment and workstations were arranged to establish a robust experimental setup. The experimental setup employed two distinct VR headsets, namely the HTC VIVE Cosmos and the Meta Quest 2. The HTC headset is classified as a computer-supported VR headset and was configured and launched using the SteamVR platform. This platform offers users the opportunity to engage in a wide array of interactive games, with the flexibility to choose between VR or non-VR modes. To meet the minimum requirements for the HTC VIVE cosmos headset, an Alienware PC was procured, characterized by its high resolution and formidable processing power. A listing of all the hardware and software equipment utilized in the experiment is provided in Table 2 and table 3.

In this experimental configuration, a controlled setting was created, engaging the participation of two users. These users logged in using two sterile accounts created solely for the experiment. Various interactions occurring within the VRChat application were systematically recorded.

User A was assigned an HTC VIVE cosmos headset launched via SteamVR, a virtual reality platform available through the Steam gaming platform. A username skykrash22 was created with the Steam account and registered to the VRChat application. The Meta Quest 2 headset supported the second user with the display name targ.bob116. The VRChat application was installed and launched on both headsets simultaneously. Once all the initial stages of creating and verifying accounts were completed, we used the HTC VIVE account to initiate a new instance of Home Worlds. This is a private chamber where users can extend invitations to their friends and online users, inviting them to join the room. During the

Table 2. Computer system details

Devices	Details
Model	Alienware windows 10
Processor	Intel Core i9 8950HK CPU, 2.9GHz
System type	64-bit OS, x64 processor
Graphics Card	NVIDIA GeForce GTX 1080
Manufacturer	Dell
Installed Memory RAM	32.0 GB

Table 3 Virtual reality devices

Devices	Description
HTC VIVE cosmos	VR headset by Valve corporation vive_cosmos5A99SAM00686
VIVE cosmos controller HTC	Two controllers VIVE_cosmos_ controller000432V399V06920
Meta Quest 2	Firmware N/A

experiment, an invitation was sent to user targ.bob116 and the user joined in the private room. During the VRChat session, the users interacted with voice commands and instant chats that are prompted and navigated through the digital controllers of both headsets. Our analysis is primarily focused on the HTC VIVE headset, and the Windows PC utilized to launch the headset. The objective is to identify relevant artifacts, which will aid in supporting the investigation and present valid evidence of the series of activities undertaken during the VRChat session.

The investigation process encompassed the use of diverse forensic tools, including memory acquisition tools, to attain a comprehensive understanding of the test activities and events. While both users were together in the private room engaging in various activities such as voice conversations, chatting, and virtual room exploration, a memory dump was captured and extracted using AccessData FTK Imager . In addition, FTK was also utilized in conjunction with OSForensics, to analyze the memory dump along with the Steam client folders. We identified the user account which was used to register for the VRChat application. Moreover, we collected and analyzed artifacts related to the user's activity in the virtual reality environment, including logs, configuration files, and other data. These are further discussed below.

VRChat Forensic Artifacts Collection

While the VRChat session was ongoing, the memory dump was extracted from the host computer, thereby capturing relevant forensic artifacts, while other artifacts and logs were saved in the Steam client folder as well. We established that the HTC VIVE headset is dependent on a host computer to operate and launch games, thus major files and folders used by the headset are stored in client folders. Most of the folders are associated with user data, apps installed in Steam, and configuration files.

Steam and Steam VR Forensic Artifacts

Steam VR is the software used in this study for launching VR applications and for initializing and controlling virtual reality hardware. It offers convenient game switching, access to the Steam Store, and the ability to interact with a virtual environment using a portable computer. Steams offers various features that generate numerous artifacts, many of which are stored on the Steam Cloud service. In the next subsection, we will present the key findings related to these artifacts.

In the folder C:\Program Files (x86)\Steam, various files related to the configuration, logs, music, and other information about the Steam application were discovered. Additionally, within the folder C:\ProgramFiles(x86)\Steam\appcache\httpcache, we discovered thousands of files in multiple subfolders. Most of these subfolders appear to be empty, but one specific folder, named "00," contained a file that appeared to be a combination of binary data and HTTP response headers. The content of this file was not readable as plain text and it might be related to a file or image request made through the VALVE/Steam HTTP Client user agent to the server at avatars.akamai.steamstatic.com.

One of the most important folders which contained relevant forensic evidence is the C:\Program Files (x86)\Steam\config. This folder contained numerous settings and configurations for the Steam client, such as gamer profiles, chaperone info, steam apps, shader cache sizes, VR settings, and server connection information. A particular file named "loginusers", consisting of the configuration information of the Steam user was also extracted. This file contained information about the user's account that was used to log into the Steam app using the Steam ID "76561199488552016". The user's account name was shemus221 along with the persona name (display name) as skykrash22. In the same config folder, we also found the configuration of the chaperone written in JSON format. This JSON code seems to define the collision bounds of an object in a virtual environment. The object is defined as being composed of several "universes" which appear to represent different parts or aspects of the object. Each universe is defined by a list of coordinates that represent the boundaries of that part of the object. The coordinates appear to be in three dimensions and are defined as a series of points in space, where each point is represented by an array of three values: x, y, and z. This JSON code is likely being used to establish the boundaries of a 3D object within a virtual environment, ensuring that other objects can interact with it without intersecting it.

VRChat Forensic Artifacts

As we further explored the host computer, it was evident that most folders and configuration files associated with specific games or applications installed in Steam (such as VRChat in our case) were stored in another directory under the local user of the host computer. These artifacts were found under the path directory C:\Users\avuser\AppData\LocalLow\VRChat. This directory included folders, and files containing data related to the user activities in the virtual environment. Some folders contained cookies, avatar data, and VRChat worlds configuration, among others. However, the most significant findings were the output logs where all processes, connection requests, and activities of the user were saved. These files contained logs of every activity or event that occurred since the application has been launched, and separate files were created whenever a new session was initiated by the user.

In the context of our experiment, a new file outputlog.txt was created when VRChat was launched, and as test activities progressed, the logs were updated continuously. These logs encapsulated details of the virtual room, encompassing elements such as display names, server responses, initiation of rooms and worlds, as well as avatar properties. While all the social activities performed during the experiment were reflected on the logs, the incident that occurred can be reconstructed using timestamps. However, these output logs were produced upon the completion of a particular VRChat session and were found to disappear as soon as the session ends, and a new session is initiated. So, to prevent the loss of these files we created a backup for all the output logs.

A general timeline and description of the log events are shown in Table 4 and are further discussed below.

During our testing, the HTC headset user (skykrash22) created a new instance of a customized home world. Initialization of the VRChat application and joining of the user (Event 1 in Table 4), are reflected by the creation of the log. The timestamp indicates the exact date and time when the user logged in to the application. This is relevant to the forensic investigation as it represents the time when the user joined the room. Once the application has been initialized, the user is directed to a virtual world called VRChat home world (Event 2). It seems that the world instances have a unique room id with a series of characters classified into several strings.

Event 3 represents a customized invite message received from user targ.bob116 to join the room, with a request stating, 'I'd like to chat'. These log entries provide forensic investigators with evidence that an invitation was received from the second user (targ.bob116), at a particular time along with the invite message. The invite message inferred that user targ.bob116 wanted to join the session to chat with skykrash22. Events 4 and 5 showed that the user entered the private room and that both users were in the VRChat home world. The entry logs showed the display name of the user along with some activities (behaviors) such as entering and joining the VRChat room. It is clear from Event 6 logs that the guest user

Table 4. VRChat activities and forensic artifacts

Events	Artifacts
1. User opens application	2023.04.25 19:01:35 Log - [Behaviour] OnPlayerJoined skykrash22 30ff 2023.04.25 19:01:35 Log - [Behaviour] OnPlayerJoinComplete skykrash22 30ff 2023.04.25 19:01:35 Log - [Behaviour] Initialized PlayerAPI "skykrash22 30ff" is local
2. Creating and joining room	2023.04.25 19:03:27 Log - [Behaviour] Entering world 2023.04.25 19:03:28 Log - [Behaviour] Entering Room: VRChat Home 2023.04.25 19:03:28 Log - [Behaviour] Joining wrld_4432ea9b-729c-46e3-8eaf-846aa0a37fdd:06450~friends(usr_71e97a1c-047c-4228-bd6d-2cd67df530ff)~nonce(6A38FAFE86521D45219DE551ECB46B3F2E2390490-5191770) 2023.04.25 19:03:28 Log - [Behaviour] Joining or Creating Room: VRChat Home 2023.04.25 19:03:28 Log - [Behaviour] Successfully joined room
3. Invite message	2023.04.25 19:11:08 Log - AcceptNotification for notification:<Notification from username:targ.bob116 b072, sender user id:usr_ebc84b06-8705-41bb-9ccf-97bfe647b072 to usr_71e97a1c-047c-4228-bd6d-2cd67df530ff of type: requestInvite, id: not_db43e3fe-c6ae-4b5c-b087-025ff8872891, created at: 04/25/2023 19:11:08 UTC, details: {{requestMessage=I'd like to chat!}}, type:requestInvite, m seen:True, message: "">
4. Second user joining room	2023.04.25 19:13:10 Log - [Behaviour] OnPlayerEnteredRoom 2023.04.25 19:13:11 Log - Voice DeliveryMode: UnreliableUnsequenced 2023.04.25 19:13:11 Log - [Behaviour] OnPlayerJoined targ.bob116 b072 2023.04.25 19:13:11 Log - [Behaviour] Initialized PlayerAPI "targ.bob116 b072" is remote
5. Complete joining	2023.04.25 19:13:13 Log - [Behaviour] OnPlayerJoinComplete targ.bob116 b072
6. Second user leaving room	2023.04.25 19:24:42 Log - [Behaviour] OnPlayerLeftRoom 2023.04.25 19:24:42 Log - [Behaviour] Cleaning up held messages 2023.04.25 19:24:42 Log - [Behaviour] OnPlayerLeft targ.bob116 b072 2023.04.25 19:24:42 Log - [Behaviour] Removed player targ.bob116 b072 2023.04.25 19:24:42 Log - [Behaviour] Unregistering targ.bob116 b072
7. Close application	2023.04.25 20:44:49 Log - VRCApplication: OnApplicationQuit at 2262.249

left the room and was unregistered from the private world. Event 7 shows the log when the application was closed. Figure 3 also shows the hardware and software equipment utilized as a part of the output logs. These artifacts present the specific device model and system specifications of the host computer used to launch the application. Figure 4 illustrates multiple logs of the specific behavior uspeak, which record when the microphone was switched from the standard host computer to the headset and vice versa. The events "stop microphone" and "start microphone" seem to indicate muting and unmuting the microphone when the players were interacting with each other.

Although the output logs provided details of events, the contents of actual chats exchanged in the virtual room were not available despite an extensive forensic analysis of local storage. We also performed a memory dump while the VRChat session was in progress, and we were able to retrieve some information related to the local user by using a keyword search. We used OSForensics to extract a string format of the memory dump which was then exported it as a text file (Figure 5). This file contained the steam id, which is the same id discovered previously in steam client folders, the username of the steam account (skykrash22), and some snippets of the output logs. Additionally, the file contained a JSON format configuration and status of the VRChat home world. It showed the name of the virtual world, current occupants, general private occupants, and other statuses such as the region of the home world.

In light of the above, the absence of forensic evidence related to the exchanged text/voice chat records (whether in the client folders or in volatile memory) represents a key challenge for VRChat forensic investigators. To circumvent this obstacle, an investigator may need to follow an alternative approach

Figure 3. Artifact containing system information

```
2023.04.25 18:52:35 Log        -  [UserInfoLogger] Environment Info:
    VRChat Build: 2023.2.1p2-1299-2d201ab09b-Release
    Store: Steam
    Platform: standalonewindows
    Device Model: Alienware 17 R5 (Alienware)
    Processor Type: Intel(R) Core(TM) i9-8950HK CPU @ 2.90GHz
    System Memory Size: 32630MB
    Operating System: Windows 10  (10.0.18363) 64bit
    Graphics Device Name: NVIDIA GeForce GTX 1080
    Graphics Device Version: Direct3D 11.0 [level 11.1]
    Graphics Memory Size: 8079MB
    Supports Audio: True
    XR Device: None
    API Status: Available: ("pong")
    CloudFront Status: Available: (pong)
```

Figure 4. Log of microphone usage in chat

```
2023.04.25 12:55:01 Log        -  [Always] Microphones installed (2 total)
2023.04.25 12:55:01 Log        -  [Always] -- [0] device name = 'Microphone (2- VIVE Cosmos
Multimedia Audio)' min/max freq = 44100 / 44100
2023.04.25 12:55:01 Log        -  [Always] -- [1] device name = 'Microphone (Realtek(R) Audio)'
min/max freq = 48000 / 48000
2023.04.25 12:55:01 Log        -  [Behaviour] uSpeak [499][1934194477]: Stop Microphone:
2023.04.25 12:55:01 Log        -  [Behaviour] uSpeak [499][1934194477]: Start Microphone:
Microphone (2- VIVE Cosmos Multimedia Audio)
```

Figure 5. Memory dump of the VRChat home world

```
"lastWorldId":"wrld_4432ea9b-729c-46e3-8eaf-846aa0a37fdd"
Occupants":1
"lastWorldName":"VRChat Home"
PrivateOccupants":663
"lastWorldRegion":"eu"
 "lastWorldSDKVersion":"SDK3"
"lastWorldStatsrunningTime":500.428009033203
 "lastWorldStats stat meanfps":59.3675994873047
 "lastWorldStats stat mean ping":141.902679443359
 "lastWorldStats stat total net_bytes avatar_interaction_list":78
"lastWorldStats stat total net_bytes player_properties":2388
```

such as requiring access to the VRChat backend cloud servers. Such a process would necessitate legal authorization and would entail filing a motion in a court of law, justifying the relevance of and the need for accessing the servers to gather evidence. It should be noted that in their terms of service agreements, most metaverse platforms inform users that they can disclose any information about them to law enforcement agencies or government officials at their discretion and when it is deemed necessary or appropriate to do so, or as otherwise required by law (Leenes, 2007).

Case Study #2: AltspaceVR Forensic Investigation

AltspaceVR is a social VR platform released in 2015 that allows users to attend an "endless array of virtual events" including but not limited to conferences, workshops, tech talks, festivals, meditation sessions, and school events. Each event can be joined using a 6-character entry code. The platform also consists of user-generated spaces called Worlds, which can be visited by other users.

Figure 6. The user interface of AltspaceVR

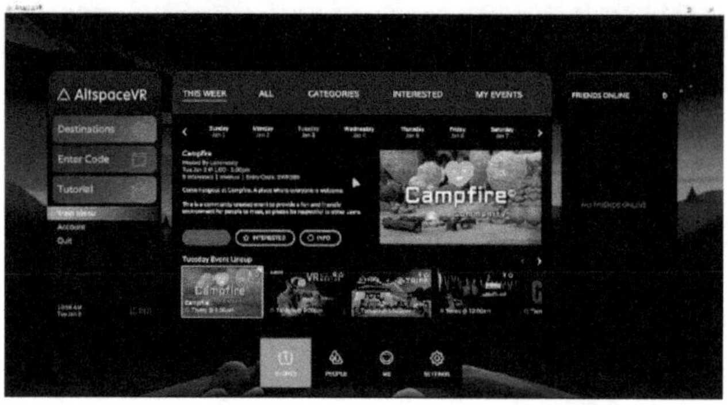

Users must have a Microsoft Account (MSA) to sign into AltspaceVR. The application can be freely downloaded and installed from the Microsoft Store. After choosing a Display Name and Username upon registering, users may (1) customize their avatars, (2) attend events, (3) create events, and (4) build worlds. Figure 6 shows the 'Main Menu' of the AltspaceVR user interface.

AltspaceVR supports many headsets including Oculus devices (Quest, Rift), Windows Mixed Reality (WMR), HTC VIVE, and Apple and Windows PCs in 2D.

Experimental Setup

To simulate a bullying scenario, two AltspaceVR test accounts were registered on separate end devices to represent the victim and abuser.

Test users A (victim) and B (abuser) got acquainted and added each other as "friends". A joined B in a private event called X at location Y. During audio and video conversations between both test users, A was subjected to simulated virtual intimidations by B, after which user A exits the space, blocks user B from his friends' list, and then logs out AltspaceVR.

The simulation was performed in a scenario where the "victim" was using a laptop PC (Windows 11 OS) as an end device, while the "offender" was using a VR headset (Oculus Quest) as an end device. The case study aimed to analyze the victim's PC. Both memory and disk space were subsequently analyzed for forensic artifacts.

We used AccessData FTK Imager to create memory dumps and disk images of the victim's PC upon completion of the simulated incident scenario. For forensic analysis, we employed several tools such as Volatility and Autopsy.

AltspaceVR Forensic Artifacts

We successfully performed a memory forensic analysis and identified two relevant AltspaceVR running processes namely AltspaceVR.exe and UnityCrashHandler64.exe. The execution timestamps of the running processes (carved using Volatility) indicated when the application was run on the PC. The Process IDs confirmed the origin of the application. Images/photos in the memory (at the time the memory dump was captured) were also carved (using Photorec) and consisted of AltspaceVR application logos/icons. In addition, some DLL files, and executables of the application were also extracted.

Figure 7. Manually extracted memory artifacts

```
maple@kali:~/Desktop$ strings -f memdump.mem | grep "UserB"
memdump.mem: ry_denied_because_full":false,"entry_denied_because_role":false},"display_name":"UserB","streaming":false,"usertZ
memdump.mem: UserB**y
memdump.mem: Player [UserB] (Blocked)
memdump.mem: Nametag UserB[1]
memdump.mem: Nametag UserB[1]
maple@kali:~/Desktop$ strings -f memdump.mem | grep "TestUserB"
memdump.mem: TestUserBs
memdump.mem: UserName:        TestUserB
memdump.mem: UserName:        TestUserB
memdump.mem: UserName:        TestUserB
memdump.mem: UserName:        TestUserB
memdump.mem: UserName:        TestUserB
```

As shown in Figure 7, the artifacts that we were able to extract manually from the victim's test PC, using strings and grep tools, were limited to the following:

1. Display the name and Username of test users A (victim) and B (abuser)
2. UserIDs of test users
3. List of blocked user(s)
4. Device and OS details of test user A

It is worth noting that the artifacts extracted were not in a very elaborate/particular string format. This may lead to difficulties in performing string extractions of the artifacts using a repetitive pattern of string searching or creating an automated tool. In addition, the analysis of the memory dump did not reveal any stored audio or chat conversations that took place during the simulated scenario. Once again, this limitation represents a significant challenge for forensic investigation and the assurance of non-repudiation, which are essential for the establishment of a strong base in legal proceedings.

We next carried a forensic disk analysis which enabled us to discover some AltspaceVR files in the Local and Locallow folders in the AppData directory (C:\Users\[HP]\AppData\). In the Local folder, an AltspaceVR package with a 13-character code (seemingly the package ID) was stored at \AppData\Local\Packages\Microsoft.AltspaceVR_8wekyb3d8bbwe. From the directory shown in Figure 8, we were able to access stored cache, cookies, internet history, and settings among other information but no forensically-relevant user activity data was found.

In the Locallow folder, a sub-folder named Microsoft_AltspaceVR (\AppData\LocalLow\Unity\Microsoft_AltspaceVR) stored some UnityFS files that contained 'world data' of various Worlds and events that were visited by the test user such as "meditation forest night" and "campfire" which are necessary for the worlds/events to be loaded onto the PC. This is indicative of what events the test user may have joined.

The AltspaceVR folder at \AppData\LocalLow\Microsoft\AltspaceVR stored some event logs with timestamps which may be indicative of the times the user interacted online with the platform.

Figure 8. Directory of AltspaceVR package on disk space

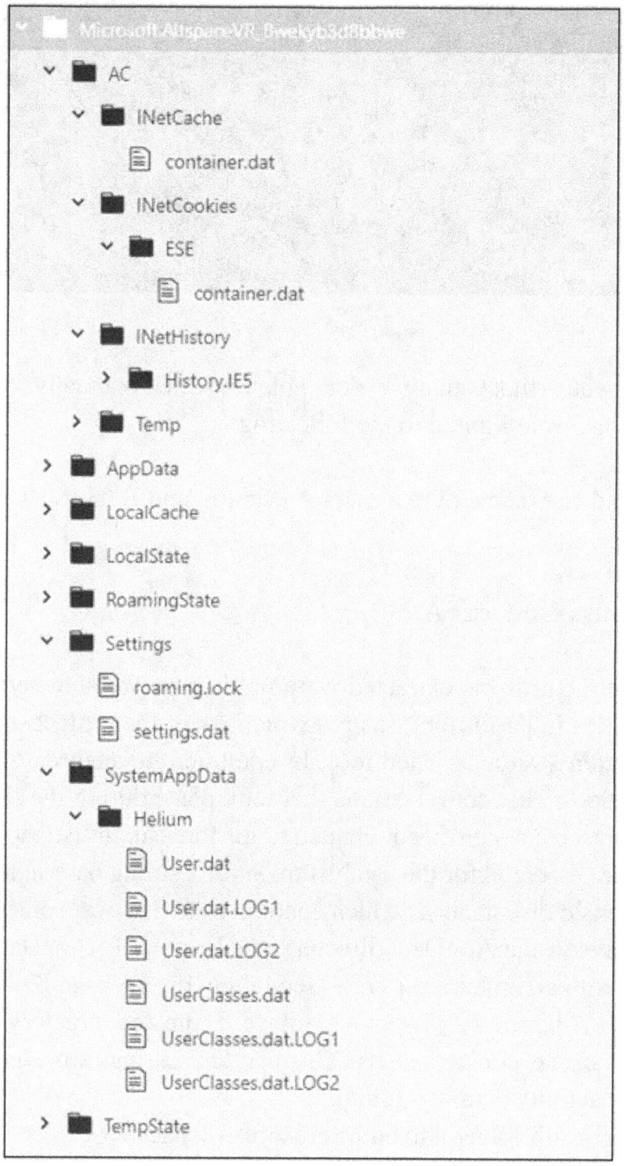

CONCLUSION AND FUTURE WORK

The metaverse offers new flavors of mixed interaction between virtual and physical worlds, leading to new innovative applications and exciting user experiences. At the same time, the misuse of the metaverse has raised serious concerns related to cybersecurity, privacy, ethics, safety, governance, and law. Digital forensic researchers and investigators need to continuously adapt their methods and tools to adequately address the unique cybersecurity challenges posed by the metaverse. This study was, to the best of our knowledge, the first initiative that aimed at exploring the forensic aspects of the metaverse through two case studies related to the VRChat and AltspaceVR applications. The extracted forensic artifacts highlighted that some incriminating (and possibly attributable) forensic evidence reside in the disk space. However, the forensic analysis of the memory dump did not divulge as much. This might be attributed to the fact that the relatively small memory size of the VR headsets favors the discard of memory processes sooner, resulting in the loss of data that may be of forensic relevance.

One of the key challenges faced during our investigations was the inability to extract forensic evidence related to actual chat conversations from memory or hard disks, whether on VR headsets or on PCs. It is most likely that these conversations are stored exclusively in the metaverse platforms' cloud servers as VRChat and AltspaceVR may have specific privacy measures that hinder the visibility of chat logs. In this case, upon filing a motion with the court and if the court grants permission, investigators can proceed with retrieving the required data from the cloud servers, enabling them to conduct thorough forensic analysis and uncover relevant information for the investigation. Though cloud forensics is beyond the scope of this study, we refer interested readers to the earlier research reported in (Wu et al, 2022), (Zawoad & Hasan, 2013), (Chou et al, 2017), (Manral et al, 2019) (Khan et al, 2016) and (Simou et al, 2016) and the references cited therein for additional details.

This work can be further explored in many directions. First, it would be interesting to extend our study beyond the VRChat and AltspaceVR applications. Such research can establish a solid groundwork for an insightful comparative analysis of the prominent metaverse platforms from a digital forensic perspective. By doing so, we can gain new insights into the unique characteristics, strengths, and weaknesses of these platforms, enabling a thorough understanding of their forensic implications. Second, it would be interesting to explore the usage of Artificial Intelligence and machine learning algorithms in facilitating metaverse forensic investigations, specifically by automating the collection and analysis of digital evidence, as well as extracting relevant textual information. Lastly, the potential attack trend in virtual worlds requires the development of a comprehensive and formal approach to investigating crimes in the metaverse. Forensic frameworks, models, and metamodels are often leveraged to develop such an approach.

ACKNOWLEDGMENT

This research was supported by Zayed University [Research Incentive Fund # R21111].

REFERENCES

Barr, K. (2022). Interpol Wants in on the 'Metaverse', *Gizmodo*. https://www.gizmodo.com.au/2022/10/interpol-wants-in-on-the-metaverse/

Basu, T. (2022). The metaverse has a groping problem already. *MIT Technology Review*. https://www.technologyreview.com/2021/12/16/1042516/the-metaverse-has-a-groping-problem/

Bertino, E., & Islam, N. (2017). Botnets and internet of things security. *Computer*, *50*(2), 76–79. doi:10.1109/MC.2017.62

Bono, S., Caselden, D., Landau, G., & Miller, C. (2009). Reducing the attack surface in massively multiplayer online role-playing games. *IEEE Security and Privacy*, *7*(3), 13–19. doi:10.1109/MSP.2009.75

Braud, L. H. T., Zhou, P., Wang, L., Xu, D., Lin, Z., & Hui, P. (2021). All one needs to know about metaverse: A complete survey on technological singularity, virtual ecosystem, and research agenda. *arXiv, 2110, 05352.* [Online]. https://doi.org//arXiv.2110.05352 doi:10.48550

Buck, L., & McDonnell, R. (2022). *Security and privacy in the metaverse: The threat of the digital human.* In 1st Workshop on Novel Challenges of Safety, Security and Privacy in Extended Reality, New Orleans, LA, USA.

Casey, P., Baggili, I., & Yarramreddy, A. (2021). Immersive virtual reality attacks and the human joystick. *IEEE Transactions on Dependable and Secure Computing*, *18*(2), 550–562. doi:10.1109/TDSC.2019.2907942

CCDH. (2022). *Facebook Metaverse is unsafe.* CCDH. https://www.counterhate.com/metaverse

Cheong, B. C. (2022). Avatars in the metaverse: Potential legal issues and remedies. *International Cybersecurity Law Review*, *3*(2), 467–494. doi:10.136543439-022-00056-9

Choo, K. R., Esposito, C., & Castiglione, A. (2017). Evidence and forensics in the cloud: Challenges and future research directions. *IEEE Cloud Computing*, *4*(3), 14–19. doi:10.1109/MCC.2017.39

Dailybrief. (2022). Metaverse adoption will multiply Ccybersecurity risks. *Daily Brief.* https://dailybrief.oxan.com/Analysis/GA266968/Metaverse-adoption-will-multiply-cybersecurity-risks

Debuire, D. (2022). Terrorist use of the metaverse: New opportunities and new challenges. *The Security Distillery*. https://thesecuritydistillery.org/all-articles/terrorism-and-the-metaverse-new-opportunities-and-new-challenges

Di Pietro, R., & Cresci, S. (2022). Metaverse: Security and privacy issues. [Online]. Available: https://arxiv.org/pdf/2205.07590.pdf

Dwivedi, Y. K., Hughes, L., Baabdullah, A. M., Ribeiro-Navarrete, S., Giannakis, M., Al-Debei, M. M., Dennehy, D., Metri, B., Buhalis, D., Cheung, C. M. K., Conboy, K., Doyle, R., Dubey, R., Dutot, V., Felix, R., Goyal, D. P., Gustafsson, A., Hinsch, C., Jebabli, I., & Wamba, S. F. (2022). Metaverse beyond the hype: Multidisciplinary perspectives on emerging challenges, opportunities, and agenda for research, practice and policy. *International Journal of Information Management*, *66*(C), 102542. doi:10.1016/j.ijinfomgt.2022.102542

Elson, J. S., Doctor, A. C., & Hunter, S. (2022). The metaverse offers a future full of potential – for terrorists and extremists, too, *The Conversation.* https://theconversation.com/the-metaverse-offers-a-future-full-of-potential-for-terrorists-and-extremists-too-173622

Euronews. (2022). Russian teen jailed for 5 years over 'terrorism' plot to blow up virtual spy HQ on Minecraft. *Euronews.* https://www.euronews.com/next/2022/02/10/russian-teen-jailed-for-5-years-over-terrorism-plot-to-blow-up-virtual-spy-hq-on-minecraft

Falchuk, B., Loeb, S., & Neff, R. (2018). The Social metaverse: Battle for privacy. *IEEE Technology and Society Magazine*, *37*(2), 52–61. doi:10.1109/MTS.2018.2826060

FernandezB. C.HuiP. (2022). Life, the metaverse and everything: An overview of privacy, ethics, and governance in metaverse. *arXiv:2204.01480v1.* https://arxiv.org/pdf/2204.01480.pdf doi:10.1109/ICDCSW56584.2022.00058

Fineman, B., & Lewis, N. (2018). *Securing your reality: Addressing security and privacy in virtual and augmented reality applications.* Educause. https://er.educause.edu/articles/2018/5/securing-your-reality-addressing-security-and-privacy-in-virtual-andaugmented-reality-applications

Frenkel, S., & Browning, K. (2021). The Metaverse's dark side: Here come harassment and assaults. *The New York Times*. https://www.nytimes.com/2021/12/30/technology/metaverse-harassment-assaults.html

Gadekallu, T. R., Huynh-The, T., Wang, W., Yenduri, G., Ranaweera, P., Pham, Q. V., da Costa, D. B., & Liyanageet, M. (2022). *Blockchain for the metaverse: A review*. arXiv. https://arxiv.org/pdf/2203.09738.pdf

GaronJ. M. (2022). Legal implications of a ubiquitous metaverse and a Web3 future. [Online]. Available at SSRN: https://ssrn.com/abstract=4002551. http://dx.doi.org/ doi:10.2139/ssrn.4002551

Gulhane, A. (2019). Security, privacy and safety risk assessment for virtual reality learning environment applications. In the *16th IEEE Annual Consumer Communications Networking Conference (CCNC).* IEEE. 10.1109/CCNC.2019.8651847

Hu, J., & Iosifescu, A., & LiKamWa, R. (2021). Lenscap: split-process framework for fine-grained visual privacy control for augmented reality apps. In *Proceedings of the 19th Annual International Conference on Mobile Systems, Applications, and Services* (MobiSys '21). ACM. 10.1145/3458864.3467676

Huq, N. Reyes, R., Lin, P., & Swimmer. M. (2022). Metaverse or metaworse?: Cybersecurity threats against the Internet of experiences. *Trend Micro Research Paper*. https://documents.trendmicro.com/assets/white_papers/wp-metaverse-or-metaworse-cybersecurity-threats-against-the-internet-of-experiences.pdf

ISO/IEC 23005. (2020). *MPEG-V standards.* ISO. https://mpeg.chiariglione.org/standards/mpeg-v

IT-Online. (2022). *Meta safety; meta security; metaverse*. IT Online. https://it-online.co.za/2022/02/08/meta-safety-meta-security-metaverse

Jeon, S.-E., Oh, Y. S., & Lee, I. G. (2022). A Study on the policy measures for the prevention of industrial secret leakage in the metaverse. *Journal of Digital Convergence*, *20*(4), 377–388. doi:10.14400/JDC.2022.20.4.377

Joshua, J. (2017). Information bodies: Computational anxiety in Neal Stephenson's snow crash. *Interdisciplinary Literary Studies*, *19*(1), 17–47. doi:10.5325/intelitestud.19.1.0017

Kasiyanto, S., & Kilinc, M. R. (2022). The legal conundrums of the metaverse. *J. Central Bank. Law Institutions*, *1*(2), 299–322. doi:10.21098/jcli.v1i2.25

Katterbauer, K., Syed, H., & Cleenewerck, L. (2022). Financial cybercrime in the Islamic Finance Metaverse. *Journal of Metaverse*, *2*(2), 56–61. doi:10.57019/jmv.1108783

Khan, S., Gani, A., Abdul Wahab, A. W., Iqbal, S., Abdelaziz, A., Mahdi, O. A., Abdallaahmed, A. I., Shiraz, M., Al-Mayouf, Y. R. B., Khan, Z., Ko, K., Khan, M. K., & Chang, V. (2016). Towards an applicability of current network forensics for cloud networks: A SWOT analysis. *IEEE Access : Practical Innovations, Open Solutions, 4*, 9800–9820. doi:10.1109/ACCESS.2016.2631543

Kunthara, S. (2021). VCs will spend Billions more to make the metaverse a reality. *Crunchbase News.* https://news.crunchbase.com/news/metaverse-startups-funding-investors

Lavoie, R., Main, K., King, C., & King, D. (2021). Virtual experience, real consequences: The potential negative emotional consequences of virtual reality gameplay. *Virtual Reality (Waltham Cross), 25*(1), 69–81. doi:10.100710055-020-00440-y

Lee, H., Lee, J., Kim, D., Jana, S., Shin, I., & Son, S. (2021). AdCube: WebVR ad fraud and practical confinement of Third-Party ads. In the *30th USENIX Security Symposium (USENIX Security 21).* ACM.

Leenes, R. (2007). Privacy in the metaverse. In S. Fischer-Hübner, P. Duquenoy, A. Zuccato, and L. Martucci (Eds). The Future of Identity in the Information Society. Springer. doi:10.1007/978-0-387-79026-8_7

Lim, J., Yun, H., Ham, A., & Kim, S. (2022). Mine yourself!: A role-playing privacy tutorial in virtual reality environment. In: *CHI Conference on Human Factors in Computing Systems Extended Abstracts*, New Orleans, LA, USA. 10.1145/3491101.3519773

Liu, A., Xia, L., Duchowski, A., Bailey, R., Holmqvist, K., & Jain, E. (2019). Differential privacy for eye-tracking data. In *Proceedings of the 11th ACM Symposium on Eye Tracking Research & Applications*. New York, NY, USA. 10.1145/3314111.3319823

Mackenzie, S. (2022). Criminology towards the metaverse: Cryptocurrency scams, grey economy and the techno-social. *British Journal of Criminology*, *62*(6), 1537–1552. doi:10.1093/bjc/azab118

Manral, B., Somani, G., Choo, K. K. R., Conti, M., & Gaur, M. S. (2019). A Systematic survey on cloud forensics challenges, solutions, and future directions. *ACM Computing Surveys*, *52*(6), 1–38. doi:10.1145/3361216

Miller, M.R., Herrera, F., Jun, H. et al. (2020). Personal identifiability of user tracking data during observation of 360-degree VR video. *Scientific Reports. 10*, 17404. doi:10.1038/s41598-020-74486-y

MurrayM. D. (2022). Ready lawyer one: Lawyering in the Metaverse. [Online]. https://ssrn.com/abstract=4082648 doi:10.2139/ssrn.4082648

Mystakidis, S. (2022). Metaverse. *Encyclopedia*, *2*(1), 486–497. doi:10.3390/encyclopedia2010031

NairV.Munilla GarridoG.SongD. (2022). Exploring the unprecedented privacy risks of the metaverse. arXiv:2207.13176. [Online]. Available: https://arxiv.org/pdf/2207.13176.pdf

NingH.WangH.LinY.WangW. (2021). A Survey on metaverse: The state-of-the-art, technologies, applications, and challenges. arXiv:2111.09673. https://arxiv.org/ftp/arxiv/papers/2111/2111.09673.pdf.

Reid, D. (2021). *Who is going to police the metaverse?* Liverpool Hope University. Available at: https://www.hope.ac.uk/news/allnews/who-is-going-to-police-the metaverse.html

Shen, M. (2022). Sexual harassment in the metaverse? Woman alleges rape in virtual world. *USA Today*. https://www.usatoday.com/story/tech/2022/01/31/woman-allegedly-groped-metaverse/9278578002/

Simou, S., Kalloniatis, C., Gritzalis, S., & Mouratidis, H. (2016). A survey on cloud forensics challenges and solutions. *Security and Communication Networks*, *9*(18), 6285–6314. doi:10.1002ec.1688

Sparkes, M. (2021). What is a metaverse? *New Scientist*, *251*(3348), 18.

Stanage, N. (2007). From Second Life to second-degree murder. The Guardian. [Online]. Available: https://www.theguardian.com/commentisfree/2007/jan/16/fromsecondlifetoseconddegr

Statista. (2022). *Dangers of the metaverse according to internet users worldwide in 2021*. Statista. https://www.statista.com/statistics/1288822/metaversedangers/

Techcrunch. (2006). Metaverse breached: Second life customer database hacked. *Techcrunch*. https://techcrunch.com/2006/09/08/metaverse-breached-second-life-customer-database-hacked/

Threatpost. (2022). NFT investors lose $1.7m in OpenSea phishing attack," Threatpost. https://threatpost.com/nft-investors-lose-1-7m-in-opensea-phishing-attack/178558

Time. (2016). Game developer saddened by virtual reality sex assault: 'This must never happen again.' *Time*. https://time.com/4545943/virtual-reality-sex-assault-developer/

Valluripally, S., Gulhane, A., Mitra, R., & Hoque, K. A. (2020). *Attack trees for security and privacy in social virtual reality learning environments. In 2020 IEEE 17th Annual Consumer Communications & Networking Conference*. CCNC., doi:10.1109/CCNC46108.2020.9045724

Wang, Y., Su, Z., Zhang, N., Xing, R., Liu, D., Luan, T. H., & Shen, X. (2022). A survey on metaverse: fundamentals, security, and privacy. arXiv:2203.02662. doi: /arXiv.2203.02662. doi:10.48550

Wu, S., Sun, W., Ding, Z., & Liu, S. (2022). Cloud evidence tracing system: An integrated forensics investigation system for large-scale public cloud platform. *Forensic Science International Digital Investigation*, *41*, 1–9. doi:10.1016/j.fsidi.2022.301391

Zawoad, S., & Hasan, R. (2013). *Cloud forensics: a meta-study of challenges, approaches, and open problems*. arXiv preprint arXiv:1302.6312. https://doi.org//arXiv.1302.6312 doi:10.48550

KEY TERMS AND DEFINITIONS

Brain Computer Interface (BCI): A Human Machine Interface (HMI) technology that establishes a direct link between the brain's neural activity and an external computing device, enabling bidirectional information exchange and control without using traditional physical hardware like a keyboard or mouse.

Cyberbullying: A form of online harassment and intimidation facilitated by digital communication technologies to threaten, embarrass, humiliate, or target individuals or groups through online threats, rude texts, verbal abuse, impersonation, and offensive content.

Non-Fungible Tokens (NFTs): Unique digital assets or tokens that are used to certify ownership and authenticity of digital or physical assets in the metaverse, typically using blockchain technology.

Virtual Avatar: A digital representation of a character that users can embody to navigate and interact with the virtual environment and other users within the metaverse.

Web 3.0: It is the next evolution of the world wide web, a public network built on distributed ledger technology and a semantic architecture, enabling decentralization, democratization, personalization, and immersiveness.

Chapter 11
Machine Learning-Based Prediction Analysis of Unlawful Activities to Aid Law Enforcement

Vijayalakshmi G. V. Mahesh
https://orcid.org/0000-0002-1917-7506
BMS Institute of Technology and Management, India

Shilpa Hiremath
https://orcid.org/0000-0002-1577-8523
BMS Institute of Technology and Management, India

Chandra Prabha R.
https://orcid.org/0000-0003-4236-2782
BMS Institute of Technology and Management, India

ABSTRACT

One of our society's most significant and pervasive issues is crime. Numerous crimes are perpetrated often each day. The development of policing strategies and the implementation of crime prevention and control depend greatly on crime prediction. The most popular prediction technique right now is machine learning. Little research, however, has rigorously contrasted various machine learning approaches for crime prediction. The dataset in this instance consists of the date and the annual crime rate for the corresponding years. The crime rate used in this project is only based on robberies. Utilising historical data, the authors employ the linear and random forest regression algorithms to estimate future crime rates. The algorithm receives the date as input, and the result is the total number of crimes that year.

DOI: 10.4018/979-8-3693-0220-0.ch011

1. INTRODUCTION

Crime poses a serious threat to humanity. They are growing and dispersing quickly and widely. Crime occurs everywhere, in both tiny towns and large cities. There are many distinct forms of crimes, including robbery, manslaughter, assault and false imprisonment. Due to the increase in crime rates, cases must be resolved significantly and more quickly. In order to manage and lessen crime, which has been growing at an increasingly rapid rate, law enforcement has to take necessary measures to control and reduce the crime activities. The primary goal of law enforcement is crime prevention and criminal identification. Due to the vast amount of data available on crime, technology is required so that case solving can be completed more quickly.

The biggest drawback noticed is that as the population grows daily, crimes likewise grow in various locations, making it impossible for officials to anticipate the crime rate with any degree of accuracy. The authorities may not be able to forecast future crimes because they are focused on so many different issues. Even when the authorities and police personnel work to lower the crime rate, they may not fully succeed.

For law authorities, predicting the future crime rate may be challenging. Numerous works have been done in relation to crimes. To aid in the tracking of law enforcement, extensive datasets have been evaluated and information like location and crime nature have been extracted. These databases have been exploited by existing techniques to locate crime hotspots and identify them. There are numerous maps programs that display the precise crime scene as well as the type of crime for every specific city. Despite the fact that crime scenes have been located, there is no information on the day and time the crime really occurred or any methods for reliably predicting future crimes.

It has been established via numerous studies and situations that data science and machine learning may expedite and simplify the task. With the aid of a machine learning(ML) system, this approach aims to forecast crime. The goal of this work would be to create a prediction model. The test dataset will be used to validate the training on the training data set. For the purpose of predicting crime, multiple linear regression and random forest regression is used. By assisting law enforcement organizations in predicting and detecting crime per capita in a community, this work aids in lowering the crime rate.

The rest of the chapter is organized into four sections. Section 2 details about the related works on crime prediction based on machine learning. The process followed in the implementation and the related information is presented in section 3. The experimental results and discussion are provided in section 4. The chapter is finally concluded in section 5.

2. RELATED WORK

To address the issue of crime prediction and to minimize crime, various researchers have offered numerous approaches, and several crime-prediction algorithms have also been proposed. The type of data used and the attributes used for prediction affect the prediction's accuracy.

According to (Bogomolov et al, 2014), mobile network activity was utilized to gather information on human behavior that was then used to predict the hotspot for crime in London with an accuracy of roughly 70%. The key innovation of the suggested method was how it approached the problem of crime prediction by using aggregated and anonymized human behavioral data obtained from mobile network activity. The results of earlier research projects, which either used historical context or offender profiling, reinforced the idea that aggregated human behavioral data collected from the mobile network infrastructure.

The first study to use data mining to analyze and forecast crime was by (Sathyadevan et al, 2014). Here the Naive Bayes algorithm and decision trees were used to predict and categorize crime using data gathered from various websites and newsletters, and it was discovered that Naive Bayes algorithm performed better. The algorithm could identify places with a high likelihood of crime and could depict crime-prone zones.

In order to address issues with various crime datasets, (Yadav et al, 2017) investigated a variety of crime prediction techniques based on Support Vector Machine (SVM) and Artificial Neural Networks (ANN). The algorithms were trained by feeding it data from prior years' record of crimes gathered from a reliable Indian web portal detailing different crimes including murder, kidnapping and abduction, dacoits, robbery, burglary, rape, and other such crimes. A regression model was developed and the crime rate in different states was forecasted using data from Indian statistics, which provides data on numerous crimes.

A review of supervised machine learning algorithms based approaches and unsupervised learning strategies has been provided by (Singh et al,2016). The creation of algorithms for supervised machine learning uses examples from the outside world to create general patterns and assumptions about what will happen to further examples in the future. Algorithms for supervised machine learning classification are designed to classify data based on prior knowledge. In data science issues, classification is commonly used.

As per (Li et al,2014), the crime records produced would show linkages between crime and crime patterns for the goal of knowledge discovery, which would help to improve the predictability of crime. In order to help the fault diagnosis information system to locate precisely the event reports of each protection device, they provided an unsupervised learning technique for the classification of the protection device. According to the automation relaying parameters, the algorithm categorizes the protective devices with little or no samples. The categorization of protective devices distinguishes between devices with the same type from the same company but distinct purposes in addition to grouping them according to the types of various firms.

(Varshitha et al,2017) proposed that there are various methods for predicting crime, including data mining, deep learning, crime casting, and sentiment analysis. It was discovered that each method has some advantages and disadvantages. Every technique produces superior outcomes in a specific situation. Crime was detected using clustering techniques, and crime was predicted using classification techniques.

(Iqbal et al, 2013) conducted an experiment in which K-Means clustering was used, and their performance was assessed based on accuracy. When analyzing the results of several clustering methods, DBSCAN produced the most accurate results, and the KNN classification technique is employed for crime prediction. As a result, this approach aids in more precise and effective crime analysis for law enforcement authorities.

In order to anticipate a future crime using data mining, (Malathi and Santhosh Baboo, 2011) has utilized enhanced Algorithms. Using the data mining programme WEKA, a comparison of the classification methods Naive Bayes and decision tree was carried out. The US Census of 1990 provided the datasets for this investigation.

(Thongsatapornwatana, 2016) suggested that it is important to choose the right data mining techniques in order to maximize the effectiveness of crime detection. The author reviewed the literature on various applications of data mining, particularly those that were used to solve murders. The survey also highlighted the limitations and difficulties of crime data mining. In addition, he gave advice on how to utilize data mining to identify patterns and trends in crime, which will be useful for newcomers doing research on crime data mining.

According to (Cahill and Mulligan, 2007) used Geographically weighted regression(GWR) process to estimate a local model, resulting in a set of mappable parameter estimates and spatially variable t-values of significance. It is discovered that a number of structural factors have associations with crime that differ greatly by place. The findings suggested that the most accurate representation of crime may come from a mixed model that includes both fixed and spatially variable characteristics.

(Morimoto et al., 2019) presented a novel approach for crime prediction and to establish a model flexible enough to apply under different circumstances. To achieve the goal, a information propagation model was built which incorporates a concept of information entropy. This research helped security organizations to address or react to crime occurrence proactively and helps local policy-makers to prevent or manage crime risks, which would eventually improve public security and safety.

KNN, Decision trees, and other algorithms were utilized for crime prediction, as described by (Pratibhaet al., 2020) The major goal here was to emphasize on the value and efficiency of machine learning in forecasting violent crimes occurring in a certain area so that it can be used by police to reduce crime rates in society.

(Shukla et al., 2021) suggested that, different mathematical and statistical models can be utilized to forecast the probability of the crime and crime patterns. Authors aimed to check different statistical parameters and figure out the most common factors that affect crime. The univariate and bivariate exploratory analysis was used for extracting the most dominant features. The Akaike Information Criteria method was used to drop out unimportant attributes followed by testing of model through Mean Absolute Error, Median Squared Error and Root Mean Squared Error techniques. The work concluded that these mathematical and statistical models can aid in the process of making society a safer place to live in.

3. MACHINE LEARNING FOR PREDICTION

The proposed work is implemented using supervised learning machine learning approach (Shalev-Shwartz and Ben-David, 2014) (Zhang et al., 2020) . Supervised learning is a process of providing input data as well as correct output data to the machine learning algorithm which finds a mapping function to map the input variable(x) with the output variable(y) for training. Once the training process is completed, the model is tested using test data that predicts the output of an unknown data. Supervised learning undergoes the following steps:

i. Choosing the training dataset's type.
ii. Data labeling for the training dataset samples.
iii. Divide the training dataset into training and validation runs for the samples.
iv. Derive the input features from samples of the dataset. The features should have sufficient details to enable reliable output prediction by the model.
v. Determine the suitable algorithm to create the model, such as support vector machine(SVM),k nearest neighbor(kNN), linear discriminant analysis(LDA), decision tree(DT), etc.
vi. Execute the algorithm on the training dataset. Sometimes validation sets are needed as the control parameters, which are the subsets of training datasets. The classifier model is created at this stage.
vii. Evaluate the performance of the model by providing the test set using appropriate metrics.

3.1 Regression Problem

Regression is a technique for investigating the relationship between independent variables or features and a dependent variable or outcome. It's used as a method for predictive modeling in machine learning, in which an algorithm is used to predict continuous outcomes. Solving regression problems is one of the most common applications of machine learning models, especially in supervised machine learning(Huang et al., 2020). Algorithms are trained to understand the relationship between independent variables(labeled features) and an outcome(class label) or dependent variable. The model can then be leveraged to predict the outcome of new and unseen input data, or to fill a gap in missing data. Regression analysis is an integral part of any forecasting or predictive model, so is a common method found in machine learning powered predictive analytics. This approach to training models required labelled input and output training data. Machine learning regression models need to understand the relationship between features and outcome variables, so accurately labelled training data is vital. Regression is a key element of predictive modelling, so can be found within many different applications of machine learning. Whether powering financial forecasting or predicting healthcare trends, regression analysis can bring organisations key insight for decision-making. It's already used in different sectors to forecast house prices, stock or share prices, or map salary changes.

4. METHODOLOGY

The methodology section provides information about the process undertaken in "Machine Learning based prediction and analysis of unlawful activities to aid law enforcement".

4.1 Architecture

The system design for the proposed work is illustrated in Figure 1. To start, the dataset was manually prepared. A regression model is developed later to forecast the likelihood of crime once the links between the variables are identified and the data are visualized. Regression models using linear and random forest are utilized here. When compared to other models, such as the Logistic Regression models, the random forest yielded the least amount of inaccuracy. By taking into account several parameters, this regression model forecasts the per capita crime rate that will occur in the future.

4.2 Crime Prediction Dataset

A collection of data is known as a data set (or dataset). In the case of tabular data, a data set relates to one or more database tables, where each row refers to a specific record in the corresponding data set and each column to a specific variable. For the proposed work, the real dataset of crime of earlier years was collected from Kaggle (https://www.kaggle.com/datasets/rajanand/crime-in-india).The dataset contains aggregated counts of different types of crime categorized by the police department of India. The dataset consists of instances or crimes that had been collected across the country. It has four predictive features and one goal feature. The four predictive features are: state, district, crime type and year. The goal feature is the predicted output that correlates to different types of crime. The data in each instance

Figure 1. System design of proposed work

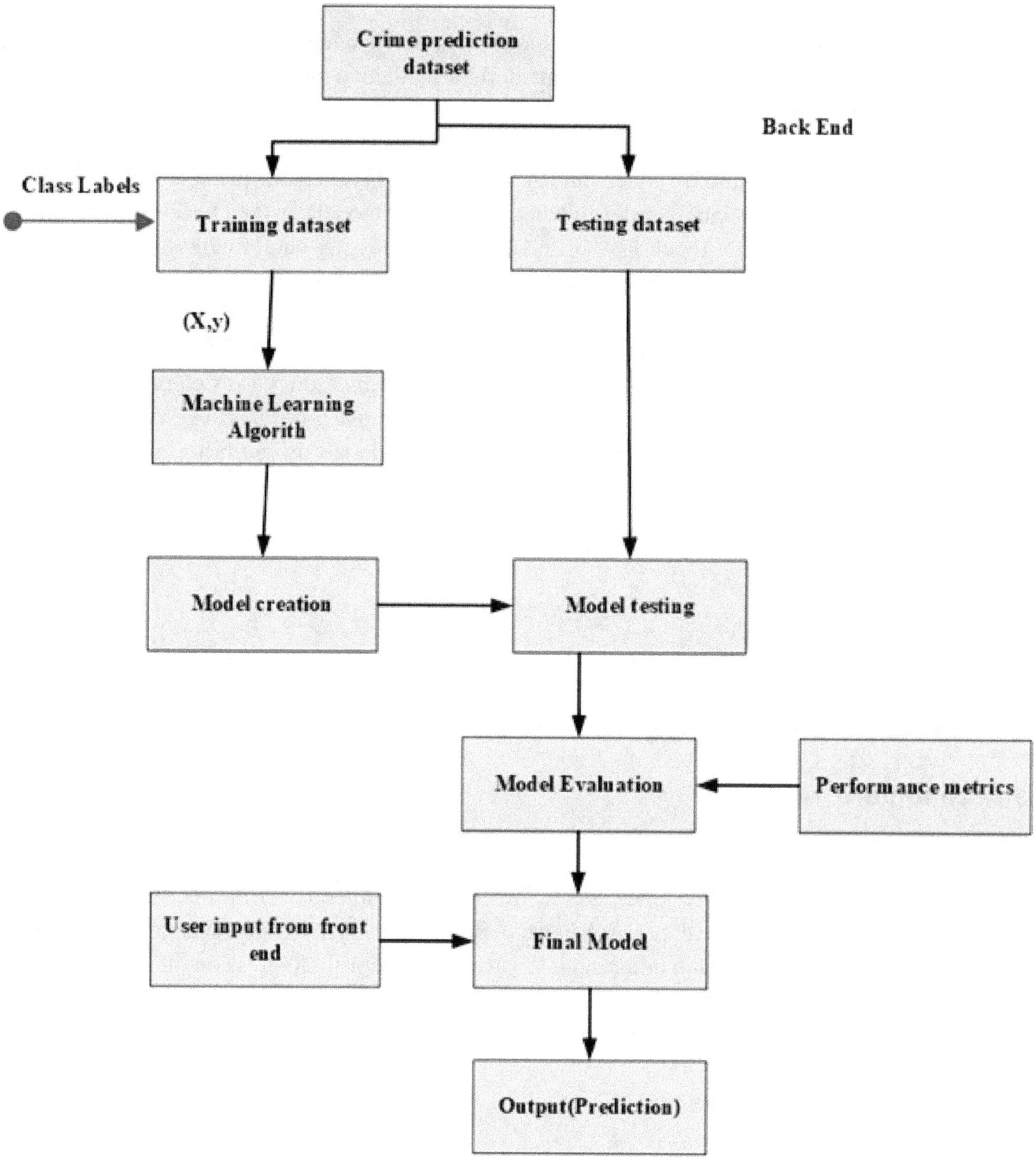

belong to different regions of India. The regions are represented in the form of a number, every number represents its perspective region of India. Snippet of Crime Dataset is displayed in Figure 2.

4.3 Training Data

Training data is an extremely large dataset that is used to train machine learning algorithm to create a predictive model.

Figure 2. Snippet of crime dataset

	A	B	C	D	E	F	G	H	I	J	K	L	M	N	O
1	Id	DISTRICT	STATE-tod	ASSAULT C	DACOITY	DOWRY DI	KIDNAPPI	MAJOR_CI	MURDER	RAPE	RIOTS	ROBBERY	THEFT	total_crim	YEAR
2	1	Ariyalur	Tamil nadu	64	0	1	26	233	27	20	19	9	76	1977	2010
3	2	Chennai	Tamil nadu	45	2	16	47	1858	103	47	60	74	1540	10869	2010
4	3	Chennai rl	Tamil nadu	2	1	2	0	250	0	0	14	58	232	647	2010
5	4	Chennai ci	Tamil nadu	61	1	18	30	1059	86	29	85	102	750	8670	2010
6	5	Coimbator	Tamil nadu	39	11	1	62	664	41	13	83	78	425	4806	2010
7	6	Coimbator	Tamil nadu	35	1	1	22	1202	22	15	23	25	1084	4180	2010
8	7	Cuddalore	Tamil nadu	8	1	8	39	530	58	27	149	16	241	6179	2010
9	8	Dharmapu	Tamil nadu	42	2	6	47	437	59	15	107	25	161	3761	2010
10	9	Dindigul	Tamil nadu	43	4	1	43	644	57	9	81	29	410	5299	2010
11	10	Erode	Tamil nadu	43	3	2	64	681	57	15	39	73	461	6702	2010
12	11	Kanchipura	Tamil nadu	23	2	1	9	494	57	17	102	21	285	5757	2010
13	12	Kanyakum	Tamil nadu	10	3	2	57	441	42	12	0	90	318	4752	2010
14	13	Karur	Tamil nadu	28	1	4	54	379	19	10	23	34	241	2974	2010
15	14	Krishnagiri	Tamil nadu	27	0	5	64	515	58	20	120	14	221	4580	2010
16	15	Madurai	Tamil nadu	62	2	14	58	726	59	17	168	95	348	5348	2010
17	16	Madurai C	Tamil nadu	12	0	11	15	592	34	3	17	77	500	2672	2010
18	17	Nagapatti	Tamil nadu	57	0	1	38	367	50	9	39	18	173	4027	2010
19	18	Namakkal	Tamil nadu	52	6	2	48	487	50	10	70	14	255	4690	2010
20	19	Nilgiris	Tamil nadu	10	0	0	8	115	11	7	18	9	61	1320	2010
21	20	Perambalu	Tamil nadu	16	2	0	10	144	13	5	7	25	93	1536	2010
22	21	Pudukotta	Tamil nadu	42	3	5	54	448	45	7	45	55	250	4808	2010
23	22	Ramnatha	Tamil nadu	14	1	1	61	402	33	16	96	26	181	3462	2010
24	23	Salem	Tamil nadu	165	9	4	140	945	81	53	281	42	221	8634	2010
25	24	Salem City	Tamil nadu	25	1	3	44	473	27	21	32	70	321	3218	2010
26	25	Sivagangai	Tamil nadu	16	3	4	32	310	38	1	21	21	198	2611	2010
27	26	Thanjavur	Tamil nadu	75	4	3	42	1183	82	7	104	141	870	6946	2010

High-quality training data is absolutely necessary to build a high-performing machine learning model, especially in the early stages, but definitely throughout the training process. The features, tags, and relevancy of the training data will be the "textbooks" from which the model will learn.

The training data will be used to train and retrain the model throughout its use because relevant data generally isn't fixed. Human language, word use, and corresponding definitions change over time, so the model will likely need to be updated with retraining periodically.

For good training data, this list needs to be checked off to make sure the dataset is:

i. **Relevant:** Data relevant to the task at hand or the problems that are to be solved is needed.
ii. **Uniform:** All data should come from the same source with the same attributes.
iii. **Representative:** The training data must have the same data points and factors as the data to be analysed.
iv. **Comprehensive:** The training dataset must be large enough for the needs and have the proper scope and range to encompass all of the model's desired use cases.
v. **Diverse:** The dataset should reflect the training and user base, or the results will end up skewed. It is to be ensured that those tasked with training the model have no hidden biases or bring in a third party to audit the criteria.

4.4 Test Data

A test set in machine learning is a secondary (or tertiary) data set that is used to test a machine learning program after it has been trained on an initial training data set. The idea is that predictive models always have some sort of unknown capacity that needs to be tested out, as opposed to analysed from a programming perspective.

4.5 Training and Testing the Model

This is the stage where the ML algorithm is trained by feeding datasets. This is the stage where the learning takes place. Consistent training can significantly improve the prediction rate of the ML model. The weights of the model must be initialized randomly. This way the algorithm will learn to adjust the weights accordingly. A training model is a dataset that is used to train an ML algorithm. It consists of the sample output data and the corresponding sets of input data that have an influence on the output. The training model is used to run the input data through the algorithm to correlate the processed output against the sample output. The result from this correlation is used to modify the model. This iterative process is called "model fitting". The accuracy of the training dataset or the validation dataset is critical for the precision of the model. Model training in machine language is the process of feeding an ML algorithm with data to help identify and learn good values for all attributes involved. There is no definite period or a prefixed set of iterations for training an ML model. The factors influencing the duration of training could be the quality of training data, proper definition of the measures of success and complexity of model selection. Factors like method of training, allocation of weights and complexity of the model also play an important role. Other factors that are extraneous to the data or the models like computing power and skilled resources can also have an impact on the training duration. There is always a scope for optimizing training a model as the number of parameters influencing its duration are too many. The trained model is tested using test dataset and accuracy is calculated.

4.6 Model Evaluation

A machine learning model cannot be 100% effective; otherwise, it would be a biased model. It also incorporates the ideas of underfitting and overfitting. Although accuracy on training data must be attained, it is equally crucial to achieve a true and approximative result on unobserved data; otherwise, the model is useless. Therefore, it is necessary to test the model on many metrics in order to better optimize the performance before building and deploying a generalized model. Multiple measures are not necessary if one metric is ideal. To comprehend the pros and disadvantages of assessment metrics since various evaluation metrics are suitable for various datasets.

The evaluation metrics(Alzoubi et al., 2022) used in the proposed work for evaluation are presented here:

i. **Mean Absolute Error (MAE):** MAE is a relatively straightforward technique that finds the absolute difference between actual and predicted values. It is most robust to outliers.

$$MAE = \frac{1}{n}\sum_{i=1}^{n}\left|y_i - \hat{y}_i\right| \tag{1}$$

n = Total number of data points

y = Actual Output
ŷ = Predicted Output

ii. **Mean Squared Error (MSE):** MSE is the widely used metric that finds its use in Regression problems. It computes the square of the difference between actual and predicted value. MSE represents the squared distance between actual and predicted output values. It is computed to avoid the cancellation of negative terms and it is the benefit of MSE.

$$MSE = \frac{1}{n}\sum_{i=1}^{n}\left(y_i - \hat{y}_i\right)^2 \tag{2}$$

iii. **R Squared (R^2):** R^2, also known as Coefficient of Determination or Goodness of fit is a metric that indicates the performance of the regression model rather than loss in an absolute sense that how many wells did the model perform. The metrics MAE and MSE are dependent on the context whereas R^2 score is independent of it. Thus, with the R2 metric there exists a baseline regression model to compare a model which none of the other metrics provided. Basically, R^2 calculates how the regression line is better than a mean line. Hence,

$$R^2 = 1 - \frac{SS_r}{SS_m} \tag{3}$$

where

SS_r = Squared sum error of regression line $= \sum_{i=1}^{n}\left(y_i - \hat{y}_i\right)^2$

SS_m = Square sum error of mean line $= \sum_{i=1}^{n}\left(y_i - \bar{y}_i\right)^2$

A value of $R^2 = 0$, indicates the worst performance where as a value of 1 shows a perfection.

iv. **Root mean squared error(RMSE):** RMSE is the average root-squared difference between the real value and the predicted value. It is obtained by computing the square root of MSE. It is required for RMSE to be as low as possible. Lower the RMSE value, better the model with its predictions. A Higher RMSE indicates the presence of large deviations between the predicted and actual value.

$$RMSE = \sqrt{\frac{1}{n}\sum_{i=1}^{n}\left(y_i - \hat{y}_i\right)^2} \tag{4}$$

4.7 User Input from Front End

To carry out this work, a front end is developed using Flask and HTML. The user can enter the input values in the front end. The collected data from the user is provided as input to the finalized algorithm to predict the crime. Finally, the predicted crime output is displayed on the website as illustrated in Figure 3.

Figure 3. User input in the website

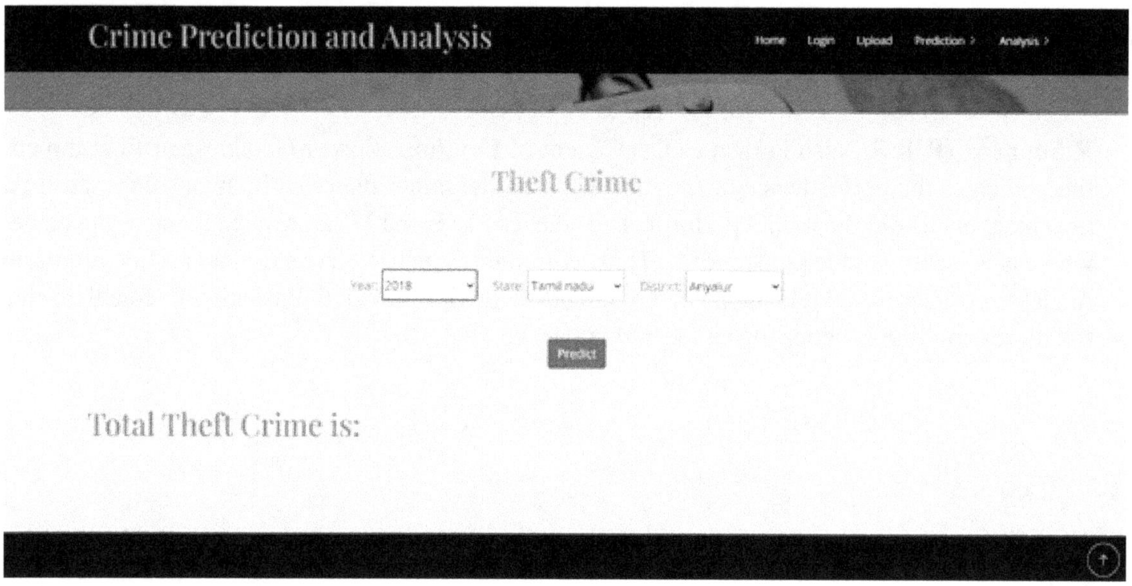

5. IMPLEMENTATION OF PROPOSED METHODOLOGY

This section presents the details of the implementation of the methodology proposed. The work on Machine learning based prediction and analysis of unlawful activities to aid law enforcement was implemented in two phases using Python:

i. Phase-1: Back-End
ii. Phase-2: Front-End

and finally integrated Front-End and Back-End

5.1 Phase One: Back-End

Data Collection

Data collection is the first real step towards the development of a machine learning model. This is a crucial phase since how well the model performs will be influenced by how much more and better data

Figure 4. Crime dataset

Id	DISTRICT	STATE-todel	ASSAULT ON WOMEN	DACOITY	DOWRY DEATHS	KIDNAPPING AND ABDUCTION	MAJOR_CRIMES_TOTAL	MURDER	RAPE	RIOTS	ROBBERY	THEFT	total_
1	Ariyalur	Tamil nadu	64.0	0.0	1.0	26.0	233.0	27	20	19.0	9.0	76	1977
2	Chennai	Tamil nadu	45.0	2.0	16.0	47.0	1858.0	103	47	60.0	74.0	1540	10869
3	Chennai rly	Tamil nadu	2.0	1.0	2.0	0.0	250.0	0	0	14.0	58.0	232	647
4	Chennai city	Tamil nadu	61.0	1.0	18.0	30.0	1059.0	86	29	85.0	102.0	750	8670
5	Coimbatore	Tamil nadu	39.0	11.0	1.0	62.0	664.0	41	13	83.0	78.0	425	4806
6	Coimbatore City	Tamil nadu	35.0	1.0	1.0	22.0	1202.0	22	15	23.0	25.0	1084	4180
7	Cuddalore	Tamil nadu	8.0	1.0	8.0	39.0	530.0	58	27	149.0	16.0	241	6179
8	Dharmapuri	Tamil nadu	42.0	2.0	6.0	47.0	437.0	59	15	107.0	25.0	161	3761
9	Dindigul	Tamil nadu	43.0	4.0	1.0	43.0	644.0	57	9	81.0	29.0	410	5299
10	Erode	Tamil nadu	43.0	3.0	2.0	64.0	681.0	57	15	39.0	73.0	461	6702
11	Kanchipuram	Tamil nadu	23.0	2.0	1.0	9.0	494.0	57	17	102.0	21.0	285	5757
12	Kanyakumari	Tamil nadu	10.0	3.0	2.0	57.0	441.0	42	12	0.0	90.0	318	4752

we can collect. The data can be collected using a variety of methods, including manual interventions and web scraping.

A snippet of the dataset used in the project is displayed in Figure 4. The dataset used in this project is taken from Kaggle and used in .csv format. The dataset consists of different features(columns), which are described below.

i. **State:** Shows the name of state in India
ii. **District:** Shoes the name of district in the state of India.
iii. **Year:** Shows the year of occurrence of crime (2001-2018)
iv. **Murder:** Total number of murder cases.
v. **Assault:** Total number of assault cases.
vi. **Theft:** Total number of theft cases.
vii. **Total Crime:** Total number of cases.

Data Pre-Processing

Preprocessing is required to handle the missing data, delete the non-required columns/rows and to standardize the data. To do this a list of column names is prepared that needs to be retained. Next, all the columns are dropped except for the columns that need to be retained.

Training and Building Model

After preprocessing, the data is prepared for training and building the model for which two datasets are created, one for training and other for testing. So, the dataset is split into two with a ratio of 70:30 at random to assure that datasets are a representative sample (e.g. random sample) of the original dataset, which in turn, should be a representative sample of observations from the problem domain. Thus 30 percent of the dataset will be allocated to the test set and 70 percent will be allocated to the training set. This work uses two machine learning algorithms that include Linear regression and Random Forest Regression for crime prediction.

Case One: Linear Regression

In the proposed work the Scikit Learn Linear Regression function is used to create a linear regression model for crime prediction. This includes (i)initializing the model (ii)train the model with the input(training) data and (iii)make predictions.

Case Two: Random Forest Regression

The scikit-learn Python machine learning library provides an implementation of Random Forest algorithm. It is available in modern versions of the library. Here Random Forest Regressor(RFR) is imported from the ensemble library of sklearn to create a regressor object using the RFR class constructor. The parameters considered during training include number of estimators, error criteria and random state.

Once the models: linear and random forest regression are trained, the model is tested for making the predictions.

Prediction

After the model is built using the above process, prediction is done using a model using predict(xtest), where xtest is the testing dataset. Next, the accuracy is calculated using accuracy_score imported from metrics - metrics. accuracy_score (ytest, predicted). In the actual dataset, we chose only 3 features: State, District and Year. The prediction part will give us the total number of murder cases, theft cases, assault cases and number of cases in total once confident enough to take the trained and tested model into the production-ready environment.

Phase Two: Front-End

The results will be visualized on the webpage where the user will be able to provide the required details in the input field. The machine learning model will analyze the data and the predicted value will be printed.

The home page is created on the website for prediction which is displayed in Figure 5. The page was created using HTML and CSS. Two buttons have been implemented in the navigation bar 'HOME' and 'LOGIN' to take the user to the corresponding pages.

The login page is shown in Figure 6 that can be accessed by pressing the **login** button. The login page a user can log in using the credentials: username and password. Once the user has logged into the website, a page is opened where a file can be uploaded as shown in Figure 7. The dataset that has to be used for prediction should be uploaded here. An upload button is implemented using input type as submit to upload the file once the file has been selected. Once the data is uploaded, it leads to the prediction page, where an option is available to enter year, state and district based on which the predictions are made which is illustrated in Figure 8.

Figure 5. Home page

Figure 6. Login page

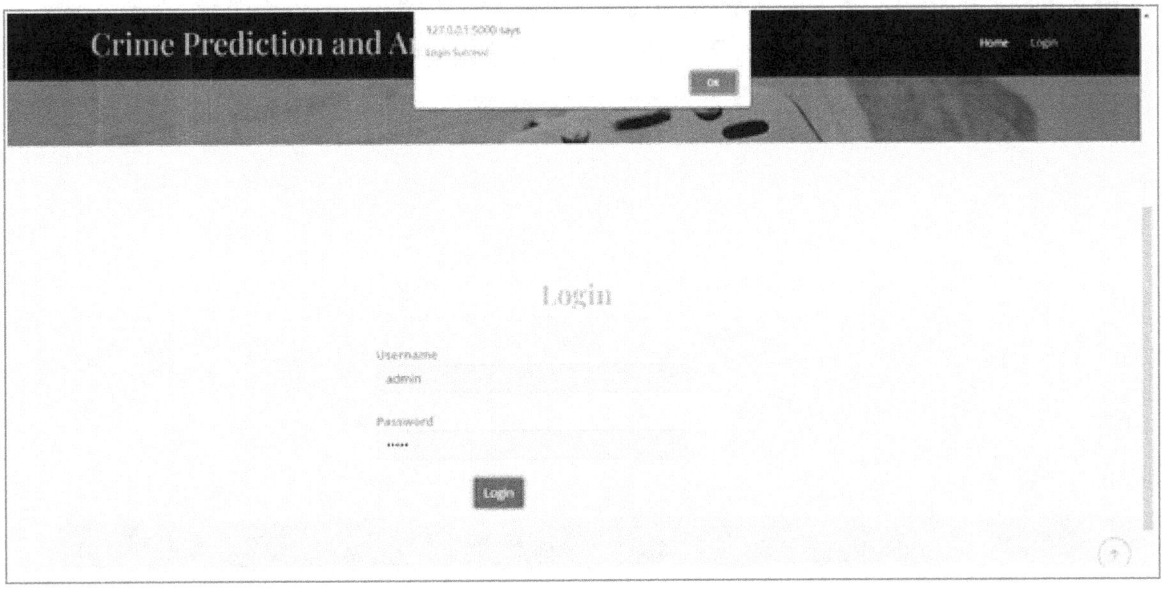

Finally, the front end and back end are integrated to carry out the complete task of learning and prediction. The complete work was implemented using a Pentium IV 2.4 GHz system with hard disk and Ram capacity of 40GB and 4 GB respectively. Python version 3.8.0 was used with machine learning packages NumPy, Pandas, Sklearn, Flask, PymySql using Notepad++, Jupyter Notebook.

Figure 7. Upload page

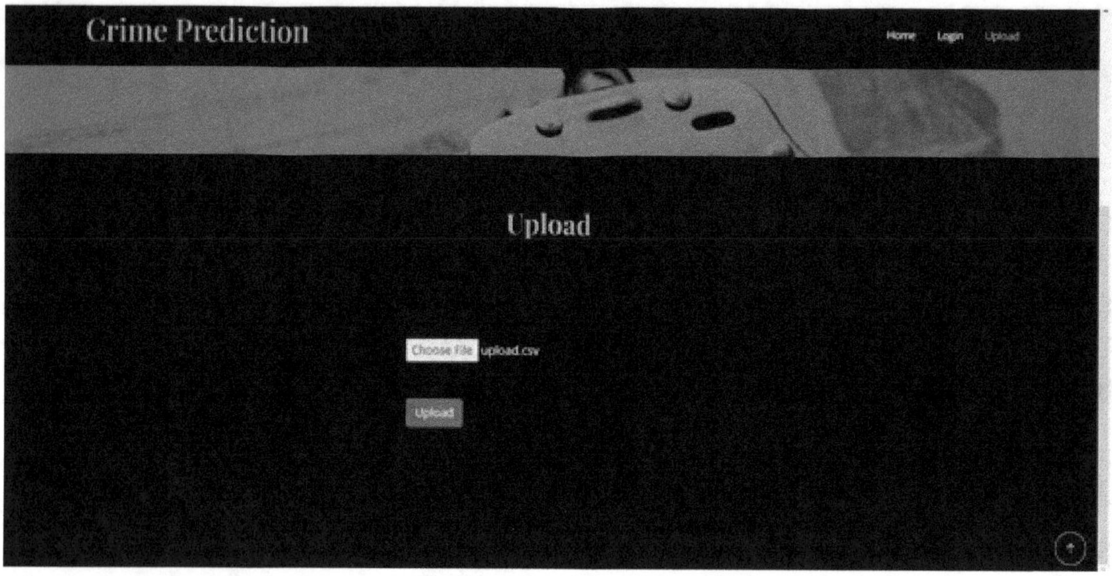

Figure 8. Prediction page

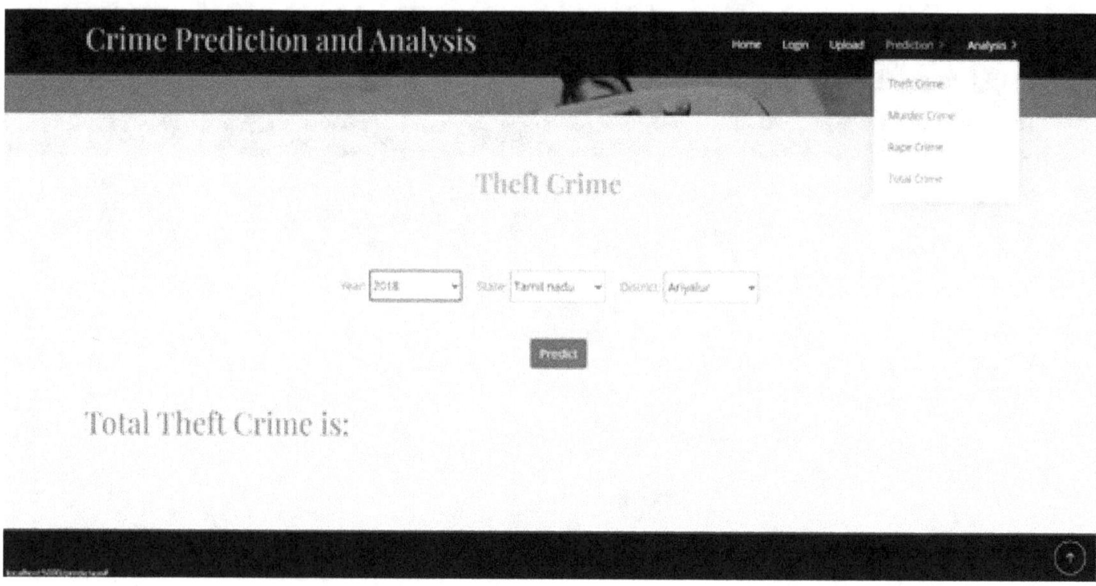

6. RESULTS AND DISCUSSION

The results of the work Machine Learning based prediction and analysis of unlawful activities to aid law enforcement was implemented according to the process flow indicated in Figure 2. As per the flow, the crime data was analyzed and the performance metrics were computed using the equations (1) through (4) as tabulated in Table 1

Table 1. Performance parameters

Performance Parameters	Linear Regression	Random Forest Regression
Mean Absolute Error	1967.42	346.58
Mean Squared Error	10760559.47	872273.37
R^2 Score (Accuracy)	88.73%	92.61%
Root mean Squared Error	3280.33	933.95

Figure 9. Crime prediction based on states

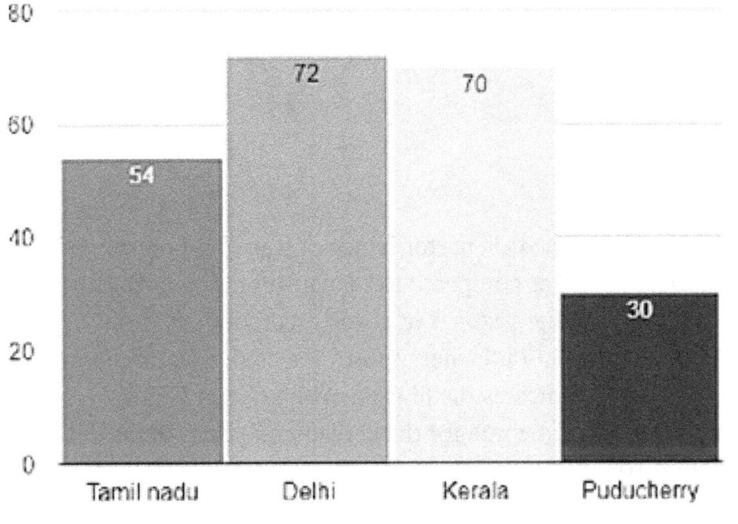

Figure 10. Crime prediction based on year

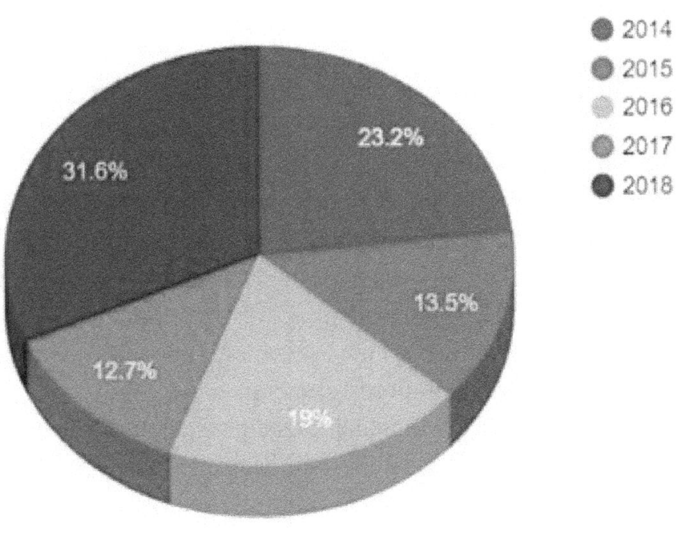

Figure 11. Total crime prediction based on year and place

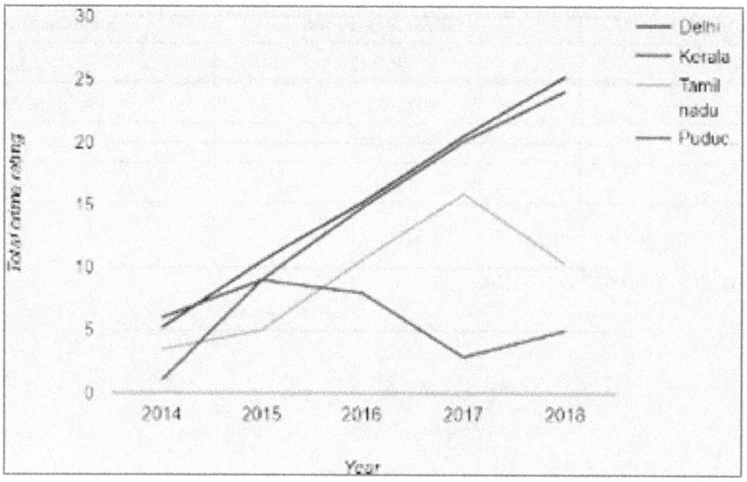

The results presented indicates the best performance of Random Forest regression that provided a R^2 value of 92.61 which is close to 100 as compared to Linear Regression. Also the MSE, RMSE and MAE is lower in case of Random Forest regression. For crime prediction Analysis, years from 2014-2018 and states Tamil nadu, Delhi, Kerala and Puducherry were selected, The prediction rate based on states is provided in Figure 9. The figure indicates the highest crime rate in Delhi.

The model also predicted the crime rate for the considered years, the result indicated highest rate in 2018 as depicted in Figure 10.

Further, the model was used to predict the crime based on year and the location and is illustrated in Figure 11. The rate is high in Delhi in the year 2018.

7. CONCLUSION

Crime prediction plays an important role in society. Crime prediction intends to reduce crime occurrences. With the help of machine learning technology, it has become easy to find out relation and patterns among various data. The work here mainly revolving around predicting the type of crime and crime per-capita which may happen in future. Using the concept of machine learning a model is built using training data set that has undergone data cleaning and data transformation using Linear Regression and Random Forest Algorithm. The model predicts the type of crime and Data visualization helps in analysis of data set and prediction of crimes. The proposed work was tested on dataset acquired from Kaggle. The results indicate that the proposed work was able to predict crime with an accuracy of 88.73% using Linear regression and 92.61% using Random Forest regression.

Along with the present scope of our work, which is the prediction of the number of crimes occurring in an area, we can also predict the exact location of the crime taking place as a future scope. Also the accuracy of frequent item-sets and predict based on different test datasets can be tested. So, the system will automatically learn the changing patterns in crime by examining the crime patterns. Also, the crime factors change over time. By shifting through the crime data, new factors that lead to crime can be identified.

REFERENCES

Alzoubi, H. M., Sahawneh, N., AlHamad, A. Q., Malik, U., Majid, A., & Atta, A. (2022, October). Analysis Of Cost Prediction In Medical Insurance Using Modern Regression Models. In *2022 International Conference on Cyber Resilience (ICCR)* (pp. 1-10). IEEE. 10.1109/ICCR56254.2022.9995926

Bogomolov, A., Lepri, B., Staiano, J., Oliver, N., Pianesi, F., & Pentland, A. (2014, November). Once upon a crime: towards crime prediction from demographics and mobile data. In *Proceedings of the 16th international conference on multimodal interaction* (pp. 427-434). 10.1145/2663204.2663254

Cahill, M., & Mulligan, G. (2007). Using geographically weighted regression to explore local crime patterns. *Social Science Computer Review*, *25*(2), 174–193. doi:10.1177/0894439307298925

Huang, J. C., Ko, K. M., Shu, M. H., & Hsu, B. M. (2020). Application and comparison of several machine learning algorithms and their integration models in regression problems. *Neural Computing & Applications*, *32*(10), 5461–5469. doi:10.100700521-019-04644-5

Iqbal, R., Murad, M. A. A., Mustapha, A., Panahy, P. H. S., & Khanahmadliravi, N. (2013). An experimental study of classification algorithms for crime prediction. *Indian Journal of Science and Technology*, *6*(3), 4219–4225. doi:10.17485/ijst/2013/v6i3.6

Li, B., Guo, Y., Wu, Y., Chen, J., Yuan, Y., & Zhang, X. (2014, September). An unsupervised learning algorithm for the classification of the protection device in the fault diagnosis system. In *2014 China International Conference on Electricity Distribution (CICED)* (pp. 817-823). IEEE. 10.1109/CICED.2014.6991823

Malathi, A., & Santhosh Baboo, S. (2011). An enhanced algorithm to predict a future crime using data mining. *International Journal of Computer Applications*, *21*(1), 1–6. doi:10.5120/2478-3335

Morimoto, S., Kawamukai, H., & Shin, K. (2019, August). Prediction of crime occurrence using information propagation model and gaussian process. In *2019 14th Asia Joint Conference on Information Security (AsiaJCIS)* (pp. 80-87). IEEE. 10.1109/AsiaJCIS.2019.000-2

Pratibha, Akanksha Gahalot, Uprant, Suraina Dhiman, Lokesh Chouhan, "Crime Prediction and Analysis", Institute of Electronics and Electricals Engineers, February 2020.

Sathyadevan, S., Devan, M. S., & Gangadharan, S. S. (2014, August). Crime analysis and prediction using data mining. In *2014 First international conference on networks & soft computing (ICNSC2014)* (pp. 406-412). IEEE. 10.1109/CNSC.2014.6906719

Shalev-Shwartz, S., & Ben-David, S. (2014). *Understanding machine learning: From theory to algorithms*. Cambridge university press. doi:10.1017/CBO9781107298019

Shukla, A., Katal, A., Raghuvanshi, S., & Sharma, S. (2021, June). Criminal Combat: Crime Analysis and Prediction Using Machine Learning. In *2021 International Conference on Intelligent Technologies (CONIT)* (pp. 1-5). IEEE. 10.1109/CONIT51480.2021.9498397

Singh, A., Thakur, N., & Sharma, A. (2016, March). A review of supervised machine learning algorithms. In *2016 3rd international conference on computing for sustainable global development (INDIACom)* (pp. 1310-1315). IEEE.

Thongsatapornwatana, U. (2016, January). A survey of data mining techniques for analyzing crime patterns. In *2016 Second Asian Conference on Defence Technology (ACDT)* (pp. 123-128). IEEE. 10.1109/ACDT.2016.7437655

Varshitha, D. N., Vidyashree, K. P., Aishwarya, P., & Janya, T. S., KR, D. G., & Sahana, R. (2017). Paper on Different Approaches for Crime Prediction system. [IJERT]. *International Journal of Engineering Research & Technology (Ahmedabad).*

Yadav, S., Timbadia, M., Yadav, A., Vishwakarma, R., & Yadav, N. (2017, April). Crime pattern detection, analysis & prediction. In *2017 International conference of Electronics, Communication and Aerospace Technology (ICECA)* (Vol. 1, pp. 225-230). IEEE. 10.1109/ICECA.2017.8203676

Zhang, X., Liu, L., Xiao, L., & Ji, J. (2020). Comparison of machine learning algorithms for predicting crime hotspots. *IEEE Access : Practical Innovations, Open Solutions*, *8*, 181302–181310. https://www.kaggle.com/datasets/rajanand/crime-in-india. doi:10.1109/ACCESS.2020.3028420

Chapter 12
Investigating Forensic Evidence in Metaverse: A Comparative Analytical Study

Ramy Metwally El-Kady
https://orcid.org/0000-0003-2208-7576
Police Academy, Egypt

ABSTRACT

The chapter deals with the issue of investigating forensic evidence in metaverse. The importance of the chapter stems from its handling of the Metaverse technology, as one of the most prominent technological topics on the global scene at present, which is expected to shine in the coming times as the most prominent form of the development of the internet, which moves humanity to new technological dimensions. Spatial and temporal boundaries. The importance of this chapter is evident in light of the legislative vacuum that exists in the face of all forms of violations that occur in the Metaverse. The chapter aims to shed light on ways to collect digital evidence in the Metaverse. The chapter concluded with a set of recommendations, most notably: the need for concerted international efforts to amend international conventions on cybercrime, led by the Budapest Convention, or to aspire to develop a new international convention that regulates the responsibility of Metaverse service providers and obliges them to comply with cooperation in combating crimes.

INTRODUCTION

Metaverse is one of the vast technological transformations that humanity is witnessing during the twenty-first century. This new technology launched by Meta or Facebook previously, without a doubt represents a great revolution in human life. It transforms the individual from a user of technology, such as the Internet, to a participant and contributor to its development through the use of virtual reality tools that allow him to access the Internet and transform it into a community or virtual environment in which the sexes can live and interact with others in a new life experience that is sure to turn the life of humanity upside down (Marshall, 2023: 1).

DOI: 10.4018/979-8-3693-0220-0.ch012

There is no doubt that the current witness indicates the extent of the interest of the countries of the world in this technology to find some countries are moving to adopt their virtual experiments on the application of the Metaverse technology; Japan, the United States, South Korea, Singapore, and Indonesia (Egyptian Cabinet Information and Decision Support Center report, 2022: 55), and some other countries are developing strategies to expand the use of this technology; As Dubai's strategy for Metaverse in the UAE, third countries are starting to enhance their experiences in using this technology, such as Egypt.

Positive economic indicators highlight the trend of the global economy towards expanding the use of this technology; According to Some international estimates, the market for Metaverse is estimated to be $39 billion in 2021 and $47 billion in 2022 and is expected to rise during 2023 to $56.6 billion until reaching $679 billion in 2030 (Egyptian Cabinet Information and Decision Support Center report, 2022: 6), which highlights the positive economic outlook associated with Metaverse technology and its significant impact on the global economy(El-Kady, 2023: 5).

Amid the growing optimism of the majority of supporters of this technology, some expect the potential for VR environments (the Metaverse) to become new environments for criminal activity (Marshall, 2023: 1), so some question whether the metaverse opens new dimensions to the already known Internet criminality, and expect the danger of a quantitative increase of criminality in the Internet, but only low potential for the development of completely new forms of criminality (Laue, 2011: 19).

Other concerns have emerged about the appearance of some types of virtual crimes created by this technology, and then questions have become about how to prove this new type of virtual crime and collect and extract the evidence obtained about it. In light of the Metaverse technology, which opens the way to enter a virtual world of 3D using virtual reality (VR) and augmented reality (AR) tools, as well as the risks of privacy violations for users in light of the novelty of this technology and it is still under development (Abdel Majeed, 2023:76), with the expectation that the potential threat of crime in the world of Metaverse will be a concern in human reality; Given its great similarity to the real world, the real world can be influenced by events that take place in the virtual world (Seo et al., 2023:9468).

THE IMPORTANCE OF THE STUDY

The study focuses on the Metaverse, which is expected to shine during the coming period as the most prominent image of the development of the Internet, which will move humanity to new technological dimensions(Marshall, 2023: 1), despite the existence of legal provisions governing the confrontation of crimes in cyberspace, However, these rules are perceived to be incapable of confronting modern criminal phenomena across Metaverse, which are based on non-traditional alphabets and different elements in terms of people, facts, and spatial and temporal limits (Jibril, 2023: 103).

The importance of this study also is evident in light of the legislative vacuum that exists in the face of all forms of violations that occur in the world of Metaverse, There is no doubt that the current criminal laws are idle in the face of successive technological developments that cannot be dealt with criminally, except through existing criminal provisions due to the principle of criminal legality, that means only the law can define a crime and prescribe a penalty, not to mention that all criminal proceedings to confront all forms of violations that occur in the world of the Metaverse must be by law due to the same principle (procedural legitimacy), Metaverse is seen as taking the world to different and unconventional horizons that will undoubtedly raise unlimited problems from the perspective of criminal law(El-Kady, 2023: 6).

It also highlights the importance of researching digital evidence in this new virtual world in light of the new means used in accessing it, which are virtual or augmented reality tools, mobile phones, and gaming platforms, where this technology uses devices and tools for perception, sensation, and recall, such as Glasses, gloves, jackets, sensors, and sensors combine Internet of Things (IoT), VR, AR, and 3D technology.

It is therefore expected that this issue will become more important with the expected developments of the Metaverse when the users will be capable of engaging in any activity and will be capable of handling anything they need from one place. When the Metaverse reaches the ideal state, it can be applied to anything, and the Metaverse will become the new hypothetical conception of human life.

Although no cases related to Metaverse have yet been brought before the courts, the use of this technology is expected to be problematic, including the digital forensics of Metaverse. This is in light of the rapid technological changes in which the world is moving towards a total dependence on Metaverse and rapid steps to the stage of virtual life.

PROBLEMS OF STUDY

Metaverse raises several legal problems in the context of criminal law, most notably: the lack of criminal provisions related to this technology and offending behaviors committed through it, in addition to the inadequacy of traditional criminal adaptations for crimes committed through Metaverse technology, in particular crimes of assault on persons, as well as for the time and place conditions in Metaverse crimes.

Metaverse has created a new concept of the crime scene, in that the conduct of a single actor may have an effect in several places at a single moment, unlike the temporal dimension of the act, which varies from state to state due to the timing between states, with the consequence that the legal description of the act differs(Jibril, 2023: 104), the changing and volatile nature of this new virtual space will undoubtedly affect the reliability of digital evidence of new crimes within it, which will undoubtedly reflect on how digital evidence is collected and extracted in this virtual world.

STUDY INQUIRIES

The study raises many questions related to:

- How do crimes occur in the world of Metaverse?
- What are the types of these crimes?
- Is it different from other crimes that occur in cyberspace?
- Does the special nature of Metaverse affect the nature and form of digital evidence from crimes occurring in this virtual space?
- Will digital evidence in Metaverse be affected by this nature?
- Will digital evidence from crimes in Metaverse differ from other digital evidence in ordinary cyberspace?
- What are the methods and procedures for collecting forensic evidence from Metaverse crimes?
- What are the limits of law enforcement authorities in this world run by private companies?

- What are the limits of cooperation between these companies and law enforcement authorities in the Metaverse world?
- Will law enforcement agencies have the ability and powers to enforce the state's laws in Metaverse, which are controlled by the various virtual platforms affiliated with private companies?
- What are the limits of cooperation between these companies and law enforcement authorities in the world of Metaverse?
- Will law enforcement challenges about social media platforms become the same, or will they create more significant legislative, executive, and operational challenges in the field of prosecution, seizure procedures, and evidence extraction?

Other legal questions related to the subject of the study, imposed by the special nature of the Metaverse technology, which led some to argue that Metaverse may bring new dimensions to the concept of cybercrime and that there is a possibility that there is some risk of increasing types of cybercrime and that there is a possibility of some risk of increasing types of cybercrimes, it is also expected that entirely new types of such crimes will be developed.

Although most of the above questions are not answered at this time, it is expected that shortly, these answers will be present in light of the rapid developments in the Metaverse world, and the danger of this world is that more human depends on technology, The more fertile the space for the growing number of virtual crimes envisaged in this new world, the more important it is to examine the role of digital evidence in the world of Metaverse; This is what human life will look like in this new virtual world.

All of the above questions, from the researcher's point of view, can be answered at present that Metaverse, like the virtual cyber environment, any crime that falls within it, is a cybercrime to which all legal rules of criminal proof apply in the virtual environment. All the legal rules concerning the admissibility and reliability of this evidence before the criminal courts also apply.

OBJECTIVES OF THE STUDY

The research mainly aims to study the subject of digital forensics in Metaverse, and branch from this goal a set of sub-goals, most notably:

A- Shed light on the Metaverse technology, its dimensions, characteristics, and risks of its use.
B- Investigate the criminal patterns that can arise in the Metaverse technology and ways to counter them.
C- Highlight ways to collect and extract digital evidence in the Metaverse technology.

STUDY HYPOTHESES

The study hypothesizes that the evolution toward Web3 creates an environment that may have severe implications for crimes in the metaverse as well as severely diminishing law enforcement's ability to apprehend suspects who commit them, and that affects the process of collecting digital evidence of crimes in Metaverse, which is expected to face difficulty, given the novelty of this technology, and the development and integration of its elements.

Law enforcement agencies expect to face other difficulties due to the 3D nature of the metaverse, which affects the process of collecting data from different sources, such as user devices, service providers' servers, and the Metaverse platform itself, and due to the massive data needed to be analyzed from these sources, and the new tools which are designed and utilized to collect data from these modern devises and platforms (Europol, 2021:20).

In addition, the presentation of the evidence which was gathered from the crime scene in Metaverse in 3D form presented to the courts, may lose some information or alter its content when presented in a 2D paper form.

Add to that, the international interest in this new technology, which may tempt criminal elements to exploit it to commit various criminal activities for profit (Europol, 2021:13), which will place the burden on investigators and criminal justice agencies to confront these crimes as a priority and collect the evidence of them.

DIFFICULTIES OF THE STUDY

The difficulties of the study center on the novelty of its subject, as it deals with the Metaverse technology as one of the latest current technologies, the accompanying occurrence of some new criminal patterns that occur in its environment, and the difficulties facing law enforcement agencies in collecting and extracting evidence obtained from their commission, as well as the lack of Arabic literature dealing with the subject of the study.

STUDY METHODOLOGY

The methodology of the study is the use of the analytical descriptive approach, which deals with the phenomenon of the Metaverse in all its aspects and dimensions, with the use of the comparative method through the review of comparative experiments organized on this subject, and the analytical descriptive method is defined as: "To study the phenomenon as it exists in reality and describe it closely and express it qualitatively or quantitatively to reach conclusions that contribute to understand and develop this reality" (Obeidat et al., 1996), this approach aims to research and analyze Metaverse from its legal aspects, and the preparation of this study has been assisted by available legal references, from general literature in the field of criminal law or specialized in the subject of the study, whether Arab or foreign references related to the subject of the study.

STUDY PLAN

The detailed plan of the study follows two requirements:

- **The first part** deals with the essence of the Metaverse in two sections, the first of which presents the definition of the Metaverse and its characteristics, and the second section deals with the dangers of Metaverse technology in criminal terms.

- **The second part** presents the digital evidence in the world of Metaverse and the procedures for its collection and extraction, in three sections. Section I presents the definition and characteristics of digital evidence, Section II deals with the procedures for collecting digital evidence, its legitimacy, and its admissibility before a criminal judge, and Section III deals with the authority of digital evidence and international cooperation in its collection.

INTRODUCTION TO METAVERSE

Definition of Metaverse

Many idiomatic definitions describe Metaverse according to how researchers look at it, some of them focus on considering it an information network, and a developed model of the Internet, and this is the perspective of Mark Zuckerberg who defines it as the immersive embodied Internet, and the thing that people can jump to or achieve it through virtual reality or augmented reality when international interest is aroused in it" (Chayka, 2021).

Rabindra Ratan (Associate Professor of Media and Information at Michigan State University) defines it as a huge and interconnected network of virtual spaces", and there is another trend that defines it as a digital platform, as some go to define it as a completely new platform or framework that meets the physical and virtual worlds (Li, B. J. et al., 2022).

Some define it as: "a digital platform that is very similar to the real world and connected to it extensively, to which people can enter or bring virtual elements through a device that acts as an intermediary through the concept of digital twinning" (Seo et al., 2023: 9468).

It can be defined as: "A parallel 3D digital virtual world, which facilitates the user to log in it with the help of certain tools, and by using an animated avatar that represents him (avatar), to perform some operations such as shopping, meeting people, games, and many other activities without moving from his place." (Jibril, 2023: 16).

Others define it as: "A virtual world in which objects can appear alive and live as if they were real. It is a combination of virtual reality, augmented reality, mixed reality, and the web". (Salem, 2022: 396).

The metaverse is often described as a hypothetical iteration of the internet as a single, universal virtual world that presents the user with an immersive experience that feels 'real', usually through the use of a headset. In its very recent definition, it can blur the lines between the physical and virtual world to create a single blended, extended, or mixed reality. As a result, the metaverse is now just focused on virtual reality (VR) but is increasingly being defined in terms of augmented reality (AR) or extended or mixed reality (XR) (Europol, 2022: 7).

In terms of linguistic meaning, the word "Metaverse" means the metaphysical world, and it consists of two parts: the first is "meta" (meaning beyond, or the most descriptive), and the second "Verse" is coined from "Universe" and means "beyond the world" (Khalifa, 2022:8). The term was used for the first time in the 1992 science fiction novel "Snow Crash" by Neil Stephenson, in which humans, as avatars, interact with each other and with software, in a virtual 3D space similar to the real world (Sparkes, 2021: 18).

Characteristics of Metaverse

It is clear from the previous definition some distinct characteristics of the Metaverse technique, the most prominent of which are the following (see Figure 1):

Metaverse is a Parallel Virtual World

Metaverse technology is distinguished by that it creates a third world for the user between two worlds: the first is a tangible material world, which is the natural life that humans live in, and the second is a virtual world created by modern technology, which is cyberspace.

Then comes the metaverse as a parallel 3D virtual world, which facilitates the user to log in with certain technological tools, and by using an animated avatar that represents it, which is a shape that every user creates his own space or contents (avatar), which means ensuring anonymity and independence from the world (Abdel Majeed, 2023: 77).

Also, Metaverse transfers the individual from just a user of the Internet to a part of it, and a participant in it, where users who turn into avatars participate in the same experience in the same place and at the same time as is the case in the real world.

The virtual world is just a fantasy, but it carries with it many realistic applications that will provide a person with a distinct civilized world. Hence, it is not an absolute reality, nor is it an absolute fantasy, but a third world (El-Kady, 2023: 8).

Some believe that the use of Metaverse may bring about a significant development in human life and behavior, in state human interactions being realistic and tangible through physical convergence, or being immaterial and intangible through digital convergence through smartphones and computer screens, there will be a third way.

It bridges the gap between these real and digital worlds, to reveal a third, virtual, parallel world that takes something from reality, and from imagination, the Internet, smart technologies, things, and other characteristics (Khalifa, 2022: 3).

Through Metaverse, it opens the door wide to create a virtual third world, in which individuals can create a virtual life for themselves across different areas of the Internet, allowing them to meet, work, teach, and entertain within it while providing an experience that allows them not only to watch remotely through smart devices as is happening now but by entering this world in the form of an animated image that represents the person (avatar) in the 3D world through virtual metaverse techniques (Abdel Sadik, 2022: 404).

Metaverse Is One of the Applications of Modern Technology

It can be said that Metaverse is an advanced form of the Internet. Rather, it is the modern generation of this network that enables the person to enter it, and to practice an integrated virtual life, allowing the user to carry out all the activities and operations that he used to undertake in his normal physical life.

One of the characteristics of Metaverse is that it relies upon the process of using a cryptographic technology based on electronic technology on Internet platforms, so a person can carry out his activity via the Internet using certain tools that help him enter the virtual world, despite the availability of this technology of complete confidentiality (El-Kady, 2023: 9).

However, the absence of legal regulation that governs it loses its users the necessary protection, which exposes them to fraud, which will raise a problem about how to extract and collect evidence in light of this new digital environment with complex technologies.

Metaverse relies on certain technological means

One of the peculiarities of Metaverse is that it is a technology that is based on two important elements: the Internet and virtual and augmented reality tools. (Jibril, 2023: 18).

The connection of the Metaverse with the Internet has led to the Metaverse environment becoming part of a global village on the Internet that is governed by a virtual reality, that is not subject to the traditional concepts that set geographical and political borders to separate countries, regions and different continents, as these separations are not compatible at all with an electronic society that is divided into websites and platforms and electronic networks.

On the other hand, Metaverse technology relies on the use of some technical tools, such as virtual reality glasses and augmented reality, and wearing jackets and gloves equipped with sensors, through which the user can live a real experience, in which these smart technologies act as a mediator between users in Metaverse world, to convey a feeling of physical sensation, so the user can feel through the gloves the texture and temperature of things and its weight, and he can see through the special glasses the things around him in a 3D image.

He can also feel sensory physical stimuli through the jacket or suit, such as the feeling of falling into the water or being punched in the face, or other things, through the sensors in the jackets and gloves he wears, so he gets an experience more like realism, even if it is indirect (Khalifa, 2022: 7).

Figure 1. Metaverse properties

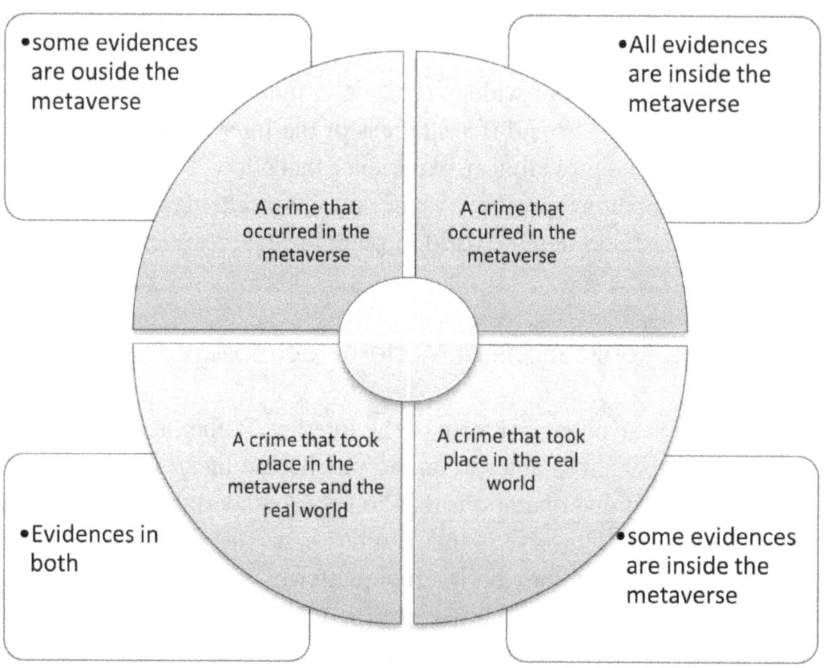

Visualization of Using Metaverse

Metaverse is based on a new technological strategy that relies on the unprecedented development of third-generation web (web-3.0) applications, which will allow websites and applications to deal with information in a human-like manner, through machine learning techniques and big data, where the data will be interconnected with dealing protocols in a decentralized manner based on blockchain technologies and crypto-currency.

Users will be able to interact with tools, equipment, and data in a way that reshapes social media, allowing its users to move, enter, and interact within the metaverse world interactively in a digital environment that simulates the natural or physical environment in which we live through the use of Avatar characters for interaction and interaction (Hijazi, 2022: 9).

Some explain the perception of the world of Metaverse, and how to deal with and coexist within it, that it is like turning the Internet into a community that surrounds a person with a three-dimensional feature, and then the user enters this world in his virtual image (avatar) and using virtual reality technologies; such as glasses, jackets, and gloves, to find himself inside a group of interconnected virtual worlds that have no end (El-Kady, 2023: 9).

He can also meet a large number of people in their avatar image as well, and deal with them, so that the user of the Metaverse is part of the virtual world, and the user may become a participant and maker of this world if his requirements of a suit, glasses, headphone, and gloves are provided. With fast internet from the fifth generation and beyond, technology will change in its dealings with the user, so that he turns from a mere user or viewer into an integral part of this virtual life (Jibril, 2023:25).

Instead of entering cyberspace through computer screens and smartphones, as is the current situation on the Internet, it will be entered through virtual reality glasses, which are currently used in video games, but instead of using them as a means of playing, they will be redesigned to become an alternative to smartphones, it becomes connected to the Internet, and augmented reality technologies will be integrated with it, which displays all information about anything that your eye falls on in real reality. A mixed world is a metaphysics (Khalifa, 2022: 9).

Challenges and Concerns Related to The Metaverse

The metaverse, a new technology, presents numerous challenges, including privacy, data protection, and security. Companies implementing this technology face criticism for its potential to collect biometric data, making individuals vulnerable to cybercrimes. Governments must prepare a strong network infrastructure, and financial and technical capabilities, and ensure a sound regulatory environment.

Data privacy, security, and integrity concerns are also significant. Companies like Meta's virtual reality headsets collect sensitive data, such as location, physical features, and audio recordings, which can be used to target users with personalized ads. Cyberattacks can cause physical harm, and attackers can influence users' activities.

Additionally, the metaverse may lead to addiction and the end of direct communication between individuals. There is no final vision of the metaverse environment, and no frameworks, ethics, or controls have been defined. The metaverse will also enable the purchase of virtual property in the form of NFTs, but challenges arise in granting ownership rights to creators and verifying ownership in the metaverse. Content creators may struggle to protect their intellectual property due to the difficulty of tracking instances of copyright infringement in the virtual realm.

RISKS OF METAVERSE FROM A CRIMINAL PERSPECTIVE

The Dangers of Metaverse

Despite the many advantages claimed by supporters of Metaverse, the most prominent of which are: (see Figure 2)

- Removing geographical barriers between people and each other.
- The possibility of finding and getting to know people with similar interests and ideas.
- Social media development.
- Creating many business opportunities.
- Providing new forms of marketing and advertising on social media platforms.
- Developing the online teaching and learning system.

Figure 2. Advantages of metaverse

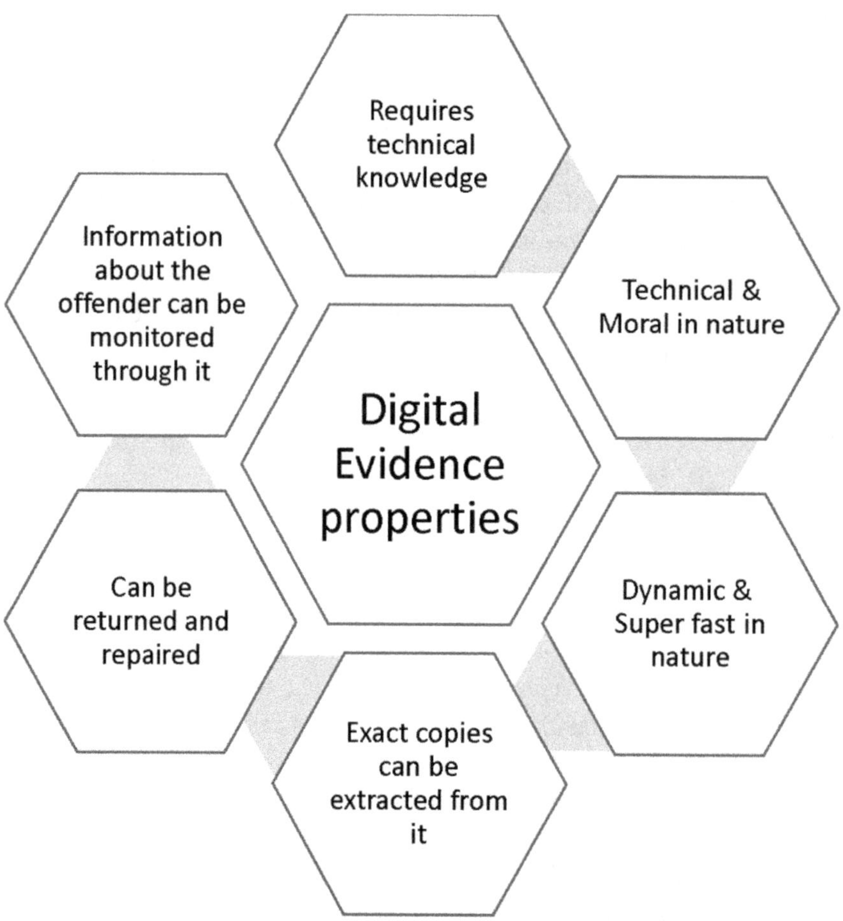

However, the reality of the metaverse is not rosy, as the most prominent negative of the Metaverse is the ease of committing crimes through it, as the person logins Metaverse in a secret encrypted way, and interacts with programmable avatars with other people in a virtual three-dimensional space (see Figure 3).

Some believe that many crimes may be committed through the Metaverse; Such as sexual crimes, immoral practices, deliberately disturbing others, insulting and defamation, violating public morals, outrageous modesty, public indecency, breaching the modesty of a woman in private, incitement to immorality and prostitution, sexual exploitation of children, eavesdropping, breach of family values, theft, and fraud, as well as other money crimes (Al-Marri, 2020: 78).

Hence, some expect an increase in the risks of cybercrime with the presence of Metaverse, marking the emergence of a new term, "Metacrimes"(Abdel Sadek, 2022: 405).

This new world - which is still under development - does not have advanced security levels, which may make it a wide arena for committing many illegal activities such as Identity impersonation, fraud, virtual theft, vandalism of virtual works and art collections, money laundering, counterfeiting virtual currencies, exploitation of children in prostitution, trafficking in illegal goods and drugs, etc. (Abdel Majeed, 2023: 78).

Among the images of the new Metaverse crimes are impersonation crimes, where some link the use of avatars in metaverse to identity impersonation operations, where users have a symbolic identity that represents them in the world of metaverse "avatars", usually in a 3D human form, and users customize it in a unique way of color skin to attachments in detail when first registering in Metaverse, and they recognize each other through an avatar when forming a relationship with others or making transactions; Because the user only enters simple data; Such as ID, age, and gender when registering in Metaverse(El-Kady, 2023: 10).

Since all actions of an avatar are exposed to all users in Metaverse, unique characteristics such as appearance, behavior patterns, and gestures can be recognized by users for malicious purposes only, through simple observation.

In addition, the user's personal information is easily displayed to other users on Metaverse, as the unique pattern of the profile picture and personal information can be used for impersonation or social engineering attacks, such as phishing and persistent threats to obtain financial gain, where it is difficult to identify social engineering attacks more than reality; Because the metaverse has no restrictions on avatar changes (Seo et al., 2023:9472).

Adding that, the crimes of virtual theft, namely: the act of violating the virtual property of others by stealing virtual things in Metaverse, as some indicate that there are cases in which virtual theft was punished as a criminal act in actual courts (Lodder, 2011:79).

Some reports also indicate the possibility of sexual crimes occurring in Metaverse, such as the crime of virtual Rape and Sexual Harassment, where an English woman claimed that her avatar was raped by other people's avatars and that she was subjected to severe psychological damage and trouble as a result of the rape she went through while she was in the metaverse world. and demanding that these avatars be punished for the crime of rape they committed (Hijazi, 2022: 10).

Where the facts of the incident are summed up in the fact that the woman, as soon as she entered the world of the Metaverse, and within a minute of entering, was verbally and sexually harassed by four symbolic personalities through their avatar, and they were not satisfied with verbal or sexual harassment, but they went too far and her avatar was raped (Europol, 2022: 17).

The Europol sees that these kinds of virtual experiences pose serious questions about the applicability of current legislation. Rape requires physical contact, while by definition an avatar is virtual. However, as the embodied internet is one of the ways of describing the metaverse, one can imagine that, as the technology gets more sophisticated, this crude delineation between physical and virtual will become increasingly problematic.

As these experiences become more embodied, and start to feel more real, we will have to decide at which point virtual experiences will be equally impactful as those of the physical realm. It will be important to have a clear idea of what is considered criminal behavior in the metaverse and to have matching laws to provide the means to prosecute these transgressions (Europol, 2022: 17).

In addition to digital money laundering, the Metaverse can be a central space or area of communication between money launderers (Laue, 2011: 20), where illegal money laundering criminal groups can carry out purchases and sales of virtual assets on metaverses by uploading virtual content to the Metaverse market and then buying through fictitious companies or companies with suspicious ownership in the currency used only within the Metaverse, or the so-called Metaverse Coin.

Which is expected to be misused in illegal money laundering operations in the future, because the user creates avatars anonymously, and the Metaverse currency can be purchased with real money and exchanged for real money, for example, criminals can buy Metaverse currencies through multiple accounts that they get from shareholders or Mixed companies, selling pre-made fake virtual objects (El-Kady, 2023: 11).

Terrorists will always try to exploit new technological options to facilitate their activities; in the case of the metaverse, this may lead to new opportunities for terrorist organizations, primarily for propaganda, recruitment, and training. With more immersive technology and related generated data at their disposal, it will become easier for terrorists to select and target vulnerable people and tailor their messages to their biases. That will enable them to more effectively target their propaganda and recruit people (Europol, 2022: 19).

Figure 3. Metaverse dangers

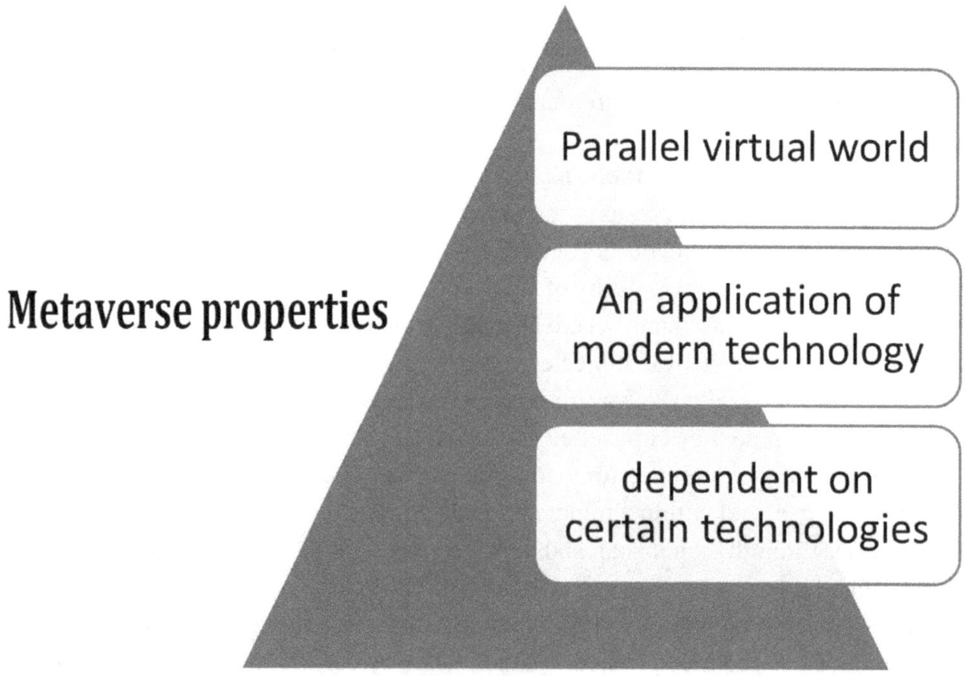

Adding that, this is the expectation of an increase in cyberattacks (Criminal and Terrorist); This raises the expected risk of cybersecurity, due to the absence of oversight in this new world. Monitoring a very large number of users at one time will not be an easy task, but it is almost impossible, especially since this technology is modern, and no organized controls have been established to operate it yet, and then we conclude from that that Metaverse may be one of the causes of increasing the risk and spread of cybercrime in our world today to a greater extent than what exists at present.

Question: Is It Possible to Describe Some Behaviors in The Metaverse World Under the Description of Crime

Some have raised an important question about the extent to which crimes can occur within the Metaverse because the metaverse is a fictional virtual world, Criminal Law is directed only at external material behavior in real society, and the consequence that the law does not take into account intentions, and does not apply to what it takes place within the secrets of man or his dreams and aspirations.

Likewise, the law has nothing to do with a person's psychological feelings that do not appear to reality and take an external appearance, or his fears or delusions that do not appear in reality, and then it can be said in conclusion that the law may not govern what a person does in the virtual world, as long as it does not cause harm. to others, or did not represent behavior that constitutes a crime according to the provisions of the law.

Then the previous opinion - which the researcher agrees with - ends by subjecting the world of metaphysics to the rule of law, and then the permissibility of punishing behaviors that occur through the metaphysical environment if they constitute criminal behavior according to the law (Jibril, 2023: 62).

Others argue with the previous opinion, that the virtual worlds can be regarded as separate societies for which the effects of deviant behavior can be analyzed by criminology, resulting in severe conceptual and methodical problems, and conclude that the findings of criminology in the real world can hardly be applied to the conditions of the virtual world (Laue, 2011: 19).

Question: The Extent to Which It Is Possible to Say That the Avatar Is Granted Legal Personality

Another question emerges from the previous question about the extent to which the people of Metaverse, especially the avatar, enjoy legal personality. The symbol of a person, his image, or any of the things that represent him, such as his image, or the symbol that indicates him in Metaverse.

Hence, the real person remains criminally liable for the actions that he commits through Metaverse. As for the avatar, which is the symbol that represents the real person, his actions, and his transgression, it is not considered unless it is issued by a real person. Or issued against him, and the implication of the foregoing is that the crimes that occur on the avatar may not represent a crime at all, such as the crime of rape, which is only imagined to occur on a female, and that it takes place on her real body, and not her symbol through Metaverse, as well as the crime of murder, so it does not occur except for a living person (Europol, 2022: 17).

The answer to the last question is of great importance in the context of criminal law, and it is expected that these rules will evolve with the development of Metaverse, and the ramifications of its use in all aspects of life, which may be reflected in the rules of criminal law in the future, and we find from jurisprudence those who may call for granting Avatars limited legal personality (El-Kady, 2023: 12).

The digital virtual metaverse environment casts a shadow over the forensic evidence obtained from the crimes that occur within it, as the nature of the metaverse crime scene is that it is a virtual world that has no spatial boundaries, and research in it focuses on the means and tools by which the crime is carried out through electronic devices and international electronic networks, using electronic devices, so the digital evidence may be a message or a picture loaded on a computer or a cell phone receiving the message from any remote country.

In summary, forensic evidence in the world of the metaverse is divided into two parts: the first is physical evidence obtained from the use of virtual and augmented reality tools; such as glasses, jackets, gloves, headphones, etc., and the second is the digital evidence obtained from the virtual Metaverse world and smartphone applications, which we will discuss.

INTRODUCTION TO DIGITAL EVIDENCE IN METAVERSE AND THE PROCEDURES FOR COLLECTING AND EXTRACTING IT

Definition of Digital Evidence and its Characteristics

Definition of Forensic Evidence

Before defining digital evidence, we should define forensic evidence, which refers to the means that link facts to the conviction or innocence of individuals during criminal trials.

It is also a set of clues, through which a set of facts about the crime can be established, in addition to the ability to attribute it to a specific offender.

Or it is a set of proofs accepted by the rule of law that the facts of the crime cannot be proven except by using it before the judicial authorities, whether the courts or the Public Prosecution, and it varies according to the variety of crimes.

Hence, forensic evidence is every procedure recognized by law to convince the judge of the truth of the incident in question, and the evidence is obtained from the crime scene, which is defined as: “The place where the crime occurred or was committed”.

Given the great importance of forensic evidence for the judicial authorities to reach the truth, it has been restricted by a set of restrictions and controls, and this means that this forensic evidence must be based on proof and logic, and the mind must be convinced of it (El-Kady, 2023: 12).

Definition of Digital Evidence

Several legislations developed a definition of digital evidence, among which we mention the Egyptian legislation, which defined digital evidence as: “any electronic information that has evidentiary value or power that is stored, transmitted, extracted or taken from computers or information networks and the like, it can be collected and analyzed using special technological devices, programs, or applications” (Article 1 of Law No. 175 of 2018 regarding combating information technology crimes).

It is noted that the legislator was keen to highlight the essence of digital evidence, which is the information extracted from technical devices, whether they are computers, automation information networks, and the like.

Properties of the Digital Evidence

The digital evidence in Metaverse is characterized by several characteristics as follows (see Figure 4):

1- Dealing with digital evidence requires specialized scientific and technical knowledge, and it cannot be extracted or even discovered, except through specialized experts (Younis, 2004: 977),

2- The digital evidence is technical and consists of information that is embodied in an electronic image, which is not perceived except by using information technology (Naguib, 2014: 52), and the digital evidence is only in a digital environment (Ibrahim, 2020: 40).

3- The digital evidence consists of data and information of an intangible electronic form that is not perceived by the ordinary senses, but rather its realization requires the use of HARDWARE devices and equipment, and the use of SOFTWARE computer software systems (Farghali, 2007: 14), Digital evidence is not only less physical than physical evidence, but also reaches the degree of imaginary in its shape, size, and undeclared location. Which achieves this link between it and the perpetrator (Younis, 2006: 14),

4- The digital evidence is of a high-speed dynamic nature, moving from one place to another through communication networks that transcend the limits of time and space (Naguib, 2014: 55).

5- The possibility to extract copies of digital evidence that are identical to the original and have the same scientific and evidentiary value and this matter is not available in traditional evidence. Which constitutes a highly effective guarantee for preserving the evidence against loss, damage, and change, using exact copies of the evidence (Farghali, 2007: 15).

6- The digital evidence can be retrieved after erasing, repaired after being destroyed, and shown after concealment, which leads to difficulty in Getting rid of it, which is the most important characteristic of digital evidence, and this is done through the use of computer programs whose function is to recover data that has been deleted or canceled, which means that it is difficult for the perpetrator to hide his crime from the eyes of criminal justice men (Al-Husseini, 2019: 157),

7- Through digital evidence, it is possible to monitor the information about the offender and analyze it at the same time. The digital evidence can also record the individual's movements, behaviors, and some personal matters about him (Abdul Muttalib, 2003: 649).

The Importance of Digital Evidence in Metaverse

The importance of digital evidence can be rooted in the fact that the widespread use of technology in aspects of life, and the spread of electrical and technological devices and the Internet has led to a logical conclusion, to the effect that it is inconceivable that a traditional or modern crime will occur, without leaving digital evidence behind, which through this digital evidence, the perpetrator of the crime can be identified.

It is expected that the importance of digital evidence will increase in the criminal field, with the widespread use of new technologies, such as the IoT, dark web networks, high-level encryption, virtual currencies, and even Metaverse technology in committing crimes, which will require law enforcement agencies to make radical changes in the methods of collecting evidence and mechanisms of international cooperation in criminal matters, in a manner commensurate with the nature of this new type of forensic evidence (Meiklejohn, 2013: 9), which is characterized by its changing moral nature, as the information

Figure 4. Digital evidence properties

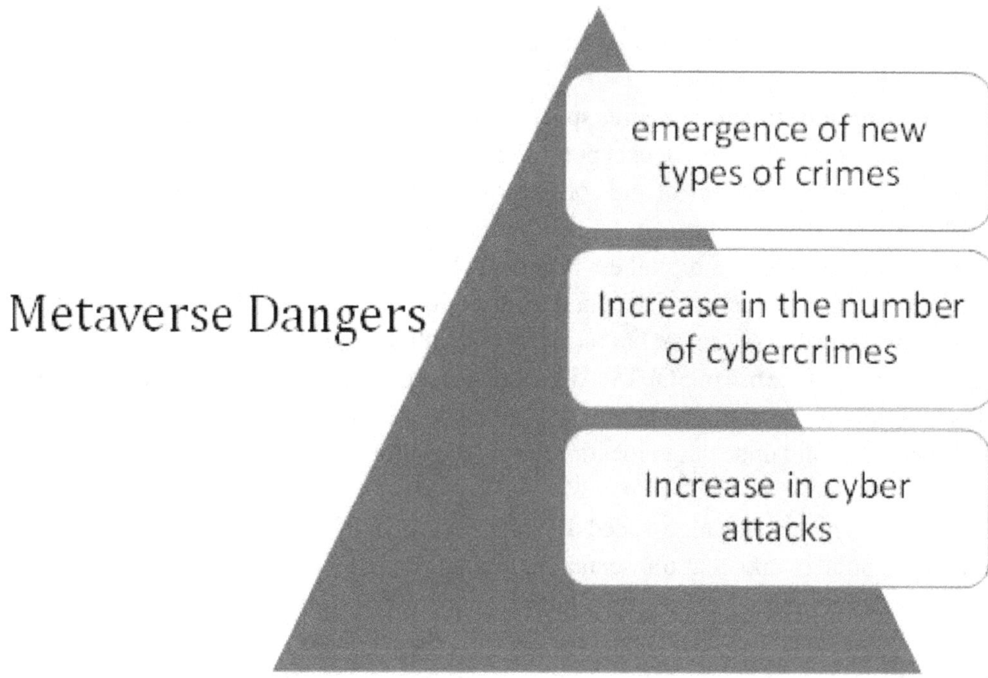

stored on computers or cloud computing servers via the Internet is volatile (Quéméner, 2014:63), and it is easy to tamper with and change during investigations.

Indeed, this evidence is fragile and is subject to destruction through mishandling or improper examination (UNODC, 2013: 230).

Hence, the importance of digital evidence is evident, as it is the means that enables law enforcement authorities to know how cybercrime occurred, prove it, and attribute it to the perpetrator, especially since it is committed in a non-physical virtual environment (Al-Saghir, 2002: 11), and it was necessary to set specific rules and conditions for dealing With this digital evidence to ensure its admissibility before criminal justice, as well as taking special precautions to document, collect, preserve and examine it (El-Kady, 2023: 13).

Collecting Digital Evidence, Its Legality, And Admissibility Before a Criminal Judge

Collecting Digital Evidence in Metaverse

Researchers divide the stages of collecting digital evidence in the world of Metaverse into three stages: the first is the data collection stage, the second is the stage of examining and retrieving evidence, and the third stage is data analysis and preparation of reports to present the evidence to the court, which will be reviewed as follows: (see Figure 5)

Figure 5. Stages of Digital Forensic Investigation

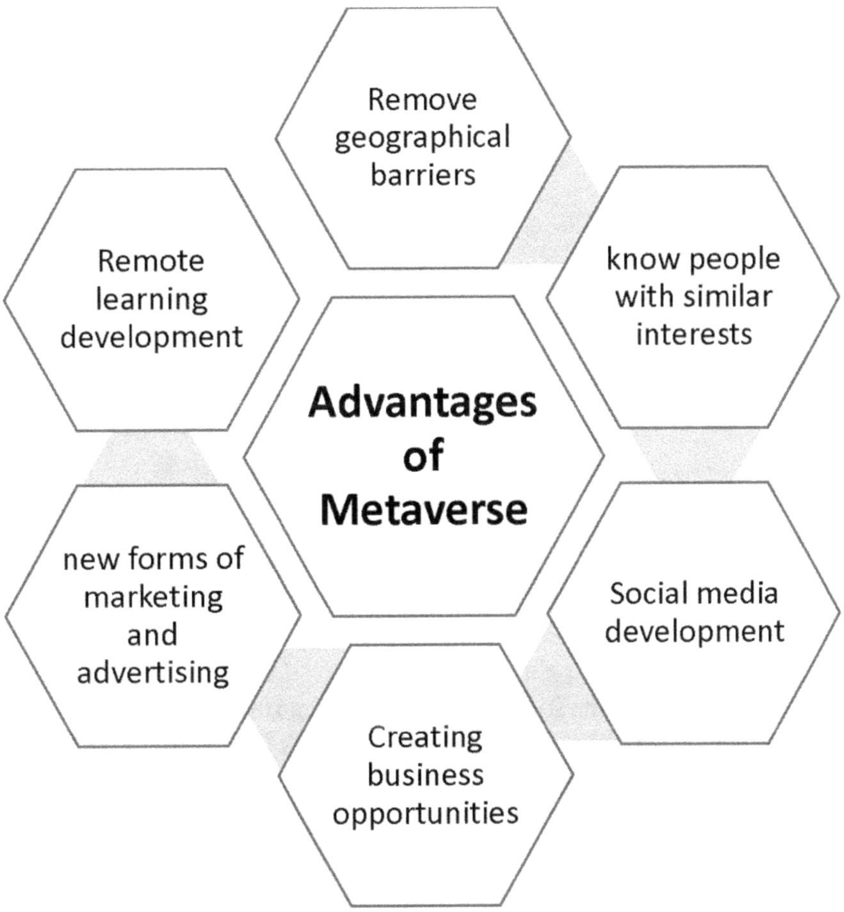

The Phase of Collecting Data in Metaverse

The first step in collecting evidence is to collect data on the occurrence of crime in the world of Metaverse, which requires the need to identify the sources that appear to have evidence, which can be a physical device, an information system, or a service.

Then, the party involved in collecting the evidence (whether they are judicial officers or experts specializing in collecting electronic evidence) must obtain evidence from the sources, and ensure that it is in a format that can be easily copied while preserving the original state as an image while preserving the integrity of the data (SEO et al.,2023:9477).

Some point out that, there is a relationship between physical evidence in the real world and their analogs of digital evidence in the Metaverse world.

Metaverse data may include evidence of traditional crimes in the real world, due to the mutual influence between them and the real world.

Figure 6. Types of evidence of Metaverse crimes according to the location of the crime

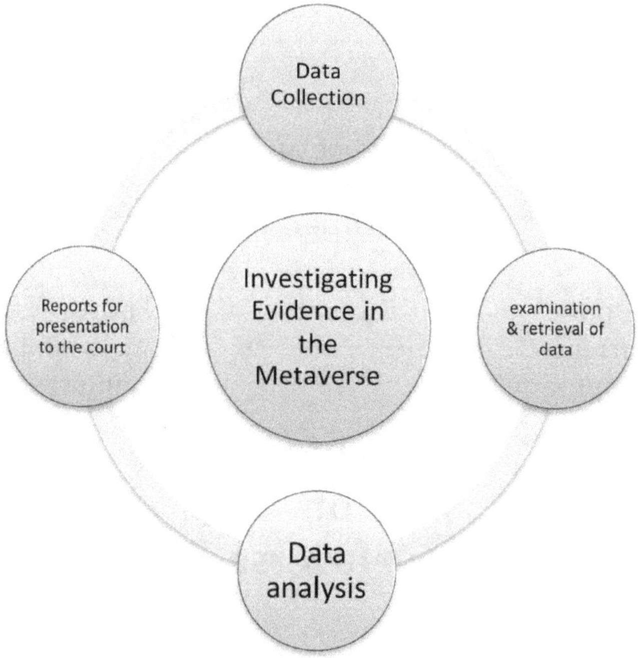

Real-world data is a guide when investigating a case that occurred in the Metaverse, so investigators will need to analyze all evidence from both worlds in some cases (Seo et al., 2023:9469).

Then the researchers divide the evidence of Metaverse crimes according to the location of the crime according to four hypotheses: (see Figure 6)

1. A crime that occurs in the Metaverse and all evidence is inherently within the Metaverse.
2. A crime that occurs in the Metaverse, and some evidence outside the Metaverse.
3. A crime that occurred in the real world, some of which is evidence from the Metaverse.
4. A crime that occurred through the Metaverse and the real world, and the evidence is from both (Seo et al., 2023: 9475).

On the other hand, the procedures for collecting digital evidence in Metaverse are particularly specific and linked to the special nature of this world.

As the procedures for collecting digital evidence extend to include three sources or constituent domains of the Metaverse, which are user devices, service providers' servers, and the Metaverse platform itself, it is possible to distinguish between the following three domains: (see Figure 7)

User Domain

It contains everything that users in the real world can do and the avatars they control in the Metaverse. It consists of a connection layer, which represents the connection of users to Metaverse, all communication actions, and an interaction layer, which represents the interactions between users in Metaverse.

Figure 7. Data resources in the Metaverse

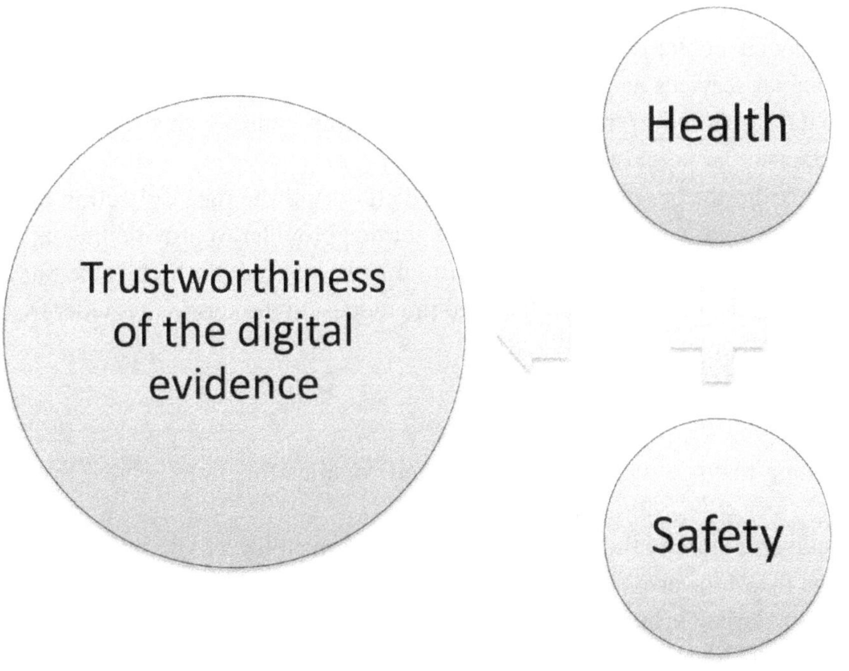

The communication layer can be implemented through augmented reality glasses, jackets, or sensors, as users access and communicate with the Metaverse through devices containing processors, and random access memory to perform their functions.

Augmented reality glasses, for example, connect users to Metaverse, on a memory of 128 GB or more, and it is expected that different types of crime-related data will be stored in the memory of those devices used to interact with the real world, as for the procedures and methods used to collect data from these devices.

They are similar to those used with the Internet of Things and mobile devices, except that given the successive technical developments in such interactive devices, it must take into account the peripheral devices that are linked to these devices in the real world, where the data of those interactive devices is transmitted on other devices (Seo et al., 2023: 9477).

Domain of Service

It includes everything related to the services provided by the platform, in addition to the services provided by third parties, and the service layer requires technologies such as e-commerce, p2p payment systems, open-source technology, and encrypted currencies; Because the contents of trading and shopping are provided as services, due to the many services provided by Metaverse to users simultaneously, which are difficult to operate with only Metaverse resources.

External service providers have resorted to providing them to users, as these providers rely and are relying on the basic information provided by the Metaverse platform about these services, such as display and user interactions to implement service functions, which may be an essential resource to provide the service smoothly from their side, which may constitute a source for investigators in collecting and extracting evidence obtained about crimes occurring in the world of Metaverse (El-Kady, 2023: 14).

Investigators may encounter difficulties in obtaining some data, which is related to managing user data, such as financial services and payment services, if the service involved in the incident uses its resources, as the data is stored in the provider's infrastructure, and for this reason, investigators must request relevant data.

The connection from the service provider immediately, and the data collection procedure may be impossible when there is no legal obligation on the service provider to provide the data.

On the other hand, the data collection procedure may be not only in Metaverse but also in the real world, then the investigators in this case must send the request to the service provider for the data stored outside the Metaverse (Seo et al., 2023:9478).

Metaverse Platform Domain

It refers to everything that operates the Metaverse and contains functions related to the system or administrator.

To put the Metaverse close to the real world, the management layer is an implementation of the system that maintains the Metaverse and requires Artificial intelligence (AI) technology to automatically manage problems too large for humans to handle, and the data layer is a layer that manages all the data that is generated and stored on Metaverse platform, and in the data layer, there is a need for technologies such as Blockchain, Edge Computing, and cloud concept to ensure the integrity and stability of data up to the zettabyte level and beyond in Metaverse (Seo et al., 2023:9471).

Since the Metaverse contains a volume of data that must be communicated with the user, the data on the objects executed in the virtual space and the contents created by the user must be stored and managed in real time.

Thus, the Metaverse has a much larger amount of data to process and store than any other platform, and when a crime occurs in the Metaverse, it is likely difficult or even impossible to collect and verify all the data stored on this platform; Given that the Metaverse data center servers use basic blockchain and cloud computing technologies distributed in different countries (El-Kady, 2023: 15).

Thus, the relevant data will be distributed across several servers from different countries, so it is difficult to access the server and collect the data; Due to time and money constraints, and because of the long distances involved and the possibility of legal problems between countries, therefore, investigators should collect data generated by the Metaverse platform through the data management system.

On the other hand, investigators should collect only crime-related data selectively, when considering time and cost, It may also be needful to request the relevant data from the Metaverse system again based on the results of the analysis of the gathered data, which may have to perform this process frequently, so when collecting data on the Metaverse platform, it is important to decide which data will be collected from the system in particular, and it is also necessary to provide the system with units or information for data selection, such as a specific location or region of the Metaverse and specific content for the specified period (Seo et al., 2023:9479),

There is no doubt that the collection of data on the crimes of Metaverse requires law enforcement agencies to work on all three levels to collect evidence obtained about crimes committed in the context of the Metaverse.

Examination and Retrieval of Digital Evidence in Metaverse

The phase of examination and retrieval of digital evidence includes extracting and evaluating crime-related data elements from the collected raw data set. The collected data may be in a form that cannot transmit meaningful information due to coding, or compression. It also contains the process of neutralizing those that hinder the interpretation of the data.

In the data collection stage, the types of data gathered by investigators differ in the domains (the user, service providers, and the Metaverse platform), according to the considerations of each domain.

For user domain data, the method differs. Interpretation of the collected data by the operating system and file system of the data source.

As for service providers' domain data, the data type, directory structure, and file format can vary depending on how the service framework technical stack is implemented in the Metaverse platform and what type of local storage is provided, if the server uses an encoding method or file format developed by the provider instead of a package provided by Metaverse platform, a tool or method will be required to interpret the collected data (El-Kady, 2023: 15).

When a service provider compresses or encrypts the data for protection or to increase storage efficiency, research is required to interpret the data.

For data provided by the service provider using an independent type of infrastructure, it is specified procedures for extracting and evaluating data according to the type provided by the provider.

As for the Metaverse platform, the data extraction and evaluation procedures are determined according to the data format provided, if the data management system operates based on data mining or artificial intelligence, the data collected will be more formatted than the data collected from the user domain (Seo et al.,2023:9479).

The Phase of Data Analysis and Preparation of Reports on Digital Evidence in the Metaverse

The analysis stage is based on analyzing the data and evidence extracted from each of the three domains that investigators in the world of Metaverse work on, and conclusions are drawn about the case by collecting data, during which approval is made during this stage.

On the most data and outputs to be examined at the outset, which depend on the type of crime committed in the metaverse, prioritization and the order of data analysis and the obtained outputs depend on the investigator's intuition and experience.

Evidence gathered from different sources in the Metaverse may have meaning in itself, but new meanings can also be created for it through correlation analyses between it and other outputs obtained from other Metaverse domains (user domain, service domain), where the investigator can determine the user's conduct at a specific time by linking the evidence obtained from the three different domains of the Metaverse.

While the reporting phase Indicates how to present and explain the conclusion that results from the analysis phase, through that phase, there is a concern about how the evidence in 3D form gathered from the crime scene in Metaverse will be presented to the courts, when the 3D data is presented in a 2D paper form, it may raise concerns about losing some information or altering its content (Ebert et al., 2014:623), particularly for fragmentary 3D images or a single shot of a scene collected in the Metaverse.

As the meaning of the information can become ambiguous depending on the angle and distance the VR/AR glasses are exposed to, it is, therefore, necessary to study the methodology and special considerations related to 3D data before it is recognized as evidence in court (Seo et al., 2023:9480).

Finally, those in charge of criminal investigations of Metaverse crimes face some related challenges, the most prominent of which are: the reliability of the evidence obtained from Metaverse, and the amount and quality of the main data collected (El-Kady, 2023: 16).

Within the domain of the Metaverse platform, big and distributed data from Metaverse must be collected selectively with consideration to time and cost efficiency, and since selective data collection depends on the data management system of the Metaverse platform, all data collection procedures may be opaque, so when presenting evidence in Court - Proving the suitability of selective data collection on the Metaverse platform, as well as some discussion about the reliability of results in the Metaverse world when data is collected selectively using technologies such as machine learning and artificial intelligence.

In addition, the investigators - at the phase of collecting information from Metaverse regarding their direct access to data sources, are restricted to the extent of cooperation of the companies that own data and information within the Metaverse platform.

Since these companies may reserve cooperation with the investigation authorities and provide the required data from them, unless the company is directly involved in the case, due to the lack of a legal obligation on it to cooperate with the investigation and trial authorities.

Therefore, data on the Metaverse platform can only be collected in cooperation with the company that owns the data. The same applies to third-party companies that provide Metaverse service if they store data outside the Metaverse platform, bearing in mind the commitment of these companies to consider the subscribers' rights to privacy.

And then it refrained from disclosing any data about them, even if it was related to existing investigations or trials. For example, in 2016, Apple refused to cooperate with the FBI when it was asked to analyze the iPhone data of a dead terrorist due to its considerations of user privacy (Seo. et al.,2023:9481).

Add to that, the more volatile data generated in the Metaverse than the data recorded in the real world, and the impossibility of recording all of the data that occurs in the Metaverse; As the movements of all avatars, plus real-time streaming data such as video conferencing and voice chats are all volatile if not recorded by the user, and it is not easy to develop a technology to monitor tens of thousands of terabytes of data generated in chunks, of a thousandth of a second in the Metaverse.

Hence, if Metaverse does not operate a separate logging system or forensic data center for incident responses, the computing resources of the Metaverse model must be used to investigate incidents or problems.

Information about the operational process of the developed system is also required to develop a custom analysis tool. If the manufacturer does not publish the official documentation of the file system, investigators must reverse engineer against the operating system binary, which takes a lot of time and effort.

On the one hand, If the analysis technology is not fully developed, the analyst will not be able to collect or analyze data from the input or output device.

This is in addition to the issue of protecting the privacy of users in Metaverse, and the extent to which investigators can be allowed to access information and evidence recorded on screens carried on the user's head, in addition to following the movement of other components on Metaverse, where backgrounds play an important role in the criminal investigation process, which often includes information unintentional, such as movements of other avatars, markers, surroundings, crime scenes (El-Kady, 2023: 16).

Also, the user may reveal some sensitive personal information through the background screen, and the user's gestures and movement patterns of the head or eyes can be observed through the avatar, this information can also be used to track the actual identity of the user outside the Metaverse through eye tracking in Avatar and pattern recognition Gestures using biometrics (Pfeuffer et al., 2019:12) such as fingerprints and the user's iris, and new privacy-preserving techniques such as avatar cloning, locking, camouflage, teleportation, and concealment sometimes lead investigators to make incorrect decisions or cause confusion during the analysis process (Falchuk et al., 2018: 55).

The Legality of the Digital Evidence

The digital evidence requires that the means of obtaining it be legitimate, that the procedures for obtaining it were implemented due to the law (Naguib, 2014: 56), and that access to it was done through free will without any assault on the will of the accused or the will of others, Such as the use of violence with the suspect to decode an information system, access the encryption solution circuit, or access stored data files (Naguib, 2014: 56).

The legality of the procedures for obtaining it is limited to merely following the established legal rules, rather, it must also agree with the established rules in the conscience of society (Minshawi, 2012: 552).

From the comparative judiciary, the position of the Belgian Court of Cassation ruled that: "The description of the illegal act is not limited to the act that the law expressly prohibits, but rather includes all an act that contradicts the fundamental rules of criminal procedures, or legal principles" (Al-Saghir, 2002: 110).

Among the judicial applications about the legality of procedures for obtaining evidence, what was decided by an American court regarding the legality of law enforcement agencies collecting information about the occurrence of a crime, among the information and data that the accused shares with his friends on social networking sites, where the court ruled that: "If the settings related to privacy on the social networking site (Facebook) allow viewing of correspondence by "friends" so that state agencies can access this information through the cooperation of one of the "friends" of the accused on the social networking site without this violating the Fourth Amendment.

While the accused undoubtedly believes that his account will not be shared by law enforcement, there is no justification for expecting that "friends" will keep the account confidential, and the larger the circle of "friends", the greater the likelihood that the accused's correspondence will be seen by someone He is not expected to see it, and that the accused's legitimate expectations of maintaining his privacy end when he publishes his correspondence to his "friends"; Because these "friends" are free to use this information however they like, including sharing that information with state agencies" (United States v. Meregildo, No. 11 Cr. 576 WHP, 2012 WL 3264501, at *2 S.D.N.Y. Aug. 10, 2012).

Admissibility of Digital Evidence Before Criminal Courts

The criminal judiciary in some countries tended to set some rules or standards to assess the acceptability of digital evidence and ensure its reliability, and to examine the extent to which it can be relied upon in judicial procedures.

The most important rules for determining the admissibility of digital evidence before criminal courts are The need for the court to be certain of the integrity and authenticity of the digital evidence, and not to be subjected to any attempt to tamper with it, and it is the responsibility of the accusing authority to prove that this evidence was initially obtained by a legitimate means, and secondly to prove what is called the continuity of the evidence; That is, the status of the digital information as evidence has not undergone any modification or change that casts doubt on its credibility in revealing the facts of the crime throughout judicial procedures, from the date of its seizure until the issuance of a judgment in the case(El-Kady, 2023: 17).

Those in charge of collecting digital evidence from the crime scene must take the necessary measures to preserve the integrity of the digital evidence, starting from the moment of its creation and up to the stage of its submission before the court, which is known as the continuity of the evidence and the stability of its condition and that it is not subject to modification, distortion or tampering with it, as they must preserve Continuity of evidence on both the physical devices containing the data (when it was received or captured) and the data stored on the devices (US Department of Justice, National Institute of Justice, 2007: 16).

The investigating authority must present to the court the procedures applied to preserve the integrity of the digital evidence, indicate the mechanism applied to preserve the evidence and document its chronological history, and that it has not undergone any change or tampering with it.

So the Public Prosecution must present to the court that the data obtained from the device is a true and proper representation of the original data contained in the device (health) and that the device and the data to be presented as evidence are the same as those that were originally discovered, preserved and documented in their chronological history (safety) (see Figure 8), because of this having a direct impact on The court favored the idea of reliability and trustworthiness of the digital evidence (Greenfield RS, 2002: 136).

Figure 8. Trustworthiness of the digital evidence

Then its admissibility before the criminal judiciary and the court in its investigation of the case in the session may hear the witnesses and experts who collected and extracted the digital evidence and discuss with them what they proved in their reports to verify its validity and integrity and that access to it was done legitimately (El-Kady, 2023: 17).

In sum, for the acceptance of digital evidence before the criminal courts, the evidence collection procedures must be carried out in a manner that guarantees the legal validity of the collection procedures, the preservation of the integrity of the evidence, the non-change of its form, and the continuity of its condition throughout the entire period separating its seizure and its use in the trial.

The importance of addressing the issue of the reliability of the digital evidence before the criminal courts is evident in the precedent of an appeal before an American court regarding the reliability of computer-generated and stored information on the basis of security gaps in operating systems and programs that could lead to threats to the integrity of digital information, where the court considered the issue of the vulnerability of digital information to manipulation during the submission of electronic evidence, and the need to demonstrate the validity of the computer with regard to its ability to retain and restore the information in question (the case of Deptor American Express Travel Land Services v. Fei Vinhe Company, Session 16/ 12/2006), It ruled that: The acceptability of computer-generated information (such as log file records) gives details of the activities of the computer, network, and other devices that could be vulnerable if the system generating the information did not contain strong security controls (Chaykin, 2006: 239).

Finally, some point out that the American judiciary relied on five basic conditions for accepting digital evidence before it, of any kind (Al-Ojali, 2016: 31-40), and these conditions are:

1- **It is related to the incident** to be proven, whether directly or indirectly;
2- **It must be original**; That is, the extracted evidence should be the same as the original data that was seized, without any change since it was seized and compiled.
3- **It must be reliable**, and it must not have been tampered with or altered.
4- **It must be best**, that the evidence presented be an original copy, as it is one of the best data and information available on which courts can rely in their judgments, which is a rule established in Article 1002 of the US Federal Rules of Evidence, Which provides that: The original is required when proving the content of messages, records or images.

Article 1003/3 of the aforementioned rules stipulates that: If the information is stored on a computer or similar device, any print or extract from it that is visually readable and shows the data accurately is considered an original copy.

5- **It should not be an auditory testimony**; That is, digital evidence cannot be accepted if it is a word sent or just a rumor.

The approval of these conditions is due to what was decided by an American court in a case between Lorrinace and Markel American Insurance, as this ruling is an important judicial precedent.

For dealing in detail with the requirements for the admissibility of evidence extracted from electronic devices; such as e-mail and Internet sites, the contents of chat rooms and recordings are stored and transmitted (Keiko. L. Sugisaka, p.1458).

Figure 9. Conditions for accepting digital evidence

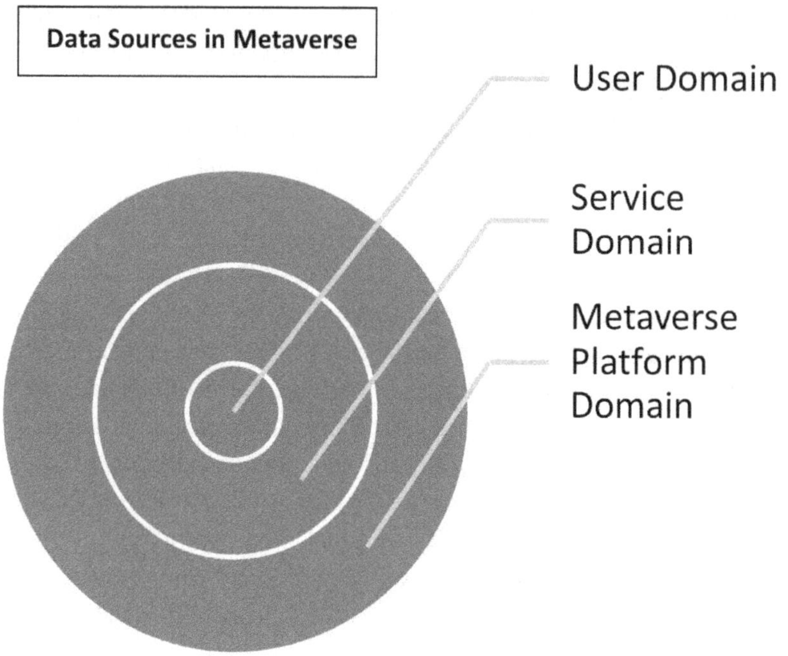

THE AUTHORITATIVENESS OF THE DIGITAL EVIDENCE IN PROOF AND INTERNATIONAL COOPERATION IN ITS COLLECTION

The Authoritativeness of Digital Evidence in Criminal Proof

Computer and electronic communications data - that may be related to a crime - contain many pictures, videos, e-mail messages, conversation records, and system data, and this data and information constitute, to a large extent, digital evidence, however, in the context of criminal law, the question arose whether these new digital evidence enjoy the same legal authority as traditional evidences in proving crime, despite the moral nature of these evidences, which differs from traditional evidences.

Legislators have answered this question in anti-information technology legislation, by giving it the legal authority prescribed for traditional physical evidence over digital evidence of an intangible nature in criminal evidence.

We mention among them the Egyptian legislator who decided in Article (11) of Law No. 175 of 2018 that: "Evidence derived or extracted from devices, equipment, media, electronic supports, information systems, computer programs, or any means of information technology has the value and authority of physical forensic evidence in criminal evidence when it meets the technical conditions stipulated in the executive regulations of this law.".

The Saudi judiciary took this approach, as the General Authority of the Supreme Court in the Kingdom of Saudi Arabia issued Decision No. 34 of 4/24/1439 AH regarding digital evidence and its validity, which stipulates that: "Digital evidence is a valid argument in proof when it is free from symptoms and varies in strength and weakness according to the incident, its circumstances, and the evidence it contains." Safety from accidents means that the evidence is free from modification and change and that it is reliable.

International Cooperation for Collecting Digital Evidence

The importance of international cooperation in criminal matters related to digital evidence and Metaverse crimes is evident, given the transnational nature of these crimes, which are most often used to commit the Internet, and digital evidence exists, resulting from these crimes outside the legal jurisdiction of law enforcement agencies, which requires the existence of legal rules regulating issues of cooperation between countries, taking into account the unstable nature of digital evidence, which requires a quick response on the part of the investigation authorities, and the ability to request investigative measures specialization requires strengthening the mechanisms of international cooperation on a large scale between different countries.

In this context, it is worth noting that United Nations Office on Drugs and Crime (UNODC) - in one of its studies on cybercrime - rightly believes that relying on traditional means of formal international cooperation in matters of cybercrime, including Metaverse crimes, is not currently sufficient to respond promptly to the requirements obtaining ephemeral and changing digital evidence, located in multiple geographic locations, which will constitute a procedural problem for all crimes, not just cybercrimes (UNODC, 2013: 15).

The aforementioned study indicated that the majority of countries (over 70%) use the mechanism of formal mutual legal assistance requests, which usually takes about 150 days, to respond to these requests, and that often these periods may exceed the period of retention of the data by the service provider, or during which the perpetrators of the crime may be able to destroy digital evidence.

The importance of international cooperation in combating Metaverse crimes is due to its special nature as a transnational crime, which requires rapid investigations characterized by unprecedented experience and cooperation, which requires the need for law enforcement agencies to cooperate quickly and effectively across national borders (Pinter, 2005: 66), as well as cloud computing poses an increasing challenge to international cooperation because computer services are increasingly moved to geographically distributed servers and data centers, making it difficult to locate digital evidence (UNODC, 2013: 216).

In addition to limiting the scope of applicability of criminal rules to the territory of the state (the principle of territoriality of the criminal rule), which results in procedural difficulties in confronting these crimes, represented in the inability of the judicial authorities in the country to conduct some procedural judicial acts within the territories of other countries, such as inspection and seizure procedures to others. This is a criminal procedure (Al-Shorbaji, 2003: 10).

Most bilateral, regional, and international agreements often include provisions requiring the need to resort to mutual judicial assistance, to achieve speed and effectiveness in the prosecution of offenders, and the collection of digital evidence (Al-Saghir, 1999: 79).

The exchange of information in the field of Metaverse crimes is one of the most prominent forms of international cooperation in confronting them, and it may take place bilaterally or multilaterally, through the International Criminal Police Organization or other counterpart bodies at the regional level such as Europol, Afripol, and the Arab Bureau for Combating Crime, and it means the exchange of information International security cooperation, which takes place through the exchange of information between the security agencies about the criminal activities undertaken by informatics criminals, to achieve effective security cooperation in confronting them.

Given the special nature of Metaverse crimes, international cooperation in combating them should not be limited to international security cooperation in the field of information exchange and international judicial cooperation in the field of judicial delegation and extradition of criminals. Rather, it requires international cooperation in the field of training security and judicial cadres to detect and investigate Metaverse crimes.

The international community has been interested in activating international cooperation in the field of combating cybercrime through several solutions, most notably: the Budapest Agreement, the European Union's framework decision, legislative activities, and capacity-building activities in the field of combating, which are supported by some regional international organizations such as the Organization of American States, and the Asia-Pacific Group, as well as the efforts of the International Working Group on Training in Cybercrime, and the efforts of the International Criminal Police Organization "Interpol" (Pinter, 2005: 66).

The Role of INTERPOL in Dealing With Digital Evidence

INTERPOL is working to enhance international police cooperation among its members - 195 countries - by providing field support services, where specialized assistance in the field of forensic evidence can be provided in the INTERPOL Digital Forensic Laboratory, and the field by fielding incident response teams.

The INTERPOL also assists and guides member countries in setting up and maintaining state-of-the-art laboratories, in line with procedures adopted at the international level, to better support investigations and prosecutions.

The INTERPOL develops training programs that focus on unified curricula and solutions in the field of digital forensics, in close collaboration with the INTERPOL Capacity Building Unit and its partners from law enforcement agencies, the private sector, and university circles, and to achieve communication between specialized experts, as the INTERPOL Forensic Laboratory provides links between experts in all fields, around the world to share their knowledge and discuss ways to improve their daily work.

The INTERPOL works in combating Cybercrimes by preparing publications related to dealing with digital evidence, the most prominent of which are: Global Guidelines for Digital Forensic Laboratories, which present the procedures for establishing and managing a digital forensic laboratory, and provide technical methods for managing electronic evidence and its handling, and the Guidelines for First Insights in Digital Forensics, which provide advice on the search, seizure, identification, and treatment of digital evidence using methods to ensure its integrity to be admissible in the context of judicial proceedings.

In the same context, the INTERPOL organizes several forums related to dealing with digital evidence, most notably: the INTERPOL Digital Forensics Expert Group Meeting (annual meeting), which is open to specialists and managers from law enforcement agencies, government agencies, digital forensics companies and university institutions to which you are invited, and the meeting is a suitable place for establishing relationships, exchanging experiences, and providing updated information on technology and new techniques in the field of digital forensic evidence.

CONCLUSION

The study reviewed the issue of digital forensic evidence in the era of Metaverse through two parts that dealt with the nature of Metaverse technology and the procedures for collecting and extracting evidence obtained from crimes committed within it. The research resulted in a set of results and recommendations, as follows:

RESULTS

1- The emergence of Metaverse technology as a virtual world parallel to the real world, amid speculation that it could be misused in committing more cybercrimes and violating the privacy of users, given that it has not reached the ideal state for its operation.
2- The absence of legal texts regulating the use of this technology and confronting the new forms of cybercrime committed during it, and the inability of the existing legal texts to confront them.

RECOMMENDATIONS

1- Working to update legislative frameworks to make them more suitable for application in the virtual environment provided by metaverse technology, and this includes collecting and processing data that takes place through virtual reality systems.
2- Inviting countries to develop strategies that regulate the use of Metaverse technology and define ways to deal with it and the areas in which Metaverses must be created to develop them and the areas in which they are prohibited, in a way that ensures the formulation of a pattern of direct relationship with the developing companies to enhance the state's oversight role over its citizens within the Metaverse without this detracts from their digital rights and freedoms.
3- The need for concerted international efforts to amend international conventions on cybercrime, especially the Budapest Convention (the European Convention for Combating Cybercrime), or to aspire to develop a new international agreement that regulates the responsibility of Metaverse service providers and obliges them to comply with cooperation in combating crimes, following up on infringements and violations, exchanging evidence and information related to these cases, and identifying the applicable laws in those cases and the controls based on them.
4- Calling on the Arab Parliament to update the provisions of the Arab Convention on Combating Information Technology Crimes of 2010 to ensure confronting the new forms of cybercrime, on top of which are Metaverse crimes.
5- Call on Arab legislators to make appropriate amendments to the texts of the laws to combat information technology crimes, to accommodate the crimes of Metaverse, and to achieve an effective confrontation in the face of cybercrime committed within the technology of Metaverse.
6- Continuing to hone the self-capabilities of law enforcement officers and criminal investigators concerned with dealing with cybercrimes, and developing their technological skills to enable them to perform their role in confronting Metaverse crimes.
7- The necessity of strengthening international judicial and security cooperation and facilitating the exchange of information between countries to reduce the types of Metaverse crimes, especially in countries where servers are operating this new technology.
8- Building an international network of law enforcement experts on the subject to exchange these experiences will help build knowledge faster and more efficiently which requires setting up an online policing network to help build and exchange experience on the subject.

REFERENCE

Abdel Sadik, A. (2022, January). What impact does the Metaverse have on the human future in the digital age? Future Horizons Magazine. *Information and Decision Support Center of the Egyptian Council of Ministers*, (2), 401–408.

Abdul-Muttalib, M. (2003). *Using the TCP IP Protocol in Researching and Investigating Computer Crimes*. Center for Research and Studies at the Dubai Police Academy.

Al-Awjali, S. (2016). Admissibility of Digital Evidence in Criminal Courts. Journal of Legal Studies, Benghazi University, Libya.

Al-Husseini, A. (2013). Procedural aspects of crimes arising from the use of electronic networks, [Dissertation, Cairo: Ain Shams University].

Al-Marri, B. (2022). *Social Media Crimes*. Cairo: Dar Al-Ahram for Legal Publications.

Al-Saghir, J. (1999). *Procedural Aspects of Internet-related Crimes*. Dar Al-Nahda Al-Arabiya.

Al-Saghir, J. (2002). *Criminal Evidence and Modern Technology*. Dar Al-Nahda Al-Arabiya.

Al-Shorbaji. (2003). Prospects and Mechanisms of International Cooperation against Crime. Judges Quarterly Magazine.

Chaiken, D. (2006). Network Investigations of Cyberattacks - The Limits of Digital Evidence. *Crime, Law, and Social Change*, *46*(4-5), 239–256. doi:10.100710611-007-9058-4

Chayka, K. (2021). Facebook Wants Us to Live in the Metaverse, what does that even mean? *The New Yorker*. https://www.newyorker.com/culture/infinite-scroll/facebook-wants-us-to-live-in-the-metaverse

Ebert, L. C., Nguyen, T. T., Breitbeck, R., Braun, M., Thali, M. J., & Ross, S. (2014). The forensic holodeck: An immersive display for forensic crime scene reconstructions. *Forensic Science, Medicine, and Pathology*, *10*(4), 623–626. doi:10.100712024-014-9605-0 PMID:25315842

El-Kady, R. (2023). Digital Forensics in Metaverse Technology, AJSS. *Naif University for Security Studies*, *39*(2), 4–20.

Europol. (2022). *Policing in the metaverse: what law enforcement needs to know, an observatory report from the Europol Innovation Lab*. Publications Office of the European Union, Luxembourg.

Falchuk, B., Loeb, S., & Neff, R. (2018). The social metaverse: The battle for privacy. *IEEE Technology and Society Magazine*, *37*(2), 52–61. doi:10.1109/MTS.2018.2826060

Farghali, A. N. (2007). *Criminal Evidence with Digital Evidence from the Legal and Technical Points - A Comparative Applied Study*. Naif Arab University for Security Sciences.

Greenfield, R. S., & Marcella, A. J. Jr. (2002). *Electronic Forensic Evidence, A Field Guide to Collecting, Studying and Preserving Computer Crime Evidence*. CRC Press.

Ibrahim, K. (2020). *Electronic Evidence in Criminal and Civil Matters*. Dar Al-Fikr Al-Jamei.

Jibril, M. (2023). *The Legal Challenges of Metaverse Technology from the Criminal Point of View.* Cairo: Dar Al-Ahram for Legal Publications.

Khalifa, I. (2022). The Metaverse of the Future of Human Urbanization in a Post-Internet World. Abu Dhabi: The Future Center for Research and Advanced Studies.

Laue, C. (2011). Crime potential of metaverses. Springer. doi:10.1007/978-3-642-20823-2_2

Li, B. J., Ratan, R., & Lwin, M. O. (2022). Virtual game changers: How avatars and virtual coaches influence exergame outcomes through enactive and vicarious learning. *Behaviour & Information Technology, 41*(7), 1529–1543. doi:10.1080/0144929X.2021.1884290

Lodder, A. R. (2011). Conflict resolution in virtual worlds: general characteristics and the 2009 Dutch convictions on virtual theft.

Marshall, A. M., & Tompsett, B. C. (2023). The metaverse—Not a new frontier for crime. *WIREs Forensic Science, 1505*, e1505. doi:10.1002/wfs2.1505

Meiklejohn, S., & ... (2013). A fistful of bitcoins: characterizing payments among men with no names. *Proceedings of the 2013 ACM SIGCOMM conference on Internet measurement conference.* New York, ACM. 10.1145/2504730.2504747

Minshawi, M. (2012). The Authority of the Criminal Judge in Estimating Electronic Evidence. Journal of Laws, 36(2).

Naguib, H. (2014). The Authenticity of the Electronic Evidence (Cairo: National Center for Social and Criminological Research). National Criminal Journal, 57.

Pfeuffer, K., Geiger, M. J., Prange, S., Mecke, L., Buschek, D., & Alt, F. (2019) Behavioural biometrics in VR: identifying people from body motion and relations in virtual reality. In: *Proceedings of the 2019 CHI Conference on Human Factors in Computing Systems*, (pp 1–12). ACM. 10.1145/3290605.3300340

Pinter, C. (2005). *The threat posed by information crime and the need for international cooperation, (Cairo: Police Academy).* Sixth International Conference on Information Crime organized by the International Criminal Police Organization “Interpol,” Cairo.

Quéméner, M. (2014). Les spécificités juridiques de la prevue numérique. *AJ Pénal*, (1).

Salem, M. (2022, January). The future of technological development in light of metaverse technology, Future Horizons Magazine. *Information and Decision Support Center of the Egyptian Council of Ministers*, (2), 395–400.

Seo, S., Seok, B., & Lee, C. (2023). Digital forensic investigation framework for the metaverse. *The Journal of Supercomputing, 79*(9), 9467–9485. doi:10.100711227-023-05045-1

Sparkes, M. (2021). “What is a metaverse” 251. *New Scientist, 3348*, 18.

The Information and Decision Support Center of the Egyptian Council of Ministers. (2022). World Trends - Metaverse World.

United Nations Office on Drugs and Crime. (2013). *Study on Cybercrime*. United Nations Organization.

United States v. Meregildo, No. 11 Cr. 576 WHP, 2012 WL 3264501, at *2 S.D.N.Y. Aug. 10, 2012.

US Department of Justice. (2007). *Digital Evidence in the Courtroom, A Business Guide for Law Enforcement and Prosecutors*. National Institute of Justice.

Yunus, O. (2004). Crimes arising from the use of the Internet. (Dissertation, Cairo: Ain Shams University].

Yunus, O. (2006). *Notes on Criminal Evidence via the Internet*. [Dissertation, Cairo: League of Arab States].

Compilation of References

Abdel Sadik, A. (2022, January). What impact does the Metaverse have on the human future in the digital age? Future Horizons Magazine. *Information and Decision Support Center of the Egyptian Council of Ministers*, (2), 401–408.

Abdul-Muttalib, M. (2003). *Using the TCP IP Protocol in Researching and Investigating Computer Crimes*. Center for Research and Studies at the Dubai Police Academy.

Aburayya, A., Salloum, S., Alderbashi, K., Shwedeh, F., Shaalan, Y., Alfaisal, R., Malaka, S., & Shaalan, K. (2023). SEM-machine learning-based model for perusing the adoption of metaverse in higher education in UAE. *International Journal of Data and Network Science*, *7*(2), 667–676. doi:10.5267/j.ijdns.2023.3.005

Aiken, M., Mc Mahon, C., Haughton, C., O'Neill, L., & O'Carroll, E. (2019). A consideration of the social impact of cybercrime: examples from hacking, piracy, and child abuse material online. In *Crime and Society* (pp. 91–109). Routledge. doi:10.4324/9781351207430-7

Alabdulatif, A., Thilakarathne, N. N., Lawal, Z. K., Fahim, K. E., & Zakari, R. Y. (2023). Internet of nano-things (iont): A comprehensive review from architecture to security and privacy challenges. *Sensors (Basel)*, *23*(5), 2807. doi:10.339023052807 PMID:36905010

Al-Ahram newspaper. (2021). The private data of more than 533 million users was leaked. *Al-Ahram Newspaper*.

Al-Awjali, S. (2016). Admissibility of Digital Evidence in Criminal Courts. Journal of Legal Studies, Benghazi University, Libya.

Al-Husseini, A. (2013). Procedural aspects of crimes arising from the use of electronic networks, [Dissertation, Cairo: Ain Shams University].

Al-Marri, B. (2022). *Social Media Crimes*. Cairo: Dar Al-Ahram for Legal Publications.

Al-rimy, B. A. S., Maarof, M. A., & Shaid, S. Z. M. (2018). Ransomware threat success factors, taxonomy, and countermeasures: A survey and research directions. *Computers & Security*, *74*, 144–166. doi:10.1016/j.cose.2018.01.001

Al-Saghir, J. (1999). *Procedural Aspects of Internet-related Crimes*. Dar Al-Nahda Al-Arabiya.

Al-Saghir, J. (2002). *Criminal Evidence and Modern Technology*. Dar Al-Nahda Al-Arabiya.

Al-Shorbaji. (2003). Prospects and Mechanisms of International Cooperation against Crime. Judges Quarterly Magazine.

Alzoubi, H. M., Sahawneh, N., AlHamad, A. Q., Malik, U., Majid, A., & Atta, A. (2022, October). Analysis Of Cost Prediction In Medical Insurance Using Modern Regression Models. In *2022 International Conference on Cyber Resilience (ICCR)* (pp. 1-10). IEEE. 10.1109/ICCR56254.2022.9995926

Amalia, R. F. (2023). Legal Protection for Virtual Land Trading Investment Transactions in the Metaverse. *3rd International Conference on Business Law and Local Wisdom in Tourism (ICBLT 2022)*, 488–496. 10.2991/978-2-494069-93-0_58

AnidjarL. Y.PackinN. G.PaneziA. (2023). The Matrix Of Privacy: Data Infrastructure In The Ai-Powered Metaverse. *Available at* SSRN. doi:10.2139/ssrn.4363208

Ansari, A. P. (2023). A Critique on Cybercrimes Concerning Online Games and Content: Need for Comprehensive Legal Framework in India. *Res Militaris*, *13*(3), 82–95.

Arfeen, A., Ahmed, S., Khan, M. A., & Jafri, S. F. A. (2021). Endpoint Detection & Response: A Malware Identification Solution. *2021 International Conference on Cyber Warfare and Security (ICCWS)*. Semantic Scholar.

Ariesta, W., & Tuti, T. (2023). Penerapan Doktrin Vicarious Liability Untuk Pertanggungjawaban Pelaku Tindak Pidana Dunia Maya. *Jurnal Penelitian IPTEKS*, *8*(1), 39–45.

Arkvik, I. (2021). What is financial cybercrime and how to prevent it. VISMA.

Aslam, M. M., Tufail, A., Kim, K. H., Apong, R. A. A. H. M., & Raza, M. T. (2023). A Comprehensive Study on Cyber Attacks in Communication Networks in Water Purification and Distribution Plants: Challenges, Vulnerabilities, and Future Prospects. *Sensors (Basel)*, *23*(18), 7999. doi:10.339023187999 PMID:37766053

Awadallah, A. M., Damiani, E., Zemerly, J., & Yeun, C. Y. (2023, March). Identity Threats in the Metaverse and Future Research Opportunities. In *2023 International Conference on Business Analytics for Technology and Security (ICBATS)* (pp. 1-6). IEEE. https://doi.org/10.1109/ICBATS57792.2023.10111122

Babylonian, A. (2020). *Space security email*. Studies Institute Arabic, League of Arab States.

Barr, K. (2022). Interpol Wants in on the 'Metaverse', *Gizmodo*. https://www.gizmodo.com.au/2022/10/interpol-wants-in-on-the-metaverse/

Basu, T. (2022). The metaverse has a groping problem already. *MIT Technology Review*. https://www.technologyreview.com/2021/12/16/1042516/the-metaverse-has-a-groping-problem/

Baughman, J. (2022). Enter the Battleverse: China's Metaverse War. *Military Cyber Affairs: 5*(1).

Bele, J. L. (2021). Cryptocurrencies as facilitators of cybercrime. In *The 3rd Eastern European Conference of Management and Economics (EECME 2021) – Sustainable Development in Modern Knowledge Society*. (*Vol. 111*, p. 01005). SHS Web of Conferences. EDP Sciences. 10.1051hsconf/202111101005

Bernik, I. (2014). *Cybercrime and cyber warfare*. John Wiley & Sons. doi:10.1002/9781118898604

Bertino, E., & Islam, N. (2017). Botnets and internet of things security. *Computer*, *50*(2), 76–79. doi:10.1109/MC.2017.62

Betül, C. A. N. (2023). Metaverse Sosyal Alanına Meta Ekonomik Sermaye Açısından İslam Ülkeleri Ne Kadar Hazır? Ürün Uzayı Bağlamında Kesitsel Bir Değerlendirme. *Eskişehir Osmangazi Üniversitesi İlahiyat Fakültesi Dergisi*, *10*(1), 10–41. doi:10.51702/esoguifd.1213159

Bhattacharya, S., Hegde, P., & Maddikunta, P. K. R. (n.d.). *Metaverse for Healthcare: A Survey on Potential Applications*. Challenges and Future Directions.

Bogomolov, A., Lepri, B., Staiano, J., Oliver, N., Pianesi, F., & Pentland, A. (2014, November). Once upon a crime: towards crime prediction from demographics and mobile data. In *Proceedings of the 16th international conference on multimodal interaction* (pp. 427-434). 10.1145/2663204.2663254

Bolton, D. (2021). Targeting ontological security: Information warfare in the modern age. *Political Psychology*, *42*(1), 127–142. doi:10.1111/pops.12691

Bono, S., Caselden, D., Landau, G., & Miller, C. (2009). Reducing the attack surface in massively multiplayer online role-playing games. *IEEE Security and Privacy*, *7*(3), 13–19. doi:10.1109/MSP.2009.75

Bovenzi, G. M. (2023, April). MetaCrimes: Criminal accountability for conducts in the Metaverse. In *Companion Proceedings of the ACM Web Conference 2023 (pp. 565-567).* ACM Digital Library. 10.1145/3543873.3587535

Brenner, S. W. (2008). Fantasy Crime: The Role of Criminal Law in Virtual Worlds. *Vanderbilt Journal of Entertainment and Technology Law*, *11*(1), 61–65. https://scholarship.law.vanderbilt.edu/cgi/viewcontent.cgi?article=1317&context=jetlaw

Buck, L., & McDonnell, R. (2022). *Security and privacy in the metaverse: The threat of the digital human.* In 1st Workshop on Novel Challenges of Safety, Security and Privacy in Extended Reality, New Orleans, LA, USA.

Buck, L., & McDonnell, R. (2022). Security and privacy in the metaverse: The threat of the digital human. *Proceedings of the 1st Workshop on Novel Challenges of Safety, Security and Privacy in Extended Reality.* ACM.

Buhalis, D., Leung, D., & Lin, M. (2023). Metaverse as a disruptive technology revolutionising tourism management and marketing. *Tourism Management*, *97*, 104724. doi:10.1016/j.tourman.2023.104724

Bussolati, N. (2015). The Rise of Non-State Actors in Cyberwarfare: Cyber War: Law and Ethics for Virtual Conflicts. Oxford University Press. doi:10.1093/acprof:oso/9780198717492.003.0007

Caglar, E. (2023). Analysis of Metaverse Technology: Is It Real or Virtual? In Strategies and Opportunities for Technology in the Metaverse World (pp. 1–12). IGI Global.

Cahill, M., & Mulligan, G. (2007). Using geographically weighted regression to explore local crime patterns. *Social Science Computer Review*, *25*(2), 174–193. doi:10.1177/0894439307298925

Calderoni, F. (2010). The European legal framework on cybercrime: Striving for an effective implementation. *Crime, Law, and Social Change*, *54*(5), 339–357. doi:10.100710611-010-9261-6

Casey, P., Baggili, I., & Yarramreddy, A. (2021). Immersive virtual reality attacks and the human joystick. *IEEE Transactions on Dependable and Secure Computing*, *18*(2), 550–562. doi:10.1109/TDSC.2019.2907942

CCDH. (2022). *Facebook Metaverse is unsafe.* CCDH. https://www.counterhate.com/metaverse

Chaiken, D. (2006). Network Investigations of Cyberattacks - The Limits of Digital Evidence. *Crime, Law, and Social Change*, *46*(4-5), 239–256. doi:10.100710611-007-9058-4

Chandra, A., & Snowe, M. J. (2020). A taxonomy of cybercrime: Theory and design. *International Journal of Accounting Information Systems*, *38*, 100467. doi:10.1016/j.accinf.2020.100467

Chayka, K. (2021). Facebook Wants Us to Live in the Metaverse, what does that even mean? *The New Yorker.* https://www.newyorker.com/culture/infinite-scroll/facebook-wants-us-to-live-in-the-metaverse

Chen, Z. (2023). Metaverse office: Exploring future teleworking model. *Kybernetes.* Advance online publication. doi:10.1108/K-10-2022-1432

Cheong, B. C. (2022). Avatars in the metaverse: Potential legal issues and remedies. *International Cybersecurity Law Review*, *3*(2), 467–494. doi:10.136543439-022-00056-9

Choo, K. R., Esposito, C., & Castiglione, A. (2017). Evidence and forensics in the cloud: Challenges and future research directions. *IEEE Cloud Computing*, *4*(3), 14–19. doi:10.1109/MCC.2017.39

Chopra, A. (2021). Cyberattack-Intangible Damages in a Virtual World: Property Insurance Companies Declare War on Cyber-Attack Insurance Claims. *Ohio St. LJ*, *82*, 121.

Chow, Y. W., Susilo, W., Li, Y., Li, N., & Nguyen, C. (2022). Visualization and Cybersecurity in the Metaverse: A Survey. *Journal of Imaging*, *9*(1), 11. doi:10.3390/jimaging9010011 PMID:36662109

Chukwunonso, A. G., Njoku, J. N., Lee, J.-M., & Kim, D.-S. (2022). *Security in Metaverse: A Closer Look* (Conference Paper). Research Gate. https://www.researchgate.net/publication/358948229SecurityinMetaverseACloserLook?enrichId=rgreq-1532b32e0303a88ccfddf15ca27f8419XXX&enrichSource=Y292ZXJQYWdlOzM1ODk0ODIyOTtBUzoxMTI5MDAwNDU4MDI3MDA4QDE2NDYxODYwOTMxNTU%3D&el=1x2&esc=publicationCoverPdf

Collard, A. (2022, August 18). *Crime in the Metaverse is Very Real. But How Do We Police a World With No Borders or Bodies?* World Economic Forum. https://www.weforum.org/agenda/2022/08/crime-punishment-metaverse/

CorkD. A. D.FianiC.KhamisM.McGillM.MurdochS.RashidA.SaegheP. (2023). *REPHRAIN*.

Council of the European Union. (2022). *The Metaverse in the Context of the Fight Against Terrorism.* EU. https://data.consilium.europa.eu/doc/document/ST-9292-2022-INIT/en/pdf

Czosseck, C., Ottis, R., & Talihärm, A.-M. (2013). Estonia after the 2007 cyber attacks: Legal, strategic and organisational changes in cyber security. *Case studies in information warfare and security: For researchers, teachers and students, 72.*

DaCosta, B., & Seok, S. (2020). Cybercrime in Online Gaming. In M. Khosrow-Pour D.B.A. (Ed.), Encyclopedia of Criminal Activities and the Deep Web (pp. 881-892). IGI Global. doi:10.4018/978-1-5225-9715-5.ch059

Dailybrief. (2022). Metaverse adoption will multiply Ccybersecurity risks. *Daily Brief.* https://dailybrief.oxan.com/Analysis/GA266968/Metaverse-adoption-will-multiply-cybersecurity-risks

Dao, T. H. D., & Thill, J. C. (2022). CrimeScape: Analysis of socio-spatial associations of urban residential motor vehicle theft. *Social Science Research, 101*, 102618. doi:10.1016/j.ssresearch.2021.102618 PMID:34823669

Datta, P. (2022). Hannibal at the gates: Cyberwarfare & the Solarwinds sunburst hack. *Journal of Information Technology Teaching Cases*, *12*(2), 115–120. doi:10.1177/2043886921993126

Dayani, R., Chabra, N., Kadina, T., & Kaushal, R. (2015). Rumor Detection in Twitter: An Analysis in Retrospect. In *2015 IEEE International Conference on Advanced Networks and Telecommunications Systems (ANTS)*. IEEE. 10.1109/ANTS.2015.7413660

Debuire, D. (2022). Terrorist use of the metaverse: New opportunities and new challenges. *The Security Distillery*. https://thesecuritydistillery.org/all-articles/terrorism-and-the-metaverse-new-opportunities-and-new-challenges

Décary-Hétu, D. (2017). *Online crime monitoring. The Routledge International Handbook of Forensic Intelligence and Criminology*. Routledge. doi:10.4324/9781315541945-20

Demetis, D. (2023). Organised crime-the cyber dimension. *A Research Agenda for Organised Crime*, 177–194.

Denning, D. E. (2010). Terror's web: how the Internet is transforming terrorism. In Y. Jewkes & M. Yar (Eds.), *Handbook of Internet Crime* (pp. 194–213). Willan Publishing.

Di Pietro, R., & Cresci, S. (2021). Metaverse: security and privacy issues. *2021 Third IEEE International Conference on Trust, Privacy and Security in Intelligent Systems and Applications (TPS-ISA)*. IEEE.

Di Pietro, R., & Cresci, S. (2022). Metaverse: Security and privacy issues. [Online]. Available: https://arxiv.org/pdf/2205.07590.pdf

Dolata, M., & Schwabe, G. (2023). What is the Metaverse and who seeks to define it? Mapping the site of social construction. *Journal of Information Technology*, 02683962231159927.

Duranton, M., De Bosschere, K., Coppens, B., Gamrat, C., Gray, M., Hoberg, T., Munk, H., Robinson, C., Vardanega, T., & Zendra, O. (2023). *HiPEAC Vision 2023.*

Dwivedi, Y. K., Hughes, L., Baabdullah, A. M., Ribeiro-Navarrete, S., Giannakis, M., Al-Debei, M. M., Dennehy, D., Metri, B., Buhalis, D., Cheung, C. M. K., Conboy, K., Doyle, R., Dubey, R., Dutot, V., Felix, R., Goyal, D. P., Gustafsson, A., Hinsch, C., Jebabli, I., & Wamba, S. F. (2022). Metaverse beyond the hype: Multidisciplinary perspectives on emerging challenges, opportunities, and agenda for research, practice and policy. *International Journal of Information Management*, *66*(C), 102542. doi:10.1016/j.ijinfomgt.2022.102542

Ebert, L. C., Nguyen, T. T., Breitbeck, R., Braun, M., Thali, M. J., & Ross, S. (2014). The forensic holodeck: An immersive display for forensic crime scene reconstructions. *Forensic Science, Medicine, and Pathology*, *10*(4), 623–626. doi:10.100712024-014-9605-0 PMID:25315842

El Gataa, I. (2022). *Non-state actors & cyber-warfare.*

Eling, M., & Wars, J. (2019). What are the actual costs of cyber risk events? *Eur. J. Opera. Res.*, *272*. 1109–1119.www.scopus.com

Elisa Orofino, E. (2021). nanoelectronics warfare. *Lebanese National Defense Journal, 118.*

El-Kady, R. (2023). Digital Forensics in Metaverse Technology, AJSS. *Naif University for Security Studies*, *39*(2), 4–20.

Elson, J. S., Doctor, A. C., & Hunter, S. (2022). The metaverse offers a future full of potential – for terrorists and extremists, too, *The Conversation.* https://theconversation.com/the-metaverse-offers-a-future-full-of-potential-for-terrorists-and-extremists-too-173622

Elson, J., Doctor, A., & Hunter, S. (2022). The metaverse offers a future full of potential – for terrorists and extremists. *The Conversation.* https://theconversation.com/themetaverse-offers-a-future-full-of-potential-for-terrorists-and-extremists-too-173622

Essam, A. (2021). Role The United Nations in the fight against terrorism 2001-2020. The Arab Democratic Center for Strategic, Hunting and Political Studies, Cairo.

Euronews. (2022). Russian teen jailed for 5 years over 'terrorism' plot to blow up virtual spy HQ on Minecraft. *Euronews.* https://www.euronews.com/next/2022/02/10/russian-teen-jailed-for-5-years-over-terrorism-plot-to-blow-up-virtual-spy-hq-on-minecraft

Europol. (2022). *Policing in the metaverse, what law enforcement needs to know, An Observatory Report from the Europol Innovation Lab.* Politiet. https://www.politiet.no/en/rad/trygg-nettbruk/police-online-patrol/

Europol. (2022). *Policing in the metaverse: what law enforcement needs to know, an observatory report from the Europol Innovation Lab.* Publications Office of the European Union, Luxembourg.

Fahd, W. & El-Meadowy, W. (2022). Arbitrary search titled Strategic directions to confront extremism and takfiri thought, a study in the light of the Egyptian and Emirati experience. *Police Thought Journal*, Sharjah Police Research Center.

Fahd, W. & Mustafa, W. (2021). The effectiveness of chatbot technology "conversational bots", in institutions. *Journal of Media Research, Faculty of Mass Communication, Al-Azhar University.*

Fahd, W. (2022). *Studying Artificial Intelligence... Between Terrorist Tactics and National Strategies.* Trends Center for Research and Studies, Abu Dhabi, UAE. https://trendsresearch.org/ar/insight/ai-between-terrorist-actics-and-national-strategies/

Falchuk, B., Loeb, S., & Neff, R. (2018). The Social Metaverse: Battle for Privacy. *IEEE Technology and Society Magazine, 37*(2), 52–61. https://www.semanticscholar.org/paper/The-Social-Metaverse%3A-Battle-for-Privacy-Falchuk Loeb/b4c1ade08edba966a44765e32117eb2c9cb114c2. doi:10.1109/MTS.2018.2826060

Farghali, A. N. (2007). *Criminal Evidence with Digital Evidence from the Legal and Technical Points - A Comparative Applied Study*. Naif Arab University for Security Sciences.

Farish, K. (2021). *Deepfakes and their impact on women*. Dacbeach Croft. https://www.dacbeachcroft.com/en/gb/articles/2021/august/deepfakes-and-their-impact-on-women/

Fernandes, F. A., & Werner, C. M. (2023). A Scoping Review of the Metaverse for Software Engineering Education: Overview, Challenges and Opportunities. *PRESENCE: Virtual and Augmented Reality*, 1–56.

FernandezB. C.HuiP. (2022). Life, the metaverse and everything: An overview of privacy, ethics, and governance in metaverse. *arXiv:2204.01480v1*. https://arxiv.org/pdf/2204.01480.pdf doi:10.1109/ICDCSW56584.2022.00058

Figueiredo, S. C. (2023). Rhetoric in the metaverse. *Convergence (London), 29*(1), 81–96. doi:10.1177/13548565221138399

Filipova, I. A. (2023). Creating the Metaverse: Consequences for Economy, Society, and Law. *Journal of Digital Technologies and Law, 1*(1), 7–32. doi:10.21202/jdtl.2023.1

Fineman, B., & Lewis, N. (2018). *Securing your reality: Addressing security and privacy in virtual and augmented reality applications.* Educause. https://er.educause.edu/articles/2018/5/securing-your-reality-addressing-security-and-privacy-in-virtual-andaugmented-reality-applications

Fouad, N. S. (2021). Securing higher education against cyberthreats: From an institutional risk to a national policy challenge. *Journal of Cyber Policy, 6*(2), 137–154. doi:10.1080/23738871.2021.1973526

Frenkel, S., & Browning, K. (2021). The Metaverse's dark side: Here come harassment and assaults. *The New York Times*. https://www.nytimes.com/2021/12/30/technology/metaverse-harassment-assaults.html

Fusco, M. (2023). *Moving towards virtual identity: Enabling accessible motion capture for Metaverse users and their avatars* [Master's Thesis]. University of Twente.

Gadekallu, T. R., Huynh-The, T., Wang, W., Yenduri, G., Ranaweera, P., Pham, Q. V., da Costa, D. B., & Liyanageet, M. (2022). *Blockchain for the metaverse: A review*. arXiv. https://arxiv.org/pdf/2203.09738.pdf

GaronJ. M. (2022). Legal implications of a ubiquitous metaverse and a Web3 future. [Online]. Available at SSRN: https://ssrn.com/abstract=4002551. http://dx.doi.org/ doi:10.2139/ssrn.4002551

Gee, A. P., Escamilla-Ambrosio, P. J., Webb, M., Mayol-Cuevas, W., & Calway, A. (2010, October 29). *Augmented Crime Scenes: Virtual Annotation of Physical Environments for Forensic Investigation.* In MiFOR'10 Conference, Firenze, Italy. https://www.researchgate.net/publication/228418927_Augmented_crime_scenes_Virtual_annotation_of_physical_environments_for_forensic_investigation

Gerstenfeld, J. (2023). Understanding the Connection Between Hackers and Their Hacks: Analyzing USDOJ Reports for HackerProfiles. *International Journal of Cybersecurity Intelligence & Cybercrime, 6*(1), 59–76.

Göknur, E. G. E., YOUSSOUF, M. M., & DARNADJI, D. (n.d.). DIGITAL DIVIDE AND AFRICA IN THE UPCOMING METAVERSE ERA: A STUDY ON THE EXAMPLES OF CHAD AND DJIBOUTI. *Prof. Dursun KOSE, Ph. D.*, 388.

Greenfield, R. S., & Marcella, A. J. Jr. (2002). *Electronic Forensic Evidence, A Field Guide to Collecting, Studying and Preserving Computer Crime Evidence*. CRC Press.

Grover, A., Arora, N., & Sharma, P. (2023). Social Commerce and Metaverse in a New Virtual World: Exploring Women's Adoption Intentions. In *Cultural Marketing and Metaverse for Consumer Engagement* (pp. 262–286). IGI Global. doi:10.4018/978-1-6684-8312-1.ch019

Gulhane, A. (2019). Security, privacy and safety risk assessment for virtual reality learning environment applications. In the *16th IEEE Annual Consumer Communications Networking Conference (CCNC)*. IEEE. 10.1109/CCNC.2019.8651847

Gümüşbaş, D., Yıldırım, T., Genovese, A., & Scotti, F. (2020). A comprehensive survey of databases and deep learning methods for cybersecurity and intrusion detection systems. *IEEE Systems Journal*, *15*(2), 1717–1731. doi:10.1109/JSYST.2020.2992966

Guo, W., Xu, J., Pei, Y., Yin, L., Jiang, C., & Ge, N. (2022). A distributed collaborative entrance Defense framework against DDoS attacks on satellite internet. *IEEE Internet of Things Journal*, *9*(17), 15497–15510. doi:10.1109/JIOT.2022.3176121

Gupta, S. (2016). A literature survey on social engineering attacks: Phishing attack. 2016 international conference on computing, communication, and automation (ICCCA). IEEE.

Gupta, A., Khan, H. U., Nazir, S., Shafiq, M., & Shabaz, M. (2023). Metaverse Security: Issues, Challenges and a Viable ZTA Model. *Electronics (Basel)*, *12*(2), 391. doi:10.3390/electronics12020391

Haataja, S. (2017). The 2007 cyber attacks against Estonia and international law on the use of force: An informational approach. *Law, Innovation and Technology*, *9*(2), 159–189. doi:10.1080/17579961.2017.1377914

Haber, E. (2023). (Forthcoming). The Criminal Metaverse. *Indiana Law Journal (Indianapolis, Ind.)*.

Han, Q.-L. (2023). The Era of Quality and Metaverse. *IEEE/CAA Journal of Automatica Sinica*, *10*(1), 1–2.

Han, J., Liu, G., & Gao, Y. (2023). Learners in the Metaverse: A Systematic Review on the Use of Roblox in Learning. *Education Sciences*, *13*(3), 296. doi:10.3390/educsci13030296

Hanke, J. (2022). *Value Creation in the Metaverse: The Real Business of the Virtual World*. McKinsey & Company. https://www.mckinsey.com/~/media/mckinsey/business%20functions/marketing%20and%20sales/our%20insights/value%20creation%20in%20the%20metaverse/Value-creation-in-the-metaverse.pdf

Herzog, S. (2011). Revisiting the Estonian cyber attacks: Digital threats and multinational responses. *Journal of Strategic Security*, *4*(2), 49–60. doi:10.5038/1944-0472.4.2.3

Hidayat, W., Ramli, H., Ikhram, P. M. B., Ridhawi, A. R., Mukhtar, N. A., & Junedy, R. (2023). Analisa Clustering Phising Untuk Meningkatkan Kesadaran Mahasiswa Terhadap Keamanan Data Pribadi Mahasiswa Universitas Negeri Makassar. *Vokatek: Jurnal Pengabdian Masyarakat*, *1*(1), 28–33. doi:10.61255/vokatekjpm.v1i1.29

Hu, J., & Iosifescu, A., & LiKamWa, R. (2021). Lenscap: split-process framework for fine-grained visual privacy control for augmented reality apps. In *Proceedings of the 19th Annual International Conference on Mobile Systems, Applications, and Services* (MobiSys '21). ACM. 10.1145/3458864.3467676

Huang, J., Sun, P., & Zhang, W. 2022, March. Analysis of the Future Prospects for the Metaverse. In *2022 7th International Conference on Financial Innovation and Economic Development (ICFIED 2022)* (pp. 1899-1904). Atlantis Press. 10.2991/aebmr.k.220307.312

Huang, J. C., Ko, K. M., Shu, M. H., & Hsu, B. M. (2020). Application and comparison of several machine learning algorithms and their integration models in regression problems. *Neural Computing & Applications*, *32*(10), 5461–5469. doi:10.100700521-019-04644-5

Huang, Y., Li, Y. J., & Cai, Z. (2023). Security and Privacy in Metaverse: A Comprehensive Survey. *Big Data Mining and Analytics*, *6*(2), 234–247. doi:10.26599/BDMA.2022.9020047

Huq, N. Reyes, R., Lin, P., & Swimmer. M. (2022). Metaverse or metaworse?: Cybersecurity threats against the Internet of experiences. *Trend Micro Research Paper*. https://documents.trendmicro.com/assets/white_papers/wp-metaverse-or-metaworse-cybersecurity-threats-against-the-internet-of-experiences.pdf

Huq, N., Reyes, R., Lin, P., & Swimmer, M. (2023). Cybersecurity Threats Against the Internet of Experiences. *Trend Micro*. https://documents.trendmicro.com/assets/white_papers/wp-metaverse-or-metaworse-cybersecurity-threats-against-the-internet-of-experiences.pdf

Huq, N., Reyes, R., Lin, P., & Swimmer, M. (2022). *Cybersecurity Threats Against the Internet of Experiences*. Trend Micro Res.

Hutson, J., Banerjee, G., Kshetri, N., Odenwald, K., & Ratican, J. (2023). Architecting the Metaverse: Blockchain and the Financial and Legal Regulatory Challenges of Virtual Real Estate. *Journal of Intelligent Learning Systems and Applications, 15*.

Ibrahim, K. (2020). *Electronic Evidence in Criminal and Civil Matters*. Dar Al-Fikr Al-Jamei.

Iqbal, R., Murad, M. A. A., Mustapha, A., Panahy, P. H. S., & Khanahmadliravi, N. (2013). An experimental study of classification algorithms for crime prediction. *Indian Journal of Science and Technology*, *6*(3), 4219–4225. doi:10.17485/ijst/2013/v6i3.6

Islam, C., Babar, M. A., & Nepal, S. (2020). *Architecture-centric support for integrating security tools in a security orchestration platform*. Software Architecture: 14th European Conference, ECSA 2020, L'Aquila, Italy.10.1007/978-3-030-58923-3_11

ISO/IEC 23005. (2020). *MPEG-V standards*. ISO. https://mpeg.chiariglione.org/standards/mpeg-v

IT-Online. (2022). *Meta safety; meta security; metaverse*. IT Online. https://it-online.co.za/2022/02/08/meta-safety-meta-security-metaverse

Jaipong, P., Siripipattanakul, S., Sriboonruang, P., Sitthipon, T., Jaipong, P., Siripipattanakul, S., Sriboonruang, P., & Sitthipon, T. (2023). A Review of Metaverse and Cybersecurity in the Digital Era. *International Journal of Computing Sciences Research*, *7*, 1125–1132. doi:10.25147/ijcsr.2017.001.1.122

Jeon, S.-E., Oh, Y. S., & Lee, I. G. (2022). A Study on the policy measures for the prevention of industrial secret leakage in the metaverse. *Journal of Digital Convergence*, *20*(4), 377–388. doi:10.14400/JDC.2022.20.4.377

Jibril, M. (2023). *The Legal Challenges of Metaverse Technology from the Criminal Point of View*. Cairo: Dar Al-Ahram for Legal Publications.

Joshua, J. (2017). Information bodies: Computational anxiety in Neal Stephenson's snow crash. *Interdisciplinary Literary Studies*, *19*(1), 17–47. doi:10.5325/intelitestud.19.1.0017

Jovanovic, V., Kuzlu, M., Cali, U., Utku, D. H., Catak, F. O., Sarp, S., & Zohrabi, N. (2023). Digital Twin in Industry 4.0 and Beyond Applications. In Digital Twin Driven Intelligent Systems and Emerging Metaverse (pp. 155–174). Springer.

Jun, Y., Craig, A., Shafik, W., & Sharif, L. (2021). Artificial intelligence application in cybersecurity and cyberdefense. *Wireless Communications and Mobile Computing*, *1*, 1–10. doi:10.1155/2021/3329581

Kalinaki, K., Thilakarathne, N. N., Mubarak, H. R., Malik, O. A., & Abdullatif, M. (2023). *Cybersafe capabilities and utilities for smart cities. Cybersecurity for Smart Cities.* Springer., doi:10.1007/978-3-031-24946-4_6

Kalyvaki, M. (2023). Navigating the Metaverse Business and Legal Challenges: Intellectual Property, Privacy, and Jurisdiction. *Journal of Metaverse*, *3*(1), 87–92.

Kasiyanto, S., & Kilinc, M. R. (2022). The legal conundrums of the metaverse. *J. Central Bank. Law Institutions*, *1*(2), 299–322. doi:10.21098/jcli.v1i2.25

Katterbauer, K., Hassan, S. Y. E. D., & Cleenewerck, L. (2022). Financial cybercrime in the Islamic finance metaverse. *Journal of Metaverse*, *2*(2), 56–61. doi:10.57019/jmv.1108783

Kaur, P., Dhir, A., Tandon, A., Alzeiby, E. A., & Abohassan, A. A. (2021). A systematic literature review on cyberstalking. An analysis of past achievements and future promises. *Technological Forecasting and Social Change*, *163*, 120426. doi:10.1016/j.techfore.2020.120426

Kennedy, J. (2023). Metaverse Property: Advocating for the Regulation of Metaverse Land and Property through a Real Estate Legal Regime. *Ohio St. Bus. LJ*, *17*, 323.

Khalid, F. (2023). Metaverse is the Next Normal and Digital Future: A Systematic Review. In *2023 IEEE International Conference on Emerging Trends in Engineering, Sciences and Technology (ICES&T)* (pp. 1-7). IEEE. https://doi.org/10.1109/ICEST56843.2023.10138832

Khalifa, I. (2022). The Metaverse of the Future of Human Urbanization in a Post-Internet World. Abu Dhabi: The Future Center for Research and Advanced Studies.

Khan, S., Gani, A., Abdul Wahab, A. W., Iqbal, S., Abdelaziz, A., Mahdi, O. A., Abdallaahmed, A. I., Shiraz, M., Al-Mayouf, Y. R. B., Khan, Z., Ko, K., Khan, M. K., & Chang, V. (2016). Towards an applicability of current network forensics for cloud networks: A SWOT analysis. *IEEE Access : Practical Innovations, Open Solutions*, *4*, 9800–9820. doi:10.1109/ACCESS.2016.2631543

Koohang, A., Nord, J. H., Ooi, K.-B., Tan, G. W.-H., Al-Emran, M., Aw, E. C.-X., Baabdullah, A. M., Buhalis, D., Cham, T.-H., Dennis, C., Dutot, V., Dwivedi, Y. K., Hughes, L., Mogaji, E., Pandey, N., Phau, I., Raman, R., Sharma, A., Sigala, M., ... Wong, L.-W. (2023). Shaping the metaverse into reality: A holistic multidisciplinary understanding of opportunities, challenges, and avenues for future investigation. *Journal of Computer Information Systems*, *63*(3), 1–31. doi:10.1080/08874417.2023.2165197

Kumari, P., & Jain, A. K. (2023). A comprehensive study of DDoS attacks over IoT network and their countermeasures. *Computers & Security, 127.*

Kunthara, S. (2021). VCs will spend Billions more to make the metaverse a reality. *Crunchbase News.* https://news.crunchbase.com/news/metaverse-startups-funding-investors

Laeeq, K. (2022). *Metaverse: why, how and what.* How and What.

Laue, C. (2011). Crime Potential of Metaverses. In K. Cornelius & D. Hermann (Eds.), *Virtual Worlds and Criminality* (pp. 19–25). Springer-Verlag Berlin Heidelberg. doi:10.1007/978-3-642-20823-2_2

Lavoie, R., Main, K., King, C., & King, D. (2021). Virtual experience, real consequences: The potential negative emotional consequences of virtual reality gameplay. *Virtual Reality (Waltham Cross)*, *25*(1), 69–81. doi:10.100710055-020-00440-y

Lee, H., Lee, J., Kim, D., Jana, S., Shin, I., & Son, S. (2021). AdCube: WebVR ad fraud and practical confinement of Third-Party ads. In the *30th USENIX Security Symposium (USENIX Security 21)*. ACM.

Lee, L. H. (2022, October). The Digital Big Bang in the Metaverse Era. In *2022 IEEE International Symposium on Mixed and Augmented Reality Adjunct (ISMAR-Adjunct) (pp. 55-55)*. IEEE. 10.1109/ISMAR-Adjunct57072.2022.00020

Lee, L.-H., Braud, T., Zhou, P., Wang, L., Xu, D., Lin, Z., Kumar, A., Bermejo, C., & Hui, P. (2021). All one needs to know about metaverse: A complete survey on technological singularity, virtual ecosystem, and research agenda. *arXiv preprint arXiv:2110.05352.*

Lee, W. S. (2022). A Study on the Role of criminal law in Metaverse. *Institute for Legal Studies Chonnam National University, 177-202.* doi:10.38133/cnulawreview.2022.42.3.177

Lee, H., & Choi, K.-S. (2021). Interrelationship between Bitcoin, ransomware, and terrorist activities: Criminal opportunity assessment via cyber-routine activities theoretical framework. *Victims & Offenders, 16*(3), 363–384.

Leenes, R. (2007). Privacy in the metaverse. In S. Fischer-Hübner, P. Duquenoy, A. Zuccato, and L. Martucci (Eds). The Future of Identity in the Information Society. Springer. doi:10.1007/978-0-387-79026-8_7

Leenes, R. (2010). *Privacy in the Metaverse: Regulating a Complex Social Construct in a Virtual World.* Springer. https://link.springer.com/content/pdf/10.1007/978-0-387-79026-8_7.pdf

Levy, S. (2022). Neal Stephenson Named the Metaverse. Now, He's Building It. *Wired.* https://www.wired.com/story/plaintext-neal-stephenson-named-the-metaverse-now-hes-building-it/

Li, T., Yang, C., Yang, Q., Zhou, S., Huang, H., & Zheng, Z. (2023). MetaOpera: A Cross-Metaverse Interoperability Protocol. *ArXiv Preprint ArXiv:2302.01600.*

Li, B. J., Ratan, R., & Lwin, M. O. (2022). Virtual game changers: How avatars and virtual coaches influence exergame outcomes through enactive and vicarious learning. *Behaviour & Information Technology, 41*(7), 1529–1543. doi:10.1080/0144929X.2021.1884290

Li, B., Guo, Y., Wu, Y., Chen, J., Yuan, Y., & Zhang, X. (2014, September). An unsupervised learning algorithm for the classification of the protection device in the fault diagnosis system. In *2014 China International Conference on Electricity Distribution (CICED)* (pp. 817-823). IEEE. 10.1109/CICED.2014.6991823

Lik-HangL.TristanB.PengyuanZ.LinW.DianleiX.ZijunL.PanH. (2021). All One Needs to Know about Metaverse: A Complete Survey on Technological Singularity. Virtual Ecosystem, and Research Agenda. *Latex Class Files, 14.* https://pengyuan-zhou.github.io/papers/metaversearxiv.pdf

Lim, J., Yun, H., Ham, A., & Kim, S. (2022). Mine yourself!: A role-playing privacy tutorial in virtual reality environment. In: *CHI Conference on Human Factors in Computing Systems Extended Abstracts*, New Orleans, LA, USA. 10.1145/3491101.3519773

Liu, A., Xia, L., Duchowski, A., Bailey, R., Holmqvist, K., & Jain, E. (2019). Differential privacy for eye-tracking data. In *Proceedings of the 11th ACM Symposium on Eye Tracking Research & Applications.* New York, NY, USA. 10.1145/3314111.3319823

Li, Y., Yang, X., Sun, P., Qi, H., & Lyu, S. (2020). Celeb-df: A large-scale challenging dataset for deepfake forensics. *Proceedings of the IEEE/CVF conference on computer vision and pattern recognition.* IEEE.

Lodder, A. R. (2011). Conflict resolution in virtual worlds: general characteristics and the 2009 Dutch convictions on virtual theft.

Loozen, T., Chedid, F., & Buchanan, L. (2022). *Journey to the Centre of the Metaverse: A Perspective on the Metaverse and What It Means for Telcos*. Ernst & Young., https://assets.ey.com/content/dam/ey-sites/ey-com/en_gl/topics/telecommunications/ey-metaverse-for-telcos.pdf?download

Lusthaus, J., & Varese, F. (2021). Offline and local: The hidden face of cybercrime. *Policing. Policing (Oxford, England), 15*(1), 4–14. doi:10.1093/police/pax042

Mackenzie, S. (2022). Criminology towards the metaverse: Cryptocurrency scams, grey economy and the techno-social. *British Journal of Criminology, 62*(6), 1537–1552. doi:10.1093/bjc/azab118

Macpherson, I., & Puplampu, A. (2023). *15 Better than the Real You? VR, Identity, Privacy, and the Metaverse*. Virtual Identities and Digital Culture.

Majun, M. (2022). Incitement to hatred and violence in social networks. The Islamic Military Coalition to Combat Terrorism, Riyadh.

Malathi, A., & Santhosh Baboo, S. (2011). An enhanced algorithm to predict a future crime using data mining. *International Journal of Computer Applications, 21*(1), 1–6. doi:10.5120/2478-3335

Manral, B., Somani, G., Choo, K. K. R., Conti, M., & Gaur, M. S. (2019). A Systematic survey on cloud forensics challenges, solutions, and future directions. *ACM Computing Surveys, 52*(6), 1–38. doi:10.1145/3361216

Marr, B. (2022). *The fascinating history and evolution of Extended Reality (XR) – covering AR*. VR and MR.

Marshall, A. M., & Tompsett, B. C. (2023). The metaverse—Not a new frontier for crime. *WIREs Forensic Science, 1505*, e1505. doi:10.1002/wfs2.1505

Masera, R. (2023). Web 1.0, 2.0, 3.0; InfoSphere; Metaverse: An Overview. Monetary, Financial, Societal and Geopolitical Transformation Cusps. *Monetary, Financial, Societal and Geopolitical Transformation Cusps (January 14, 2023).*

Mccormick, T. Y. (2013). The Darknet: A Short History. *Foreign Policy.*

McGuire, M., & Dowling, S. (2013). Cyber crime: A review of the evidence. *Summary of key findings and implications. Home Office*. Research Reports (Montgomery), 75, 1–35.

Meiklejohn, S., & ... (2013). A fistful of bitcoins: characterizing payments among men with no names. *Proceedings of the 2013 ACM SIGCOMM conference on Internet measurement conference*. New York, ACM. 10.1145/2504730.2504747

Meta. (2021). *Introducing Meta: A Social Technology Company*. Meta.

Meta. (2021). *Our vision for the metaverse*. Meta. https://tech.fb.com/ar-vr/2021/10/connect-2021-our-vision-for-the-metaverse/

Miller, M.R., Herrera, F., Jun, H. et al. (2020). Personal identifiability of user tracking data during observation of 360-degree VR video. *Scientific Reports. 10*, 17404. doi:10.1038/s41598-020-74486-y

Minshawi, M. (2012). The Authority of the Criminal Judge in Estimating Electronic Evidence. Journal of Laws, 36(2).

Mitchell, A. R., Ahlert, D., Brown, C., Birge, M., & Gibbs, A. (2023). Electrocardiogram-based biometrics for user identification–Using your heartbeat as a digital key. *Journal of Electrocardiology, 80*, 1–6. doi:10.1016/j.jelectrocard.2023.04.001 PMID:37058746

Mittal, G., & Bansal, R. (2023). *Driving Force Behind Consumer Brand Engagement.*

Morgan, R. A. (2021). *Exploring the Feasibility of Developing a Customized IDS/IPS Security Control for Computer Network Security*. Colorado Technical University.

Morimoto, S., Kawamukai, H., & Shin, K. (2019, August). Prediction of crime occurrence using information propagation model and gaussian process. In *2019 14th Asia Joint Conference on Information Security (AsiaJCIS)* (pp. 80-87). IEEE. 10.1109/AsiaJCIS.2019.000-2

Mukherjee, S. (2022). Fighting Cybercrime in the Metaverse: As More Money Enters the Metaverse, the More Hackers Will Try to Take Advantage of Everyday Crypto Users. *Analytics India.* https://analyticsindiamag.com/fighting-cybercrime-in-metaverse/

Murray, M. D. (April 2022). *Ready Lawyer One: Lawyering in the Metaverse* (pp. 2-5). Research Gate. https://www.researchgate.net/publication/359931632

MurrayM. D. (2022). Ready lawyer one: Lawyering in the Metaverse. [Online]. https://ssrn.com/abstract=4082648 doi:10.2139/ssrn.4082648

Mystakidis, S. (2022). Metaverse. *Encyclopedia, 2*(1), 486–497. doi:10.3390/encyclopedia2010031

Naguib, H. (2014). The Authenticity of the Electronic Evidence (Cairo: National Center for Social and Criminological Research). National Criminal Journal, 57.

NairV.Munilla GarridoG.SongD. (2022). Exploring the unprecedented privacy risks of the metaverse. arXiv:2207.13176. [Online]. Available: https://arxiv.org/pdf/2207.13176.pdf

Naqvi, A. A. (n.d.). *A COMPREHENSIVE ANALYSIS OF METAVERSE TECHNOLOGIES TO ATTEMPT A TREND ANALYSIS OF THE EMERGING CONCEPTUAL AND APPLIED ASPECTS OF METAVERSE.*

Narang, N. K. (2023). Mentor's Musings on Role of Standards, Regulations & Policies in Navigating Through Metaverse and its Future Avatars. *IEEE Internet of Things Magazine, 6*(1), 4–11. doi:10.1109/MIOT.2023.10070410

NingH.WangH.LinY.WangW. (2021). A Survey on metaverse: The state-of-the-art, technologies, applications, and challenges. arXiv:2111.09673. https://arxiv.org/ftp/arxiv/papers/2111/2111.09673.pdf.

Ning, H., Wang, H., Lin, Y., Wang, W., Dhelim, S., Farha, F., Ding, J., & Daneshmand, M. (2023). A Survey on the Metaverse: The State-of-the-Art, Technologies, Applications, and Challenges. *IEEE Internet of Things Journal.*

Nobles, C. (2019). Establishing human factors programs to mitigate blind spots in cybersecurity. *MWAIS 2019 Proceedings, 22.*

OlubuseO. (2023). The Role of the Nigerian Lawyer in the Metaverse. *Available at* SSRN 4326585. doi:10.2139/ssrn.4326585

Orofino, E. (2021). International Security Confrontation of Criminal Activities Committed Through the Dark Web. *Public Security Magazine.*

Orofino, E. (2021). The Depths of the "Dark Internet", Hiring Killers and Abnormal Services in Exchange for Cryptocurrency. *Asharq Al-Awsat Newspaper, Al-Arab International Newspaper.*

Orofino, E. (2022). Digital counterfeiting and its impact on the authenticity of digital evidence in criminal cases, a comparative jurisprudence study. *Journal of Comparative Jurisprudence, Faculty of Sharia Law, Al-Azhar University, Cairo, 14.*

Orofino, E. (2022). *Online Radicalization: How to Detect and Deal with Extremist Content (United Kingdom Model).* European Eye on Radicalization Report. https://eeradicalization.com/exploring-online-radicalization-how-to-spot-extremist-content-and-what-to-do-about-it/

Orofino, E. (2022). Rumors and Cybercrime Crimes in the Arab Emirates. *Journal of Fiqh and Legal Research,* Al-Azhar University, Cairo. https://jlr.journals.ekb.eg/article_251626_ec495d5801eb0c97219e5b22d07cc5ad.pdf https://digitalwellbeing.ae/ar/digital_laws_in_uae

OSCE. (2019). *Understanding the Role of Social Communication, and Preventing Countering Violent Extremism Conducive to Terrorism.* OSCE Secretariat.

Ottis, R. (2008). Analysis of the 2007 cyber attacks against Estonia from the information warfare perspective. Proceedings of the 7th European Conference on Information Warfare,.

Pagani, F., Fedorov, O., & Balzarotti, D. (2019). Introducing the temporal dimension to memory forensics. *ACM Transactions on Privacy and Security (TOPS), 22*(2), 1-21

Pastrana, S., Hutchings, A., Caines, A., & Buttery, P. (2018). *Characterizing eve: Analysing cybercrime actors in a large underground forum.* Research in Attacks, Intrusions, and Defenses: *21st International Symposium, RAID 2018,* Heraklion, Crete, Greece.

Patel, N. (2021). The metaverse is already here — and it's full of Pokemon, says Niantic CEO John Hanke. *The Verge.* https://www.theverge.com/22832490/niantic-ceo-john-hanke-metaverse-pokemon-go-ar-vr-podcast-decoder-interview

Pfeuffer, K., Geiger, M. J., Prange, S., Mecke, L., Buschek, D., & Alt, F. (2019) Behavioural biometrics in VR: identifying people from body motion and relations in virtual reality. In: *Proceedings of the 2019 CHI Conference on Human Factors in Computing Systems,* (pp 1–12). ACM. 10.1145/3290605.3300340

Pinter, C. (2005). *The threat posed by information crime and the need for international cooperation, (Cairo: Police Academy).* Sixth International Conference on Information Crime organized by the International Criminal Police Organization "Interpol," Cairo.

Pipyros, K., Mitrou, L., Gritzalis, D., & Apostolopoulos, T. (2016). Cyberoperations and international humanitarian law: A review of obstacles in applying international law rules in cyber warfare. *Information & Computer Security.*

Poore, C. A. (2023). *Leadership in the Metaverse: Creating the Future of WebWe Through Strategy and Community Building.* Greenleaf Book Group.

Popa, M., Stoklossa, S. M., & Mazumdar, S. (2023). ChainDiscipline-Towards A Blockchain-IoT-Based Self-Sovereign Identity Management Framework. *IEEE Transactions on Services Computing, 16*(5), 3238–3251. doi:10.1109/TSC.2023.3279871

Pratibha, Akanksha Gahalot, Uprant, Suraina Dhiman, Lokesh Chouhan, "Crime Prediction and Analysis", Institute of Electronics and Electricals Engineers, February 2020.

Qamar, S., Anwar, Z., & Afzal, M. (2023). A systematic threat analysis and defense strategies for the metaverse and extended reality systems. *Computers & Security, 128,* 103127. doi:10.1016/j.cose.2023.103127

Qin, H. X., Wang, Y., & Hui, P. (2022). Identity, crimes, and law enforcement in the metaverse. arXiv preprint arXiv:2210.06134. https://doi.org//arXiv.2210.06134 doi:10.48550

Quéméner, M. (2014). Les spécificités juridiques de la prevue numérique. *AJ Pénal,* (1).

Radanliev, P. (2023). *The Metaverse: Economic and Social Values and Risks of New Cryptocurrencies and Blockchain Technologies.*

Rahman, F. (2022). The future of cybersecurity in the age of quantum computers. *Future Internet, 14*(11), 335.

Ratan, R. & Lei, Y. (2021). *What is the metaverse? 2 media and information experts explain.* Down to Earth.

Rawat, D. B., & El Alami, H. (2023). Metaverse: Requirements, Architecture, Standards, Status, Challenges, and Perspectives. *IEEE Internet of Things Magazine*, *6*(1), 14–18. doi:10.1109/IOTM.001.2200258

Reid, D. (2021). *Who is going to police the metaverse?* Liverpool Hope University. Available at: https://www.hope.ac.uk/news/allnews/who-is-going-to-police-the metaverse.html

Report, E. M. (2022). *The Future of Financial Crime in the Metaverse, Fighting Crypto crime in Web3.0* Elliptic. https://www.elliptic.co/hubfs/Crime%20in%20the%20Metaverse%202022%20final.pdf

Robinson, M., Jones, K., & Janicke, H. (2015). Cyber warfare: Issues and challenges. *Computers & Security*, *49*, 70–94. doi:10.1016/j.cose.2014.11.007

Rosenberg, L. (2022, March). Regulation of the Metaverse: A Roadmap: The risks and regulatory solutions for largescale consumer platforms. In *Proceedings of the 6th international conference on virtual and augmented reality simulations* (pp. 21-26). ACM. 10.1145/3546607.3546611

Saad, M., Njilla, L., Kamhoua, C., Kim, J., Nyang, D., & Mohaisen, A. (2019). Mempool optimization for defending against DDoS attacks in PoW-based blockchain systems. *2019 IEEE international conference on blockchain and cryptocurrency (ICBC)*. IEEE.

Sabillon, R., Cano, J. J., Cavaller Reyes, V., & Serra Ruiz, J. (2016). Cybercrime and cybercriminals: A comprehensive study. *International Journal of Computer Networks and Communications Security, 2016, 4(6).*

Saharan, S., & Yadav, B. (2022). Digital and cyber forensics: A contemporary evolution in forensic sciences. In Crime Scene Management within Forensic Science: Forensic Techniques for Criminal Investigations (pp. 267-294). Springer. doi:10.1007/978-981-16-6683-4_11

Saini, H., & … . (2012). Cyber-crimes and their impacts: A review. *International Journal of Engineering Research and Applications*, *2*(2), 202–209.

Salem, M. (2022, January). The future of technological development in light of metaverse technology, Future Horizons Magazine. *Information and Decision Support Center of the Egyptian Council of Ministers*, (2), 395–400.

Sá, M. J., & Serpa, S. (2023). Metaverse as a Learning Environment: Some Considerations. *Sustainability (Basel)*, *15*(3), 2186. doi:10.3390u15032186

Samtani, S., Abate, M., Benjamin, V., & Li, W. (2020). Cybersecurity as an industry: A cyber threat intelligence perspective. The Palgrave Handbook of International Cybercrime and Cyberdeviance. Palgrave.

Sathyadevan, S., Devan, M. S., & Gangadharan, S. S. (2014, August). Crime analysis and prediction using data mining. In *2014 First international conference on networks & soft computing (ICNSC2014)* (pp. 406-412). IEEE. 10.1109/CNSC.2014.6906719

Scharfman, J. (2023). Additional Case Studies in Cryptocurrency Fraud. In *The Cryptocurrency and Digital Asset Fraud Casebook* (pp. 161–172). Springer. doi:10.1007/978-3-031-23679-2_11

SchmittM. (2023). Big Data Analytics in the Metaverse: Business Value Creation with Artificial Intelligence and Data-Driven Decision Making. *Available at* SSRN 4385347. doi:10.2139/ssrn.4385347

SchmittM. (n.d.). Securing the Digital World: Protecting Smart Infrastructures and Digital Industries with Artificial Intelligence (Ai)-Enabled Malware and Intrusion Detection. *Available at* SSRN 4397870. doi:10.1016/j.jii.2023.100520

Segal, A. (2013). The code not taken: China, the United States, and the future of cyber espionage. *Bulletin of the Atomic Scientists*, *69*(5), 38–45.

Seigfried-Spellar, K. C., Holt, T. J., & Bossler, A. M. (2022). *Cybercrime and Digital Forensics: An Introduction. (n.p.)*. Taylor & Francis.

Senno, S. (2022). *The Metaverse, an opportunity for society or terrorism?* AMISTADES report. https://en.amistades.info/post/metaverse-an-opportunity-for-society-or-terrorism

Seo, S., Seok, B., & Lee, C. (2023). Digital forensic investigation framework for the metaverse. *The Journal of Supercomputing*, *79*(9), 1–19. doi:10.100711227-023-05045-1

Sethuraman, S. C., Mitra, A., Ghosh, A., Galada, G., & Subramanian, A. (2023). MetaSecure: A Passwordless Authentication for the Metaverse. *ArXiv Preprint ArXiv:2301.01770.*

Sfetcu, N. (2023). *Intelligence Info, Volumul 2, Numărul 1, Martie*. Nicolae Sfetcu.

Shafik, W. (2023). Cyber Security Perspectives in Public Spaces: Drone Case Study. In *Handbook of Research on Cybersecurity Risk in Contemporary Business Systems, 79–97*. IGI Global. doi:10.4018/978-1-6684-7207-1.ch004

Shalev-Shwartz, S., & Ben-David, S. (2014). *Understanding machine learning: From theory to algorithms*. Cambridge university press. doi:10.1017/CBO9781107298019

Shen, M. (2022). Sexual harassment in the metaverse? Woman alleges rape in virtual world. *USA Today*. https://www.usatoday.com/story/tech/2022/01/31/woman-allegedly-groped-metaverse/9278578002/

Shinde, N., & Kulkarni, P. (2021). Cyber incident response and planning: a flexible approach. *Computer Fraud & Security*, *2021*(1), 14–19.

Shukla, A., Katal, A., Raghuvanshi, S., & Sharma, S. (2021, June). Criminal Combat: Crime Analysis and Prediction Using Machine Learning. In *2021 International Conference on Intelligent Technologies (CONIT)* (pp. 1-5). IEEE. 10.1109/CONIT51480.2021.9498397

Sia, C. C. (2023). The Role of Legal Governance Framework in the Metaverse World. In *Strategies and Opportunities for Technology in the Metaverse World* (pp. 321–330). IGI Global. doi:10.4018/978-1-6684-5732-0.ch017

Siddiqi, M. A., Pak, W., & Siddiqi, M. A. (2022). A Study on the Psychology of Social Engineering-Based Cyberattacks and Existing Countermeasures. *Applied Sciences (Basel, Switzerland)*, *12*(12), 6042. doi:10.3390/app12126042

Simou, S., Kalloniatis, C., Gritzalis, S., & Mouratidis, H. (2016). A survey on cloud forensics challenges and solutions. *Security and Communication Networks*, *9*(18), 6285–6314. doi:10.1002ec.1688

Singh, A., Thakur, N., & Sharma, A. (2016, March). A review of supervised machine learning algorithms. In *2016 3rd international conference on computing for sustainable global development (INDIACom)* (pp. 1310-1315). IEEE.

Siyaev, A., & Jo, G. S. (2021). Towards Aircraft Maintenance Metaverse Using Speech Interactions with Virtual Objects in Mixed Reality. *Sensors (Basel)*, *21*(6), 1–21. doi:10.339021062066 PMID:33804253

Smaili, N., & de Rancourt-Raymond, A. (2022). Metaverse: Welcome to the new fraud marketplace. *Journal of Financial Crime*. Advance online publication. doi:10.1108/JFC-06-2022-0124

Smith, K. T., Smith, L. M., Burger, M., & Boyle, E. S. (2023). Cyber terrorism cases and stock market valuation effects. *Information and Computer Security*, *31*(4), 385–403. doi:10.1108/ICS-09-2022-0147

Sparkes, M. (2021). "What is a metaverse" 251. *New Scientist*, *3348*, 18.

Sparkes, M. (2021). *What is a metaverse*. Elsevier. doi:10.1016/S0262-4079(21)01450-0

Sparkes, M. (2021). What is a metaverse? *New Scientist*, *251*(3348), 18.

Stanage, N. (2007). From Second Life to second-degree murder. The Guardian. [Online]. Available: https://www.theguardian.com/commentisfree/2007/jan/16/fromsecondlifetoseconddegr

Statista. (2022). *Dangers of the metaverse according to internet users worldwide in 2021*. Statista. https://www.statista.com/statistics/1288822/metaversedangers/

Stephenson, N. (2003). *Snow crash: A novel*. Spectra.

Stubbs, G. (2023). *How should we police the metaverse?* DWTC. https://www.dwtc.com/en/industry-insights/how-should-we-police-the-metaverse/

Szymanski, T. (2023). *A Software-Defined Deterministic Internet of Things (IoT) with Artificial Intelligence (AI) for Quantum-Safe Cyber-Security*.

Techcrunch. (2006). Metaverse breached: Second life customer database hacked. *Techcrunch*. https://techcrunch.com/2006/09/08/metaverse-breached-second-life-customer-database-hacked/

Teodorov., A.V. (2023). Cybercrimes in the Metaverse: Challenges and Solutions. In *Proceedings of the International Conference on Cybersecurity and Cybercrime-2023* (pp. 209-215). Asociatia Romana pentru Asigurarea Securitatii Informatiei.

The Information and Decision Support Center of the Egyptian Council of Ministers. (2022). World Trends - Metaverse World.

Thongsatapornwatana, U. (2016, January). A survey of data mining techniques for analyzing crime patterns. In *2016 Second Asian Conference on Defence Technology (ACDT)* (pp. 123-128). IEEE. 10.1109/ACDT.2016.7437655

Threatpost. (2022). NFT investors lose $1.7m in OpenSea phishing attack," Threatpost. https://threatpost.com/nft-investors-lose-1-7m-in-opensea-phishing-attack/178558

Time. (2016). Game developer saddened by virtual reality sex assault: 'This must never happen again.' *Time*. https://time.com/4545943/virtual-reality-sex-assault-developer/

Tlili, A., Huang, R., & Kinshuk. (2023). Metaverse for climbing the ladder toward 'Industry 5.0'and' Society 5.0′? *Service Industries Journal*, *43*(3–4), 260–287. doi:10.1080/02642069.2023.2178644

Tredinnick, R., Smith, S., & Ponto, K. (2019, November). A Cost-Benefit Analysis of 3D Scanning Technology for Crime Scene Investigation. *Forensic Science International. Reports*, *1*, 100025. https://www.sciencedirect.com/science/article/pii/S2665910719300258. doi:10.1016/j.fsir.2019.100025

Tugtekin, U. (2023). The Dark Side of Metaverse Learning Environments: Potential Threats and Risk Factors. In Shaping the Future of Online Learning: Education in the Metaverse (pp. 57-67). IGI Global.

Tugtekin, U. (2023). The Dark Side of Metaverse Learning Environments: Potential Threats and Risk Factors. In Shaping the Future of Online Learning: Education in the Metaverse (pp. 57–67). IGI Global.

UAE. (2021). *National Program for Artificial Intelligence*. UAE. https://ai.gov.ae/wp-content/uploads/2021/07/AI-Deepfake-Guide-AR-2021.pdf

Ulrich, F., Müller, S. D., & Flowers, S. (2023). The Professionalization of Hackers: A Content Analysis of 30 Years of Hacker Communication. *Communications of the Association for Information Systems*, *52*(1), 12.

UN. (2012). *The use of the Internet for terrorist purposes*. UNODC. https://www.unodc.org/documents/terrorism/Publications/Use_of_Internet_for_Terrorist_Purposes/ebook_use_of_the_internet_for_terrorist_purposes.pdf

United Nations Office on Drugs and Crime. (2013). *Study on Cybercrime*. United Nations Organization.

United States v. Meregildo, No. 11 Cr. 576 WHP, 2012 WL 3264501, at *2 S.D.N.Y. Aug. 10, 2012.

Upadhyay, D., & Sampalli, S. (2020). SCADA (Supervisory Control and Data Acquisition) systems: Vulnerability assessment and security recommendations. *Computers & Security*, *89*, 101666. doi:10.1016/j.cose.2019.101666

US Department of Justice. (2007). *Digital Evidence in the Courtroom, A Business Guide for Law Enforcement and Prosecutors*. National Institute of Justice.

Valluripally, S., Gulhane, A., Mitra, R., & Hoque, K. A. (2020). *Attack trees for security and privacy in social virtual reality learning environments. In 2020 IEEE 17th Annual Consumer Communications & Networking Conference*. CCNC., doi:10.1109/CCNC46108.2020.9045724

Van der Land, S., Schouten, A., & Feldberg, F. (2011). Modeling the metaverse: A theoretical model of effective team collaboration in 3D virtual environments. *Journal of Virtual Worlds Research*, *4*(3). doi:10.4101/jvwr.v4i3.6126

Varshitha, D. N., Vidyashree, K. P., Aishwarya, P., & Janya, T. S., KR, D. G., & Sahana, R. (2017). Paper on Different Approaches for Crime Prediction system. [IJERT]. *International Journal of Engineering Research & Technology (Ahmedabad)*.

Vidal-Tomás, D. (2022). The new crypto niche: NFTs, play-to-earn, and metaverse tokens. *Finance Research Letters*, *47*, 102742. doi:10.1016/j.frl.2022.102742

von Wachter, V., Jensen, J. R., Regner, F., & Ross, O. 2022. NFT wash trading: Quantifying suspicious behaviour in NFT markets. *arXiv preprint arXiv:2202.03866.*

Wang, Q., Li, R., Wang, Q., & Chen, S. 2021. Non-Fungible Token (NFT): Overview, evaluation, opportunities and challenges. *arXiv preprint arXiv:2105.07447.*

Wang, Y., Su, Z., Zhang, N., Xing, R., Liu, D., Luan, T. H., & Shen, X. (2022). A survey on metaverse: Fundamentals, security, and privacy. *IEEE Communications Surveys & Tutorials*. IEEE. 10.1007/978-3-031-35504-2_8

Wang, F. Y., Tang, Y., & Werbos, P. J. (2023). Guest editorial: cyber–physical–social intelligence: toward metaverse-based smart societies of 6I and 6S. *IEEE Transactions on Systems, Man, and Cybernetics. Systems*, *53*(4), 2018–2024. doi:10.1109/TSMC.2023.3243558

Wang, J., Makowski, S., Cieślik, A., Lv, H., & Lv, Z. (2023). Fake News in Virtual Community, Virtual Society, and Metaverse: A Survey. *IEEE Transactions on Computational Social Systems*, 1–15. doi:10.1109/TCSS.2022.3220420

Wang, Y., Su, Z., Li, J., Zhang, N., Zhang, K., Choo, K.-K. R., & Liu, Y. (2022). Blockchain-Based Secure and Cooperative Private Charging Pile Sharing Services for Vehicular Networks. *IEEE Transactions on Vehicular Technology*, *71*(2), 1857–1874. doi:10.1109/TVT.2021.3131744

Wang, Y., Su, Z., Zhang, N., Xing, R., Liu, D., Luan, T. H., & Shen, X. (2022). A survey on metaverse: Fundamentals, security, and privacy. *IEEE Communications Surveys and Tutorials.*

Weimann, G., & Dimant, R. (2023). The Metaverse and Terrorism: Threats and Challenges. *Prespectives on terrorism, 17*(2). https://pt.icct.nl/sites/default/files/2023-06/PT%20-%20Vol%20XVII%2C%20Issue%20II%20-%20June%20 2023%20A5.pdf

Weinberger, M. (2022). What Is Metaverse? A Definition Based on Qualitative Meta-Synthesis. *Future Internet*, *14*(11), 310.

Wu, S., Sun, W., Ding, Z., & Liu, S. (2022). Cloud evidence tracing system: An integrated forensics investigation system for large-scale public cloud platform. *Forensic Science International Digital Investigation*, *41*, 1–9. doi:10.1016/j.fsidi.2022.301391

Yadav, S., Timbadia, M., Yadav, A., Vishwakarma, R., & Yadav, N. (2017, April). Crime pattern detection, analysis & prediction. In *2017 International conference of Electronics, Communication and Aerospace Technology (ICECA)* (Vol. 1, pp. 225-230). IEEE. 10.1109/ICECA.2017.8203676

Yang, R., Li, L., Gan, W., Chen, Z., & Qi, Z. (2023). The Human-Centric Metaverse: A Survey. *ArXiv Preprint ArXiv:2303.11123*. doi:10.1145/3543873.3587593

Yeom, S., Shin, D., & Shin, D. (2021). Scenario-based cyber attack· defense education system on virtual machines integrated by web technologies for protection of multimedia contents in a network. *Multimedia Tools and Applications*, *80*(26-27), 34085–34101. doi:10.100711042-019-08583-0

Yoo, K., Welden, R., Hewett, K., & Haenlein, M. (2023). The merchants of meta: A research agenda to understand the future of retailing in the metaverse. *Journal of Retailing*, *99*(2), 173–192. doi:10.1016/j.jretai.2023.02.002

Yunus, O. (2004). Crimes arising from the use of the Internet. (Dissertation, Cairo: Ain Shams University].

Yunus, O. (2006). *Notes on Criminal Evidence via the Internet*. [Dissertation, Cairo: League of Arab States].

Zainurin, M. Z. L., Haji Masri, M., Besar, M. H. A., & Anshari, M. (2023). Towards an understanding of metaverse banking: A conceptual paper. *Journal of Financial Reporting and Accounting*, *21*(1), 178–190. doi:10.1108/JFRA-12-2021-0487

Zaki, M. R. S., & Santo, P. A. F. D. (n.d.). *International Labour Law Perspectives on the Metaverse*.

Zhang, X., Liu, L., Xiao, L., & Ji, J. (2020). Comparison of machine learning algorithms for predicting crime hotspots. *IEEE Access : Practical Innovations, Open Solutions*, *8*, 181302–181310. https://www.kaggle.com/datasets/rajanand/crime-in-india. doi:10.1109/ACCESS.2020.3028420

Zhang, Y., Xiao, Y., Ghaboosi, K., Zhang, J., & Deng, H. (2012). A survey of cyber crimes. *Security and Communication Networks*, *5*(4), 422–437. doi:10.1002ec.331

Zhao, L., Zhu, D., Shafik, W., Matinkhah, S. M., Ahmad, Z., Sharif, L., & Craig, A. (2022). Artificial intelligence analysis in cyber domain: A review. *International Journal of Distributed Sensor Networks*, *18*(4), 15501329221084882. doi:10.1177/15501329221084882

Zubaska, M., & Szczytno, P. (2018, January). Improvement of Crime Scene Examination and Reduction of Cognitive Deficit: The Need to Implement a New Imaging and Dimensioning Technique. *Issues in Forensic Science, 302,* 54-62.

Zytko, D., & Chan, J. (2023). The Dating Metaverse: Why We Need to Design for Consent in Social VR. *IEEE Transactions on Visualization and Computer Graphics*, *29*(5), 2489–2498. doi:10.1109/TVCG.2023.3247065 PMID:37027706

About the Contributors

Hossam Nabil ElShenraky, full Professor of Head of cybercrime Investigation science section - Dubai Police Academy, Bachelor of Law, and Police Sciences in 1992 from the Police College, Master's in cybercrime investigation, PhD in in cybercrime investigation, Specialization: cybercrime Investigation - Information Technology Crimes – cybercrime analysis, Leadership and Decision Making - Cyber Crisis Management - Digital Transformation - Cyber Security worked as investigation officer since 1996 until 2018, worked with peacekeeping forces in Darfur, Sudan for two years and 3 months, police sector commander, retired as brigadier general and worked in Dubai Police Academy, a teaching staff until now, got many training courses in criminal investigation, and information crimes, presented in many conferences and chaired many conferences internationally. peer reviewer at Journal of Cybercrime, member of the editorial board of Naif Arab University journal for Security Sciences, arbitrator at Journal of Digital Forensic, A security expert accredited by Naif Arab University for Security Sciences and listed in its database of security expert, Member of the Editorial Board of the Journal of the International Police Science Organization (IPSA) in the USA, Supervised dozens of master's and doctoral dissertations at the Dubai Police Academy in the field of police sciences and security crisis management, have more than 12 scientific research papers published in many scientific journals in Egypt and the UAE, have 5 academic books, Member of the Editorial Board of Security and Law Magazine - Dubai Police Academy, Scientific Adviser to the police Department for Future Foresight in Dubai Police In training courses, Certified trainer with Dubai Police.

***

Sened Abraham received her Bachelor of Information Technology degree from Zayed University, Abu Dhabi, United Arab Emirates in 2023. In 2019, she was awarded a scholarship to pursue her studies in the UAE. Currently, she is focusing on information security and digital forensics as her primary field of study and research. Her research interests include digital forensics, network security, artificial intelligence, and machine learning, among others

Ibtesam Alawadhi is the head of Post graduate college at the Dubai Police Academy. Previously, dr. Ibtesam worked as a digital forensics expert and consultant with over 18 years of experience in the field. She worked as a senior expert in Digital Forensics Department - Dubai Police which provides computer forensics services to organizations and individuals. Dr. Ibtesam has a PhD in Digital Forensics from the University of Central Lancashire and a Master of Science in Digital Forensics from Zayed University. Dr.

Ibtesam has worked as part time faculty member in different universities in UAE sharing the knowledge of digital investigation plus the cyber security fundamentals.

Ajay Kumar Bhandari, M.Sc. Forensic Science, Amity University, Manesar, Gurugram is the Author of THE FUTURE OF CYBER-CRIMES & CYBER WAR IN THE METAVERSE.

Akashdeep Bhardwaj is working as Professor and Head of Cybersecurity (Center of Excellence) at University of Petroleum & Energy Studies (UPES), Dehradun, India. An eminent IT Industry expert with over 28 years of experience in areas such as Cybersecurity, Digital Forensics and IT Operations, Dr. Akashdeep mentors graduate, masters and doctoral students and leads several industry projects. Dr. Akashdeep is a Post-Doctoral from Majmaah University, Saudi Arabia, and a Ph.D. in Computer Science. Dr. Akashdeep has published over 125 research works (including copyrights, patent, research papers, authored & edited books) in international journals. Dr. Akashdeep worked as Technology Leader for several multinational organizations during his time in the IT industry. Dr. Akashdeep is certified in multiple technologies including Compliance Audits, Cybersecurity, and industry certifications in Microsoft, Cisco, and VMware technologies.

Shashwath Bhaskar, born on September 19, 2003, in the picturesque state of Jammu and Kashmir, India, is a young and aspiring Software Development Engineer (SDE) with a passion for technology and a love for personal growth. His journey is a testament to his resilience, determination, and unwavering belief in equality and feminism. Early Life: Shashwath was raised in the diverse and culturally rich tapestry of India, where he developed a deep appreciation for the world's myriad perspectives. From an early age, it was evident that Shashwath was destined for greatness. He exhibited a strong intellectual aptitude, securing an impressive 93.8% in his 10th-grade examinations and further raising the bar with an impressive 94.6% in his 12th-grade examinations. Academic Pursuits: Driven by his insatiable curiosity and a love for technology, Shashwath embarked on a journey to explore the realm of computer science. Currently pursuing his B.Tech in Computer Science at VIT Bhopal University, he is honing his skills and knowledge to become an SDE par excellence. His dedication to his academic pursuits is matched only by his passion for personal growth. Passions and Interests: Beyond the realm of academia, Shashwath Bhaskar is a multifaceted individual. He is an avid reader, finding solace and knowledge in the pages of books. Simultaneously, he is a fitness enthusiast, believing in the importance of a healthy body to complement a sharp mind. His commitment to personal development extends beyond the classroom, making him a well-rounded individual. Overcoming Challenges: Shashwath's journey to self-discovery wasn't without its hurdles. He faced and overcame challenges such as stage fright, shyness, and the crippling fear of examinations. His transformation from an introverted individual to a confident and driven young man serves as an inspiring example for others facing similar obstacles. Values and Beliefs: Shashwath Bhaskar firmly believes in the principles of equality and feminism. He envisions a world where every individual is treated with respect and dignity, regardless of their gender or background. His philosophy combines elements of capitalism with a welfare approach, striving for economic growth while ensuring the well-being of all members of society. Shashwath is a firm believer in the concept of karma, recognizing the importance of actions and their consequences. Aspiration to Impact the World: While Shashwath may not have yet left a global imprint, he is diligently preparing himself to do just that. Through his education and skills, he aspires to make a positive and lasting impact on the world. His journey is a testament to the power of perseverance, self-belief, and a commitment to self-improvement.

In Shashwath Bhaskar's biography, one finds a young individual with immense potential, a passion for technology, a commitment to personal growth, and a strong belief in equality and social justice. As he continues his journey, one can only anticipate the remarkable contributions he will make to the world as an aspiring SDE.

Lakshmi D. is presently designated as a Senior Associate Professor in the School of Computing Science and Engineering (SCSE) & Assistant Director, at the Centre for Innovation in Teaching & Learning (CITL) at VIT Bhopal. She has 17 international conference presentations, and 21 international journal papers inclusive of SCOPUS & SCI (cumulative impact factor 31). 3 SCOPUS inee book chapters. A total of 24 patents are in various states and 18 patents have been granted at both national and international levels. One Edited book with Taylor & Francis (SCOPUS Indexed). She has won two Best Paper awards at international conferences, one at the IEEE conference and another one at EAMMIS 2021. She received two awards in the year 2022. She received two awards in the year 2022. She has addressed innumerable guest lectures, acted as a session chair, and was invited as a keynote speaker at several international conferences. She has conducted FDPs that cover approximately ~80,000 plus faculty members including JNTU, TEQIP, SERB, SWAYAM, DST, AICTE, MHRD, ATAL, ISTE, Madhya Pradesh Government-sponsored, and self-financed workshops across India on various titles.

Amar Yasser El-Bably PhD in Law and Police Sciences and lecturer at the Egyptian Police Academy in the field of Cyber Security, Artificial Intelligence, and Crime Forecasting.

Ramy El-Kady Head of the criminal law department in Police college, Egypt and associate professor, He rewarded The Egyptian State Incentive Award for legal and economic sciences Granted by the Supreme Council of Culture in Egypt, and he graduated from the Police College in 1999 and attained his doctoral degree in law from Cairo University. He teaches criminal law at Police College. He supervised numerous researches submitted for doctoral degree and higher diploma and authored a host of researches in criminal law field. He published a host of researches in refereed and indexed periodicals and took part in a number of international and local conferences and symposia.

Richard Ikuesan received the M.Sc. and Ph.D. degrees (Hons.) in computer science from the Universiti Teknologi Malaysia in 2012 and 2015, respectively. He is currently an Assistant Professor of Cyber Security with the Computing and Applied Technology Department at the College of Technological Innovation, Zayed University, UAE. He is an Active Researcher who also pioneers a digital policing and forensic project for developing nations, using Nigeria and South Africa, as a hub for West Africa and Southern Africa, respectively. His research interests include digital forensics, human-centered computing, and information security, among others

Farkhund Iqbal received the MSc and the Ph.D. degrees from Concordia University, Canada, in 2005 and 2011, respectively. He is an Associate Professor in the College of Technological Innovation, Zayed University, UAE and the team lead for the Cybersecurity and Digital Forensics (CAD) research group in Center for Smart Cities and Intelligent Systems, Zayed University. He has more than 15 years of teaching and research experience. He is using Artificial Intelligence, Machine Learning, Service Robotics and Data Analytics techniques for problem-solving in digital security, digital forensics, healthcare, cybercrime investigation and smart city domains. He is also an Adjunct Professor in the School of Information Studies, McGill University, Canada, and an Associate Graduate Faculty member in the Faculty of Business and IT, Ontario Tech University, Canad

Akshaya Jayakumar was born on the 26th of March 2004 as a native of the greenest land in the country, known as God's own country. Being from a place of highest-rated literacy, she is aspiring to enter the digital technology domain to become a software engineer. She is passionate about new technologies and digital transformations and firmly believes in updating herself with the subject and keeping abreast of the changes in the technical world. Her pursuit of enriching herself through various modes of acquiring knowledge bears witness to her readiness, resilience, and patience. She upholds integrity and equality to the core. Early Life: The upbringing of Akshaya has occurred with utmost care to shape the belief system of the child, uplift core values, make her emotionally more potent, and build her capacity, capabilities, and interests. Her upbringing in two culturally diverse lands such as Kerala and Madhya Pradesh offered her an amalgamated culture which played a significant role in the personality development of Akshaya as a person. Since childhood, she has been keen on nurturing a goal-seeking attitude. Academic Pursuits: Akshaya has received education and training since her formative stage to her senior classes at Atomic Energy Central School, Indore, a premier educational institute of great repute, wherein she was exposed to various learning experiences and skills by learned educators which helped her groom into an inquisitive learner. Further, the able guidance of the masters sowed the seed of interest in computational technology. Her ambition ushered her to VIT, Bhopal to explore the scope of realizing her long-cherished dream. Presently she is pursuing a B.Tech in Computer Science at VITB University. Passions and Interests: Since childhood, Akshaya has been a gifted girl of talent thereby a versatile singer and dancer. She has participated in the All India Inter School Cultural Meet every year both for dance and music for 5 consecutive years from class 8 to class 12. A sprinter who bravely participated with her much more senior counterparts to reach the semi-finals and is inclined to play basketball, volleyball, and the like. A fitness enthusiast, she believes "a sound mind can dwell only in a sound body." Apart from being a curious student, she spares time to satiate the hunger of her mind, that is reading. She finds time to fiddle her fingers on her favorite piano. She is a connoisseur who finds solace in inventing new refreshments to tickle the tastebuds. She finds new domains of culinary skills knowing that to win someone, it is better possible through one's stomach. Overcoming Challenges: Akshaya is earnest to be a self-made girl who knows the importance of self-help. She had her share of fears and apprehensions as well. But she learned that when the wind is unfavorable, one must adjust the sail. Thus, she set herself to face the challenges in her way. She is gradually trying to discover the self in her by self-evolution. Values and Beliefs: Having been brought up in a traditional household with a modern outlook, she has been reared to uphold ethical and moral values to the core. She is always encouraged to view gender equality among people irrespective of their social and economic status. Her vision and mission are to bridge the gap between the rich and poor through education. She envisions creating a ripple on this planet by being committed to her cause. Aspirations to Impact the World: As it says, "A journey of a thousand miles begins with a tiny step", No matter how big the task is, it starts when you start. Likewise, Akshaya cherishes giving to the world her share of endeavor, big or small, to make it a worthy place to live. Her commitments coupled with her creative imagination and thought system, with the sole instinct and objectivity, will realize her goal which she fondly nourished. She will commence her journey to fulfill her commitment, though in small steps, but indeed grooming herself to optimize her potential and caliber. In the biography, Akshaya portrays an inquisitive learner who always wonders about the whys and whats of life phenomenon and continues to thrive on learning. She is a person of perseverance who will bring her dream to life.

Faouzi Kamoun received the B. Eng, the M.Sc and the Ph.D. degrees in electrical and computer engineering from Concordia University, Montreal, Canada in 1988, 1991, and 1995, respectively. He also received an MBA degree from McGill University, Canada in 1999. He is a Professor, Director of ESPRIT Research Office, and Deputy General Manager of ESPRIT School of Business. He started his professional career in 1995, as Senior Systems Engineer at Nortel Networks, Montreal, Canada. He moved to the UAE in 2002, where he held various academic and administrative positions, including Dean of the College of IT at the University of Dubai and Acting Dean of the College of Technological Innovation at Zayed University. Since 2015, he has been with ESPRIT where he leads many research projects on cybersecurity and digital forensics, social innovation, smart-cities, pedagogical innovation, and technology management. He is the co-editor of one book and the co-author of more than 100 research articles. Prof. Kamoun awards and honors include the J.W. McConnell Memorial University Graduate Fellowship, 2008 IBM Faculty award, and the University of Dubai 2004 best faculty award

Zainab Khalid received the Bachelor of Electrical Telecommunication Engineering (BETE) degree from the Military College of Signals (MCS), National University of Sciences and Technology (NUST), Rawalpindi, Pakistan in 2017. She completed her post-graduate degree in Information Security at the School of Electrical Engineering and Computer Science (SEECS), NUST, Islamabad, Pakistan in 2020. Currently, her major field of research is on information security and digital forensics. Her research appeared in renowned publications such as: Annals of Telecommunications, Springer, and Forensic Science International: Digital Investigation, Springer; among many others.

Ehab Khalifa, PhD Holder in International relations (Smart Cities and National Security), and have more than 10 years' experience in research in the 4th industrial revolution technologies and its effect on national security, also expert in Cyber Politics, Cyber Warfare issues, and Social Media Analysis. Currently, Khalifa serve as head of Monitoring technological developments unit, Chief technology officer, and the head of cyber security program at Future center for advanced research and studies, Abu Dhabi, UAE, since 2014 till now. In addition, Dr Khalifa is the author of (6) published books in Arabic language on technology and international relations, most of them being taught in different universities in the Middle East, the books are: "Cyber Warfare (2021) - Smart Cities (2020) - Artificial Intelligence (2020) - Post-Information Society (2019) - Cyber Power (2017), Social Media Warfare (2015)" Besides publishing many academic papers in English language in academic journals like: "Central European Journal of International and Security Studies - Journal of Strategic Innovation and Sustainability - American Journal of Management - International Forum Affairs"

Aiesha Kuna, a dynamic and enthusiastic student pursuing her education in Computer Science and Engineering at VIT Bhopal. Hailing from the vibrant city of Hyderabad, Aiesha brings a unique blend of cultural diversity and technical acumen to her academic pursuits. Beyond the realm of technology, Aiesha is an avid traveler who has immersed herself in the rich tapestry of India's cultural landscape, exploring multiple states and gaining insights into their traditions. With a keen interest in the intersection of technology and societal development, Aiesha aspires to leverage her skills to contribute meaningfully to the field of computer science. Her goals encompass the exploration of innovative solutions to real-world challenges, with a focus on creating positive societal impact through technology. Aiesha values continuous learning, collaboration, and the application of her knowledge to address pressing issues in the digital era. Driven by a passion for exploring new horizons, both in terms of geographical landscapes and technological frontiers, Aiesha Kuna hones the spirit of a forward-thinking and culturally aware computer science student, poised to make meaningful contributions to the ever-evolving world of technology.

Vijayalakshmi G. V. Mahesh received her BE in Electronics and Communication Engineering from Bangalore University, India in 1999, and M.Tech in Digital Communication and Networking from Visvesvaraya Technological University in 2005 and the Ph.D. degree from the Vellore Institute of Technology, Vellore, India. Currently she is working as an Associate Professor at BMS Institute of Technology and Management, Bangalore, India. She has been in academics for over 19 years and has published her research in various reputed journals and conferences. Dr. Vijayalakshmi is serving as academic editor for various journals. She has edited and published two books " Handbook of Research on Deep Learning-Based Image Analysis Under Constrained and Unconstrained Environments" and " Aiding Forensic Investigation Through Deep Learning and Machine Learning Frameworks" with IGI Global publishers. Her research interests include Machine Learning, Image Processing, Pattern Recognition and Deep learning, Affective computing.

Chandra Prabha R. is an Assistant Professor, currently pursuing PhD in Deep Learning.

Sameer Saharan is a dedicated researcher in Forensic Science, specializing in fingerprint analysis, cyber forensics, and DNA fingerprinting. He holds a Ph.D. in Forensic Science from Amity University, Haryana, and has authored several research papers and book chapters. With a passion for continuous learning, Dr. Saharan actively contributes to the advancement of forensic science through his expertise and knowledge. He is committed to nurturing the next generation of forensic scientists and making a positive impact in the field.

Wasswa Shafik is an IEEE member. He has a bachelor of science in Information Technology Engineering with a minor in Mathematics in 2016 from Ndejje University, Kampala, Uganda, a master of engineering in Information Technology Engineering (MIT) in 2020, from the Computer Engineering Department, Yazd University, Islamic Republic of Iran and PhD in Computer Science at school of Digital Science, Universiti Brunei Darussalam. He is an associate researcher at the Computer Science department, Network interconnectivity Lab at Yazd University, Islamic Republic of Iran, and at Information Sciences, Prince Sultan University, Saudi Arabia. His areas of interest are Pattern Recognition, Plant Pathology, Anomaly Detection, Drones (UAVs), Machine/Deep Learning, AI-enabled IoT/IoMTs, IoT/IIoT/OT Security, Cyber Security and Privacy. Shafik is the chair/co-chair/program chair of some Scopus/EI conferences. Also, academic editor/ associate editor for set of indexed journals (Scopus journals' quartile ranking). He is the founder and lead investigator of Digital Connectivity Research Laboratory (DCR-Lab) since 2019, the Managing Executive director of Asmaah Charity Organisation (ACO).

Shailja Singh is an accomplished individual who has dedicated her life to the pursuit of knowledge and academic excellence. As an Assistant Professor, she has made significant contributions to the field of education, inspiring and shaping the minds of young learners. Born with an innate curiosity and a passion for learning, Shailja's journey has been one of determination, hard work, and continuous self-improvement. Shailja Singh completed her Master of Science (MSc) degree in a Forensic Science, which laid the foundation for her expertise in Forensic Science. Her academic prowess and thirst for knowledge led her to achieve great heights in her educational journey. To further enhance her skills and broaden her horizons, Shailja successfully qualified the UGC NET examination, a prestigious national-level eligibility test for aspiring lecturers in India.

Bhuvnesh Yadav is currently working as an Associate Professor in the Department of Forensic Science at Amity University Haryana. She has 18 years of experience in Forensic academics and research. Dr. Yadav completed her PhD in population genetic diversity analysis from the prestigious All India Institute of Medical Sciences, India in 2010. Her area of research is forensic genetics, Molecular Biology, microdeletion, heteroplasmy analysis, and population diversity. She has been involved in many medicolegal cases during her PhD. She has received the Young Scientist award in the field of Forensic Genetics from SARC. She is a published author on numerous forensic topics and has around 60 publications in genetic diversification with Autosomal and Y markers, allelic variation, serological aspects of populations and cyber forensics. She has also published a patent on forged fingerprint detection and contributed Six polymorphism databases for Indian populations to the international YHRD database. Prior to Amity University, she had associated with SGT University from 2012-2016 and contributed as a founder member in the development of the faculty of Allied Health Sciences and had been a member of the core committees of the University.

Siem Zeresenay received his Bachelor of Information Technology degree from Zayed University, Abu Dhabi, United Arab Emirates in 2023. Currently, he is a Graduate Research Assistant at Zayed University, where his primary focus of study and research is on machine learning and digital forensics. His research interests include security technologies, natural language processing, digital forensics, and applications of artificial intelligence in healthcare

Index

www.ingramcontent.com/pod-product-compliance
Lightning Source LLC
LaVergne TN
LVHW081328021026
849161LV00010BA/2649